SEARCH FOR SECURITY

SEARCH FOR SECURITY

SAUDI ARABIAN OIL AND AMERICAN FOREIGN POLICY, 1939–1949

AARON DAVID MILLER

The University of North Carolina Press

Chapel Hill

Manufactured in the United States of America

ISBN 0-8078-1415-6

Library of Congress Catalog Card Number 79-18144

Library of Congress Cataloging in Publication Data
Miller, Aaron David.
  Search for security.

  Bibliography: p.
  Includes index.
  1. Petroleum industry and trade—Saudi Arabia.
2. Petroleum industry and trade—United States.
3. United States—Foreign relations—Saudi Arabia.
4. Saudi Arabia—Foreign relations—United States.
I. Title.
HD9576.S33M54   382'.42'28209538   79-18144
ISBN 0-8078-1415-6

For My Mother and Father

CONTENTS

ACKNOWLEDGMENTS

In preparing this book I have acquired debts to friends and family that I could not possibly repay. To Bradford Perkins and Richard Mitchell, I am deeply grateful. Their insights and suggestions facilitated both my research and writing. During the past seven years, each has extended me the benefits of his particular expertise, guidance, and friendship. To Gerald Linderman I owe special thanks. His sensitivity, humanity, and scholarship were a constant source of encouragement and inspiration. Thanks as well are due to John DeNovo, William Walt, George Grassmuck, Paul Claussen, Bernard Reich, Peter Iseman, David Patterson, Bruce Kuniholm, Robert McMahon, and David Painter for their invaluable suggestions.

A great many archivists facilitated my research and went to great lengths to fill the needs of an often demanding researcher. Patricia Dowling and Kathie Nicastro of the Diplomatic Branch, National Archives, were helpful in sorting through State Department material. Edward J. Reese and John E. Taylor of the Modern Military Branch were particularly helpful in locating pertinent OSS and JCS material. Michael Goldman of the National Archives helped me with PAW and Interior documents and William G. Lewis assisted in locating valuable military intelligence files. Special thanks go to John Davies for his assistance with material in the Public Records Office in London. I am grateful to Herbert A. Fine, formerly of the Office of the Historian, and Wilmer Sparrow of the Foreign Affairs Document and Reference Center for locating and preserving material vital to my research.

There is simply no way to thank my friends and family. Alan Clive, Alan Makovsky, and Will Rollman endured long hours of conversation about the manuscript; my brothers Richard and Abe and sister Gabrielle all contributed in their own special way. I owe special thanks to Deborah and Brian Ratner who not only helped me adjust to the National Archives but also to life in Washington, D.C. I am also grateful to Nancy Reilly who prepared the original manuscript and gave me moral support and a sense of balance throughout, and to Nancy Kleinman for suggestions on cover design.

I owe everything and more to my wife, Lindsay. Her support, confidence, and willingness to sacrifice filled a good many lonely days with joy and with love.

A final note. Since November 1978 I have been employed as a historian at the Department of State. The views expressed in this book, however, are solely my own and in no way reflect or represent those of the Office of the Historian or the Department of State.

INTRODUCTION

O N the morning of 14 February 1945, the American destroyer U.S.S. *Murphy*, carrying Abd al-Aziz ibn Abd al-Rahman al Faisal al Saud, king of Saudi Arabia, steamed north through the Suez Canal and drew alongside the U.S.S. *Quincy* anchored in the Great Bitter Lake. The crew of the *Quincy* lowered their gangway and stood silently at attention as the Arabian king drew his heavy six-foot-three-inch frame from his gilded chair and moved slowly to greet Franklin Delano Roosevelt aboard the presidential cruiser.[1] There was little ceremony and no artillery salute—only the bosun's piping—yet the encounter was nonetheless impressive. The contrast between the navy's blue uniforms and the splendid attire of the king and his party, the Cairo daily *Al-Ahram* noted, was a "magnificent sight." Similarly, Michael Reilly, chief of the White House Secret Service, recollected that with flowing black robes and red and black turban, Ibn Saud was certainly the "most impressive" foreign statesman he had ever seen.[2]

The historic meeting between Roosevelt and Ibn Saud at Great Bitter Lake represented more than Roosevelt's fascination with the colorful pageantry of desert monarchs. The president's decision to rendezvous with Ibn Saud, coupled with his earlier meetings with King Farouk of Egypt and Haile Selaisse of Ethiopia, seemed to reflect the United States' increasing awareness of the importance of the entire Middle Eastern area. Roosevelt was exhausted from the strain and tension of the Yalta Conference, yet he seemed intent on plying the "Kings of the Orient" with his diplomatic skills and personal charm.[3] The president was particularly interested in wooing Ibn Saud. Not only did the king, as guardian of the holy cities of Mecca and Medina, wield considerable influence in the Muslim world, but also he had granted an oil concession of enormous potential to an American oil company. More important, the president seemed to believe he could gain Ibn Saud's help in resolving the already tortuous problem of Palestine.

1. W. Barry McCarthy, "Ibn Saud's Voyage," pp. 59–64. For a detailed account of the meeting see William A. Eddy, *FDR Meets Ibn Saud*. Although the king is more properly referred to as Abd al-Aziz, I have used the name by which he was popularly known in the West—Ibn Saud.

2. *Al-Ahram*, 21 Feb. 1945, p. 1. See also Michael Reilly, *Reilly of the White House*, p. 222.

3. *New York Times*, 22 Feb. 1945, p. 26.

Although Harry Hopkins, Roosevelt's closest adviser, believed the meeting to be a "lot of horseplay," it was clear there were far more serious matters at hand.[4]

For Ibn Saud the meeting was of even greater significance. The king had left Saudi Arabia only once before during a brief trip to Basra in British-controlled Mesopotamia. Now for the first time he had permitted an American warship to enter the Red Sea port of Jidda and to carry him hundreds of miles from his capital at Riyadh to meet with an American president. Jidda buzzed with rumors that the king had abdicated or been kidnapped by the Americans, yet Ibn Saud no doubt had his own reasons for risking the journey.[5] Not only might the American oil companies make him rich but the American government might strengthen his kingdom and send him support against his enemies. What better way to woo the leader of a prospective ally than over roast lamb and Arab coffee. "Behind the robes and beneath the draped headgear," the *New York Times* noted, "was a very practical man."[6]

The conversations aboard the *Quincy* ranged from Palestine to farming, yet the emerging relationship between the United States and Saudi Arabia was firmly based on the already impressive reports of Saudi crude reserves. In the 1930s the California Arabian Standard Oil Company (CASOC), a subsidiary of Standard of California and the Texas Company, had secured a concession in the al-Hasa area of eastern Saudi Arabia.[7] Although by 1939 the concession was considered to be one of the most promising in the world, interest in Saudi petroleum was largely confined to oilmen and to those government officials actively involved in Middle Eastern affairs.

World War II, however, drastically altered the American view of Arabian oil and fundamentally changed the course of the relationship between the United States and Saudi Arabia. Disturbed by the possi-

4. Robert Sherwood, *Roosevelt and Hopkins*, pp. 871–82.
5. David Howarth, *The Desert King*, p. 254.
6. *New York Times*, 22 Feb. 1945, p. 26.
7. Standard Oil of California (SOCAL) acquired the concession in May 1933. By November 1933 the concession was assigned to the California Arabian Standard Oil Company (CASOC), a subsidiary of SOCAL. In 1936, the Texas Oil Company became a half-partner in CASOC and in July an additional agreement was concluded establishing the California Texas Oil Company (CALTEX), a marketing subsidiary. SOCAL received a half interest in the Texas Company's marketing operations east of Suez. In return Texas obtained a half interest in the Bahrain Petroleum Company (BAPCO), a Canadian subsidiary of SOCAL. On 31 January 1944, CASOC changed its name to the Arabian American Oil Company (ARAMCO).

bilities of declining domestic reserves and accelerating wartime demand, the Americans began to attach new importance to Middle Eastern oil. The enormity of the area's reserves and the prospect of using this oil to conserve the more strategically vital reserves of the Western Hemisphere convinced officials that the all-American enterprise in Saudi Arabia was too important to be left entirely to the companies or to the British. Joined by the army, the navy, the Interior Department, and Harold Ickes's Petroleum Administration for War, the United States Government launched a variety of wartime projects designed to secure and develop the American concession in Saudi Arabia. By 1946, disturbed by the problems of Palestine and the emerging cold war, the Americans set out to protect and consolidate an already valuable interest.

The importance of the American interest in Middle Eastern oil, however, cannot be measured solely in the production and control of Arabian crude. The colossal discoveries of the 1950s and 1960s at Khursaniyah, Safaniya, and the Ghawar complex would dwarf production figures of the earlier years and add global significance to Arabian oil. In 1948, Saudi fields produced roughly 390,000 barrels per day (b.p.d.) with estimates of proven reserves ranging from 4,000,000,000 to 30,000,000,000 barrels; by 1978, Saudi output averaged more than 8,000,000 barrels daily while boasting known reserves of 170,000,000,000 barrels. Nor was the United States dependent upon Saudi or Middle Eastern petroleum. In 1948, the nation imported roughly 6 percent of its oil; crude imports from Saudi Arabia totaled approximately 29,300 b.p.d.—8.3 percent of total imported crude.

Far more significant during these early years was the extent to which Saudi Arabian oil had come to shape American perceptions and policies toward the entire Middle East. Oil was only part of the increasing national stake in the area, yet it quickly became an important element in the broadening concept of national security which dominated Washington's view of the world in the postwar years. The United States' new and expanded definition of its national security needs quickly encompassed the Middle East. In view of the critical role of petroleum in industrial and military power and signs of increasing Soviet interest in the eastern Mediterranean and Middle East, the Americans began to attach new importance to the security of their petroleum reserves in Saudi Arabia and the Persian Gulf. Postwar plans for the reconstruction of Europe only highlighted the necessity of developing a prolific source of energy closer to the Continent. Although by 1950 the value of Arabian oil was still measured largely in terms of the future, the significance of Saudi Arabia and its crude reserves could no longer be ignored. If any oil lubricated American diplomacy between 1939 and 1949, it was indeed Saudi Arabian oil.

This book is an account of how Saudi Arabia and its oil shaped United States' attitudes and policies toward the Middle East during World War II and the immediate postwar years. My purpose is not to examine every aspect of United States' relations with the Saudi kingdom nor to trace the history of the oil companies' relations with Saudi Arabia. The relationship between the companies and the king—the conflicts and common interests among them—is indeed an important part of the story, but it is not its central theme. Although I do examine the process by which the oil companies influenced and were influenced by United States' attitudes and policies, my primary concern is not to detail the history of CASOC and the Arabian American Oil Company's (ARAMCO) interaction with the federal government.

I have chosen instead to focus on the view from Washington, specifically on the emerging interests of the Departments of State, War, and Navy in Saudi Arabian oil. In an effort to explore this official interest, I have concentrated on two general and interrelated questions: first, how did the need to maintain Ibn Saud's friendship and access to his oil alter traditional attitudes toward Saudi Arabia and the Middle East; and second, to what extent did these changing perceptions influence American policies toward the Saudis, the British, and the oil companies. In this sense, U.S. interest in Arabian oil not only affected matters of foreign policy, but also raised vital questions about the relationships between private and public interest and between domestic and foreign oil policy. Finally, in addressing these themes, I will explore the origins of the much acclaimed and controversial "special relationship" between the United States and Saudi Arabia—a relationship which undoubtedly had its roots in the war and immediate postwar years.

Although the United States was first drawn into the Middle East by the wartime challenges of supply and communications, it was the oil of Saudi Arabia and the Persian Gulf that assured the nation a permanent interest in the area. Arabian oil quickly provided both the pretext and vehicle for greater American involvement in the affairs of the Saudi kingdom. Although the Department of State and military services were eager to strengthen official ties with Saudi Arabia and determined to see that the concession remained in American hands, not all officials seemed willing to accept the attendant responsibilities of this new role. Neither the domestic petroleum industry nor its supporters in Congress were prepared to accept the government's view of the

crucial importance of Saudi oil or the measures officials believed necessary to secure and develop the American interest. Still, disturbed by
the prospect of declining domestic reserves and increasing wartime
consumption, State Department and military representatives set out to
defend what they believed to be a new national interest.

The maturing of this national interest during the 1940s fell roughly
into three phases. The first phase, which extended from CASOC's campaign to obtain government aid for Ibn Saud in 1941 to the extension
of lend-lease assistance to Saudi Arabia in 1943, reflected the Roosevelt
administration's gradual recognition of the importance of Saudi Arabia
and its oil. During these years, American interests were defined primarily by those of Great Britain. Led by the Department of State, the
United States, in the interest of the Allied cause, sought to support the
British position in Saudi Arabia and to determine an appropriate role
for itself in the area. During the second phase, 1943 to 1945, the Allied
interest in Saudi Arabia became a peculiarly national concern. These
years revealed a determined but clumsy campaign to gain greater security for American oil interests through a variety of ill-fated government projects such as the Petroleum Reserves Corporation and the
Anglo-American Petroleum Agreement. Concerned about the prospective decline in domestic reserves and disturbed by the lack of
American influence in an area traditionally dominated by Great Britain, the Department of State, spurred by its Division of Near Eastern
Affairs, sought to reduce the king's dependence on Britain and to
create a closer relationship with Saudi Arabia.[8] Finally, the immediate
postwar years, 1945–1949, witnessed American efforts to protect a
highly valued interest against the potential threats posed by the Palestine question and the cold war.

The development of American policy was not for the most part a
story of carefully conceived decisions and well-laid plans. In fact, the
search for a national policy for Middle Eastern oil was more a record
of uncoordinated, heavy-handed diplomacy which inevitably led to
conflicts with the oilmen, Congress, and the British. The task, to be
sure, was not a simple one. During the war years, the Departments of
State, War, Navy, and the Petroleum Administration for War wrestled

8. The Division of Near Eastern Affairs (NE), created in 1909, became the
Office of Near Eastern and African Affairs (NEA) in 1944. NEA was composed
of three smaller geographic divisions—the Division of Near Eastern Affairs
(NE); the Division of Middle Eastern Affairs (ME); and the Division of African
Affairs (AF).

with the difficulties of forging a policy whose implications spanned a wide range of highly sensitive domestic and foreign policy issues. Hampered at home by congressional and oil industry opposition and limited by bureaucratic infighting, the Americans never really achieved the kind of control or influence they believed necessary to protect their stake in Saudi Arabia. Nor in retrospect does it seem that the "dangers" facing the concession justified the measures officials took to counteract them. Although the Division of Near Eastern Affairs cannot be faulted for its desire to enhance American prestige and influence, it can be criticized for an almost hysterical view of British designs and an unfailing belief in the importance of government rather than company support of the king's ailing finances.

It would be unfair, however, to be too critical of the government's actions. Charged with the responsibility of protecting a valuable American concern in an area where it had little influence and experience, Washington tended to adopt a cautious and almost "worst case" view of events. This perception, heightened by the increasing importance of oil and the companies' reports of British influence with Ibn Saud, challenged the Americans to take measures to ensure that the concession remained permanently in American hands. In short, what motivated U.S. policy toward Saudi Arabian oil throughout the 1940s was this constant search for security—a search which not only led most officials to aspire to free and unrestricted access to Arabian oil, but also challenged some to call for direct official control over Saudi Arabia's immense reserves. Underlying these varying definitions of security was a variety of economic and strategic concepts conceived in an age of war and cold war. The United States' view of its security needs no longer seemed confined to an immediate threat to its borders. The challenges of national security now encompassed the importance of preserving direct and free access to strategic resources like oil and maintaining American prestige and influence in the oil-bearing areas. The Arabian peninsula and Persian Gulf, traditionally peripheral to U.S. security needs, now became important factors in the emerging cold war contest.

As the nation's first line of defense moved farther from its shores, the potential for cooperation between government and the oil companies increased. Although there were conflicts between the bureaucrats and oilmen, the traditional view that the companies could be used to extend United States' influence abroad and export American technology and expertise gained increasing popularity—particularly among officials whose power to secure American interests seemed limited by domestic restraints. On the other hand, as official relations between the United States and Saudi Arabia were strained over the Palestine question, the Department of State, in an effort to boost sagging American prestige, began to depend more and more on the companies' nonofficial status in Saudi Arabia. Subsidizing the Saudi economy, reducing Ibn Saud's dependence on Great Britain, and pursuing a Palestine policy more attuned to Arab sensitivities, many officials argued, would provide a more favorable atmosphere for the concession. These measures, however, were not designed for the sole benefit of the companies but seemed to serve the public interest as effortlessly as private profit. As the nation's definition of its security requirements expanded, economic and strategic motives thus merged into a broader conception of what constituted the national interest.

As war turned to cold war, the search for security for Arabian oil continued. Troubled by signs of increasing Soviet activity and interest in Iran and Turkey, State and Defense Department representatives warned of the importance of maintaining American and Western influence throughout the Arab world. Convinced that American support of Zionist objectives in Palestine might not only jeopardize access to Arab oil but also throw the Arab world into the arms of the Soviets, the generals and diplomats waged a determined campaign to reverse support for partition. Although the Americans may have overestimated Soviet capabilities in the Middle East and exaggerated the immediate danger to their oil interests, they genuinely believed that a pro-Zionist policy would disrupt the development of Middle Eastern oil and ultimately threaten American access to the area's reserves.

Arabian oil thus provided a convenient rallying point around which these antipartition forces could gather. Although Saudi oil was too vulnerable a factor to be relied upon in an actual conflict with the Soviet Union, strategic planners highlighted the importance of using it to conserve the more strategically vital reserves of the Western Hemisphere. Similarly, postwar planners began to praise its potential as a prolific and accessible source of energy for European recovery. By 1949, the strategic and economic advantages of Arabian oil were still untested, yet the Americans had little doubt about its value in an emerging cold war contest. At the very least, military planners argued, Saudi reserves must be denied to the enemy. In this sense, Arabian oil challenged policymakers to examine traditional attitudes and policies toward the Middle East and to redefine them according to what they believed to be the strategic realities of their day. Their search to secure Saudi oil, however elusive it proved to be, established a new relationship with Saudi Arabia and laid the foundation of more active American involvement throughout the Middle East.

A brief note on terminology and transliteration. During the 1940s, State Department and military planners frequently referred to the oil of Iraq, Bahrain, Kuwait, and Saudi Arabia as a distinct unit—using the term Persian Gulf oil. In this study I have used the term "Persian Gulf oil" to refer to the oil of Saudi Arabia as well. The term Middle Eastern oil as used here, refers to the oil of Iraq, Bahrain, Kuwait, Saudi Arabia, and Iran.

Romanization of Arabic names presents a problem for the area specialist and layman alike. The difficulty lies in part with different systems of transliteration and the transcriptions of vowels—thus the King of Jordan has been variously rendered Husain, Husayn, or Hussein. I have left personalities and place names which appear in quoted source material in their original form. To simplify matters, however, I have imposed a uniform style of transliteration in my own writing which generally reflects a recognizable usage in the West. Thus the King of Jordan is rendered as Hussein; Ibn Saud's son and Foreign Minister of Saudi Arabia as Faisal. I have not used diacritical marks.

SEARCH FOR SECURITY

IRAN

Ras Tanura

mmam
Dhahran
Abqaiq

BAHRAIN

QATAR

AL HASA

PERSIAN
GULF

A

RUB AL-KHALI

SULTANATE OF MUSCAT AND OMAN

TECTORATE

ARABIAN SEA

CHAPTER 1

THE UNITED STATES AND MIDDLE EASTERN OIL, 1900–1939

AMERICA'S entrance into the Middle East, like its own rise to prominence in world affairs, spanned the first fifty years of the twentieth century. Throughout the early years of the Republic, the Arab East, Turkey, and Iran held little attraction for the United States and its nationals. Unlike emerging American interests in China or Latin America, the Middle East seemed to hold little promise of potential markets or of fabled trade in silk, tea, and spices. Tied by culture and history to Europe and preoccupied with events in their own hemisphere, the Americans expressed only casual interest in the political and commercial affairs of the Eastern Levant. While the British, French, and Russians struggled for influence and power from Cairo to Constantinople, Americans were engulfed in the challenges of civil war, westward expansion, and industrialization. Although on the eve of the United States' entry into World War I the Middle East was no longer *terra incognita*, American interests were largely confined to the activities of missionaries and educators, and to those entrepreneurs and adventurers who dared risk their fortunes at the courts of sultans and desert shaikhs.[1]

World War I briefly challenged the Americans to play a more active role in Middle Eastern affairs, yet for the most part they continued to avoid entanglement in the politics of the area. The United States did not declare war on Turkey nor was it prepared to assume responsibility for the fate of the disintegrating Ottoman Empire. Despite President Wilson's grand design for international trusteeships and some official and popular interest in Armenia and Palestine, the Americans withdrew from Versailles, leaving the Middle East to the Europeans. Determined to resolve the troublesome "Eastern Question" once and for all, the British and French eagerly divided the Arab provinces according to their own imperial designs.[2]

The Great War, however, held important consequences which would permanently alter the development of American interests. The new importance of mechanized and industrial power in modern warfare enhanced the value of petroleum and stimulated interest in the untapped oil wealth of the Mesopotamian Basin. Supported by their governments, British, French, and Dutch companies set out to secure concessions and to ensure European dominance in Middle Eastern petroleum. Eager to stake their claim to the oil of the East and faced with resistance from the Europeans, American oilmen appealed to their own government for assistance. Between 1920 and 1928 the companies, supported by the Department of State, attempted to gain entry into the oil fields of Iraq. During the 1930s the oilmen continued their efforts to obtain concessions in Bahrain, Kuwait, and Saudi Arabia.

For the Americans the new significance of Middle Eastern petroleum did not lie in its value as a source of supply. Resting on billions of barrels in proven reserves and supported by the world's most advanced petroleum technology, the domestic industry supplied the bulk of the nation's petroleum requirements. In the event foreign oil was required to supplement domestic production, the wells of the Caribbean and South America offered a more prolific and accessible source of supply.

More important, the emerging American interest in Middle Eastern oil, particularly Arabian oil, laid the foundation of a more active national role in Middle Eastern affairs. For more than a century, the Americans had been content to watch the British, French, and Russians maneuver through the maze of Levantine politics. The development of the all-American oil enterprise in Saudi Arabia, however, challenged the United States to secure and develop its newfound interest. The Americans, to be sure, were sometimes reluctant to accept the political responsibilities of their new role. Nonetheless, with the coming of World War II, Middle Eastern oil had begun to give new direction and focus to American policy. Although the Americans were neither prepared nor eager to rush headlong into the madhouse of Middle Eastern politics, it was equally clear that they would not continue to regard the area as the exclusive domain of the European powers.

"The Arabia which once trafficked in spices and perfumes, for the service of the gods and dead of the ancient world," the great English Arabist H. St. John Philby wrote, "has risen at last from her long sleep to serve man and Mammon from the new-found sources of her hidden wealth."[3] Despite its meteoric rise to world prominence, Arabian oil, as Philby observed, emerged late in the history of international petroleum. The first Arabian well was not spudded until April 1935; by 1938, production was trickling in at 1,357 barrels per day (b.p.d.). Commercial export of Saudi crude did not begin until 1939 and even then Arabian output contributed only a fraction of Middle Eastern production.[4]

Far more significant in the early years was the development of the American petroleum industry and its rise to a dominant position in world oil. While CASOC's (California Arabian Standard Oil Company) geologists struggled with the frustrations and dangers of a hostile Arabia, oilmen at home had already developed the world's most prolific wells and efficient refineries. Underlying their energy and resourcefulness was a strong faith in the capacity of American wells to supply the nation's requirements. There were, to be sure, periods of disillusionment and concern, marked by fears of domestic shortages and shrinking reserves, yet the first seventy-five years of petroleum development in America were far more a story of the achievements of both the wildcatter and large producer. The character which the industry acquired in its early years, particularly its views of foreign oil, would help to shape the attitudes with which the government and the companies confronted Arabian oil on the eve of American entry into World War II.

Although developments in the exploitation of petroleum can be traced back to ancient Mesopotamia, the modern petroleum industry had its roots in the wooded foothills of northwestern Pennsylvania. In August 1859 an unemployed railroad conductor, E. L. Drake, drilled the first successful commercial oil well.[5] Developments over the next fifty years in production, refining, and transport removed any doubts about the significance of Drake's discovery at Titusville. By 1890, the United States' crude production rose to 125,545 b.p.d.; of the three largest foreign producers—Canada, Poland, and Russia—only the latter hoped to rival the American achievement with an output of 78,605 b.p.d. Between Titusville and the turn of the century, American oil wells yielded over a billion barrels of crude.[6] Of the 35,704,000 barrels of oil produced worldwide in 1882, all but 5,000,000 came from the prolific wells of Pennsylvania.[7] Similarly, the Americans figured prominently in the export trade. Between 1892 and 1914, half of the nation's oil production was marketed abroad.[8] Spurred by new techniques in production, the American industry, led by the powerful Standard Oil Trust, continued to dominate world oil. Of the almost 1,117,000 barrels produced daily in the world in 1914, American companies accounted for 728,117 b.p.d.—over 65 percent of the total.[9]

Equally impressive was the increasing demand for petroleum and its

derivatives. The development of the internal combustion engine ush-
ered in the age of mechanized transport and initiated the American
love affair with the automobile. Between 1899 and 1919 the number of
cars and trucks on American roads jumped from 8,000 to 7,600,000.
The future direction of petroleum consumption was already unmistakably clear. Although at the turn of the century petroleum accounted
for only 4.5 percent of the nation's total energy requirements, by 1919
it had increased its share to 12 percent.[10]

During the early years of the industry the importance of foreign oil
was overshadowed by the remarkable success of the American fields.
New drilling opportunities in Kansas, Oklahoma, Texas, and California had catapulted production from 63,621,000 barrels in 1900 to
265,763,000 in 1914.[11] Although American companies continued to
expand their foreign marketing outlets, the risks of producing abroad
and the undeveloped state of world oil provided little incentive to
explore new foreign sources. As late as 1914 no profitably exploitable
oil had even been found in Venezuela, Arabia, or Iraq and little in
Canada, Trinidad, or the Argentine.[12]

American oilmen, however, were not wholly uninterested in foreign
reserves. By 1900, Americans had invested in the oil of Mexico and
Romania, and interest in the reserves of Peru, Argentina, and Colombia was soon to follow. The industry's drilling methods were also widely
used in Poland, Romania, and Russia. Still in 1910 American companies owned 2.8 percent of all the petroleum produced abroad—a total
of 9,000 b.p.d. On the eve of World War I the bulk of the nation's
foreign production was drawn from only two sources—Romania and
Mexico.[13]

The coming of the Great War dramatically altered the American
view of foreign crude and initiated an intense rivalry for the reserves
of South America, the Dutch East Indies, and particularly the Middle
East. With the employment of mechanized transport, submarines, and
aircraft, World War I established the strategic importance of oil both
in modern warfare and diplomatic planning of the great powers. While
Russia directed her attack upon Austria-Hungary at the Galician oil
fields, Germany invaded Romania in 1916 in an effort to secure Romanian crude. The Allies, Lord Curzon, British foreign secretary, informed the Inter-Allied Petroleum Council in November 1918, had
"floated to victory on a wave of oil."[14]

The significance of Curzon's remark was perhaps most obvious to
the United States. If the Allies had floated to victory on a wave of oil it
was indeed an American wave. Between 1914 and 1919 the domestic

petroleum industry increased its production of crude from 265,763,000 barrels to 378,367,000 barrels. By the end of the war Britain was receiving almost 80 percent of its petroleum requirements from the United States.[15]

Although the American petroleum industry responded quickly to the challenges of fueling the Allied war effort, the new importance of oil in peace and war aroused considerable anxiety about the availability of domestic reserves. The basis for the new concern was not at all justified by the performance of the industry. Over 70 percent of the new wells drilled in 1919 and 1920 were productive. Postwar discoveries had even pushed proven reserves from almost 6,000,000,000 barrels in 1917 to 7,200,000,000 in 1920.[16] Nonetheless, frightened by prospects of increasing domestic demand and sensitive to the new strategic importance of petroleum, industry and government representatives began to focus greater attention on the importance of foreign crude reserves. In May 1919, David White, chief geologist of the United States Geological Survey, noting that output from domestic fields was declining, urged American companies to move "more aggressively" into the reserves of South America and the Middle East.[17]

American anxieties over crude supplies would not have reached crisis dimensions had it not been for European success in staking out foreign reserves and discriminating against American interests. Between Royal Dutch-Shell and the Anglo-Persian Oil Company (APOC), the Dutch and British had laid claim to the Persian reserves, the oil of the Dutch East Indies, and the potentially rich concession in Mesopotamia. Acutely aware of the power of the American industry from the days of the Standard Trust, the Europeans, supported by their governments, seemed determined to protect themselves by protecting their sources of crude. By 1920 it was clear that a full-fledged oil war was already in the making. Eager to secure future crude supplies and to maintain their competitive position abroad, the American companies led by Standard Oil of New Jersey (SONJ) and Standard Oil of New York (SOCONY), set out to stake their claim to the fields of Mexico, the Dutch East Indies, and the Mesopotamian Basin.[18]

It seemed only natural that the quest for foreign crude would first lead American oilmen south across their own borders toward Mexico. Americans had been involved in Mexican oil since the turn of the century, yet it was not until the immediate postwar period that interest increased. In 1918 the president of SONJ's Mexican subsidiary predicted that Mexico's potential production might even be greater than the actual production in the United States.[19] Between 1914 and 1919, Mexico's oil production more than tripled, making it the second largest producer in the world. By 1920 nearly every major American oil company had some investment there.

Yet the Mexican boom was short-lived. The political turmoil of revolution together with the problems of mining and export taxes began to discourage investment. By the 1920s, labor problems, the appearance of salt water in the wells, and increasing controversy over ownership of subsurface rights, forced even the most adventurous entrepreneurs to seek their fortunes further to the south, particularly in Venezuela. Between 1921 and 1929 Mexican production declined from 193,000,000 barrels annually to 45,000,000. By 1929 Venezuela had replaced Mexico as the leading supplier of oil to the United States.[20]

The search for potential sources of crude also drew American oilmen west across the Pacific. Eager to compete with the Europeans, particularly Royal Dutch-Shell, and determined to build a fully integrated company, Standard of New Jersey, under the driving leadership of Walter C. Teagle, was attracted by the possibilities of concessions in the Dutch East Indies. A SONJ subsidiary had been drilling in the area before the war and had discovered oil in Java in 1914. The parent company, however, was far more intrigued by Shell's discovery in April 1920 of the rich Djambi fields of Sumatra.

Neither Shell nor the Dutch government had any intention of aiding their strongest American competitor. Despite official support from the Department of State, SONJ could not prevent the Dutch Parliament from granting a monopoly for the Djambi fields to a subsidiary of Royal Dutch-Shell. The attitude of the Dutch together with the difficulties of operating in the tropics soon convinced SONJ that competing with the Dutch on their own ground might be far more difficult and expensive than anticipated. Although it did acquire holdings in southern Sumatra, the company did not market a barrel of this oil until 1926. Moreover, the Americans had already been tempted by other sources of crude which seemed to offer even greater potential than Djambi. Among the most promising of these new areas seemed to be the oil-laden regions of the Mesopotamian Basin.[21]

Although surface signs indicating the presence of oil had existed in the Middle East throughout history, it was not until the last quarter of the nineteenth century that serious surveys were made in the area.[22] During the 1870s German geologists conducted surveys of the Ottoman *vilayets* of Mosul and Baghdad. But it was in Persia that the significance of Middle Eastern oil was first realized. In 1901, William

Knox D'Arcy, an Englishman who had made a fortune in Australian gold, received a sixty-year concession covering the whole of Persia with the exception of the five northern provinces. Preliminary drilling led to the discovery of oil in May 1908 at Masjid-i-Sulaiman and the formation of APOC.[23]

In 1904, as part of the growing rapprochement between Berlin and Istanbul, the German Deutsche Bank received an option on oil and mineral rights in the Mosul and Baghdad areas. The Germans soon allowed their option to lapse and competition for the renewal of this concession initiated one of the most complex periods in the history of Middle Eastern oil. The complications which surrounded the Meso-potamian concession were not only a result of the administrative confusion of the Ottoman system, but also the conflicting and competing claims of the great powers themselves. The early history of petroleum in the Middle East is far less a story of the development of oil in the field than it is a record of the financial and political battles of governments and entrepreneurs.

The conflicting claims to the Mosul-Baghdad concession finally led to the formation of the Turkish Petroleum Company (TPC) in 1912. Organized by Sir Ernest Cassel, German-born governor of the Bank of England, in order to acquire concessions within the Ottoman Empire, TPC ultimately encompassed the interests and claims of the German Deutsche Bank, Royal Dutch-Shell, and APOC. TPC's success was facilitated considerably by the efforts of Calouste Sarkis Gulbenkian, an Armenian entrepreneur, who not only succeeded in bridging Anglo-German differences, but also in pleading TPC's case with the Turks. In this sense, Gulbenkian's efforts, like TPC itself, represented a European attempt to resolve internal conflicts and to maintain a united front against the Americans who had already expressed an interest in oil concessions in the area.[24]

Aided by Gulbenkian's negotiating skill, and supported by the British government, then in the process of planning to convert its fleet from coal to oil, the parties came together in March 1914 under the auspices of the British Foreign Office. The product of their efforts, the Foreign Office Agreement, provided for an enlarged TPC with APOC acquiring 50 percent, Royal Dutch-Shell 25 percent, and the Deutsche Bank 25 percent. For his extraordinary efforts, Gulbenkian received a tiny but fateful 5 percent—2.5 from the Dutch and an identical share from the British. This development would not only earn the Armenian the title "Mr. Five Per Cent," but would ensure him a degree of immortality in the history of Middle Eastern oil. In the summer of 1914, the Germans and British sought formal assurances that the Turks indeed recognized their claim, yet the outbreak of war prevented official ratification of the concession by the Turkish Parliament—a development which would have significant consequences for American oil diplomacy in the postwar years.[25] However, the British had purchased not only a potential source of crude petroleum, but also a new role in the oil diplomacy of the Middle East.[26]

Despite its increasing importance, on the eve of World War I the potential of Middle Eastern oil was largely unrealized. In 1915 the wells of Persia and Egypt, then the only two producers in the area, accounted for less than 4,000,000 barrels of a total world output of 432,000,000 barrels. Even by 1920 oil from the Middle East contributed only 1 percent to the world output.[27] Yet the realities of four brutal years of military conflict impressed upon the great powers, particularly the British, the strategic importance of petroleum and challenged the Europeans to secure their stake in the future of Middle Eastern reserves. Moreover, the areas in which this oil was thought to lie coincided remarkably with the very areas necessary to preserve vital communication and supply links between Britain and her Empire. If to the French Prime Minister, Georges Clemenceau, oil was as necessary as blood, to the British, particularly to those old guard imperialists like Lord Curzon, oil may well have seemed to be one of the most important instruments for preservation of the Empire.

Eager to secure their own imperial war and postwar objectives, the British and the French entered into a series of vague but determined wartime agreements designed to divide the Ottoman Empire into spheres of influence. Oil was not the primary motive behind Anglo-French wartime maneuvering in the Middle East yet it soon occupied a prominent place in the negotiations. By 1920, after an intricate and confusing series of negotiations, London and Paris reached an agreement designed to settle their outstanding differences over Mesopotamian oil and to maintain a united front against American concession seekers. In exchange for facilitating the construction of pipelines and railways across Syria, the British agreed to give the French 25 percent of the crude output of the TPC. To the Americans, already concerned about possible crude shortages, the accord, concluded at the San Remo conference in April 1920, seemed nothing less than a European attempt to corner the oil wealth of the Eastern Hemisphere.[28]

Anglo-French maneuvering at San Remo, however, should have come as no surprise to the Americans. In 1919, while attempting to resume work on concessions in Palestine acquired from the Ottomans, SOCONY met resistance from British military authorities. Arguing that British interference endangered American property rights, the company presented its case to the Department of State. The diplomats however had even less success than the oilmen. The department initiated informal approaches through the American ambassador in London but met with delay and evasion from the authorities. Despite more formal protests, the British seemed determined to maintain a solid front against the Americans. [29]

The San Remo accord, combined with further reports of discrimination against American interests in Mesopotamia, intensified diplomatic efforts. The accord between France and Britain for the first time threatened to legitimize European domination of Mesopotamian oil. Sensitive to European efforts to use the mandates as a cover for their own imperial designs and pressured by Congress's pique over European actions, the department apparently sensed that unless it took positive action either the British or Congress or both might take the initiative with equally disastrous consequences for American interests. [30]

Between 1920 and 1922, armed with the rhetoric of the Open Door, the Department of State waged an active campaign to facilitate American entry into Mesopotamian oil. Secretary of State Bainbridge Colby plied the Foreign Office with arguments ranging from the validity of certain American claims before the war, to a direct questioning of the legality of the TPC concession. Shifting the tactics of his predecessor Secretary of State, Charles E. Hughes, in cooperation with Secretary of Commerce Herbert Hoover, attempted to gain additional bargaining power through the formation of a bloc of American companies interested in Mesopotamian oil.

At first London seemed reluctant to concede anything to the Americans. The British vigorously defended the San Remo accord and Lord Curzon, wary of American oil power, personally countered American charges. Washington's persistence, however, and the already tenuous status of the TPC concession, presumably persuaded the British to see the advantages of compromise. By early 1922 against the background of efforts to defuse Anglo-American naval rivalry, the British position seemed to soften. The Foreign Office dropped its objections to continued work by SOCONY's geologists in Palestine. [31]

Although the State Department's efforts convinced the British government that it could not arbitrarily discriminate against American companies in Palestine, the Mesopotamian oil controversy was ultimately resolved not in the spirit of the Open Door but in the closed door atmosphere of company board rooms. Already uneasy over the legality of the TPC concession and disturbed by American efforts to gain entry into Mesopotamian fields, APOC, Shell, and Gulbenkian began to fear another concession scramble similar to the prewar contest. By the summer of 1922 the TPC had apparently accepted the possibility of American entry, yet the painful details of percentage and the demands of Gulbenkian had to be worked out. Resolution of these problems required almost six years of negotiations, but the final agreement provided the framework which set the pattern of Middle Eastern oil development for the next twenty years.

The agreement signed at Ostend, Belgium, in July 1928, and the subsequent marketing pact among the companies was a testament to the ability of the companies to solve the problems which official diplomacy could not resolve. The Group Agreement, more popularly called the Red Line Agreement, restricted independent operations of TPC members within the boundaries of the former Ottoman Empire.[32] This self-denying clause was designed to eliminate competition among TPC members and to prevent an unbridled oil scramble among the major companies which Calouste Gulbenkian knew might easily prejudice his own financial interests.[33] The Red Line was, in this respect, the first in a series of "non-aggression treaties" designed not only to control the flow of oil but also to protect the TPC members from each other.[34]

The July agreement, however, could only restrict production and with the glut in the world oil market in the late 1920s and the prospects of a price war, the companies turned to the problems of marketing. In August the heads of APOC, Shell, Gulf, and SONJ met at Achnacarry Castle in the Scottish highlands, ostensibly for game hunting. By September the oilmen had bagged more than grouse, and had formulated a set of principles designed to stabilize and secure the world's major marketing areas. Together with the Red Line the "As Is" Agreement laid the foundations of what one Justice Department attorney called a "vast new supra-national system whose quasi sovereign powers, policies and programs were for almost half a century to transcend national boundaries, and political and legal barriers."[35] The interaction between this "supra-national" system and the increasing national interest of the United States after 1941 would comprise an intricate part of the relationship between Middle Eastern oil and American foreign policy.[36]

Although the Department of State had waged an active campaign on behalf of American oil interests in Mesopotamia, the period 1929 to 1939 witnessed a considerable lessening of official support for American companies in the Middle East. The change was largely a result of the circumstances in which the Americans sought oil abroad in the 1930s. In Iran, both the Department of State and the companies were reluctant to become involved in an area where the British and the Russians had developed interests for over a century. Although in the Persian Gulf official diplomacy did facilitate American entry into Bahrain and Kuwait, the success of the most significant venture in the area —Saudi Arabia—was, in the minds of many State Department officials, more a result of the absence of official support.

More important, urgent cries of petroleum shortages had been drowned beneath a flood of oil which by 1936 brought United States' production over the billion barrel mark. Fed by increases in Iran and Romania, world production jumped from 688,884,000 barrels in 1920 to almost 1,500,000,000 barrels in 1929.[37] In Venezuela, as well, American and British companies began to exploit the tremendous potential of the Maracaibo Basin. By 1928 Venezuela produced 8 percent of the world's oil, replacing Russia as the second largest producer.[38] The deluge of new oil removed much of the pressure upon the State Department. In short, the development of oil in the Middle East during the 1930s was primarily a story of the oilmen themselves—of risks, maverick companies, and potential profit.

Although American companies attempted inroads into Iran during the 1920s and 1930s, it was the remote region of the Arabian peninsula and Persian Gulf that attracted American interest and permanently altered the official view of Middle Eastern oil.[39] That this region should become the last frontier of oil development was not at all surprising. Bounded by the Red Sea to the west, the Persian Gulf to the east, and rimmed in the north by the desert borderlands of Iraq and Transjordan, the Arabian peninsula stretched southward for over a million square miles toward the waters of the Arabian Sea. Skirting its southern coasts lay the Yemen, the British protectorate of Aden, Dhofar, and Oman. Farther to the east along the Persian Gulf littoral were the shaikhdoms of the Trucial coast, Qatar, Bahrain, and Kuwait— nestled in the northwestern corner of the gulf.

In contrast to the southwestern corner of the peninsula, called by the Romans *Arabia Felix* for its well-watered mountain areas, the majority of the peninsula—the area which would comprise the kingdom of Saudi Arabia—consisted of waterless plains, deserts, and plateaus. To the west, hugging the Red Sea coast, lay the Tihama, a salty humid plain which supported limited agriculture. Stretching to the north toward the Gulf of Aqaba was the Hijaz or barrier, a lowland plain extending to a mountainous ridge in the east. Here along the Red Sea coast the city of Jidda, diplomatic capital of Saudi Arabia, opened its gates to a flood of pilgrims journeying to the holy city of Mecca, fifty miles to the east. South of Hijaz was Asir, a rugged mountainous region extending south toward the Yemen. Farther to the east lay the Najd, a huge sedimentary plateau surrounded by the three great desert areas of the peninsula—Nafud, Dahna, and the forbidding expanse of the Rub al'Khali or Empty Quarter. Here in Najd was the city of Riyadh, capital of the future Saudi kingdom. Finally, sloping eastward toward the Persian Gulf were the coastal plains of al-Hasa, famous for their dates and artesian wells and soon to be famous for wells of another variety.[40]

The constraints of geography and climate together with lack of security in the area only increased the difficulties for prospective oil investors. Nor did the curious mixture of Bedouin tribalism and Islamic puritanism encourage outside investment. Arabia was very much a land of harsh extremes—with summer temperatures skirting the hundred and fifteen degree mark and a code of justice which prescribed amputation of a man's hand for theft. Equally restrictive though less harsh were the cartel arrangements of 1928. The Red Line accord had closed the door to the unilateral development of Bahrain and the Arabian peninsula by TPC members. In short, Arabia was not a particularly hospitable place for the oilmen. For centuries the peninsula had eluded the grasp of the Ottomans and even the British were fortunate to secure outposts along its southern coasts. The great interior deserts of the Nafud and Rub al'Khali had been masterless for thousands of years and not even the Bedouin would have dared lay claim to it all.

The risk and unknowns of the Persian Gulf and Arabian peninsula, however, did not stop the adventurous from coming. Concession hunting had begun in the 1920s with the efforts of a New Zealand entrepreneur, Major Frank Holmes, to obtain mineral and oil rights in Arabia and Bahrain. Receiving an option to drill wells in Bahrain in 1925, Holmes searched for an interested oil company. Neither APOC, Shell, or SONJ seemed interested and it was only in late 1927 that the Gulf Oil Corporation picked up Holmes's offer.

Gulf's rights were short-lived. By July 1928 with the company's acceptance of the Red Line, Gulf was forced to relinquish the Bahrain option. Fortunately for Gulf and for Holmes, Standard Oil of California (SOCAL), having explored unsuccessfully for oil in Latin America and Alaska, risked $50,000 to purchase the option. This eleventh-hour transfer marked the emergence of the first company outside of the TPC which would shortly dominate American interest in Middle Eastern oil. The TPC would soon learn how great a price it had paid for self-denial.[41]

SOCAL's entry into Bahrain was not without the difficulties that had plagued American oil interests in Mesopotamia and those that would later characterize the Kuwait concession. Determined to protect its influence in the gulf, Great Britain, in its treaty arrangements with Bahrain, had placed certain nationality restrictions on the granting of concessions. Not only did Standard of California learn that any company operating in Bahrain would have to be British registered, but that the managing director and a majority of the other directors would have to be British subjects.[42]

Early in 1929 on behalf of SOCAL, Gulf laid the problem before the Department of State. The department approached officials in London and after some haggling with the Colonial Office, the conditions of SOCAL's entry were defined. The Bahrain Petroleum Company (BAPCO), a subsidiary of SOCAL, was established and incorporated in Canada. By October 1931 BAPCO had commenced drilling in Bahrain.[43]

The origins of American petroleum interests in Kuwait, like those in Bahrain and Saudi Arabia, were rooted in Major Holmes's early wanderings around the Persian Gulf. Although Gulf Oil had been forced by the Red Line to relinquish its option for Bahrain, the company had secured the right to an option for Kuwait should Holmes succeed in obtaining one. Moreover Kuwait, which had been a virtual British protectorate since 1899, had been excluded from the Red Line. Unlike the earlier situation in Bahrain, however, Holmes's and Gulf's interest in a concession were now opposed not only by the British but also by APOC which feared the loss of a potential source of crude to an American competitor. Finally, Shaikh Ahmad al-Jabir al-Sabah, ruler of Kuwait, eager to secure maximum advantage from a concession, apparently decided to play APOC and Gulf against one another. By 1931 after nearly two years of negotiating, Holmes and Gulf appeared no closer to obtaining a concession.[44]

Late in 1931, Gulf, presumably on the advice of Holmes, sought diplomatic assistance from Washington. Once again armed with the rhetoric of the Open Door, the Department of State took up the company's case with the British, pointing out the inconsistency of nationality restrictions and equal economic opportunity. The British were not prepared to oppose the Americans openly and after some delay agreed to yield on the issue of the nationality clause.[45]

The resolution of the nationality problem, however, did not solve the question of Gulf's entry into Kuwait. The negotiation of a concession was still wrapped in the complex relations between Gulf and APOC and between Shaikh Ahmad and the two companies. Discovery of oil in Bahrain in May 1932 not only increased the shaikh's bargaining power but steeled APOC's determination to prevent Kuwait from slipping entirely out of its control.

In fact it would take almost three years to settle matters in Kuwait. Finally, after a compromise between the companies designed to eliminate competition in production and marketing, an agreement was signed in December 1934 between APOC, Gulf, and Shaikh Ahmad. Gulf's efforts were not without cost. As the price of its new partnership, Gulf gave APOC the right to supply its crude requirements from Iran or Iraq, thus limiting the development of Kuwait oil. This agreement had little impact at the time, yet by 1945 both Gulf and the State Department would be chafing at the limits of such restrictions.[46]

State Department efforts on behalf of SOCAL and Gulf had no doubt facilitated American entry into Bahrain and Kuwait. By maintaining pressure on the British, the department had prevented them from summarily excluding American oil interests. The limitations of American diplomacy were nonetheless obvious. Although John Loftus, of the department's Petroleum Division, later observed that the "continued representations" of the United States government had secured "equal American participation" in Kuwait, it was apparent that Gulf's entry was largely a result of oil company politics.[47] The rhetoric of the Open Door had yielded once again to the closed door strategies of cartel and company. The department's efforts did have indirect benefits for American oil interests. Although Bahrain and Kuwait would become crude oil giants in their own right, they served for the present as stepping stones to an even larger treasure.[48]

In his travels around the gulf, Major Frank Holmes had secured an option for a concession in eastern Arabia, but it was not until the early 1930s that interest in mainland Arabia increased. The discovery of oil in Bahrain in the summer of 1932 had directed SOCAL's interest across the narrow shallows to the mainland. The possibility of negotiating a concession increased with the favorable reports of Karl S. Twitchell, a Vermont mining engineer and emissary of the millionaire Arabist Charles R. Crane, who had broached the idea of concessions to Ibn Saud, King of Saudi Arabia. The king, who had also been told as early as 1930 by the illustrious Arabist and traveler, H. St. John Philby, about the possibilities of wealth beneath his feet, was sympathetic to Twitchell's suggestion. By early 1933, SOCAL had sent Lloyd Hamilton, a California attorney, and Twitchell to Arabia in hopes of negotiating a concession from King Ibn Saud.[49]

The Arabia into which Twitchell and Hamilton poured their entrepreneurial energies was an unlikely candidate for economic opportunity and development. The very nature of society on the peninsula, with its strong currents of tribalism, nomadism, and Islam, seemed to produce institutions better suited to stability and status quo than to the process of economic or political change. So, too, the daily challenges of survival in a hostile desert clime had for centuries consumed the energies of tribal shaikh, pastoralist, and villager alike, drastically limiting the horizons of their economic and political worlds.

In the middle of the eighteenth century, however, certain forces were loosed on the peninsula which were destined to change its political and economic life. In the 1730s, Muhammed Ibn Abd al-Wahhab, a qadi's son who had become disillusioned with what he believed to be the corruption of Islam, began to espouse a new doctrine based on a return to the original principles of Islam and a resistance to all practices contrary to those of the Prophet Muhammed.[50] The new doctrine of Wahhabism might have remained obscure had Ibn Abd al-Wahhab not come into contact with a local Najdi shaikh, Muhammed Ibn Saud. The shaikh, ruler of the town of Dariyya, recognizing the potential appeal of this Islamic fundamentalist, mobilized his Bedouin followers in the service of the new creed. In 1764, Muhammed Ibn Saud, now carrying the Wahhabi banner, occupied Riyadh. By 1806, almost fifteen years after the death of Ibn Abd al-Wahhab, the Saudis had taken Mecca, Medina and laid claim to the Hijaz.[51]

The success of the Wahhabi-Saudi alliance brought its Bedouin warriors into direct conflict with the Ottoman rulers in Istanbul. Keenly aware of the expansionist nature of the new movement, and disturbed by its challenge to the authority of the Ottoman Sultanate, the Ottomans recruited the services of their nominal viceroy of Egypt, Muhammed Ali, to suppress the revolt. By 1818 Egyptian armies under the control of Muhammed Ali's sons had retaken the Hijaz, captured Abdullah, the reigning Saudi leader, and brought to an end the first phase of Saudi efforts to dominate the peninsula.[52]

Throughout the nineteenth century, Arabia was plagued by a continuous series of intertribal rivalries and conflicts. The situation was made even more complex by new forces which had begun to influence the area. In an effort to counter Muhammed Ali's growing influence in Arabia and to protect the route to India, the British occupied Aden in 1839 and entered into a series of treaties and protective arrangements with the shaikhs of south Arabia and the Persian Gulf. This increasing British role in the area would not only have significant consequences for the house of Saud but also would affect petroleum development on a local and international level. Equally important, with the death of Muhammed Ali in 1849, the Ottomans regained control of the Hijaz. Mecca reverted to the nominal control of the local Hashemite family, thus intensifying the Saudi-Hashemite rivalry —an important element of Saudi Arabia's foreign policy in the twentieth century.[53]

In the Najd, traditional stronghold of Saudi loyalties, the tribal struggles continued. The Saudi-Wahhabi banner was again raised in 1824 when Turki, the son of Abdullah Ibn Saud, regained power. Saudi success, however, was only temporary, declining in 1865 after the brilliant reign of Turki's son, Faisal. More important, by the 1880s a new leader, Muhammed Ibn Rashid of the Shammar tribes, set out to consolidate large areas of the Najd. In 1891, the Rashidis routed the Saudis and their allies driving Abd al-Rahman al Faisal al Saud and his small son Abd al-Aziz, known to the West as Ibn Saud and founder of the modern Saudi state, into exile in Kuwait.

The Saudi exile did not last long. In 1902 with the dramatic capture of Riyadh, the twenty-two-year-old Ibn Saud, now heir to the house of Saud, began his campaign to reestablish Saudi influence and unite the tribes of the Hijaz and Najd. Relying on the Bedouin tribes, who were drawn by the appeal of Wahhabism and the charisma of a strong leader, Ibn Saud restored Saudi influence in the Najd, and by 1913, extended his control to al-Hasa. During World War I, ultimately allying himself with the British in exchange for a subsidy and promises of support against his enemies, Ibn Saud launched a campaign against the pro-Ottoman Rashidis.[54] By 1924, Ibn Saud had turned his forces against his greater rival, the Hashemite Sharif of Mecca, and, after a two-year struggle, finally assumed control of the Hijaz. In January 1926, Ibn Saud consolidated his patrimony and was proclaimed "King of the Hejaz and Sultan of Najd and Its Dependencies." Six months before the arrival of Twitchell and Hamilton, the king formally changed the name of his realm to the kingdom of Saudi Arabia.[55]

The man with whom the Americans had come to deal was not by nature easy to please. Hardened by years of exile and desert warfare, the young prince had quickly learned the dangers of weakness and indecision in the hostile environment of the Arabian peninsula. His campaign to reestablish Saudi influence in the Najd and to unite the tribes had taught him to trust no one—not even the Bedouin Ikhwan on whom he relied. Although his commitment to the Islamic puritanism of his followers was tempered by the realities of survival in a world of great power diplomacy, Ibn Saud remained suspicious of foreign influence.[56] There was to be sure another side to the king, reflected in his personal charm, his passion for hunting and women, yet Ibn Saud was above all fervently devoted to a single aim—maintaining the independence and integrity of his realm. It was this commitment and strength of purpose which had enabled him to subdue the Rashidis, triumph over Hussein and by 1932 to found the modern kingdom of Saudi Arabia.[57]

The 1930s, however, challenged Ibn Saud to temper some of his old ways and to adopt some of the new. Despite his remarkable political success, the king faced serious financial problems. In the wake of worldwide depression, the number of pilgrims that had flooded Mecca in the late twenties subsided, cutting deeply into Ibn Saud's chief source of revenue—the pilgrimage.[58] By 1930 the king found himself with a considerable foreign debt and insufficient monies to support the tribes or his minor officials. Moreover, four years of border clashes with Yemen had placed an additional burden on his treasury.

Ibn Saud appeared to have little interest in the complexities of budget and finance as long as his personal needs were met. As a result he had delegated responsibility for finance to Shaikh Abdullah Sulaiman, a Najdi by birth, who enjoyed his complete confidence. Sulaiman, who reportedly kept the treasury of Maria Theresa dollars under his bed, developed the kingdom's finances along the lines of a large family business.[59] Eager to find additional sources of revenue, Sulaiman and Ibn Saud began to explore other options. Writing to the Department of State in 1933, Raymond Fox, American consul at Aden, took note of the new Saudi attitude: "It seems that the Saoudian government is taking a leaf out of the book of occidental economic teachings and is bent upon diversifying; one step in getting away from a one crop program is through the building up of other activities by means of government concession."[60] By 1933 Ibn Saud had apparently taken Philby's and Twitchell's advice to convert underground resources into revenue.

The developments which led to the signing of the al-Hasa concession agreement in May 1933 between SOCAL and Ibn Saud seem to lack the complexity and confusion of the Kuwait and Mesopotamian ventures. Although the Iraq Petroleum Company (TPC had become IPC in 1929) had sent a negotiator to Jidda to compete against the Americans, IPC's offer of rupees could hardly match SOCAL's bid in gold. Nor was IPC enthusiastic about reports of its own geologists. SOCAL thus remained the only American competitor in the field. In May 1933 for an immediate payment of £35,000 gold, £5,000 of which was a rental fee, and the promise of future loans, SOCAL concluded a sixty-year concession for a substantial part of al-Hasa—the heart of future Arabian American Oil Company operations.[61]

The king's decision to deal with the Americans undoubtedly lay in SOCAL's offer of gold. The entire matter, Philby later noted, "turned on the down payment."[62] Ibn Saud also considered himself an astute judge of people and liked and trusted Crane and of course Philby who was then representing SOCAL. Yet Ibn Saud's view of British and American objectives in the area may also have influenced his thinking. The king's view of British policy was based on a curious mixture of fear and respect. While the British had subsidized him in his campaign against the Turks and Rashidis, Ibn Saud also knew that they had supported the claims of his enemy, King Hussein of Hijaz, and were currently supporting his Hashemite rivals in Transjordan and Iraq, both uncomfortably close to his borders. Although the Saudi king must have realized that Britain's position in the area depended partly on maintaining his goodwill, he could never free himself of the notion that British power and influence might be used to compromise or threaten his own independence. Ibn Saud had no intention of alienating a valuable ally and benefactor, yet neither did he welcome the prospect of increasing British influence and involvement in his own affairs. Writing to William T. Wallace of Gulf Oil, the ever-present Major Holmes noted of the king's attitude: "If the oil industry of his country is developed by Americans who have no political axe to grind he risks less of his country's independence. On the other hand he does not wish to be without the British influence entirely . . . he is certain that the mixture of American and English Capital will intrigue him immensely." [63]

What "intrigued" Ibn Saud, however, was the prospect that American influence and resources, free from any trace of the political and strategic objectives of British policy, might be used to fill his coffers and perhaps someday even to maintain his own independence. [64] Although both State Department and CASOC officials would later exaggerate the king's infatuation with the Americans and overestimate his regard for the purity of their motives, it is difficult to see how Ibn Saud could have missed the advantages of dealing with the United States. Already aware of British power and influence, the king realized that their interests might inevitably conflict with his own expansionist designs on the peninsula. In contrast to the British, whose interests depended upon maintaining influence and control throughout the Middle East, the Americans must have seemed distant and uninvolved. They had not come seeking alliances or treaties with his neighbors but as businessmen, travelers, and well-intentioned philanthropists. The king, to be sure, had no great love for the Americans. Sensitive to even the appearance of uncontrolled foreign influence within his realm, Ibn Saud had no intention of allowing the Americans to flood his country with western men, machines, and mores. Yet, he no doubt realized that the United States, wealthy and aloof, was one great power whose interests did not directly impinge upon his own. Although Ibn Saud would not risk his friendship with Great Britain and would with considerable delight play the two Christian powers against one another for his own advantage, the increasing development of American oil interests in Saudi Arabia would ultimately convince him that his economic, if not political interests, lay with the United States.[65]

Had Ibn Saud judged American interest in his country or its oil resources solely by the official reaction of the United States, he might have continued to search for support from another foreign power. The Department of State followed the SOCAL negotiations with interest, yet it saw little reason to interfere in an area where it might do far more harm than good. Events in Saudi Arabia had revealed none of the restrictionist strategy of British campaigns in Mesopotamia, Bahrain, or Kuwait. More important, in view of the king's suspicion of great power motives, the department felt well advised to confine itself to the role of interested observer.[66]

The absence of official involvement in Saudi Arabia also resulted from the nature of the American approach to the Middle East. The United States would maintain American prestige and protect the interests of its nationals there as in other areas of the world, yet there were no immediate interests challenging the nation to move from isolation to involvement in Middle Eastern affairs. Moreover, to many State Department officers, the area was a playground for the European powers, complete with the kinds of spheres of influence which were believed to be contrary to the interests of the United States and to world peace. In view of the strong isolationist sentiments of the interwar years, officials were hesitant to become involved in the complex web of relations of the European powers. The department would protest British and French handling of the mandates and wax indignant over what the officials believed were excesses of European imperialism, but for the most part they pursued a policy of watchful waiting.

Nor were the diplomats adequately prepared to maneuver through the maze of Middle Eastern politics. Unlike their British counterparts, American officials had little tradition of service east of Cairo and little Arabic or Turkish language training. By the time the Department of State established a Division of Near Eastern Affairs (NE) in 1909, the British had been in Egypt almost thirty years, in Istanbul well over a hundred, and had developed political and commercial relations with the shaikhs of south Arabia and the Persian Gulf. As late as 1944 the division could claim only three Near Eastern language specialists and had not been able to detail a single officer for Arabic language study since 1935. The Americans were confident, eager, and quick to learn, but they could never hope to rival a tradition of British service which had produced a William H. Shakespear or T. E. Lawrence.[67]

The character and development of the Division of Near Eastern Affairs, created under Secretary of State Philander Knox, seemed to reflect the American ambivalence and uncertainty toward the entire Middle Eastern area. The primary function of the new division, a departmental order noted, was to handle the diplomatic and consular correspondence relating to Germany, Austria-Hungary, Russia, Romania, Serbia, Bulgaria, Montenegro, Turkey, Greece, Italy, Abyssinia, Persia, Egypt, and colonies belonging to any of these countries.[68] Russia was detached and reassigned to the newly created Division of Russian Affairs in 1919, but the year before, Poland and Czechoslovakia had been placed under the charge of the Near Eastern area. For many officials, it seemed, the Middle East remained an extension of Europe.

By 1939, NE had acquired a much more distinctly Middle Eastern flavor. India, Greece, Afghanistan, and Burma were still within its purview, but so were Iraq, Iran, Palestine, Transjordan, Saudi Arabia, other areas of the Arabian peninsula, Syria, Lebanon, and Turkey.[69] Still the division was hardly prepared to grapple with the potential problems of the areas under its charge. On the eve of World War II, it consisted of a chief, an assistant chief, seven desk officers, and four clerks—a staff of thirteen to cover an area which stretched from the Atlantic Ocean to the Arabian Sea. Recalling his early years in the foreign service, J. Rives Childs, later minister to Saudi Arabia, noted that despite his "primary responsibility" for Palestine, Jordan, Egypt, Saudi Arabia, Yemen, Ethiopia, Libya, and Tunisia, he was given neither an assistant nor a secretary.[70]

During these early years, however, the men who were soon to shape the official view of the Arab East and its oil received their first exposure to the area both at home and in the field. Foremost among the emerging group of Arab hands was the "suave and efficient" Wallace S. Murray.[71] Born in Kentucky, Murray had studied at Wittenberg, Harvard, Columbia, and the Sorbonne, served overseas with the U.S. Army, and taught preparatory school before joining the foreign service in 1920. Assigned first to the American Legation in Budapest, Murray spent an additional three years in Tehran and two in the Division of Near Eastern Affairs before becoming its chief in 1929. Murray's interest and expertise lay in Iran, yet as the dominant force in the division from 1929 to 1945, he became intimately involved with affairs both in Palestine and Saudi Arabia.[72]

Equally significant were the careers of Paul H. Alling and Gordon P. Merriam, the two assistant chiefs of the division, who would play key roles in shaping American attitudes toward Saudi Arabia and its oil. A native of Connecticut, Alling had attended Trinity College and the University of Pennsylvania, and worked for banks in New York and Philadelphia before entering the diplomatic corps in 1924. After posts in Beirut, Aleppo, and Damascus, Alling was appointed assistant chief of the Division of Near Eastern Affairs in 1934, and succeeded Murray in 1942. Merriam, as well, had considerable experience in the Middle East; first as a teacher at Robert College in Istanbul and then at posts in Beirut, Damascus, Aleppo, Istanbul, Cairo, and Tehran.[73]

The 1920s and 1930s were important years for the future of relations between the United States and Saudi Arabia. During these years before the establishment of formal diplomatic relations, State Department officials received their first impressions of Arabia.[74] Perhaps most important was the State Department's view of Ibn Saud. As the tribal struggle for dominance in the Hijaz and Najd intensified, the department's Near East hands followed the career of the young Saudi leader with interest. Early reports of Ibn Saud's campaigning and appeal were not particularly favorable. Writing to the department in July 1925, the American vice-consul at Aden noted that Ibn Saud was regarded "as little more than a savage, hopelessly intolerant of the most vital principles of Islam."[75]

As Ibn Saud's prestige grew with the defeat of the Hashemites and the occupation of the Hijaz, officials began to view the king in a more favorable light. State Department representatives seemed particularly impressed by what they believed to be the significance of Ibn Saud's control of Mecca and Medina. The king's stewardship of the holy cities and the pilgrimage, officials agreed, had suddenly increased his stature in Arabia and in the Muslim world. Writing to G. Howland Shaw, chief of NE, in October 1928, Alling noted that although Ibn Saud's territory had "few economic resources," possession of the Hijaz was "politically" important. The Saudi leader, Alling continued, is frequently acknowledged as the "most powerful and unifying force in Arabia since the Prophet Mohammed."[76] In a memorandum to Secretary of State Henry Stimson, in January 1931, which argued for official recognition of the Saudi kingdom, Murray echoed a similar line: "There is little doubt that Ibn Saud is the most important factor in the Arab world today and by some observers he is considered the greatest Arab since Mohammed."[77]

The State Department's view of Ibn Saud was in no small measure a result of the active public relations campaign waged on his behalf by

American travelers, admirers, and businessmen. In the years before the establishment of diplomatic relations with the Saudi kingdom, these private citizens provided the most important source of information on Ibn Saud and his Arabia. Some, like Ameen Rihani, an American of Arab ancestry, had traveled to Arabia in search of his heritage and to promote closer cooperation between the Arabs and the Americans.[78] Others, like Twitchell, who was at one time or another associated with SOCAL, the wealthy Arabist Charles Crane, and the Saudi Arabian Mining Syndicate, had an emotional as well as financial interest in Arabia.[79] Still others, like Crane and Philby, had quickly succumbed to the lure and fascination of the desert. Whatever their motives, these men, particularly Rihani and Twitchell, gained the respect of the department's Arab hands and helped to convince officials of the importance of Ibn Saud and the economic potential of his kingdom.[80]

It was neither the philanthropists nor the adventurers, however, who would ultimately establish the foundation upon which the Saudi-American relationship would rest—it was the oilmen. These early years were also important ones for the future course of American oil diplomacy in Saudi Arabia. Although official involvement in Arabian oil would not mature until World War II, the 1930s witnessed the formation of important relationships between State Department and SOCAL representatives. Eager to gain support for their fledgling concession, the oilmen kept officials posted on the latest developments in the field and provided a constant flow of information on the economic and political situation in Saudi Arabia.

Equally important were the personal relationships which developed from such contacts. SOCAL executives like Francis Loomis and Philip Patchin, both former State Department officials, were familiar with the workings of the department and maintained and strengthened their contacts in Washington.[81] Government officials did not cater to the oilmen, nor did they accord them special privilege. In fact, sensitive to association with large oil companies, officials sought to maintain the utmost propriety in their dealings with the oil executives. Still, impressed by the potential of Saudi oil and imbued with the notion that American business might serve the national interest as easily as the profit motive, State Department officials, particularly those connected with Near Eastern affairs, frequently gave the oilmen sympathetic hearing. These lines of communication, strengthened by the increasing importance of petroleum, set patterns of accessibility and familiarity which would characterize the mutual cooperation of the war years.

During the 1930s, however, SOCAL's executives, seeking security for their concession in Saudi Arabia, were interested in far more than friendly conversation. Although the United States had recognized the kingdom of Saudi Arabia in May 1931, company officials believed that if they received a concession actual diplomatic representation would be necessary.[82] In October 1932, Francis Loomis informed the department of his company's interest in the Saudi concession and inquired about the likelihood of the United States establishing diplomatic relations with Saudi Arabia. Secretary of State Henry Stimson advised Loomis that although the department had recognized Ibn Saud's regime and maintained contacts with the Saudi ambassador in London, it had no intention in the near future of establishing consular or diplomatic contacts in Jidda. Stimson concluded that such a step would "depend upon the character and growth of American interests in the Arabian Kingdom."[83]

Through its diplomatic staff in Cairo, the department followed the negotiations for oil concessions with considerable interest. In April 1933, Gordon Merriam, acting as chargé in Cairo, informed Washington that negotiations were progressing and that Ibn Saud might even sign an agreement with SOCAL. Following the successful completion of the negotiations in May, Merriam notified the department that the concession was of "unusual interest" because it was possibly the first granted to a non-Muslim by Ibn Saud. He added that "it may prove to be the opening wedge towards the admission of foreign capital and enterprise with a view to the exploitation of the mineral and commercial resources of the Arabian peninsula proper."[84]

Despite the possibilities of oil development, the department was cautious about the prospect of representation. Writing to Twitchell and Hamilton in June to congratulate them on the success of the negotiations, Wallace Murray concluded that at present the department would find it difficult to extend representation to Jidda, "but if relations between the two countries develop as we hope they will the question of representation will certainly have to be considered within the next two or three years."[85]

Murray's predictions proved correct. Early in 1937, in response to inquiries by both the oilmen and Congress, the department dispatched Leland B. Morris, consul general at Alexandria, to investigate and report on the advisability of establishing diplomatic representation in the Saudi kingdom.[86] The report, however, was not what the oilmen had expected. Despite "potentially important operations" of American companies, Morris concluded, American interests "as they now exist" do not warrant official representation. Writing to Secretary of State

Cordell Hull in May in support of Morris's conclusions, Murray recommended that "we should let matters stand as they now are until such a time as American interests in Saudi Arabia have made further developments."[87]

Even with the increasing level of American activity in Saudi Arabia, the department could not justify representation. Neither the spudding of the first well nor the number of American citizens in Saudi Arabia indicated the need for official action. More important, not even the most enthusiastic official could justify the establishment of a consulate in Jidda, the diplomatic capital, when American oil operations were located in al-Hasa. SOCAL continued pressing its case, yet the official position remained unchanged. Sensitive to the use of its offices on behalf of a single American company, the Department of State refused to bow to SOCAL's persuasions.[88]

Still, NE continued to follow the situation in Saudi Arabia with growing interest. In July 1938, James Moffett, vice-president of BAPCO, arranged to bring Shaikh Hafiz Wahba, Saudi minister in London, to the United States for meetings with government officials.[89] Oil developments in eastern Arabia, Moffett informed Murray during a meeting on 5 July, had been progressing far beyond expectations. One large well had been brought in, and there were indications of a large dome in the north which might prove even more important than the Bahrain finds. Murray was clearly impressed by Moffett's presentation. If the oil company's expectations were realized, Murray believed, Saudi Arabia would experience great changes—the main source of revenue would shift from the pilgrimage to oil, the Bedouin might be induced to settle, and water resources might be developed. Equally important, if modernization could be facilitated by the development of petroleum, Murray concluded, "it seems possible that an end may be made to the turbulence and chaos that have been endemic in Arabia, particularly when a great chief passes away."[90]

Increasing official interest in Arabian oil did not suggest any immediate change in the department's view of representation. Oil company officials continued to ply the department with reports of German and British approaches to Ibn Saud as well as the possibility of instability in Saudi Arabia in event of the king's death. The department's officers, however, remained firm.[91] The central issue continued to be the propriety of establishing official contacts in Jidda for the benefit of a single American company, particularly a large oil company. In a memorandum to Under Secretary of State Sumner Welles and Secretary of State Cordell Hull in January 1939, Murray outlined NE's position. Establishment of consular relations in Jidda, over 1,000 miles from the

CASOC concession area, was highly impractical and simply not warranted. Neither was Murray concerned about Loomis's vague reports of British and German "designs" on the concession. Murray concluded: "Since we obviously could not establish a legation in Saudi Arabia merely to please the Standard Oil Company of California . . . there would appear to be no need for higher officials of the Department to give any time to listening to Mr. Loomis' urgent requests which merit little, if any consideration at this time."[92]

Having cross-checked SOCAL's reports that the German minister to Iraq, Fritz Grobba, had set up a legation at Jidda, the department concluded that while Grobba had indeed been accredited to Saudi Arabia no resident status was yet evident.[93] Writing to Acting Secretary of State George Messersmith in March, Murray suggested that if Loomis could produce "convincing" evidence that American interests were "suffering" because of the absence of representation, the department might consider accrediting the American minister to Egypt to Saudi Arabia as well. Loomis, Murray noted, had raised the question of representation every few months, adding that the matter seems to be almost an "obsession" with him. "I am not at all convinced," NE's chief concluded, "that such a plan is either necessary or desirable."[94]

If Murray and department officials were not yet convinced of the need or practicality of diplomatic representation, SOCAL executives seemed very concerned. The company's concession, even under the best of circumstances, rested entirely on a private agreement with a desert king whose political and economic future was still uncertain. If Ibn Saud died or was forced from power, there were no guarantees that his successor would abide by the terms of the concession agreement. Equally disturbing, Saudi Arabia seemed to be an island in a sea of British influence. Although it is unlikely that the companies feared a determined British campaign to remove American oilmen from the peninsula, they were concerned about the extent of London's financial and economic leverage over the king. Disturbed by Ibn Saud's unwieldy financial situation and his requests for royalty advances, SOCAL was uneasy about its long-term position in Saudi Arabia. The distant rumblings of war, accompanied by rumors of Italian, German, and even Japanese approaches to the king, only increased the company's apprehension.

To what extent SOCAL was actually concerned about German and Japanese influence in Saudi Arabia is problematic. Determined to marshal official support for their interests, however, the oilmen did their best to raise suspicions within the State Department. Writing to Hull in April, Loomis advised the secretary that the United States ought to display a more permanent interest in Saudi Arabia or it might risk losing the king's favor. After years of "costly effort," foreign governments were even now attempting to "take advantage of the large amount of work and great capital expenditures on the part of the Standard Oil Company of California." Actively supported by their governments, Loomis added, these "people and companies have frequent access to high Arabian officials, if they so desire."[95]

Unable to substantiate Loomis's reports and aware of SOCAL's manufactured bogeys in the past, the department remained unresponsive to the company's requests. In May 1939 Messersmith coolly advised Loomis that in the department's opinion foreigners did not have access to high Saudi officials. "We shall of course continue to follow the situation," Messersmith concluded, "and if at any time it appears necessary or desirable to reconsider the earlier decision you may be assured that we shall be prompt to do so."[96]

On 30 June 1939, on the recommendation of the Department of State, President Roosevelt approved the accreditation of the United States minister in Egypt to Saudi Arabia. The abrupt shift in official thinking was primarily a result of increasing American commitments in the area. In his formal request to the president, Hull gave the growth of the American colony in Saudi Arabia as one of the basic reasons for the need of representation. The change in the department's attitude, however, was also related to the development of oil and the growing interest of Germany and Japan in Saudi Arabia. With the development of the Dammam Dome and the construction of the Ras Tanura deep-water port, the export of Saudi crude could begin. The SOCAL concession was further strengthened in May with the signing of a supplementary agreement which added over 80,000 square miles to the company's holdings.

Early in June in an effort to dramatize these developments, the ever-present Francis Loomis left a memorandum with Welles which highlighted the concession's potential. SOCAL's Arabian holdings, the oilman wrote, "when supplemented by reasonable extensions are likely to become one of the world's largest and most important oil fields."[97] SOCAL's descriptions were supported by cables from Bert Fish, the American minister to Egypt and Paul Knabenshue, minister to Iraq. Having closely followed oil activity in al-Hasa, Knabenshue informed the State Department that the "now proven importance of our oil interests in Saudi Arabia and generally improved economic conditions which will result therefrom make it desirable in my opinion that we now enter in formal diplomatic relations with that state."[98]

Official interest in Saudi Arabia was also heightened in the spring of

1939 by rumors of reported German and Japanese activity in Saudi Arabia. In March, Fish had informed the department that the Japanese minister in Cairo had proceeded to Jidda on an "official mission" presumably with the idea of accrediting his country's diplomatic mission in Egypt to Saudi Arabia.[99] Germany's plans to accredit its minister in Baghdad to Jidda also raised American suspicions. In June the department learned, presumably from SOCAL's representatives, that both the Japanese and the British had offered Ibn Saud large sums for concessions. Barely a week before Roosevelt's decision, Knabenshue informed the department that the recent interest of Germany and Japan in Saudi Arabia "suggest in themselves the advisability of our now having more formal relations with Saudi Arabia."[100]

Eager to avoid a concession scramble with two potentially unfriendly powers and interested in protecting the growing American stake in Saudi Arabia, the Department of State advised the president to extend representation. The move was hardly a major diplomatic démarche, and, as Hull cautiously concluded, "would involve no additional expense beyond the nominal amount required to cover travel expenses of the minister and his suite," yet it indicated, nonetheless, a clear broadening of official interest in American oil holdings in the Middle East.[101]

By 1939 Middle Eastern oil, though comprising a mere 5.5 percent of world production, had made lasting impressions on both the oil companies and government. To a small but powerful segment of the oil industry, the importance of this crude as a future source of supply had already been accepted as a ground rule of international oil politics. Total assets employed by American companies in the area had risen from well over $10,000,000 in 1929 to $93,000,000 in 1939.[102] Although the American interest in Iraq, Bahrain, and Saudi Arabia comprised roughly 10 percent of the total Middle Eastern production, the potential of these areas and that of Kuwait already threatened to rival British and Dutch concessions.[103] Moreover, this oil might offer American companies cheaper production rates and a reserve-productivity ratio reported to be at least three times that of domestic fields. Eager to develop their holdings in the area and uneasy about increasing international tension, SOCAL and the Texas company looked to the United States government for assistance in securing their already valuable interests in Saudi Arabia.

Although the Department of State had responded to SOCAL's requests for diplomatic representation with considerable caution, by 1939 it was clear that officials would have to pay more attention to the

Middle East and its oil. The department did not lack precedent as it began to reexamine its attitude toward foreign oil. The intensity of official support for American companies between 1920 and 1939 was determined largely by changes in world oil supply and by the degree of resistance the Americans encountered abroad. Following World War I, uneasy over the possibility of domestic shortages and disturbed by European efforts to discriminate against American companies, the Department of State waged an active campaign to facilitate American entry into the oil fields of Mesopotamia. With the easing of the oil scare during the 1920s much of the pressure on the department subsided. Nor did it seem the British were determined to restrict American entry into the Persian Gulf. The State Department overcame British nationality restrictions in Bahrain and Kuwait with much less difficulty than in the Mesopotamian venture.

Equally important, official oil diplomacy before World War II was shaped to a great extent by the dealings of the major companies. The diplomats could insist that American companies adhere to the principles of the Open Door, yet the State Department must have realized the limitations of its diplomacy. In both Mesopotamia and Kuwait the obstacles which prevented American nationals from exploiting Middle Eastern crude were eventually overcome by the companies themselves. Washington could refuse to abide by agreements which ran counter to the principles of equal access and equal economic opportunity, yet the final arrangements which admitted American interests, and determined the pattern of oil development and marketing well beyond 1949, were not cast in the lofty spirit of the Open Door but in the closed door atmosphere of the Red Line and Achnacarry Castle.

Finally, oil diplomacy during the early years resulted from the nature of the relationship between government and the companies. The industry's suspicion and distrust of government interference prevented the kind of cooperation abroad which characterized APOC's relationship with the British or even the arrangement between the Compagnie Française des Petroles and the French. The State Department as well, carefully defining the proper role of government, responded with equal caution to the companies' requests. Of the factors which influenced American oil diplomacy in the Middle East before 1939, it was this relationship that would most dramatically change with World War II. The United States could do nothing to affect the presence of crude oil in the ground, nor little to influence company arrangements, yet it could attempt to alter its relationship with American nationals operating abroad. This changing interaction, resulting from the increasing strategic and political importance of oil, soon reshaped American attitudes toward Arabian oil and fundamentally altered the course of the United States' relations with Saudi Arabia.

CHAPTER 2
ATTITUDES TO ACTION:
BROADENING AMERICAN
INTERESTS IN SAUDI ARABIA,
1940–1943

THE beginning of World War II and the emergence of the Middle East as a vital theater of communications and supply for the Allied war effort challenged the United States to attend to its own interests in the area. During the early years of the war, American economic interests, primarily petroleum operations in Iraq and Saudi Arabia, fell comfortably under the protective wing of Great Britain. As long as the British continued to control the Persian Gulf–Mediterranean axis, the American stake remained secure. By the middle of 1941, however, early Allied military successes in North Africa were reversed, and Britain's strategic position in the eastern Mediterranean and Middle East was seriously threatened. In April 1941, Germany attacked the Balkans and by May controlled Yugoslavia and Greece. In North Africa, Rommel's panzer divisions reinforced the collapsing Italian campaign in Libya, driving the British back to the Egyptian frontier. Farther to the east, Rashid Ali al-Kilani and his nationalist pro-Axis Golden Square temporarily threatened Britain's control of the Baghdad area and the vital Habbaniya airdrome, the air link to India and the North African theater.[1]

Even before its entry into the war, the United States had good reason to be concerned about the weakening British position in the Middle East. Military planners and diplomats alike were painfully aware of the possible consequences of Axis penetration into the Iraq and Suez-Mediterranean areas. "In my eyes," Cordell Hull observed, "the Near East offered the greatest danger of the war, the possible juncture of German and Japanese forces, effectively cutting the world in two."[2] So too, the oil of Iran, Iraq, and Saudi Arabia would be a great prize for an oil-starved German war machine. The loss or even partial abandonment of vital lines of communication and supply might not only undermine Britain's position from Cairo to Karachi but also could easily lead to the collapse of the Empire itself.

Although the Americans were concerned about the security of their petroleum interests in Iraq and Saudi Arabia, oil was not the primary focus of their diplomatic efforts in the Middle East during the early years of the war. The closing of the Mediterranean to Allied shipping in 1940 seriously curtailed petroleum operations in Iraq. In Saudi Arabia as well, the difficulties of shipping and supply slowed the development of the CASOC concession.[3]

Far more important to the United States, in view of Great Britain's desperate struggle against the Axis, was the preservation of Allied influence and prestige in the oil-bearing areas. The situation seemed most crucial in Iraq, where currents of nationalism and anti-British sentiment had temporarily merged to threaten London's control, yet State Department officials began to attach new importance to Saudi Arabia. Already convinced of Ibn Saud's great prestige in the Arab and Muslim world, officials believed that the king's desert realm might become an ally of considerable value in any future Middle Eastern campaign. Underlying this view was the rather tenuous notion that as guardian of the holy cities of Mecca and Medina, Ibn Saud commanded the respect and undying loyalty of Muslims the world over—a loyalty that might easily be channeled into action against Allied interests from Cairo to Karachi. The Rashid Ali uprising in Iraq seemed to highlight the value of a stable pro-Allied government on the western side of the Persian Gulf.[4] American policy between 1941 and 1943 was thus directed primarily at supporting Allied supply lines and attempting to preserve the friendship and goodwill of Ibn Saud. Although these early years revealed an increasing awareness of the importance of petroleum and a more active American role in Saudi Arabia, the emergence of Arabian oil as a key factor in war and postwar planning would have to await the changing political and strategic circumstances of 1943.

The Department of State, led by its Division of Near Eastern Affairs, continued to follow the American stake in Middle East oil with great interest. Although domestic production still dominated world output, State Department representatives could not ignore the promise of expanding oil development in Iraq and the Arabian peninsula.[5] Officials were particularly impressed by the all-American enterprise in Saudi Arabia. Unlike Iraq, petroleum development in Arabia was not blocked by the Red Line nor complicated by IPC arrangements. Early in 1940, Bert Fish, the American minister in Egypt, submitted the first of a series of glowing reports on American interests in Saudi Arabia. "With the extensive development of the California Arabian Standard Oil Company's activities in Al-Hasa . . . ," Fish observed, "and with a steady increase in the number of American citizens . . . it can easily be said that American economic interests in Saudi Arabia now surpass those of any other country."[6] A month later, Raymond Hare, chargé in Cairo, informed the department that production from the Dammam area alone had totaled almost 4,000,000 barrels in 1939. In addition to the increase in crude production, transportation and refining facilities were planned, including a 50,000 b.p.d. pipeline and a 3,000 b.p.d. refinery at Ras Tanura.[7]

Although the department was pleased by the success of CASOC's operations in al-Hasa, it was also concerned about the war's effect on the Saudi economy. By 1940, the pilgrimage trade, already slowed by the economic depression of the thirties, was reduced even further, cutting deeply into Ibn Saud's chief source of revenue. The flow of pilgrims from the Muslim communities of India and Indonesia dropped drastically. During the 1920s it was estimated that each year some 100,000 Muslims circled the sacred Ka'ba; by 1939 their numbers had declined to 63,800. In 1940 only 37,000 journeyed to the holy cities.[8] With crude production and oil royalties not yet sufficient to balance the king's budget, it was clear, in view of Ibn Saud's payments to the tribes and the expenses of his household, that he would not be content with the small subsidies he received from the British nor with promises of aid from the oil companies. By 1940 both the Foreign Office and CASOC seemed to believe that Saudi Arabia was already on the verge of a major financial and economic crisis.

The Department of State as well was aware of the consequences of economic and political instability in Saudi Arabia and the Persian Gulf. Control of the gulf provided a vital link in the British lifeline to India. Mastery of the southern coast of the Arabian peninsula meant control of the southern entrance to the Red Sea and Suez Canal—gateway to Egypt, North Africa, and the Mediterranean. Equally important, officials believed, Ibn Saud as guardian of Mecca and Medina and protector of the Hijaz, held considerable influence in the Muslim world. Axis influence in Saudi Arabia might provide the enemy with a valuable propaganda advantage and also might seriously disrupt British control of strategically vital Muslim-populated areas.

Although it was clear to both State Department and Foreign Office officials that Ibn Saud respected Britain's power and would avoid alienating such a benefactor without firm assurances of support from another quarter, they also realized that the king harbored a suspicion and distrust of British motives in the gulf. Not only had London supported Zionist claims to Palestine, but also it had given new direction to the ambitions of his Hashemite neighbors in Transjordan and Iraq. Above all, Ibn Saud sought to preserve the territorial integrity of his realm. Any economic or political crisis which weakened his own power and prestige might force him to seek assistance from any available quarter. Writing to Assistant Secretaries Adolph Berle and Breckinridge Long and Under Secretary of State Sumner Welles, Wallace Murray appeared to have his doubts about the king's loyalties. Comparing reports of the king's attitude toward the European war, Murray reported that Philby had assured Bert Fish of Ibn Saud's "complete neutrality." A more recent report, however, from a British Overseas Airway Corporation representative indicated that the king was pro-German and might even enter the war against Great Britain.[9] Although officials believed that Ibn Saud would not easily succumb to Axis propaganda or to the reported pro-Axis inclinations of several of his advisers, neither were they eager to test the limits of the king's pro-Allied sentiments.

Throughout the fall of 1940 the situation in Saudi Arabia continued to deteriorate. With Mediterranean shipping severely curtailed and Saudi Arabia dependent upon imports for the majority of its foodstuffs, shortages of flour and rice and spiraling prices added to the king's financial problems. Fish informed the State Department in November that despite the "bargain rates" that Ibn Saud was offering pilgrims, revenue from the hajj was greatly reduced. Nor could the king, in view of wartime difficulties in shipping and supply, expect much in the way of oil royalties. Fish concluded that it was sure to be a "lean year" for Ibn Saud and added that "it would not be surprising to hear of his casting about for a loan particularly in as much as the Legation understands that he had that idea in mind last year when his financial position was not as difficult as this year."[10]

The Department of State was already aware that a good deal of "casting about" had been going on, though not directly by Ibn Saud. Fish informed the department as early as April 1940, that the king's financial difficulties had been "brought strikingly to my attention" by casoc representatives William Lenahan and Lloyd Hamilton. Although the oilmen made no direct request for financial assistance, the company was considering government support as a means of securing its investment. It is unlikely that the oilmen feared the actual loss of the concession. They were concerned, however, about the stability of the Saudi regime if Ibn Saud's financial needs were left unattended. Although the parent companies could presumably have met the king's initial needs without Washington's help, they believed that official assistance would reduce Saudi dependence on Great Britain and ultimately enhance their own position with the king and his successor.

The oilmen certainly highlighted their fear of British designs to strengthen their case in Washington, yet there is little doubt that the companies were genuinely concerned about the fate of an investment whose future rested on the whims of a desert king and on the shifting sands of his political fortunes.

As Ibn Saud's financial position continued to deteriorate, CASOC began to broaden its already well-developed channels of communication with the department. In December, Philip Patchin, a director of SOCAL and former State Department official, sent NE an historical record of CASOC's operations—hand-carried by a vice-president of the company.[11] Three days later this representative, James Terry Duce, soon to become the company's most effective and articulate spokesman in Washington, met with Paul Alling.

The problem with Saudi finances, Duce began, was more serious than the company had previously suspected. Having advanced $3,500,000 CASOC was now being asked by the king for royalty advances well above the terms of its concession contract. Duce made no request for government aid, yet left the impression that for the first time Ibn Saud's financial troubles were beginning to influence relations between the company and the king. Although Alling gave no indication of his reaction to CASOC's concerns, it seemed likely that the department, already uneasy about the king's attitude toward the war and its effect on the Allied position in the Middle East, might have to assume a larger role in the economic and financial problems of Saudi Arabia.[12]

As Ibn Saud's financial difficulties increased in the wake of reduced revenue from the pilgrimage and customs duties, Saudi pressure on CASOC began to increase. In December 1940, F. A. Davies, president of CASOC, learned during a visit to Jidda that the king was seeking $6,000,000 in royalty advances for 1941 alone. Although Davies found the king's proposed budget of $10,000,000 reasonable (the remaining $4,000,000 were to be requested from the British), Ibn Saud had also hinted that he might require additional aid to carry him through an emergency period of perhaps five years. The oil company, having reportedly paid out $6,800,000 in advances since 1939 and $27,500,000 for development of the concession since 1933, had no desire to expend an additional $30,000,000.[13]

More important, despite the company's contract with Ibn Saud, the oil in the ground belonged to the king. CASOC sensed that it could resist Ibn Saud's requests only at the risk of incurring his displeasure and perhaps jeopardizing its own investment. In view of the king's financial troubles and the anticipated reduction in oil revenues for the coming year, the company had no desire to test the limits of Ibn Saud's patience. The possibility of an Axis attack on Suez or in Iraq increased CASOC's apprehension. The attempted bombing of the Bahrain refinery by a small squadron of Italian planes in October 1940 only reminded the company how precarious its position had become.

By January 1941, CASOC concluded that it must go at least part of the way in meeting Ibn Saud's demands. Although the oilmen sought to avoid increasing royalty advances and heightening Saudi expectations that might reflect themselves in future demands, there seemed no alternative but to pay. Failure to supply the king with sufficient revenue to support his commitments to the tribes, particularly in view of the shortages of staples, might undermine CASOC's position from within. In an informal agreement between CASOC and the king, the company promised $3,000,000 for 1941 in $500,000 installments and tentatively agreed to raise an additional $3,000,000 over the coming year. CASOC, however, cabled Fred Ohliger, the company field representative in Jidda, instructing him not to leave Ibn Saud with the impression that he could expect an immediate increase in the first $3,000,000 pledge.[14]

In March company officials were dismayed to learn that the king had upped the ante—requesting an additional $1,500,000.[15] Ibn Saud's latest demands only impressed upon CASOC officials the need for a new approach to Saudi Arabia's financial problems. As a result of wartime exigencies and general financial mismanagement, the king's budget threatened to swallow CASOC operations whole. Nor had the advances to date contributed to the basic objective of the company during the early war years—securing its concession. So, too, the company had no way of estimating whether its own financial resources were sufficient to meet the king's future requirements. Whatever CASOC policy in the past, the March demands forced a reassessment of strategy. In April 1941, Davies informed Ohliger that SOCAL and CASOC executives would soon be arriving in New York to consider approaching Washington officials for the purpose of "soliciting their assistance."[16]

Despite the oilmen's traditional suspicion of government involvement in the industry, the shift in CASOC policy was not entirely unexpected. In view of the risks and hazards of operating abroad, SOCAL-CASOC interests recognized that official support might be essential to the success of their operations. With the war continuing to restrict the king's revenue, the companies began to see the advantages of an arrangement in which the company would supply the United States with oil in return for official aid to Ibn Saud, a plan which might also provide CASOC with an assured outlet for Arabian oil.

More important than commercial considerations, however, was the political attractiveness of government support. A CASOC concession, dependent upon the whims and extravagance of the king, and his relationship with the British, was no comfort to serious businessmen. Although the oilmen recognized Ibn Saud's sensitivity to great power involvement in Saudi Arabia and the gulf, they sensed that he might welcome limited American support—perhaps even as a counter to British influence. CASOC was also uneasy about Britain's leverage with the king. Although the company never believed that the British would attempt to steal the concession whole, there was some concern that Ibn Saud's sole dependence on British support might draw Saudi Arabia into the sterling bloc or result in a division or transfer of the undeveloped part of CASOC's concession. The CASOC approach to Washington not only provided a means to secure their concession, but also to preserve the "American character" of their investment.[17]

On the afternoon of 8 April, Hamilton and Davies of CASOC walked into the New York office of James A. Moffett, chairman of the board of BAPCO and the California Texas Oil Company (CALTEX), with an intriguing bit of company business. Moffett was asked to use his contacts in Washington to secure a government loan for Ibn Saud. According to Moffett, Davies and Hamilton believed that American aid might be channeled through the newly established Lend-Lease Act, through the Export-Import Bank, or through purchases of oil by the army, the navy, or the Maritime Commission.[18] Although the CASOC executives had suggested that Moffett contact Cordell Hull, secretary of state, or Jesse Jones, secretary of commerce, Moffett decided to go right to the top. As a personal friend of Franklin Roosevelt, through his work as trustee of the Warm Springs Association, an infantile paralysis foundation, Moffett was able to set up an appointment to see the president.

Neither Moffett nor Roosevelt were strangers to oil. During World War I Moffett had worked closely with Roosevelt, then assistant secretary of the navy, supervising oil purchases, and the two continued contact in the 1930s during Moffett's service as federal housing administrator. Roosevelt also had a keen interest in the question of petroleum reserves and had worked to develop the Elk Hills naval reserve in the late 1930s. According to Moffett, at the time of their April meeting, Roosevelt had a "pretty good picture of the Arabian background." On at least one occasion, Roosevelt had planned to receive Moffett and the Shaikh of Bahrain at Hyde Park.[19]

On 16 April Moffett informally discussed CASOC's proposals with Roosevelt at the White House. Although there is no official written record of the meeting, the substance of the conversation was later revealed in Moffett's own statements and State Department memoranda.[20] In exchange for a government loan to Ibn Saud in the amount of $6,000,000, Moffett suggested, CASOC would furnish the United States with an equivalent amount of oil at a rate well below the market price. Roosevelt expressed an interest in the proposal, but he cautiously informed Moffett that he had no authority to loan government money against oil in the ground. The president added, however, that if the proposal could be framed in terms of finished products, it might be possible to work something out. According to Moffett, Roosevelt even suggested that there were four Danish tankers available, presumably for transporting such products. The president requested Moffett to draw up a formal proposal for further consideration.[21]

Moffett hurried back to New York to consult with his colleagues. Responding promptly to Moffett's account of the meeting, Hamilton and Davies drafted a proposal dealing specifically with finished products and submitted it under Moffett's name to the White House.[22] The new proposal suggested that the United States advance Ibn Saud $6,000,000 per year for five years in exchange for CASOC's delivery of an amount of gasoline, diesel, and fuel oil of equal value. The letter also emphasized the urgency of the king's financial needs. "We believe that unless this is done, and soon, this independent kingdom, and perhaps with it the entire Arab world, will be thrown into chaos."[23]

The arrangement seemed particularly well-suited to the company's needs. A three-cornered deal between the United States, Saudi Arabia, and CASOC might relieve the company of much of the burden of funding the king in dollars and might strengthen the concession by creating the impression of a direct loan from the United States government to Ibn Saud. In an accompanying memorandum emphasizing the potential of the concession and the severity of the king's finances, the oilmen again played upon the importance of Ibn Saud in the Arab and Muslim world: "No other man in the Arab countries, nor among Moslems the world over, commands prestige equal to his."[24]

Roosevelt forwarded the "Moffett proposal" to Cordell Hull for consideration by the State Department's Division of Near Eastern Affairs. The reaction was prompt and positive. In a memorandum to Hull, Murray revealed his support for the CASOC plan. In view of Ibn Saud's financial requirements, the Allied situation in the Middle East, and the fact that the king was "fundamentally" anti-Axis, the NE chief concluded that "since Ibn Saud's influence is great in the Arab world a good case can be made out in favor of granting him financial support."[25] To the department's Arab hands, the advantages of CASOC's proposal were clear. The arrangement might add to the secu-

rity of a potentially valuable oil concession and would increase Allied
influence in Saudi Arabia, thus strengthening the defense of the entire
Middle East. Although Murray raised doubts about the wisdom of the
United States marketing the oil it received from CASOC, he suggested
that funds for the king might be channeled through the newly created
lend-lease administration. Murray concluded that "such help might be
extended in return for satisfactory political assurances and commitments by Ibn Saud."[26] On 25 April, Hull forwarded Murray's memorandum to Roosevelt.

The president was eager to sound out the practicality of CASOC's
proposal. On 30 April, Roosevelt, apparently with the idea of having
the navy consider the oil purchase idea, forwarded the proposal and
NE's memorandum to Frank Knox, secretary of the navy. The president instructed Knox to consider the plan, "then send for Moffett and
see if you can work out something to submit to me."[27]

In the meantime, SOCAL-CASOC representatives, in a flurry of phone
calls and personal visits, lobbied for the CASOC plan in State Department offices. Chief among the oil company lobbyists was Max W.
Thornburg, vice-president of BAPCO. In a conversation with Paul Alling, Thornburg outlined the deteriorating situation in the Near East,
particularly in Iraq. As for Ibn Saud, Thornburg advised, he was basi-
cally pro-British but if need be he would play along with the Axis.
Unless the king's financial requirements were met, Thornburg concluded, he might be tempted to adopt such a course. Already sympathetic to the CASOC plan, Alling noted that perhaps the Lend-Lease
Act could be used to assist the king.[28] In view of Rashid Ali's attempted
coup in Baghdad and the possible threat to the British position in Iraq,
NE was aware of the importance of maintaining Allied influence in
Saudi Arabia and the Gulf. Sensing NE's concern, CASOC seemed to
believe that vigorous lobbying might facilitate its proposal. In a set of
notes prepared after his visit to Washington, Thornburg outlined a
strategy: "I have the idea that once this plan or some modification of
it, has received the President's initial blessing, its progress could be
accelerated by working with Chiefs and Assistant Chiefs of Divisions,
rather than with the extremely busy top few."[29]

The Moffett proposal, however, seemed to catch the attention of
government officials on all levels. Early in May, in a meeting with
Lord Halifax, British ambassador to the United States, Hull discussed
the CASOC plan and NE memorandum. Halifax agreed with Hull's idea
that the British should assist in "keeping the King in a proper state of
mind" and offered to refer the matter of increased subsidies to his
government.[30] The idea of persuading the British to increase their

assistance seemed a natural alternative to direct American aid. British subsidies to Ibn Saud had begun during World War I as a means of securing his support against the Turks, and continued thereafter for the purpose of maintaining the king's support in the Persian Gulf area. More important, the United States was still formally neutral, and Saudi Arabia, if not the entire Middle East, was considered to be an area of primary British responsibility. Accordingly, on 12 May, Alling informed Moffett that the president had decided to defer action on his proposal until it was known precisely what action the British were prepared to take.[31]

Great Britain was quick to see the importance of increasing its assistance to Ibn Saud. Although British officials, particularly those in Treasury, were painfully aware of the king's past fiscal irresponsibility and extravagance, F. H. W. Stonehewer-Bird, British minister in Jidda, assured the Foreign Office of the seriousness of the king's situation. Revenues from the pilgrimage and customs duties had dropped "almost to the vanishing point" at a time when it was crucial that Ibn Saud maintain his subsidies to the tribes. If the king could not pay his "tribesmen," Stonehewer-Bird warned, "the Germans may well find means to do so." The minister concluded, "you will I am convinced agree that the regime must not collapse at this highly critical time and will feel it imperative to furnish immediate aid."[32]

Disturbed by the implications of the Rashid Ali movement in Iraq and determined to maintain its influence in Saudi Arabia and the gulf, the Foreign Office succeeded in obtaining a £200,000 increase in its wartime grants to Ibn Saud. Meeting with Murray in May, Neville Butler, minister-counselor at the British Embassy in Washington, noted that in view of the king's financial predicament and his loyalty to Britain, London had taken steps to increase its assistance. Butler expressed the hope that it would now be possible for the United States to consider granting financial aid to Saudi Arabia.[33]

Despite the prospect of increasing British assistance to the king, State Department officials were disturbed by the situation in Saudi Arabia. Writing to Hull, Murray noted that according to Moffett the situation in Saudi Arabia was "becoming more and more desperate." The company, Moffett had concluded, could no longer continue its "large advances."[34] That same week, Murray took the matter up with Assistant Secretary of State Adolph Berle. "Everyone seems to agree," Murray noted, "that the King is in urgent need of assistance since his ordinary income from the pilgrim traffic and duties on imported products has been substantially reduced." Berle noted his reaction in the margin of Murray's memorandum: "I think Moffett's proposal ought to be developed and carried out. If need be we could finance via RFC."[35] (The Reconstruction Finance Corporation.)

If the State Department officials were uneasy about the delay in the Moffett matter, CASOC's anxiety seemed to rise with each passing day. In May, Lenahan informed Davies from Jidda that the situation in the field was rapidly declining. Ibn Saud was insisting on the balance of the original January agreement in addition to funds for minting riyals. Although Davies instructed CASOC's field representatives to credit the king with another $500,000, the company must have realized that this advance would only temporarily satisfy Ibn Saud.[36]

Even before the news from Jidda, the oilmen had expanded and intensified their efforts to gain financial support for the king. On 14 May, in an effort to follow up his April meeting with Roosevelt, Moffett claims to have met with the president. The oilman reviewed the proposal and asked the president whether the navy might consider purchasing the oil as a naval reserve. Roosevelt seemed interested and set up an appointment for Moffett to see Knox. That same day, Moffett met with Knox and discussed the possibility of using Saudi crude. Although Moffett claimed that Knox was sympathetic to the idea of supporting the king, the navy had no appropriations for such a venture. As to the possibility of purchasing finished products, Knox informed Moffett that he would study the matter and forward his decision to the White House.[37]

The navy's response to Roosevelt's letter of 30 April dealt company efforts an even greater blow. On 20 May, Knox informed the president that the quality of the oil products proposed in the Moffett plan did not meet navy standards. Knox appreciated the seriousness of the situation in Saudi Arabia and even suggested that he would not be opposed to appropriating a small sum of money to secure the "military support" of the king. Yet the secretary of the navy concluded that "there was no sound business reason for mixing that help up with the purchase of the type of oil produced in that field."[38]

The navy's response posed a difficult problem for advocates of financial assistance to the king. By questioning the quality of CASOC's products, the navy eliminated any commercial justification for channeling American aid to Ibn Saud. Murray attempted to salvage the proposal by suggesting that the company might be willing to substitute oil from American fields in order to increase United States naval supplies in the West Indies, but the oil arrangements in the CASOC plan were simply not salvageable.[39] Although the president, the Department of State, the secretary of the navy, and the secretary of commerce clearly sought to assist Ibn Saud in some manner, it seemed that no one knew precisely how to do so. Unless the British increased their subsidies or an alternative to a quid pro quo in oil could be arranged, the burden of the king's financial troubles would once again fall on the oil company.

Despite continuing government interest in the Moffett proposal, further action seemed blocked by serious political and legal obstacles. With the United States not yet a formal belligerent, outright grants to foreign governments, or even the use of lend-lease in any but the most urgent cases, might have subjected the administration to severe pressure from isolationist critics. By early June, however, the president and the State Department, having learned that Great Britain planned to increase its subsidies to the king, continued their efforts to meet Ibn Saud's total request.[40] The only remaining legal alternative, despite the political risks, appeared to be lend-lease legislation. NE had suggested the idea in its initial reaction to the Moffett proposal, and Roosevelt seemed to be in favor of it as well. Writing to Jesse Jones in June regarding assistance to Saudi Arabia, Harry Hopkins noted that, "the President is anxious to find a way to do something about this matter." Hopkins added that some of the aid could be funded in food shipments directly under lend-lease, but quipped "although just how we could call that outfit a 'democracy' I don't know."[41]

By the middle of June it appeared that Roosevelt had approved, at least in principle, the idea of using lend-lease to assist Ibn Saud. In a conversation with Lloyd Hamilton, general manager of CASOC, Alling learned that Jones had received the "green light" from the president to pursue the extension of financial assistance to Ibn Saud.[42] The following day Hamilton again informed Alling that, in a conversation with Jones, Moffett had learned that the president had indeed approved the idea but that Jones personally could not see how it could be handled under lend-lease. Jones had added, however, that he would attempt to find another method of dealing with the matter.[43]

Eager to facilitate the transaction, the State Department pushed CASOC to have Ibn Saud submit a formal request for American aid.[44] Late in June, Alexander Kirk, American minister in Egypt, forwarded to the department an official Saudi request for a $10,000,000 line of credit. Kirk, a vigorous advocate of greater American participation in Saudi Arabia and the Middle East, echoed a familiar line: "The importance of insuring the sympathy of the Arab world at this time cannot be too strongly emphasized and the Kingdom of Saudi Arabia is the logical field for American endeavor in that regard. I am convinced that immediate financial assistance to that Government should be regarded as a profitable investment over and above all actual business considerations."[45] Only the day before, Davies of CASOC, sensing that the loan was progressing, informed Fred Ohliger that it "now appears probable loan will be made in some form . . ."[46]

In July despite NE's efforts to ensure favorable action on financial aid to the king, the matter became bogged down in the politics and technicalities of lend-lease and RFC legislation. Although Roosevelt had informed Jones that he would like to be of some assistance, loaning money to Ibn Saud was a political and legal risk for the administration.[47] RFC legislation permitted purchases of strategic materials so designated by the president, but purchasing petroleum products below acceptable military specifications would have left the administration vulnerable to a variety of undesirable charges. Davies, usually an accurate barometer of changing government attitudes, advised Lenahan "we suggest caution in communicating to King that loan is any more than good probability at present."[48] On 18 July, in a brief note to Jones, Roosevelt apparently made his final decision. "Will you tell the British I hope they can take care of the King of Saudi-Arabia. This is a little far afield for us!"[49]

The apparent shift in Roosevelt's attitude toward direct aid to Saudi Arabia seems to have been partly a result of the political risks involved in funding the king. According to Warren Pierson, chairman of the Export-Import Bank, the administration decided against lend-lease because of its fear of provoking isolationist critics. In conversation with Jesse Jones the oilmen heard a similar line—"that they [the administration] could not do anything because of the political repercussions in the Middle Western States. Even a little move like this might set off an avalanche and the isolationists would scream to high heaven. . . ."[50] With lend-lease not yet four months old and the administration already accused of interventionist sentiments, it is likely that political factors influenced Roosevelt's thinking.

Equally important was Roosevelt's belief that Saudi Arabia, if not the entire Middle East, was an area of primary British interest and responsibility. Even NE, leading a campaign for more active American involvement in Saudi Arabia and the gulf, was forced to confront circumstances in 1941. In a conversation with Davies and Hamilton of CASOC in August, Murray pointed out that "Saudi Arabia lies in an area in which British interests are much greater than ours and that the British are therefore more directly concerned." The NE chief added that London had a "long background" in the area of "political loans" while Washington had no such tradition.[51] The United States, not yet a participant in the war, was hardly prepared to assume responsibilities for an area which had been considered a British sphere of influence for almost a century and a half.

The belief that Great Britain might continue to assume the responsibility for funding Ibn Saud was reflected in the administration's last ditch efforts to aid the king. Roosevelt's request to Jones to sound out further British support for Saudi Arabia was not intended as an idle gesture. On 22 July, Jones informed Hopkins that "there appears to be no legal way that we can help the King so with the approval of the President, I suggested to Lord Halifax and Sir Frederick Phillips, also Mr. Neville Butler, that they arrange taking care of the King."[52]

What Jones meant by "taking care of the King" is not entirely clear. According to Rodgers and Moffett, Jones had been unable to find a way to extend direct financial assistance to Saudi Arabia without securing collateral from the company. Although the oilmen could certainly provide collateral in the form of petroleum products, CASOC preferred a government loan directly to the king rather than through the company. In short, the oilmen were interested primarily in the political implications of direct American aid. Jones reportedly agreed to explore the proposal.[53]

More important, there is evidence to suggest that Jones had developed a plan through which American money could be channeled to Ibn Saud without the political complications of lend-lease. In late July, a $425,000,000 RFC wartime loan to Great Britain was in the final stages of approval. On 18 July, the RFC Board, in a letter from Jones to Sir Frederick Phillips, confirmed the loan but stipulated that although $415,000,000 would be transferred to the British upon request, the remaining $10,000,000 would be forwarded when sufficient collateral had been received. Why Jones singled out the sum of $10,000,000, the precise amount requested by Ibn Saud for his 1941 budget, is not clear. Perhaps Jones had earmarked the sum for Ibn Saud, to be channeled through the British when sufficient collateral had been received from London. Nonetheless, on 25 July, Jones told Rodgers of the Texas Company that "there was no hurry, re: The Arabian situation, for according to figures J.A.M. and Writer gave him, the King of Arabia was taken care of until toward end of year by England and Joint Company!"[54] Although official records do not confirm that the RFC loan was approved with any precise stipulation that the British fund Ibn Saud, it is more than likely, in view of American efforts to assist the king, that Jones tried to arrange a gentleman's agreement in which Great Britain would fund Ibn Saud with RFC dollars.[55]

Although the oilmen had failed to secure direct American aid for the king, the Moffett affair provided an important foundation on which American oil diplomacy was soon to develop. CASOC's campaigning broadened a gradually widening channel of contact between oilmen

and government officials and set precedents of mutual cooperation
and accessibility which would characterize the war years. The Moffett
proposal not only enabled the companies to present their interests to
the president and his administration, but also it offered an opportunity
to highlight the political and strategic importance of Saudi Arabia.

Equally important, Moffett's proposal revealed the extent of official
interest in Saudi Arabia. The president, the federal loan administrator,
the secretary of the navy, and the State Department had all given
serious consideration to assisting the king. Within the Department of
State, consistent support for the oilmens' plan was largely confined to
the Division of Near Eastern Affairs, yet it was these officials who
would play the key role in shaping the department's attitude toward
Arabian oil. Although by 1941, these Middle Eastern experts were
more immediately concerned with the political advantages of Ibn
Saud's influence than with the strategic benefits of the king's oil, the
Moffett proposal further stimulated their interest in Saudi petroleum.
The idea of using lend-lease as an instrument to assist Ibn Saud laid
the basis for future consideration of aid to the king, and provided the
means to effect a new relationship between oilmen and government
and between the United States and Saudi Arabia. Despite its failure,
the Moffett affair revealed that the United States had indeed begun to
recognize a new role and interest in Saudi Arabia.

The Department of State was not altogether pleased with the events
leading to the final rejection of the Moffett proposal. In August, the
department informed Alexander Kirk in Cairo that despite consideration "from every angle"—the president, the navy, the Office of Lend-
Lease, the federal loan administrator—the United States could not
make advances to Ibn Saud against oil in the ground or through lend-
lease. Kirk was informed that the British would continue to look after
the needs of the king.[56] Already an advocate of a greater American
role in the Middle East, Kirk could not conceal his disappointment
over Washington's decision. In a telegram to the department, he
noted: "I gather that there are factors other than the actual merits of
the case which are regarded as precluding the extension of American
financial aid to Saudi Arabia. It may be presumed that the Saudi Arabian Government will so infer and that no explanation will negate that
impression or mitigate the repercussion of the refusal to respond to its
appeal especially after the lapse of time during which it has apparently
been under consideration."[57]

In September, the companies apparently sought to reopen the question of financial aid. Meeting with Roosevelt on 23 September, Moffett
again reviewed the matter and inquired whether there was any new

legislation which might permit a loan to Saudi Arabia. Although, according to Moffett, the president was "anxious" to help, the official response remained the same. The president and secretary of state were both "sympathetic" to the king's needs, Jones wrote to Moffett in early October, yet the United States could not provide Ibn Saud with a loan or advances on oil royalties.[58]

For the oilmen, however, the matter was far from closed. In a revealing letter to Reginald Stoner of SOCAL, Max W. Thornburg, a former vice-president of BAPCO and now a special assistant to the under secretary of state, outlined a future strategy. "My own view is that the approach of large-scale operations in the Near East will—in the reasonably near future—provide ample ground for the matter of our support to be raised through purely political channels—for example via Kirk in Cairo. I know that he strongly favors such support, quite apart from oil-company interests. Then, when Kirk's request hits this Dept. —in the Near East Division which also strongly supports the idea of backing Ibn Saud—it would be passed through various other divisions which have a say in matters of this kind and then start on up the line."[59] For the moment, however, the companies were prepared to let the matter rest. In a cable to Davies, Roy Lebkicher wrote from Jidda: "Strongly urge that you abandon efforts to obtain U.S. Government loan for the present and concentrate your Washington efforts convincing British that necessary Government financing over and above our reasonable flat sum contribution is their responsibility."[60]

Although, by the fall of 1941, it was clear that direct financial assistance to Saudi Arabia was not possible, State Department officials continued to advocate government support for Ibn Saud. In view of the king's inevitable disappointment over the failure of the loan and the possible loss of prestige which might result from a rejection of his personal request for funds, NE's officers believed it important to develop an alternate plan. Writing to Berle in September, Alling suggested the possibility of sending an agricultural mission to Saudi Arabia, the justification for this being the king's long-standing desire to develop the water and agricultural resources of his country. Moreover, Ibn Saud's "predominant position" in the Arab world, Alling wrote, was sufficient reason to maintain his goodwill.[61]

Even more important was the need to lessen the king's disappointment over the failure of his request for funds. In a memorandum to Welles, Alling again pushed this point. "In view of Ibn Saud's importance and influence in the critical Middle Eastern area, it would be regrettable if we should let him down completely."[62] NE's persistence seemed to have considerable influence with the higher officers in the department. On 26 September the secretary of state instructed Kirk to sound out Saudi interest in the possibility of a mission.[63]

Throughout the fall of 1941, the Division of Near Eastern Affairs continued to search for a means to assist Ibn Saud. The United States' position on direct financial aid to the king was determined, however, by factors beyond the division's control. NE nevertheless continued to do what little it could to support the position of the king. If support for Ibn Saud could not be made available in money, perhaps it could be channeled in material and supplies. Writing to the Economic Defense Board in October regarding export licenses for oil and mining equipment in the Arabian peninsula, Alling suggested that these licenses be given "as liberal treatment as possible." Because the "prestige of King Ibn Saud in the Arab world is unequaled," Alling concluded, support for the Saudi economy might also strengthen the Allied position in the area.[64]

Although the political advantages of maintaining Ibn Saud's influence and authority in the Persian Gulf continued to be the main focus of NE's attention, oil was beginning to emerge more clearly in official thinking. In a memorandum outlining American interests in Saudi Arabia, Alling noted: "Our direct material interest in Saudi Arabia is important and it would be particularly desirable in view of the important part which the Arabian oilfields would play in the Middle East campaign if the Russian and Iranian oilfields should be knocked out, to insure a sympathetic attitude on the part of Ibn Saud and his Government toward American interests."[65] Supporting BAPCO's export licenses, NE officials again emphasized the value of Persian Gulf oil. In the event the Russian and Iranian fields and refineries became inaccessible, "Bahrein would become of immense importance in supplying the Russian and the British Middle East forces with petroleum products, there being no other source of supply worth mentioning closer than the Dutch East Indies, on the one hand, and the Western Hemisphere, on the other."[66] Although the department's Middle Eastern hands viewed the oil of Saudi Arabia and the Persian Gulf as a potential source of supply, a second line of oil operations for the war effort, officials were beginning to recognize its value as a future wartime asset.

Increasing interest in the petroleum of the Persian Gulf was in no small part a result of the efforts of the oilmen themselves. In the vigorous lobbying for the Moffett proposal, CASOC representatives provided the department with the facts and figures of oil development in al-Hasa. The most curious legacy of the Moffett affair, however, was Max Thornburg, vice-president of BAPCO. Thornburg had first descended upon the department in late April of 1941 in the flurry of phone calls and visits of CASOC representatives. In July, the State Department, conducting studies on strategic materials under the direction of Herbert Feis, the department's economic adviser, decided to recruit an expert on petroleum. Thornburg, recommended to Feis by Hamilton Fish Armstrong, editor of *Foreign Affairs*, was hired, given the title of special assistant to the under secretary of state, and nominally attached to Feis's office. By September, the new petroleum consultant had already begun to operate independently of the economic adviser. Writing to Stoner, in September, Thornburg admitted that he could do nothing to salvage the Moffett proposal, "because an oil man is sort of branded around here;" yet he added that Paul Alling had recently asked him if he would be available to advise NE on its oil problems. Thornburg concluded, "I presume I shall be better posted from now on."[67]

In his new capacity as consultant on petroleum matters, Thornburg brought to the department a greater emphasis on Middle Eastern oil and directed much of his energy toward formation of a comprehensive approach toward foreign petroleum. In October, Thornburg instructed Walton C. Ferris, a young foreign service officer, to begin preparation of a study on United States' foreign oil policy. Ferris's draft, later revised by Thornburg, contained at least two of the key assumptions on which war and postwar planners would later base their view of Middle Eastern oil. First, United States' proven reserves, estimated at some 19,000,000,000 or 20,000,000,000 barrels, were declining at a rate faster than new reserves were being discovered. Unless the trend were reversed, the United States would inevitably move from a position of net exporter to net importer of crude oil. Second, in order to counteract this shift, American reserves would have to be conserved by exploiting the oil of foreign areas. Markets previously supplied with the oil of the Western Hemisphere would have to draw upon Eastern Hemisphere crude. Eventually the United States might have to increase its imports substantially. The memorandum concluded, prophetically, that as the United States moved toward a position of net importer, "our foreign oil policy will probably become more aggressive and will come more and more to resemble Great Britain's policy of the past thirty years."[68] Although State Department interest in oil from the Middle East did not evolve to the policy planning stages until 1943, these principles laid much of the theoretical foundation on which this diplomacy would rest.

If Thornburg sought to influence NE's thinking from within the department, CASOC attempted to maintain government interest in Saudi Arabia from without. Davies advised Lebkicher in Jidda in early October of 1941: "As you know we have been attempting educate Washington on King's needs and will continue to do so even in face of difficulties raised by this request and negative reply. Present situation as regards our negotiations still same. We do not consider entirely hopeless although not overly optimistic particularly as regards direct US assistance." [69] In view of Ibn Saud's increasing demands and Washington's refusal to extend financial aid, CASOC quickly realized that it had only two alternatives. The company might increase its advances and assume the majority of the king's financial requirements or it might encourage the British to shoulder the burden of Ibn Saud's budget. The company apparently decided on the latter course. [70] Although CASOC was not particularly happy about the prospect of increasing British influence in Saudi Arabia, the oilmen had cooperated with London in the past, coordinating subsidies and discussing methods of stabilizing the king's finances.

More important, the company sensed that the greatest threat to the security of their investment was not Great Britain, but the instability which might result from a financial or economic crisis. Corruption, financial irresponsibility, and mismanagement might easily jeopardize the concession, particularly after Ibn Saud's death. "My impression is that Government unique is being held together by personal strength of King," Lebkicher cabled Davies, "but with very little integrity or really active interest in country's welfare elsewhere." After reporting that the British had suggested the possibility of a financial adviser for the king, Lebkicher concluded that London "might be able tactfully to make him understand need for better organization by appealing to his probable interest in the future preservation of country he has created." [71]

There is little doubt that many of CASOC's anxieties about British influence in Saudi Arabia were expressly manufactured for the Department of State. The company had employed the British bogey since Moffett's April 1941 meeting with Roosevelt and would use it time and again. In a conversation with Alling in late November, James Terry Duce and Davies explained that in addition to British aid for 1942, the company would make advances of almost $3,000,000. When Alling asked why such advances were necessary, Davies noted that CASOC "desired to avoid, if possible, having the British be the only source of income to the King for fear that they would attempt to exact certain *quid pro quos*." [72]

The oilmen had considerable success in stimulating NE's suspicion of British motives in Saudi Arabia. In part, NE's susceptibility was a result of traditional Anglo-American competition over oil. So too,

State Department officers were eager to safeguard what they believed to be an increasing American stake in Saudi oil. Finally, like many American officials facing new responsibilities in areas of the world in which they had little experience and influence, NE seemed to adopt a cautious, almost "worst case" view of the course of events. Whatever "quid pro quos" the company feared the British might exact from the king, it was clear that CASOC's concerns were beginning to have an effect on officials. Echoing the company's suspicions, Gordon Merriam concluded that "the possibility must be squarely faced that if the British alone . . . get Ibn Saud through his present difficulties they may seek a future recompense at the expense of American interests in that country." [73]

The entrance of the United States into the war in December 1941, and the possibility that the Middle East might become an active military theater in 1942, increased American interest in Saudi Arabia and the Persian Gulf. Shortly after Pearl Harbor, Murray concluded that the "political conditions" which compelled the department to look favorably on aid to Saudi Arabia had now intensified. All of the chief supply lines to the Allies with the exception of the Atlantic connection lay across the Middle East and Muslim world. The friendship of Ibn Saud and loyalty of his government, Murray concluded, were now most important to the Allied cause. [74]

The new significance of Saudi Arabia lay primarily in the political importance of its king and in its strategic location. Sandwiched between two vital bodies of water, the Red Sea with its crucial aperture at Suez, and the Persian Gulf, warm water supply outlet to the Soviet Union, Saudi Arabia appeared to offer a key link in Allied supply lines and air routes. By the end of 1941, the United States had made plans to deploy two military supply missions in the area—the United States Military Iranian Mission under the direction of Colonel Raymond A. Wheeler; and the United States Military North African Mission under the command of Brigadier General Russell L. Maxwell. With the Saudi-Transjordanian frontier only fifty miles from the Kirkuk-Haifa pipeline, and the Saudi-Iraqi border within one hundred miles of the British air station at Shu'aiba, the importance of the Arabian peninsula as a second line of defense for Egypt and the Suez Canal increased. Hitler's invasion of the Soviet Union in June 1941 and the successful advance of German panzer divisions toward the Caucasus threatened to expose the entire northern rim of the Middle East to Nazi attack. In January 1942, the second British retreat in Cyrenaica only emphasized the necessity of maintaining Allied positions in Saudi Arabia and the gulf. [75]

The Department of State, already conscious of the wartime significance of Saudi Arabia, continued to search for a means to assist the
king. The War Department as well was becoming interested in the
possibility of air routes across the peninsula. In light of the new American military missions bordering Saudi Arabia, the Army Air Corps
and the Air Transport Command attached new importance to securing
overflight rights and emergency landing privileges.[76] Although NE officials still favored consideration of direct financial aid to Ibn Saud, the
only feasible course at the time seemed to be reconsideration of the
agricultural mission. Prospects for the success of such a mission
brightened in mid-December with information from Alexander Kirk
that the Saudi chargé in Cairo had inquired about the possibility of
obtaining American irrigation experts. Writing to Harold Ickes, secretary of the interior, in January 1942, in support of an agricultural mission, Hull concluded that with Saudi Arabia lying between two
strategic bodies of water and with its "important oil production," both
the War and the State Department thought it advisable to secure the
goodwill of the king.[77]

The War Department's interest in the possibility of air transit rights
across Saudi Arabia only accelerated the department's efforts to gain
approval for an agricultural mission. Technical assistance to Ibn Saud,
particularly in an area vital to the development of Saudi Arabia, might
serve to recover any American prestige lost in the Moffett affair as well
as to "pave the way" for War Department requests for air rights. In
February, Welles formally presented the idea of a mission to the president.[78]

Roosevelt not only approved the dispatch of agricultural experts but
also supported the department's idea of establishing a permanent legation at Jidda.[79] Writing to Welles, expressing his pleasure with the
president's decision, Murray noted: "As you know, matters are developing very rapidly in relation to that country and it seems to be perfectly clear that it will be necessary for us to have someone on the
spot."[80] Murray recommended that the post be filled by James Moose,
an Arabic-speaking foreign service officer then serving as consul in
Tehran. Plans were thus initiated to establish a legation at Jidda in the
late spring. Kirk was to remain minister to Egypt, accredited also to
Saudi Arabia; Moose would serve as chargé for all of Saudi Arabia. In
the meantime, the department informed Kirk that an agricultural mission headed by Karl Twitchell would depart for Cairo in March.[81]

The dispatch of an agricultural mission and the decision to establish
a legation, as well as the presence of military missions, reflected an
increasing American involvement not only in Saudi Arabia, but

throughout the Middle East. The American role in the area focused primarily on supply and communications. With lend-lease beginning to supply the British and Russian war effort, American commitments in the area rose dramatically. By 1942 there were 30,000 American troops in the Persian Gulf, the largest single military unit stationed in any sector of the Middle East theater.[82] This Persian corridor became a vital supply link in the campaign to support Soviet forces against the German invasion. Of the 7,900,000 long tons of supplies which passed through Persian Gulf ports between 1941 and 1945, more than half were handled by the United States Army.[83] Writing to Assistant Secretary of State Dean Acheson in April 1942, Frederick Winant, soon to become the American representative on the British-controlled Middle East Supply Center (MESC), reflected the changing American role. "With the increasing aid to that territory through Lend-Lease shipments and the substitution of United States suppliers for the former European suppliers, United States interests in the Near East have become of increasing importance. As far as the future may be appraised, the present trend will undoubtedly continue. From the point of view of self-interest, therefore, the United States should consider the possibility of playing a more important role in Near Eastern affairs."[84]

Despite its increasing commitments, Washington continued to regard most areas of the Middle East as spheres of British responsibility. Although the United States formally joined MESC in the summer of 1942, many officials sought to avoid any unilateral American commitment in the area. In fact, with the opening of the North African campaign, the escalation of the war in Europe, and the long struggle ahead in the Pacific, the Americans were more than happy to support British hegemony in Egypt, Palestine, and Transjordan. Even in Syria and Lebanon, areas in which Great Britain had only recently acquired some measure of control, the State Department was reluctant to challenge British military policy.[85]

To many of the foreign service officers in the field and to those in the Division of Near Eastern Affairs, however, American concern and interest in the Middle East was far too passive and undefined. From the perspectives of Kirk in Cairo, George Wadsworth in Beirut and Damascus, and later James Moose in Jidda, American policy was dangerously casual. Writing to Acheson in the spring of 1942, Kirk vented his frustration. "The fact is that the Middle East means the Mediterranean, it means the richest oil fields, it means the communications to India and China and on to Japan and it means the springboard for offensives against Germany and Italy which after all happen to be the spots which are germinating the hell to which we have been reduced. I ask again are we going to laugh off this area for if so my job is merely one of discreet preparation for a possible evacuation of Americans."[86] Although these men recognized the necessity of cooperating with Great Britain for the benefit of the allied cause, they also became staunch advocates of safeguarding interests which they believed were more national in character. Nowhere was this more apparent than in the emerging view of American petroleum interests, particularly in Saudi Arabia. Here competition rather than cooperation seemed the rule; suspicion rather than trust. And here, more than in any other area, it was becoming increasingly clear that the United States was beginning to shed its image as Britain's junior partner and was preparing to assume a greater role in the affairs of the Middle East.

Although the importance of petroleum in modern warfare was obvious to Allied strategists and military planners, the role of Middle Eastern oil as a source of supply for Allied operations was far less clear. The closing of the Mediterranean in 1940 had severely curtailed petroleum development in the area. Iran and Iraq had both suffered drastic cuts in production.[87] Iraq, whose oil fields produced 30,791,000 barrels in 1939, yielded only 12,650,000 barrels in 1941.[88]

The problem was only partly a result of wartime difficulties in shipping and supply. For the most part, by 1939 Middle Eastern oil had not undergone consistent development in either crude production or refining capacity. Although Iran and Iraq were among the world's five largest crude producers, progress in Saudi Arabia, Kuwait, Qatar, and Bahrain was measured more in terms of potential reserves than actual production. In 1942, Saudi Arabia, Egypt, and Bahrain contributed a total of 19,046,000 barrels—about one-fourth of Iran's yield. Production in Qatar was still in its early stages; in Kuwait, crude output was halted entirely. In 1942, the total Middle Eastern production including Iran was approximately 91,302,000 barrels. Venezuela alone yielded 147,625,000 barrels for the same year.[89]

Middle Eastern oil was nonetheless a factor in Allied plans and operations during the early years of the war. The refining facilities at Abadan, the largest crude refinery in the Eastern Hemisphere, combined with its subsidiary units at Bandar Shahpur and Kermanshah, had a total refinery run of some 330,000 b.p.d. As a result of their strategic location and capacity to produce aviation gasoline, the Iranian facilities became a valuable source of supply for the Soviet Union as well as for American and British air squadrons throughout the Middle and Far East.[90]

The significance of this oil, however, was measured far more in terms of its potential as a source of supply and its value as a prize of war than as an immediate source of oil for campaign operations. With the critical shortage of tankers and lack of adequate pipeline facilities, oil development seemed less urgent than its denial to the enemy. The Axis need for petroleum was well known and it was clear that Hitler's southward push toward the Caucasus was partly directed at the Russian oil fields between the Caspian and Black Sea. Allied fear of further German penetration into the oil-laden areas of Iran, Iraq, or even the Persian Gulf was no idle concern. Writing to Roosevelt in December 1941, Ickes concluded that "All of these [South American] oil reserves, added together would not equal the total that Germany would possess if Germany should defeat Russia and then proceed to add . . . the reserves of Arabia, Iran, Iraq and the Persian Gulf area."[91]

Although some American intelligence reports indicated that Axis control of Middle Eastern oil fields and refineries would be more important for the future "New Order" than for the immediate prosecution of war, others suggested that German access to the oil might offer the enemy a valuable strategic advantage. In view of the expanding Axis military threat to North Africa and to the northeast through the Caucasus, control of Middle Eastern oil might provide a strategic source of crude for Axis operations from Africa to the subcontinent. In July 1942, an American intelligence study bluntly warned that, "the acquisition of the undamaged Middle East oil fields would solve the oil problem of the Axis."[92]

Although the potential of oil in the Middle East was an important consideration in Allied planning, it had little tangible effect on United States petroleum planning or operations between 1939 and 1942. Middle Eastern oil production paled before the capacity of the domestic industry. In 1941, American production exceeded 3,800,000 b.p.d.— 63 percent of the world crude output. More important, particularly after the United States entered the war, was the industry's maximum efficient rate of production (MER)—the maximum rate at which reserves could be extracted from the ground without permanently damaging the reservoir. By December 1941, the MER was estimated at 4,760,000 b.p.d., almost one million barrels in excess of actual production.[93]

This crucial margin not only enabled the United States to meet the majority of its civilian and military requirements but also to fuel the Allied war effort. With estimates of proven reserves between eighteen and twenty billion barrels, the highest reserve level in the industry's history, there seemed to be little need for Middle Eastern oil reserves.

If and when the United States was forced to search out foreign areas of supply, the rich fields of Venezuela offered a more likely alternative. In January 1942, with Western Hemisphere production supplying the British and other Allied forces with almost a million b.p.d. in crude and refined products, dependence on Eastern Hemisphere crude appeared highly unlikely.[94]

Although both government and oil company officials expressed great confidence in the ability of the American petroleum industry to supply the nation's wartime needs, the realities of war had already begun to complicate the picture. At first the problem appeared to be transportation. Losses to U-boats and priority scheduling diversions, in early 1942, curtailed the availability of tankers. The east coast in particular, receiving almost 95 percent of its oil requirements via ocean tanker from the Gulf of Mexico and Western states, faced serious cutbacks in consumption. In February 1942, Harold Ickes, petroleum coordinator for national defense, in conjunction with the War Production Board (WPB) issued a directive reducing deliveries of gasoline to east coast service stations. With petroleum stocks on the Atlantic Seaboard below the 1941 level, further restrictions on nonessential civilian consumption were expected.[95]

Transportation was not the only area which troubled government officials. Testifying before the Petroleum Subcommittee of the House Interstate and Foreign Commerce Committee in February, Ickes raised an entirely new set of disturbing questions: "When we talked of oil reserves in 1934, we could measure them in terms of years' supply without feeling too much concern over a difference of a year or two. . . . Our oil reserves now must be measured in terms of present production: how much can we produce now, and can we maintain that production at the full, necessary level until the war is over?"[96] The concern about domestic reserves did not involve the actual level of proven reserves, but had more to do with productive capacity. The nation's proven reserves gave only a rough indication of the long-range ability to produce oil. Far more telling, particularly in a wartime situation, was the measure of the industry's capacity to extract oil from the ground efficiently. Although the industry's maximum efficient rate of production was secure, the relationship between new discoveries and recovery rates seemed to provide cause for some concern. In 1934, 86 new pools were discovered with an average recovery rate of 19,400,000 barrels per pool. In 1941, however, with the discovery of 340 pools, the rate had declined to only 1,200,000 barrels per pool. Not all government or industry experts agreed as to the seriousness of the downward trend, yet the American Petroleum Institute concluded that the chances of finding a major field between 1938 and 1940 were 2.5 times less likely than in the period 1934 to 1936.[97]

The fact that the immediate problem continued to be one of transportation and supply rather than an actual shortage of oil was no source of comfort to millions of Americans forced to restrict their driving. In May 1942, the first formal rationing of gasoline was introduced. To officials of the Interior Department and War Production Board, the shortage, whether a result of transportation or availability, still forced the United States to draw upon reserve stocks in order to balance consumption and production. The average monthly demand for the first seven months of 1942 was 4,110,000 b.p.d. Production was averaging only 3,870,000 b.p.d., leaving a deficit of some 240,000 b.p.d.[98]

The situation was by no means critical, yet the new demands and challenges of world war heightened American concern over the availability of oil. The new uses of petroleum derivatives—toluene for TNT, butadiene for synthetic rubber—combined with marked increases in the demand for aviation gasoline and fuel oil called for a shift in the type and quantity of petroleum production. Concern with the problem of transportation now began to merge with anxieties over the availability and supply of crude. The rising military and domestic requirements of a nation at war and the added responsibility of exporting oil to its Allies challenged the United States for the first time in twenty years to take a hard look at the potential of its own crude reserves.

Increasing concern over wartime domestic reserves and production capacity inevitably focused attention on the importance of foreign oil. The United States had already recognized Venezuelan crude as a means to supplement exports and to conserve its own reserves. Tanker shortages combined with increased submarine activity in the Atlantic, however, clearly indicated the need for a potential source of crude closer to the military theaters. Despite difficulties of supply and transportation, oil in the Middle East seemed to offer a potential source of supply in a strategic location. The area's proven reserves, even by the most conservative standards, totaled 15,000,000,000 barrels, with unproven estimates as high as 40,000,000,000. With increased refinery capacity and crude output, Middle Eastern oil had the potential to supplement wartime needs and relieve the drain on Western Hemisphere reserves. In July 1942, an intelligence study by the Board of Economic Warfare estimated that the area's "productive potentialities" were greater than the Caucasus fields and perhaps as great as those of the United States. The report concluded: "Middle East oil production constitutes the only available substantial oil resources of the United

States in the Eastern Hemisphere for use of British or American armed forces."[99]

The increasing interest in oil in the Middle East was reflected in a meeting held in early January in the office of Wallace Murray. The conference, attended by representatives of the War and State Departments, Lend-Lease Administration, SOCAL, CASOC, and the Texas Company, was called to discuss the postwar implications of building military pipelines in Iran and Iraq. Discussion soon focused, however, on the importance of the oil and the necessity of protecting American interests after the war. Having catalogued Britain's attempts to exclude American companies from Middle Eastern oil following World War I, Murray emphasized that the State Department's main concern was to protect the "long-range interests" of the United States in oil, not the interests of individual companies. NE's chief also reminded the group that "competent authorities" had indicated that domestic oil supplies were not "inexhaustible" and that it was important to consider securing access to foreign supplies.[100]

The Department of State, largely through the efforts of Max Thornburg and the officers of NE, was rapidly becoming aware of the potential of foreign petroleum, particularly Middle Eastern oil. Throughout 1942, Thornburg, as petroleum adviser, had attempted to focus the department's attention on the problems of foreign oil, and to coordinate official petroleum planning. In early February 1942, apparently on Thornburg's advice, a program of petroleum attachés was developed. These representatives, attached to various diplomatic missions, were to gather information on petroleum operations and to report special oil-related problems to the department.[101]

Thornburg's particular interest and area of expertise, however, was the Middle East. Writing to Alling in April of 1942, Thornburg urged that there was need for "aggressive action" toward "safeguarding oil supplies for war in the Middle East," and throughout that year he continued to urge a more energetic American policy toward Middle Eastern petroleum.[102] By November, the petroleum adviser called the department's attention to diminishing domestic production and warned that domestic output would not continue to support the United States as an oil-exporting nation. In order to maintain American dominance in world petroleum, he advised, American oil policy must be more "realistic." After reviewing the situation in Latin and South America, Thornburg offered an example of the new realism as it pertained to the Middle East. The most important single piece of equipment for controlling the flow of world oil, Thornburg noted, was the twelve-inch valve on the Mediterranean end of the Kirkuk-Haifa pipe-line. Thornburg concluded:

> The hand on that valve, and it is not an American hand, can head the tanker fleets of the world in almost any direction it wishes by raising or lowering the level of supply in Europe. American interests have, nearly enough, as much oil in the Middle East as any other power, but another pipeline to the Mediterranean would require rights-of-way which probably could not be acquired without the intercession of this Government. Are we interested in having an American valve on the Mediterranean, through which "equal access" might take on an American meaning?[103]

Although the Department of State lacked the immediate resources to change the flow of oil between continents or to consider seriously the construction of an American pipeline, NE continued to advocate a more active policy in the one area where it might influence the course of events—Saudi Arabia. If for some reason the refineries of Abadan or Kermanshah were endangered, Bahrain and later Ras Tanura might become the only petroleum bunkers nearer than Karachi, which was over a thousand miles to the east. The abundance of Persian Gulf reserves and their potential for development might also provide a means to conserve and even supplement United States domestic reserves. The traditional reasons underlying NE's consideration of direct financial aid to Saudi Arabia since the Moffett proposal were still predominant, yet oil now began to have greater influence in shaping official thinking.

In December, in a memorandum to Berle and Acheson, Murray again presented the case for the extension of lend-lease to Saudi Arabia. Murray first reviewed the political and strategic reasons for strengthening ties with Ibn Saud, yet this time he focused on the potential importance of securing the American interest in Saudi petroleum. The Dhahran area, Murray began, "gives every promise of being one of the world's most important oilfields." Although domestic reserves, to be sure, were not on the point of exhaustion, "it is beyond dispute" that the United States might have to look abroad for supplies "long before our own fields are exhausted." With the British continuing to support the king with three to four million pounds sterling annually, there was a definite possibility, Murray warned, "that the British will demand a quid pro quo at the end of the war, and as petroleum is the only resource of interest in Saudi Arabia, the British demand, if met, would be at the expense of an American interest of the highest importance." Finally, in perhaps the first description of Arabian oil as a national concern, Murray concluded that: "It is our strong belief that the development of Saudi Arabian petroleum resources should be viewed in the light of broad national interest and that we should safeguard the position in every way possible." Acheson's immediate reaction to the idea of lend-lease is not known, but Berle noted in the margin of Alling's memorandum, "I fully agree the move is overdue." [104]

Similarly, the military had also begun to reveal a greater interest. Sensitive to the increasing military demand and the possibility of declining domestic reserves, planners had begun to consider the possible advantages of encouraging the development of foreign oil. Both the Caribbean area and the Mesopotamian Basin, the Potentials Committee of the Army-Navy Petroleum Board (ANPB) observed in December, offered a considerable amount of excess daily production. Although Western Hemisphere sources were more secure, Middle Eastern crude was nearer the United Kingdom and the Central Mediterranean military theater. Moreover, the abundance of reserves was well known. "Known reserves of crude oil within the Mesopotamian Basin . . . ," the ANPB Committee concluded, "are, for practical purposes, unlimited." [105]

American interest in Saudi Arabia before Pearl Harbor was firmly rooted in the belief that the maintenance of Ibn Saud's prestige and influence in the Muslim and Arab world was important to the stability of an area vital to the Allied war effort. This view of the king's role, already complemented by the heroic mold into which Ibn Saud had been cast, became a fundamental and unchallenged part of American policy toward Saudi Arabia. Although the oil companies had their own motives for fostering the king's image, NE's officers had come to believe that as the "outstanding leader in the Arab world," Ibn Saud could protect Allied and American interests. This belief in the king's influence within the Arab world even led some to the conclusion that Ibn Saud might be persuaded to temper Arab animosity toward the Jews of Palestine and toward the idea of a Jewish homeland. [106]

The entry of the United States into the war only increased the importance of preserving the goodwill and support of the king. With the Arabian peninsula lodged between the Red Sea and the Persian Gulf, Saudi Arabia lay astride vital air and supply links connecting North Africa and the Far East. Throughout 1942, American interests were gradually shaped by two additional considerations. First, the oil of Saudi Arabia, if not the entire Middle East, was beginning to emerge as a significant element in war and postwar planning. Increasing wartime requirements combined with what appeared to be disturbing decreases in the productive capacity of new wells heightened concern about domestic reserves and indicated a need to maintain a strong position in foreign petroleum. Saudi Arabian oil, with its vast reserve potential, seemed to offer considerable security for the future.

Second, and perhaps of more immediate concern, was the State Department's increasing uneasiness over the security of American oil interests in Saudi Arabia. Although the only immediate threat to the CASOC concession seemed to be possible Axis penetration into the Middle East, NE's officers were becoming more and more concerned about British intentions toward Saudi Arabia. The new concern was based largely on CASOC's own fears and on traditional Anglo-American rivalry over oil, rather than on tangible evidence of British designs. Nevertheless, there was a growing awareness among some that if the United States did not attend to its own petroleum interests abroad, the British most certainly would. These attitudes, soon to be set within the context of a broadening war and an increasing concern with domestic reserves, provided the basis for the emerging American interest in Saudi Arabian oil.

CHAPTER 3
CRUDE DIPLOMACY:
THE UNITED STATES AND
ARABIAN OIL, 1943

AMERICAN interest in Middle Eastern petroleum, aroused by the uncertainties of world war, increased during 1943 with the broadening American combat role in Europe and the Pacific. The lessons of the new war not only reinforced the ideas of Curzon and Clemenceau, but also added new significance to the use of oil as a strategic resource. In a war of movement and mechanization, petroleum quickly became a vital ingredient of industrial power and military strength. An army, Ralph Davies, deputy petroleum administrator, declared, "no longer marches on its stomach; an army marches, a navy sails, and an air force flies on oil."[1] If to Clemenceau oil was the lifeblood of the armies of the Great War, it had become an instrument of national survival in a world of blitzkrieg and panzer assault.

Although American wells continued to supply the majority of the nation's petroleum requirements, oil from the Middle East began to assume new importance in American war and postwar planning. The expanding naval war in the Pacific increased the importance of securing potential sources of military resupply. Moreover, the gradual reopening of the Mediterranean revealed new possibilities for the use of Middle Eastern oil. As the war progressed, this petroleum began to fuel British and American naval units in the Mediterranean and Indian Ocean. Oil from the refineries of Abadan, Haifa, and Suez supplied the Persian Gulf command, the ninth U.S. Air Force in Egypt, and the British eighth, ninth, tenth, and fourteenth armies. Persian Gulf crude also met the requirements of the Air Transport Command, the twentieth U.S. Air Force, the Africa-Middle Eastern Service Command, and provided large quantities of aviation gasoline to Soviet air units via the Persian corridor. In 1941, the refineries of the Middle East produced 38,000 b.p.d. of fuel oil and 1,600 b.p.d. of aviation gasoline for Allied military units. By 1945, the area's fuel oil output alone totaled 112,000 b.p.d.[2]

Interest in Middle Eastern petroleum was heightened by a growing concern about the situation in the United States. Despite dramatic increases in domestic production and refining capacity, rising industrial and military requirements in 1943 and anticipated increases for 1944 indicated the possibility of future shortage. Gloomy forecasts, based on a downward curve in new discoveries and a decrease in new drilling activity, seemed to indicate that the national oil barrel might be running dry. Although the industry's maximum efficient rate (MER) of production for 1943 was secure, the comfortable margin in excess productive capacity with which the United States had entered the war had decreased. Diminished productive capacity did not necessarily suggest an oil crisis or shortage, yet many officials, caught up in the alarming atmosphere of a national emergency, adopted a cautious view of the future. For a nation at war, forced to fill its own petroleum needs and those of its allies, sustained output above maximum efficient production might impair the potential and recovery capacity of valuable domestic reserves. [3]

Equally important were the long-range possibilities for petroleum development. Exploitation of Middle Eastern crude seemed to offer a means to slow the accelerating wartime drain on domestic reserves and to conserve strategically vital supplies of the continental United States and Western Hemisphere. In 1943, while the oil wells of the world produced 2,256,625,000 barrels of crude, the United States accounted for 1,505,613,000 barrels, almost 67 percent of the total output. The entire Middle East, on the other hand, with almost 40 percent of the world's proven reserves yielded only 322,579 b.p.d. for the same year. [4]

Although there was little agreement over the methods to implement a more active oil diplomacy, representatives of the Departments of State, War, Navy, Interior, and the Petroleum Administration for War (PAW), agreed that the protection and even development of Arabian oil were far too important to be left entirely to the private sector. This new attitude influenced by increasing uneasiness over the security of American oil interests in Saudi Arabia and the gulf, determined the direction of American oil diplomacy in 1943 and influenced its course in the immediate postwar period.

During the early months of 1943, the Department of State, led by the Division of Near Eastern Affairs, continued to press for a more active American role in Saudi Arabia and the Persian Gulf. The new interest in the area was, as previously mentioned, primarily a result of the growing concern about the availability of war and postwar petroleum reserves, yet officials were becoming more and more concerned about relations with the British in Saudi Arabia. During the early years of the war, the United States, in the interest of the allied cause, sought to support and even enhance Britain's influence and prestige within the Saudi kingdom.

By 1943, however, American perceptions of British intentions began to change. Eager to safeguard the American stake in Arabian oil, officials grew increasingly wary of Britain's predominant position in Saudi Arabia and the Persian Gulf. Already uneasy over what they believed to be Britain's self-serving imperial interests throughout the Middle East, NE officials attached a new and somewhat ominous meaning to Britain's long-standing interest in Saudi Arabia.[5] Traditional British involvement in the financial and political affairs of the Saudi kingdom, once welcomed and even encouraged at the time of the Moffett proposal, was now viewed by some as a potential threat to the development and security of the concession. If the British could not steal the concession whole, a prospect which must have seemed unlikely even to an Anglophobe like Wallace Murray, they might attempt to acquire a stake of their own in the undeveloped portions of the king's oil. Although it is more than likely that officials highlighted the extent of British influence in order to stimulate greater interest in Arabian oil, NE's officers were not prepared to run the risk of jeopardizing what they believed to be a national interest. In the event the concession were lost, stolen, or compromised in any way, it was they who might be held ultimately responsible.

The view that Britain had launched a campaign to prejudice the American character of the CASOC concession was for the most part confined to officials in the Division of Near Eastern Affairs. Many department officials, particularly in the Divisions of European and Financial and Monetary Affairs, were skeptical about NE's tales of British designs.[6] Similarly, officials in the Division of Commercial Policy and Agreements, sensitive to the provisions of the Atlantic Charter and postwar economic cooperation, were reluctant to touch off an Anglo-American oil scramble in the Eastern Hemisphere.[7] With the growing American interest in Saudi Arabia and the Middle East, there was likely to be some tension in an area formerly under Britain's charge. Yet, many officials believed these problems between Washington and London could be resolved without the necessity of engaging in an embarrassing diplomatic confrontation on the Arabian peninsula. Still, concerned about the possibility of wartime petroleum shortages and prompted by NE's misgivings, assistant secretaries like Berle and Welles began to focus greater attention on Arabia and its oil.[8] At the very least, it seemed, the Department of State would have to begin defining and coordinating its policy toward foreign oil, particularly in Saudi Arabia.

Early in January, Berle raised the question of oil policy with Hull, Welles, Feis, and Thornburg. Already, Berle noted, representatives of SONJ had expressed concern that certain "foreign interests" might "pre-empt" all of the oil fields in the Near East and others in Africa. Although the assistant secretary advised his colleagues to proceed with caution in their dealings with the American companies, he recommended that the department begin formulating its own views on petroleum policy.[9] Writing to Hull and Welles, Berle again pointed out the need for action: "We were already at grips with the problem of the distribution of oil facilities in French West Africa, which included their use after the war, as well as before; and with the policy to be pursued in respect to the oil reserves in Arabia; with respect to the undeveloped fields in Iran; and with respect to the yet undeveloped fields in Libya. These necessarily brought up the question of the method by which American interests were to be protected during and after the present war; and by which any of the pledges of the Atlantic Charter were to be fulfilled. These were not matters of theory."[10]

For officials in the Division of Near Eastern Affairs, the importance of protecting the American stake in Middle Eastern oil had long since moved beyond the realm of theory. Already concerned about the lack of American influence throughout the Middle East, officials were particularly sensitive to reports of increasing British activity in the one area where the United States had established some degree of influence —Saudi Arabia. In January, NE learned, presumably from CASOC officials, that London had sent experts to assist the Saudi government in eliminating the locust problem in certain parts of the Hijaz. Accompanying the entymologists, it was rumored, were British geologists.[11]

The locust party, together with rumors of a British bank in Jidda, only confirmed NE's belief in the necessity of a stronger American presence in Saudi Arabia. Although the division had formally recommended the extension of lend-lease for Ibn Saud in the fall of 1942, it was not until 9 January that Dean Acheson, then an assistant secretary of state, wrote to Edward Stettinius, lend-lease administrator, requesting that Saudi Arabia be declared eligible for lend-lease aid. Not only was Ibn Saud's kingdom the only "major political unit" in the Near East not yet eligible for lend-lease, Acheson noted, but the king's prestige and the strategic location of his realm might aid substantially in prosecuting the war.[12] Two days later, Stettinius sent the department's request on to the president, recommending its acceptance.[13]

Although the department's first formal request for lend-lease assistance did not emphasize the importance of Saudi petroleum, increasing American interest in Arabian oil was reflected in the formation of the first interdepartmental oil committee in January 1943.[14] Formed under the auspices of the under secretary of state and chaired by Herbert Feis, the Committee on International Petroleum Policy (CIPP) was the first of the department's organized efforts to coordinate a far-sighted policy to protect American oil interests abroad.[15] The committee functioned only in an advisory capacity, yet it provided a valuable forum for the discussion of current petroleum problems and a sounding board for testing future policy alternatives.[16]

The meetings of the new committee were attended by representatives of the various geographic divisions, yet it quickly became apparent that the CIPP would focus immediately on the problems of Middle Eastern petroleum, particularly on the formation of a policy toward Arabian oil.[17] On 14 January, in response to the CIPP's request for a forecast of emerging problems in the Near East and Africa, Gordon Merriam, now assistant chief of NE, submitted a country by country analysis of petroleum conditions in the area. The situation seemed particularly pressing in Saudi Arabia. After surveying the history of the concession, Merriam brought the committee up-to-date: "Chief cause for worry at the present time is the fact that since the commencement of the war the Saudi Arabian Government has been completely indigent, and has been kept on its feet by large subsidies from the British Government and advances from the oil company. The possibility that after the war the British may demand a *quid pro quo* at the expense of this important American interest has been very much on our minds." Merriam noted that the department had succeeded in dispatching an agricultural mission as a gesture of goodwill, yet this was only a "drop in the bucket." In addition Saudi Arabia had been recommended for lend-lease, but no action had yet been taken. "We believe," Merriam concluded, "that developments in Saudi Arabia should be followed with extreme care in order to protect an oil interest which is already important and is likely to become highly so."[18]

Although it is unlikely that officials were particularly disturbed by CASOC's vague reports of overly ambitious entymologists, reports of British plans to reorganize Saudi finances through the establishment of a central bank and currency reform were regarded far more seriously. On 14 January, the department learned that the British Foreign Office was considering a plan to institute currency reform in Saudi Arabia under the direct supervision of the Currency Control Board in London. The plan also included a proposal to channel Saudi imports directly through the United Kingdom Commercial Corporation, a British-directed supply organization.[19]

NE's reaction to the idea of financial reform was mixed. Officials were among the first to concede that Saudi Arabia was in desperate need of assistance, yet they were hesitant to permit the British alone to implement fundamental changes in the king's finances. Because the CASOC concession was entirely dependent upon Ibn Saud, it was impossible to separate the successful development of oil from his political and economic situation. Officials believed that resolution of Ibn Saud's financial problems, the perennial trouble spot in CASOC-Saudi relations, could not be left entirely to a power whose long-term objectives in the area might be in conflict with those of both the oil companies and the king. Although the ever-vigilant Kirk, an advocate of closer Anglo-American cooperation, favored the British plan provided the Americans participated, he cautioned that British-directed reforms might only add to the "increasingly discernible tendency toward British economic intrenchment in this area under war impact to a degree which might materially negate best intentioned postwar agreements for equality of opportunity." Kirk also advised the department to consider the early extension of lend-lease aid to Saudi Arabia.[20] On 27 January, Hull informed the minister in Egypt that the department favored the extension of direct assistance, and that the move had been recommended to the president.[21]

NE's concern about the lack of American influence in Saudi Arabia was more than matched by CASOC's. It is unlikely that the oilmen were particularly troubled by the locust mission, yet British proposals to establish a central bank and currency issue aroused concern. Although there is no evidence to indicate that the companies feared the loss of the concession to British interests, the oilmen apparently viewed London's involvement as a threat to the American character of their investment. In their testimony before Congress, company representatives claimed that currency reform might even draw Saudi Arabia into the sterling block and establish the kind of mercantile controls which existed in Egypt, Palestine, and India.[22] Writing to the head office to inform Davies that the king had agreed in principle to the bank scheme, Garry Owen, CASOC's Jidda representative, concluded, "I question of [sic] King and advisers fully appreciate proposal with its attendant ramifications and control."[23] The oilmen, however, seemed fully aware of the consequences of the British proposal and, as W. S. S. Rodgers later admitted, fear of the banking plan forced CASOC executives to come to Washington and "call on practically every large department head."[24]

CASOC's campaign to secure government assistance for the concession, like the earlier Moffett proposal, was primarily directed at acquiring the kind of security for its investment which only official support seemed able to provide. Although the oilmen were disturbed by increasing British activity in Saudi Arabia, it is likely that CASOC saw a perfect opportunity to acquire for their investment the long-term insurance which they had failed to achieve two years earlier. Official interest in Saudi Arabia might not only deter foreign designs on the concession, it might demonstrate to Ibn Saud that the Americans had a permanent stake in developing his oil. In addition to any loans or technical assistance which might result from ties with the government, the oilmen seemed to believe that Washington's interest would bring greater long-term security to their investment. In the event of the king's sudden death or an abrupt change in government, the presence of a concerned and rich benefactor might provide the influence and leverage necessary to ensure that the concession remained in American hands.

Early in February, Rodgers and Collier of SOCAL, through contact with Ralph Davies, deputy petroleum administrator and former SOCAL executive, met with Harold Ickes, secretary of the interior and petroleum administrator. The oilmen bluntly informed Ickes that the British were attempting to "edge in on the concession," and, according to Ickes, warned that, unless "some fast moves were made," American interests might lose the concession.[25] Ickes, already very much interested in the potential of Middle Eastern reserves, requested Collier and Rodgers to draw up a proposal which he could present to the president.

On 8 February, the SOCAL executives again met with Ickes and submitted a proposal suggesting that the United States extend direct lend-lease to Saudi Arabia. In exchange, the company's representatives offered to establish a special reserve for the United States and to grant the government options on a determined amount of oil at a rate below market price. In an accompanying memorandum, the oilmen were quick to point out the advantages of access to such a large pool: "The importance of this vast reserve of American controlled petroleum becomes increasingly apparent as demands on production within the United States point more and more to a decrease in our national reserves and an increase in our national consumption. Maximum efficient production from all domestic wells will soon be insufficient to meet this country's expanding consumption and exports." Saudi reserves, the memorandum added, are "the same order of magnitude as the great reserves of Iran and Iraq."[26] According to Rodgers, the oilmen also contacted Stettinius, and attempted to arrange appointments with Knox, Forrestal, and Welles.[27]

Although the oilmen approached Ickes with a formal lend-lease proposal, Rodgers and Collier had also been in touch with State Department representatives. On 8 February, Feis advised Thornburg that as a result of the "growing interest" in Arabian oil the CIPP might meet to consider the situation.[28] The committee's next meeting focused entirely on the problem of Saudi Arabia—specifically on a memorandum (similar to that of 14 January) prepared by NE. The draft, presented to the committee by Merriam, reviewed the financial difficulties of Ibn Saud and the proposed British banking scheme. In view of Britain's financial assistance to the king, the memo concluded, "there is a possibility that after the war the British may demand a *quid pro quo* at the expense of this American interest, which it is considered necessary to preserve as a means of assuring the United States of an ample supply of oil in the event of exhaustion of domestic reserves."[29]

Although the committee conceded that the immediate problems in Saudi Arabia were political and economic matters, involving American relations with Great Britain, it also admitted that such matters "might affect the development of our oil interests, and therefore come within the purview of foreign oil policy."[30] Discussion of Saudi Arabia was "exploratory" in nature, yet the committee agreed to consider, among other things, the extension of lend-lease and participation in the banking scheme. The committee decided to meet again on 15 February.[31]

Aware of the State Department's long-standing interest in and support for the Saudi concession, the oilmen proceeded to present their lend-lease proposal to certain influential CIPP members.[32] On 11 February, Rodgers, Collier, and Fred Davies, through contacts with Thornburg and Welles, met with Feis and Merriam to discuss the petroleum situation in Saudi Arabia. Although the oil executives, particularly Davies, expressed concern about British advances to Ibn Saud and the effects of currency schemes on American oil interests, Feis later concluded that "their anxieties were connected with vague possibilities in the future, rather than with any immediate problem."[33] The oilmen, nonetheless, requested formal lend-lease assistance for Ibn Saud as a means of securing the American petroleum position in Saudi Arabia. Collier and Rodgers also presented two additional proposals which held great significance for the future. First, the oil executives suggested that the United States government acquire a share in the actual ownership of the companies following the model of the British Anglo-Iranian (AIOC) arrangement. The idea was not a new one and had been discussed with navy representatives only the day before.

Second, the oilmen proposed a series of contract options on Saudi oil to be drawn from a reserve which CASOC would maintain for the United States.

Whether the companies made their stock offer in good faith or whether it was simply a means of enticing the government to extend lend-lease assistance is not at all clear. Feis, however, was impressed by the companies' willingness to enter into cooperation with the government. "The oil company representatives," he noted, "showed clearly they were desirous of having this Government interest itself definitely and comprehensively in the future of these companies."[34] Shortly after his meeting with the oilmen, Feis concluded: "It is plainly advisable to carry on expeditiously consideration and handling of no less than five or six matters that directly or indirectly have a bearing on the oil situation."[35] Heading Feis's six-point agenda was the decision to extend formal lend-lease assistance to Saudi Arabia.

Although the question of lend-lease aid had been stalled at the White House since early January, increasing interest in Arabian oil, strengthened by the visit of CASOC-SOCAL representatives, seemed to facilitate the decision-making process considerably. At the CIPP meeting of 15 February, the committee, having reviewed Feis's program, agreed that lend-lease should be extended to Ibn Saud.[36] On 16 February, two days before Roosevelt declared Saudi Arabia eligible for lend-lease, Ickes met with the president to discuss the matter of Saudi oil. Not only was Roosevelt "very much interested' in the Arabian situation, but, according to Ickes's later recollection, the president's "mind at once moved to the conclusion . . . that our economy and our own ability to fend for ourselves in time of war would be greatly increased if we had an interest in this big oil pool and so we moved in right away to try to acquire some interest."[37] On 18 February, at the fourth meeting of the CIPP, the committee noted that the British had been advised of United States' plans to extend formal lend-lease to Saudi Arabia and had offered no objections; the president was informed accordingly. Later that day, Roosevelt issued Executive Order 8926 declaring Saudi Arabia vital to the defense of the United States and thus eligible for lend-lease assistance.[38]

The lend-lease decision, despite its modest proportions, was the first step by the United States toward securing and preserving its stake in Arabian oil. Although Senator Owen Brewster later declared that CASOC-SOCAL efforts to secure lend-lease aid constituted one of the most remarkable selling jobs he had ever encountered, most of the credit for the decision belongs to the Department of State and to those officials like Ickes who had begun to attach new importance to Arabian oil. The timing of the decision was, to be sure, influenced by the oilmen's lobbying campaign, yet the papers for the lend-lease decision had been sitting on the president's desk since early January, almost a month before CASOC-SOCAL representatives descended on Washington.

More important than any anxieties about British intentions toward Saudi Arabia was the increasing concern about the domestic petroleum situation. Although Arabian oil did not offer a particularly accessible source for domestic supply nor even an immediate source for military use, it seemed to afford considerable security for the future. Saudi reserves, already considered among the world's largest, might provide valuable insurance for the nation's own oil barrel.[39] At the very least, it seemed, the king's oil might be utilized to conserve the more strategically valuable reserves of the United States and Western Hemisphere. It is no coincidence that while considering lend-lease aid for Saudi Arabia, officials simultaneously discussed long-range plans for government involvement in Arabian oil. Unlike the oilmen who seemed to view lend-lease as a culmination of their earlier efforts to gain government support for their investment, representatives of the Department of State, PAW, and the military saw lend-lease as the beginning of a new relationship not only between the government and the oil companies, but also between the United States and Saudi Arabian oil.

The extension of lend-lease to Saudi Arabia was certainly no radical démarche in wartime diplomacy, yet it did indicate a significant shift in the American attitude toward Saudi petroleum. Government efforts no longer aimed merely at maintaining the goodwill of Ibn Saud, but now focused as well on securing the American stake in the king's oil. Shortly after Roosevelt's decision on lend-lease, the CIPP met to consider the possible relationship of a lend-lease agreement to the question of securing the American interest in Arabian oil. In exchange for lend-lease assistance, the committee suggested, the United States might induce the king to waive his royalties on an agreed amount of petroleum which the government might then contract from CASOC. The purpose of such an arrangement, if not the motivation behind lend-lease itself, was to secure American petroleum interests in Saudi Arabia.[40]

Even more important, particularly for the immediate future, was Max Thornburg's suggestion that the United States acquire specific options on petroleum reserves. The army, navy, and PAW, Thornburg advised the committee, were now "actively interested in the matter," and he perceived no conflict with CIPP's views. With the cooperation of the interested agencies, Thornburg reasoned, the government might create a "petroleum reserves corporation" which could contract for foreign oil reserves with a single American company. Such a company, Thornburg concluded, would in turn be comprised of a board of directors representing all interested companies and one government director. The committee responded positively to the petroleum adviser's suggestion and recommended that Thornburg prepare a memorandum on foreign oil reserves for the president. The CIPP agreed that the memorandum propose the establishment of an independent corporation or agency for the purpose of contracting "at once" for reserves in Saudi Arabia, Iraq, Venezuela, and Colombia.[41]

By March the State Department's consideration of Saudi Arabian matters focused on two levels. For the present, the department sought to devise an interim method of delivering economic or financial assistance to Ibn Saud in order to stabilize the king's financial situation and maintain American prestige.[42] For the future, the department, eager to secure Saudi oil reserves on a more permanent basis, sought to involve the United States government more intimately in Arabian oil. Not only had the oilmen hinted that such participation might be welcomed but also prospective shortages seemed to call for more aggressive official action.

Early in March, in a memorandum to Acheson, James Sappington, secretary of the CIPP and assistant chief of the Office of the Petroleum Adviser, summarized the committee's position. In view of the "imminent decline" in domestic reserves, "it would be advisable to discover a means of safeguarding against any and all contingencies our prospective ability to draw on certain foreign petroleum supplies. . . ." Although Sappington regarded the idea of stock purchase of CASOC-SOCAL interests as too difficult to implement, he suggested that in the basic lend-lease agreement with Saudi Arabia, "the way be left open for the negotiation of a supplemental arrangement embodying some agreement . . . on petroleum."[43] The successful conclusion of a lend-lease agreement, however, was dependent upon factors beyond NE's or the department's immediate control. The political position of Ibn Saud, the maze of Saudi finances, and the necessity of a detailed Treasury Department study of the king's requirements indicated that the extension of aid of lend-lease might take some time. Determined to find more permanent security for American oil interests and spurred on by the added interest of the Department of the Navy and PAW, the Department of State turned its efforts toward defining a more comprehensive solution.

In March, the CIPP submitted a memorandum to Cordell Hull which would fundamentally influence American wartime oil diplomacy in the Middle East. The study, which grew out of CIPP meetings and informal discussions with navy officials and PAW, proposed the creation of a Petroleum Reserves Corporation which would deal specifically with the securing of option contracts for foreign reserves—first in Saudi Arabia and then elsewhere.[44] The memorandum pointed out that an international oil agreement was a necessary part of any comprehensive solution, yet such an accord could not at present meet the department's central objective—"current protection against the impairment of the present overseas oil production of the United States."[45] Although the committee had considered a number of alternatives, including government participation in a private company holding foreign reserves, it had decided in favor of acquiring option contracts. The CIPP presumably believed that CASOC, with more petroleum than it could presently handle and in search of additional security for its concession, might be eager to enter into some arrangement with the government. Hull forwarded the CIPP memorandum to Ickes, Henry Stimson, and Frank Knox, secretary of the navy.[46]

Although the Department of State had taken the initiative in Saudi Arabian matters since the beginning of the war, government interest in Arabian oil broadened considerably by the middle of 1943. Intrigued by the potential of the area's reserves and disturbed by the possibility of domestic shortages, the indomitable Harold Ickes, already preoccupied with the problems of domestic and foreign supply, began to devote much of his energy toward securing a more active government role in Saudi reserves. The military services as well, pressed by the requirements of new Allied offensives on the Continent and the escalating naval and air war in the Pacific, saw the advantages of a more aggressive government policy toward foreign petroleum.

Although the Army-Navy Petroleum Board (ANPB) had begun to consider seriously the development of Middle Eastern oil as early as November 1942, it was not until the spring of 1943 that the armed services, particularly the navy, disturbed by the anticipated supply needs in the southwest Pacific, began to see the potential value of this foreign crude. Writing to Hull in April, Henry Stimson, secretary of war, concluded that Saudi Arabia, with its vast American-controlled oil reserves, "is the one country where the suggested Petroleum Reserves Corporation might be made effective, and of great value to the future interest of the United States Government."[47] In early May, an ANPB subcommittee, warning that crude shortages for 1944 might reach 700,000 b.p.d., concluded that the crude deficit might best be met by using oil from Saudi Arabia, Iraq, or Iran. The advantages were

obvious—proximity to points of consumption and vast reserve potential. The ANPB had also recommended the expansion of refinery capacity at Haifa and in the Persian Gulf.[48]

Not all military planners agreed on the extent or likelihood of future
shortages. Army and particularly navy analysts, however, concurred
that projected patterns of military consumption indicated an accelerated drain on American reserves.[49] In view of a decreasing maximum
efficient rate and a decline in new discoveries, the military clothed
their assumptions in the most cautious terms. In May, F. J. Horne,
vice-chief of Naval Operations, submitted a memorandum on crude
supplies to the Joint Chiefs of Staff (JCS). Horne bluntly warned that
the United States was now faced with "an insufficient supply of crude
oil to meet the requirements of the Armed Services of the United
States and minimum essential civilian needs." Before the end of 1944,
the domestic industry might expect a shortage of anywhere between
128,000 b.p.d. to 746,000 b.p.d. The problem, Horne continued, not
only concerned insufficient productive capacity, but also touched on
domestic reserves. In 1942 alone, the reserves supply had decreased by
some 946,000,000 barrels. If the industry were forced to produce above
the MER, the reserve level might be further impaired. Horne's recommendations were remarkably direct. Because of the urgency of acquiring new reserves, a Petroleum Reserves Corporation should be
created. The PRC's "first duty" would be to negotiate a controlling
interest in the petroleum concessions of Saudi Arabia.[50] The navy's
adoption of the idea of a petroleum reserves corporation was undoubtedly a result of preliminary discussions between the Departments of
State, Navy, and Interior in March and April. Secretary of the Navy
Frank Knox and Under Secretary William Bullitt had been actively
interested in the question of Saudi petroleum since the Collier-Rodgers
visit in early February.[51]

The new military interest in Arabian oil not only facilitated formation of policy, but also added new direction to the PRC. Although the
State Department had conceived PRC as an instrument to negotiate
contract options for Saudi reserves, the armed services, led by the navy
and supported by Ickes, saw the plan as a means of negotiating with
CASOC-SOCAL interests for more direct government participation. The
navy, pressed by fears of shortage, sought more direct control of Saudi
oil. Early in June, at a meeting of the JCS, Horne formally presented
his May memorandum. Although Admiral William Leahy suggested
that the proposal be forwarded to the secretaries of War, Navy, State,
and Interior, Horne responded that their approval in principle had

already been obtained. He added that, according to Bullitt, if a proposal were sent to the Department of State it might be tied up in the Petroleum Division for months. In view of the possible interdepartmental complications of the PRC matter, however, the Joint Chiefs of Staff decided to postpone implementation of the proposal, but agreed to submit a memorandum to the president recommending formation of a corporation to acquire foreign reserves.[52] On 8 June, Leahy, on behalf of the JCS, recommended to Roosevelt that the Reconstruction Finance Corporation "be directed to organize a corporation specifically for the purpose of acquiring proven foreign reserves." This proposal, Leahy concluded, "would include the immediate acquisition of a controlling interest by the U.S. Government in Saudi Arabian oil concessions."[53]

The Department of State and the armed services concurred in the need for a government corporation to secure Arabian oil reserves, yet there was little agreement over the direction such an organization should take. The differences between the State Department and the Knox-Ickes group crystallized at a series of meetings held in the early part of June. On 11 June, Feis, Knox, Stimson, and Ickes met to exchange views on the PRC and Arabian oil. Ickes immediately called for an aggressive program of action for Saudi Arabia. In view of the wartime drain on domestic reserves and the possible threat to American petroleum interests in Arabia either from the British or as a consequence of the instability of Ibn Saud's own regime, Ickes believed it was imperative that the United States take action to safeguard its foreign reserves. A government-controlled PRC might acquire a majority interest in CASOC's concession, thus ensuring adequate protection for valuable oil reserves.

Feis, however, reflecting the views of the State Department, was quick to point out the difficulties of stock purchase. Not only was the department uneasy about the reaction of Ibn Saud and the possible conflict between the PRC and the Atlantic Charter, but also, on a more immediate level, government intervention might lead Saudi Arabia to nationalize CASOC's oil reserves. Although Feis noted that Hull had "grave hesitation" regarding the plan, he reluctantly added that the department would be "prepared to face the doubts and difficulties" of such a plan in view of the need to secure adequate foreign reserves. Nevertheless, Feis continued to press for the contract plan which he believed contained all the advantages of stock purchase without any of its risks. Ickes, however, was not prepared to accept the State Department alternative, or Feis's proposal to give the department veto power over PRC's major actions. It was only at the intercession of James Byrnes that the group adjourned to consider a compromise before a final decision on the PRC was reached.[54]

Disturbed by the possible diplomatic ramifications of the stock purchase scheme, the State Department continued to press for the contract option plan. On 14 June, Hull presented the department's views to the president. "Any negotiations," Hull cautioned, "which disturbed the present concession might have adverse results, and possibly lead to new demands either upon the Company or upon this Government under penalty of reducing the present concession or admitting representatives of other countries." Instead of stock purchase, the "simplest and most advisable" method of dealing with Saudi petroleum, Hull concluded, was to contract for military reserves through the oil companies.[55] A reserve option plan would allow the armed services to secure their petroleum needs without risking conflict with Saudi Arabia, the domestic petroleum industry, or even the great powers.

The Ickes-Knox idea, however, supported by the realities of an increasing military demand for petroleum, seemed even more convincing. Writing to Roosevelt in June, Bullitt warned that current production "barely" met requirements. As a result of increasing demands by the armed forces and essential war industry, the United States might run short before the end of 1944. "The fact is," Bullitt concluded, "that we cannot squeeze out of our own soil enough petroleum for our war needs." If the United States were able to maintain Saudi reserves "in American hands, with Government control and to exploit it successfully, the estimated oil reserves of the United States would be approximately *doubled*."[56]

Despite the State Department's efforts to retain the initiative and to implement a contract option plan, the navy seemed determined to pursue the more aggressive course of action. On 15 June, in a meeting of the newly created Special Committee on Petroleum, Bullitt again insisted on the "urgency" of the situation in Saudi Arabia and on the need to purchase CASOC stock or, at the very least, reserves in the ground. Although Feis, chairman of the committee, believed that the group should explore other areas and possibilities, such as a bilateral petroleum agreement with Great Britain, Bullitt insisted that Saudi Arabia was the "big question."[57]

In a final attempt to reach a consensus, representatives of the Departments of War, State, Navy, and Interior met on 17 June. What finally emerged in the plan for presentation to the White House was a clear-cut victory for Ickes and the navy. It was agreed that a Petroleum Reserves Corporation should be created, directed toward the acquisition of 100 percent stock ownership of CASOC's concession in Saudi Arabia. Presumably as a gesture of compromise to the State Department, the group agreed to include the alternative contract option in its presentation to the president as well as to make PRC's foreign operations subject to the approval of the secretary of state. It was clear, however, that the department had either been outmaneuvered or simply outvoted. On 26 June the secretaries of State, War, Navy, and Interior formally presented the PRC plan to Roosevelt. On 30 June Jesse Jones, the Secretary of Commerce, using funds of the Reconstruction Finance Corporation, established the Petroleum Reserves Corporation.[58]

Although the idea of a government agency to secure Saudi oil reserves had originated in the Department of State's petroleum committees, Ickes and Knox gave the PRC a new direction designed to meet their increasing concern over the availability of petroleum reserves. The State Department, sensitive to the international and domestic complications of direct government involvement in Saudi Arabian oil, was justifiably disturbed by the new emphasis of the corporation. "I have a great fear," Feis wrote in June, "that unless the Department controls the direction of this new Petroleum Reserves Corporation . . . we would run the risk of imperiling our whole post-war program."[59] The military, less concerned about the diplomatic and domestic complications of an aggressive government response in Saudi Arabia, was determined to "secure" oil reserves regardless of the price. Equally important, since the beginning of the war, the military establishment, particularly the JCS, had acquired considerably more influence with the president than the Department of State. Excluded from the War Council on military matters, Hull found himself not only left out of military decisions, but excluded on issues of great diplomatic import. Supported by the JCS, Ickes and Knox impressed upon the president the need for decisive measures to safeguard Arabian oil.[60]

Roosevelt was also receiving important information from other sources. Early in July, Patrick Hurley, former secretary of war and personal envoy of the president, submitted a report on his recent mission to the Near East. Hurley, who had considerable experience in the oil business, was greatly impressed by the size and potential of CASOC's concession: "The development of the situation in Saudi Arabia gives you, Mr. President, the possibility for a complete answer to the critics who tell us we are exhausting our oil resources at home without any hope of replacement. The development of the great oil resources of Saudi Arabia will give you a supply of this essential commodity in a strategic location. . . . And finally, after having secured all these purposes, this resource will be of great importance to our own country in the reconstruction period after the war."[61] It is likely that Roosevelt, already interested in the problem of naval reserves, and wooed by his military advisers, sought the kind of long-range solution to the acquisition of Saudi reserves that stock purchase seemed to offer.[62] Despite the reservations of the Department of State, the PRC, under Ickes, turned in the beginning of August to negotiations with CASOC and SOCAL for the purchase of their interests in Saudi Arabia.

As the Petroleum Reserves Corporation moved toward direct negotiations with the companies, the lines between the State Department and the PAW-navy group seemed to harden. The general objectives of the two groups were much the same—protection and preservation of valuable American-controlled petroleum interests in Saudi Arabia. The methods of the agencies, however, were very much in conflict, and seemed to reflect contrasts in personalities as well as policies. Supported by the armed services, Ickes, the crusty curmudgeon of the Department of Interior and PAW, advocated direct and immediate government involvement in the ownership of the companies and oil reserves. Although Ickes would later claim that the entire PRC venture was only a means to increase American negotiating strength with the British in the Middle East, the aggressiveness and persistence of PRC's approach seemed to reflect Ickes's belief that only government involvement on some level would permanently secure Saudi reserves.

On the other hand, many State Department officials, influenced by the milder internationalism of Cordell Hull, were sensitive to the possible diplomatic consequences of a heavy-handed American response. Not only might the PRC present a "clear violation" of the equal access clause of the Atlantic Charter, but also, according to Adolph Berle, the British would most likely come out ahead in a "scramble for concessions and rights."[63] The department was not unified in its own approach to the question of Arabian oil, yet it believed that strong diplomatic support, accompanied by a comprehensive petroleum agreement with the British, might provide the best possible "security" for Middle Eastern oil. By the beginning of August, however, the initiative in petroleum policy rested in the impatient hands of Harold Ickes.

Although the primary task of the PRC, according to its charter, was the purchase of 100 percent of CASOC's stock, preliminary discussions between government and company representatives indicated that the government might have to revise its original intentions.[64] On 1 September, Ickes informed the executive board of PRC that the companies,

Texas and SOCAL, might not sell their entire stock interest. In discussions with Roosevelt in August, Ickes continued, the president had advised him that negotiations should continue provided that the PRC acquire a majority of CASOC's stock or a controlling interest in Saudi reserves.[65]

Although stock purchase was the PRC's central objective, the corporation also became involved in the question of erecting a refinery in the Persian Gulf area. In August, the JCS, upon recommendation of the ANPB, decided that the establishment of a 100,000 b.p.d. refinery producing 20,000 b.p.d. of aviation gasoline, might help to supply anticipated requirements in the southwest Pacific. Already in the midst of devising ways to secure CASOC stock, Ickes seemed to believe that PRC handling of the refinery matter might increase the government's bargaining power with the companies. The cash investment required to construct the facility was so large, the PRC president reasoned, the companies would have no choice but to seek government assistance.[66] In short, to Ickes, negotiating with the companies for the refinery was a natural correlate of stock purchase.

Whatever the advantages or disadvantages of the refinery plan, it soon became clear that CASOC representatives might not even agree to the transfer of 50 percent of company interests. Early in September, Rodgers and Collier informed PRC negotiators that in view of their investment in the concession, their responsibilities to stockholders, the reaction of Ibn Saud, and the possible consequences within the oil industry of a government merger, it was doubtful that even a minority stock interest might be negotiated. At the conclusion of the meeting, Feis, Alvin Wirtz, and Mortimer Kline, general counsel to the PRC, agreed in private session that acquisition of a minority stock ownership would be pointless, involving the government in needless risks without any real measure of control. If "controlling ownership" were not possible, the government negotiators agreed, a "far-reaching contractual arrangement" might be negotiated.[67]

What led Ickes and his PRC associates to believe that CASOC might part with a controlling interest in the concession is problematic. Although CASOC representatives had broached various proposals to the Departments of State and Interior in February 1943, in an attempt to attract government interest in the concession, it was unlikely that the companies, in view of the improved situation in the Middle East and the recent lend-lease commitment, would rush to hand over an oil interest of enormous value. On 13 September, Wirtz reported to the PRC Board that while the Texas Company and SOCAL might be willing to part with one-third of their stock interest, they were opposed to yielding majority control to the government. The companies, Wirtz noted, were "fearful of Government control and political management," and to date he had been unable to reach an agreement. The PRC board agreed, however, that if the government could acquire a "substantial" stock interest in the company with an appropriate contract, then the United States' interests might be adequately protected.[68]

CASOC's reservations in yielding even partial control of the concession, however, foreshadowed the difficulties of implementing a successful stock transfer agreement. Despite the diplomatic assistance they had received from the State Department in Saudi Arabia, the companies were wary of direct government involvement in company operations. Aside from the effects such a partnership might have on CASOC's relations within the oil industry, CASOC must have feared government supervision and control of its operations in Saudi Arabia. Even if the PRC succeeded in quieting the oilmen's fears of federal controls, there was still the more practical matter of compensation. The companies, having already invested millions in the concession, sought reimbursement for the past and future worth of their investment. Even if such a value could be assessed, PRC negotiators believed, the cost to the government would be prohibitive. Despite the difficulties of stock purchase, however, Feis reported to Hull on 25 September that there was a "good prospect" that some agreement with the companies could be reached.[69]

Prospects for a stock purchase arrangement brightened as the secret PRC negotiating sessions continued. On 28 September, Alvin Wirtz announced to the PRC board that a broad basis for settlement with the companies had been reached. The reasons for the temporary change in CASOC's attitude are not clear. Perhaps the companies decided that the sale of a minority stock interest might be a profitable venture, or perhaps CASOC had learned of Ickes's negotiations with the Gulf Oil Corporation to construct a military refinery in Kuwait.[70] Whatever the companies' motives, it appeared that they had, at least temporarily, accepted in principle the sale of a substantial stock interest. According to the tentative arrangement, the PRC would acquire one-third of CASOC's common stock for an amount equal to the present investment of both Texas and SOCAL—approximately $20,000,000. The military refinery was to be constructed at government expense but owned by CASOC, with eventual repayment by the company. Moreover, the United States would have a preemptive right to purchase 100 percent of CASOC's crude production during wartime, 51 percent at all other times, and might prevent the sale of the company's products to any government if it felt such a transaction ran counter to American interests.

The agreement, Wirtz informed the PRC, was extremely beneficial to the United States and met most of PRC's original objectives. Not only was the PRC to receive a one-third interest in a company "owning concessions covering some of the largest reserves of petroleum in the world at actual investment cost without giving effect to discovery value and development," but also the government was assured a role in company policy.[71] The PRC board unanimously approved Wirtz's proposal and agreed to send Everett DeGolyer, a leading petroleum geologist and special consultant to the PRC, to Saudi Arabia and the Persian Gulf to survey petroleum operations and reserves in the area.[72]

Although both SOCAL and the Texas Company had tentatively agreed to the new stock purchase plan, early in October representatives of the Texas Company suddenly withdrew all proposals and repudiated all preliminary arrangements. According to Wirtz, the companies had suddenly requested that CASOC give income notice instead of preferred stock to the PRC and that the government agree to nine representatives on the board of directors—three from PRC and three from each company. Money was also a problem. Rodgers informed Wirtz that his company alone had invested $40,000,000 in the concession—twice the amount the government was offering.[73] Determined to maintain the companies' interest, the PRC agreed to the companies' proposals and authorized Wirtz to increase the offer to $40,000,000.[74]

The companies were apparently not interested in the compromise, and by the end of October PRC-CASOC negotiations reached an impasse.[75] On 3 November, Ickes informed the PRC board that all negotiations were suspended as a result of the "unreasonable" nature of the Texas Company's demands. Despite the collapse of negotiations, the board unanimously agreed that "the interests of the people of the United States and its foreign oil industry required the participation of the United States Government or any agency thereof in the protection of American oil reserves." Ickes was directed to continue to explore the possibilities of securing a government interest in Gulf Oil's reserves in Kuwait.[76]

Money no doubt played a role in the failure of the PRC-CASOC negotiations. Had the government met the Texas Company's financial demands, perhaps a stock purchase agreement could have been reached. However, CASOC's refusal to part with a substantial stock interest was based largely on the companies' fear of government control and on the changed circumstances of 1943. Early in the year, uneasy over British activity in Saudi Arabia and eager to add security to its investment, CASOC sought to attract government interest in the concession. The companies clearly did not anticipate the degree of official interest in Middle Eastern oil or the measures the government was prepared to take to secure Arabian reserves. According to Feis, the companies had gone "fishing for a cod and had caught a whale."[77] CASOC, to be sure, was very much interested in official diplomatic support, lend-lease aid, and even government sponsorship of petroleum facilities in the Persian Gulf; government ownership and control, however, were quite different matters.[78]

In the fall of 1943 circumstances also seemed to argue against yielding to PRC objectives. With the collapse of the Axis threat and an increase in oil production, the concession appeared relatively secure. Convinced that the oilmen were simply "pollyfoxing" with the PRC, Ickes believed that, with this new security, the companies were "more disposed to thumb their noses at us."[79] How sincere CASOC had been in offering to arrange a stock purchase is problematic; yet it is clear that inadequate financial terms and fear of government control convinced CASOC not to accept PRC's last offer. Finally, the companies undoubtedly realized that official support for their oil interests was not contingent upon government ownership of the concession. Although the PRC board had agreed to shelve the proposed contract for the refinery, the companies were wise enough to realize that the decision might only be a temporary maneuver. The government seemed to have no choice but to tend to the security and welfare of American-controlled oil reserves in Saudi Arabia and the Persian Gulf.

Breakdown of PRC plans for stock purchase may also have been a result of Ickes's own change of strategy. As the negotiations progressed and it became clear that the companies were not prepared to yield majority control of their stock, the risks of the plan seemed to outweigh its advantages. Ickes had no desire for a confrontation with the oil industry let alone with their supporters in Congress. Rumors of the secret negotiating sessions had already leaked to the press and it was only a matter of time before the independent and large producers alike would be crying out against federal intrusion and protesting favoritism toward Middle Eastern oil producers. So too, a conflict with the industry and Congress might hurt the administration politically and restrict its future initiatives. In short, when stock purchase became too costly, Ickes as a horse trader and politico par excellence, may simply have decided to shift to new and more pragmatic tactics.

Having opposed the PRC's stock purchase plans from the outset, the State Department was not particularly disappointed over the collapse of the negotiations. "My associates and I . . . ," Hull recollected, "believed that the Government should not itself enter the oil business. . . . Moreover, we considered the problem of oil a delicate element in the more important question of our over-all foreign relations."[80] Comparing the situation in the Middle East to a "finely woven Persian rug," Feis echoed Hull's feeling. "If we walked across it with heavy boots, unintended damage might be done and quarrels might follow."[81]

The idea that petroleum must be handled as a diplomatic matter, within the larger context of Anglo-American relations, had been developing in the State Department since 1941. Although the key issue for the advocates of stock purchase seemed to be the security of American oil interests in Saudi Arabia, to many State Department officials, the crucial problems of Arabian oil were woven into the larger fabric of Anglo-American competitive relationships in the Middle East. As a relative late-comer to the Middle East oil, the United States, lacking the political and economic leverage of Great Britain's century of experience in the area, was at a distinct disadvantage. The problem was highlighted by a series of restrictive agreements which had become the price of admission for American companies into the oil fields of Iraq and the Persian Gulf. The growing awareness of the necessity of a petroleum agreement with the British was not for the most part the result of a naive and doctrinaire faith in bilateral or international accords, but a practical assessment of the best methods available to solve the problems of security and development of American petroleum interests in the Middle East.

The idea of a petroleum agreement with Great Britain had been broached in the department's petroleum committees in early 1943, yet it was not until the fall that serious attention was given to the actual drafting of proposals.[82] There is little doubt that the new interest in an agreement was partly a result of Ickes's aggressive PRC maneuvering with the companies. On 21 September, Feis informed the Special Committee on Petroleum Policy that the State Department had drafted a petroleum agreement with Great Britain. The purpose of such an accord, Feis indicated, was to ensure greater protection for American interests through cooperation with the British. Such a program might guarantee adequate reserves for the postwar period and possibly facilitate the sharing of development costs. Finally, Feis stated that a "paramount reason" for a bilateral understanding was to bring about the elimination of restrictions on American-controlled oil interests, such as the Red Line agreement and the Gulf-AIOC marketing clause, and to remove British political pressure on "various political entities in the area which operate against American interests."[83] On

28 September, Feis informed the committee that the draft agreement had received Hull's approval but that he did not yet have the secretary's permission to explore the possibilities of talks with Great Britain.

The prospect of a petroleum agreement with Great Britain, however attractive, could not ease official concern about the immediate situation in Saudi Arabia. Ibn Saud's continuing dependence on Great Britain together with London's plans for currency reform provided little comfort to officials concerned with the long-range security of American interests in Arabian oil. Even more disquieting was the ever-present fear that the British might exploit the situation at the time of the king's death in order to gain a foothold in the concession. Writing to Feis, Thornburg expressed his concern and perhaps that of CASOC as well: "While Ibn Saud lives the American concession probably is secure. When he dies, however, the circumstances within his Kingdom are such that his successor will, beyond question, require support from outside if Saudi Arabia is to be held together. Our facts tell us that British policy—the policy which within the past few years, made a jig-saw pattern of Iraq, Syria, Palestine and Transjordan, and a complete muddle of the area which Ibn Saud himself later welded into a Kingdom—may or may not maintain this Kingdom under the present King's natural successor. Our facts tell us that if we recognize a national interest in Saudi Arabia's oil development, we ourselves need to see to its well being—through the British if they wish—otherwise despite them."[84] William Bullitt, in a letter intended for the president, echoed a similar line. Official reports from the field, Bullitt concluded, "seem to indicate a desire to strengthen British influence over Ibn Saud at the expense of American influence, in a manner not quite healthy for the oil concession."[85]

Throughout the summer of 1943, the Department of State, in an effort to strengthen American prestige with the king, began to formulate plans to increase American assistance to Saudi Arabia. Official efforts focused primarily on the ailing Saudi financial system, the basis of Britain's leverage with Ibn Saud. Unless a sound economic system could be established, NE officials believed, Saudi Arabia might never achieve the kind of stability necessary to ensure continued American control of Arabian oil. Of more immediate concern, Murray informed Treasury representatives in July, were certain developments under way in Saudi Arabia in which the president was personally interested. In order that these developments take place (an obvious reference to PRC activities), Murray concluded, it was "essential" that the United States support the existing Saudi regime with financial aid.[86]

Although it was obvious that Saudi Arabia's financial system was in serious need of fundamental reform, the immediate problem was the shortage of silver for minting coins. Both Kirk and Moose had repeatedly warned that without silver, Ibn Saud could neither finance the approaching pilgrimage nor dispense patronage to the tribes—developments which might adversely affect his personal prestige and control.[87] Not everyone, of course, agreed with the seriousness of the problem or the proposed solution. In a burst of skepticism, for which the Treasury and State Department's own financial officers were soon to become famous, Henry White, assistant to the secretary of the Treasury, wondered "what all the shooting was about." The oil company had a "tight concession" and could if necessary take care of the king without British or American support.[88] Still, uneasy over British proposals to establish a bank in Jidda and a currency board in London, and eager to broaden the American role in supporting the king, the State Department lobbied for increased aid. By early October, the United States had formally agreed to supply Saudi Arabia with over 5,000,000 troy ounces of silver bullion under the provisions of lend-lease.

Despite NE's suspicions of London's motives in Saudi Arabia, the British seemed to have no intention of dominating Saudi finances, let alone stealing the CASOC concession. In view of Great Britain's own financial difficulties, particularly a shortage of silver, the Foreign Office had no objection to American participation in the financial support of the king. In fact, British proposals for currency reform, D. H. Robertson of the British Treasury informed State Department representatives in September, seemed less urgent now that the Americans planned to take care of the king's silver needs through the end of the year.[89] More important, in view of the increasing interest in Arabian oil, it seemed only natural that the Americans would want to participate in plans for any long-term reform of Saudi finances.

Although British officials seemed reconciled to the inevitability and even advantages of greater American participation in the financial affairs of Saudi Arabia, they were by no means prepared to sacrifice a century of hard-earned political influence in the Middle East to their upstart American cousins. In fact, as the United States became more directly involved in Saudi affairs, the Foreign Office began to wonder whether Washington was sensitive enough to His Majesty's political and strategic interests throughout the area. Was the United States prepared to concede that despite its increasing interest in Arabian oil, British political interests were still predominant? American actions in Saudi Arabia seemed to suggest that the United States was hammering out its own policy without regard for British concerns. Anthony Eden, secretary of state for foreign affairs, informed Lord Halifax in Washington that a recent decision to consider supplying Ibn Saud with arms "takes no account of the obvious importance which His Majesty's Government . . . must always attach to preventing excessive supplies of arms from reaching the Arabian Peninsula."[90] Furthermore, Eden noted: "British interests in all the countries of the Middle East are inevitably greater than American interests, if only for geographical reasons, and it is legitimate to hope that the United States Government will take into account the fact that the responsibilities which His Majesty's Government have in that area, e.g., for the defense of India, Iraq, Transjordan, Palestine and Egypt, entitle their views to special consideration in any matters affecting these and neighbouring countries."[91]

Equally disturbing to Foreign Office officials was American suspicion and distrust of British motives—feelings which were, in the British view, totally unwarranted. One of the "American prejudices" that had to be overcome, Eden informed the War Cabinet in July, was the notion that Great Britain had exploited the Middle East for her own "imperialist ends." Another difficulty, Eden continued, was the unfriendly attitude of Wallace Murray—the source of almost all of the State Department's Anglophobia.[92] Likewise, Minister of State Casey reminded the War Cabinet that American actions "seemed to be prompted by some suspicion of our position, or even by a spirit of opposition to our interests." The only solution, Casey concluded, was to "invite the Americans to recognize that the British Commonwealth and Empire had a predominant interest in the Middle East and the American interest in this area was relatively minor and subsidiary."[93]

By the fall of 1943, it seemed clear that Britain was not about to concede her position of primacy in the Middle East to the United States. Even in Saudi Arabia where the Foreign Office freely admitted an increasing American interest in oil, London was determined to maintain influence in political and military matters. Neither, however, were the British anxious to alienate their closest ally or to compete in areas where they might conceivably lose out to the Americans. Anglo-American cooperation was crucial, particularly in Saudi Arabia where Ibn Saud or his advisers were certain to exploit any sign of tension between the two powers. For many Foreign Office officials, the gentleman's solution to Anglo-American difficulties lay in frank and friendly discussions with the Americans designed to effect a "working understanding" with respect to the Middle East. Stripped of all its diplomatic niceties, however, what the British sought was nothing short of an old-fashioned horse trade. "We cannot expect the Americans to sacrifice their interest to ours in the Middle East," Eden informed the War Cabinet, "but we may possibly hope to induce them to let us play the hand there, from a political point of view, provided that our policy commands their approval and that they are left sufficient lattitude on the commercial and cultural sides." Eden recommended that a "high official" of the State Department be invited to London for detailed discussions on Middle Eastern affairs.[94]

Although the Department of State did not object to the idea of general discussions with Britain on Middle Eastern affairs, officials were more immediately interested in initiating discussions on petroleum questions, particularly in Saudi Arabia and the Persian Gulf. Successful conclusion of a lend-lease agreement on silver had not eased NE's concerns about British motives in Saudi Arabia. In a disturbing telegram to the department in October, Kirk reported that his conversations with "high British officials" made it clear that "they have in particular developed a sudden interest in the extent and status of American oil concessions in that country."[95] Forwarding Kirk's report to Paul Alling, chief of NE, James Sappington of the Petroleum Division noted that the attached telegram "furnishes another clear indication of the strong desirability of prompt discussions with the British looking toward an agreement on oil."[96]

Official efforts to explore the possibility of petroleum negotiations with Britain were facilitated considerably by the British themselves. On 30 October in an aide-mémoire delivered to Stettinius by Halifax, Great Britain formally proposed a series of discussions to "cover not only political questions but also any other Middle Eastern questions which either Government may wish to raise."[97] Although the aide-mémoire referred to the desirability of raising Anglo-American cooperation in economic matters, it was conspicuously silent on the subject of petroleum.[98] To the Americans, this was one of the most pressing matters in Anglo-American relations, if not the most prominent source of potential friction between the two countries in the Middle East. In a memorandum to Stettinius expressing his concern over Britain's proposed agenda, Murray called attention to the obvious omission. If discussions were initiated with the British, the political adviser concluded, it should also be possible to sound out the British on a potential oil agreement.[99]

Although the British proposal for discussions was temporarily sidetracked by problems of agenda and location, State Department officials continued to push the idea of separate petroleum negotiations with Great Britain.[100] On 24 November in a lengthy memorandum to Hull and Stettinius, Murray again raised the matter. Any discussions on petroleum, Murray began, "should envisage the orderly development on the basis of sound conservation practices of the vast oil resources of the Persian Gulf area . . . with a view to assuring freely available supplies on equal terms to the United States and all other peaceful nations, and proper benefits to the countries in the area from the development of their resources." Not only would British restrictions on American companies in Iraq and Kuwait have to be considered, but Britain's use of "political pressure on local governments to further their own ends regarding oil" would have to be discussed. The oil resources of the entire area, Murray continued, "are too important from the long-range as well as from the immediate viewpoint for their development to be permitted to remain subject to existing burdens." Murray recommended that Hull advise the interdepartmental Special Committee on Petroleum of the desirability of discussions with the British, suggest to Halifax the idea of initiating informal conversations, and present the department's view to the president. Negotiations, Murray concluded, should be initiated promptly "under the firm direction of the Department."[101]

The department's preliminary view of the objectives of an Anglo-American petroleum agreement was reflected in the Special Committee on Petroleum's consideration of the proposed framework for discussions. Composed of representatives of the Departments of State, War, Navy, and PAW, the committee had met at the request of the State Department to refine its views and to coordinate interdepartmental thinking. On 30 November, Boykin Wright, the War Department's representative, forwarded a draft revised by the Departments of State and War to the secretary of war. In view of Great Britain's commercial and political power in the Middle East and the possibility of "political anarchy" upon the deaths of the "aged rulers" of Saudi Arabia and Kuwait, Wright began, American petroleum interests in the area were subject to both existing restrictions on production and marketing and "potential threats to the continuance of such holdings." PRC negotiation with these companies was clear indication itself that something more than a "private commercial effort" was needed to protect American petroleum interests. The agreement under consideration, Wright continued, was proposed "as further and more complete assurance of the U.S. position relating to Middle East oil resources." Not only might such an agreement make it possible "to offer the U.K. consideration for relaxing existing restrictions," but "by such an agreement,"

Wright concluded, "the U.S. will be enabled to consolidate its position with respect to oil reserves in an overseas area hitherto dominated by the U.K."[102]

On 1 December, writing to Murray, James Sappington confirmed the committee's belief that the loosening of British restrictions in Kuwait and Iraq, a fundamental condition for the full development of Middle Eastern petroleum, was dependent upon an agreement with Great Britain.[103] The following day, Hull, in a note to Halifax, officially invited the British government to participate in "informal and preliminary" discussions on Middle East oil.[104] Within the week, Hull had received Roosevelt's assurance that discussions with the British would be conducted under the "clear supervision and guidance" of the Department of State.[105]

Although the State Department seemed to have regained the initiative in Middle Eastern petroleum matters by keeping Anglo-American negotiations under its charge, officials were still wary of the prospects of renewed PRC maneuvering. The department was fully aware that the PRC board had authorized Ickes to continue his negotiations with Gulf Oil and that he had maintained contact with the company. On 14 December in a memorandum to Stettinius and Hull, Murray sought to gain additional insurance against PRC meddling. In view of the fact that the proposed discussions with the British were designed to protect American concessions and to eliminate Anglo-American rivalry over oil, Murray noted, they served the same purpose as the PRC. Continued unilateral action with the companies, Murray continued, might even "prove to be inconsistent with or even in conflict with the results we may wish to attain in collaboration with the British."[106] Murray recommended that Hull advise Ickes, in his capacity as PRC president, that continued negotiations for government participation in the companies holding reserves abroad be discontinued.

Faced with what seemed to be an impasse in PRC-CASOC negotiations, Ickes was by no means opposed to discussions with the British. In fact, Ickes would later claim, that the entire PRC venture was simply a means of increasing American bargaining power with the British in an effort to secure a more advantageous accord.[107] Writing to Roosevelt, Ickes noted, "I am glad that Secretary Hull has started the ball rolling with the British and I hope the proposed conferences get going speedily. We have been losing valuable ground that we are not likely to be able to recover." Ickes did insist that he be made a member of the negotiating team, adding "I have a greater interest in the subject matter and a better advisory staff on oil than anyone else in the Government. Moreover, in a sense, this is my baby."[108] Precisely what Ickes intended by the latter remark was not exactly clear, yet it would soon become apparent to both Roosevelt and to the Department of State that he was not yet prepared to relinquish his influence over American oil diplomacy in the Middle East.

In December, in an article entitled "Oil—The Search for a Policy," *Time* seemed to capture the spirit which had characterized American diplomacy toward Middle Eastern oil throughout much of 1943. "For a world still locked in a cataclysmic war that could not operate for a second without oil, the future disposition of this last great reservoir is a matter of incalculable importance—too important, perhaps for even the individualistic U.S. to leave wholly in the hands of private enterprise."[109] Despite the often conflicting approaches of the Departments of State, Interior, Navy, and PAW, most government agencies concurred in the necessity of a more active government role. The new awareness was largely a result of the growing importance of petroleum and the increasing concern about the availability of domestic supply. In this respect, the urgency which officials attached to securing Saudi reserves was a natural response to the crisis atmosphere of the war years. Although the State Department's petroleum experts would soon caution against "too facile" an acceptance of scarcity theories, even they were not prepared to court the risks of war or postwar shortages. Arabian oil was, to be sure, distant and undeveloped, yet it seemed to offer considerable security to a nation caught in the grips of a national emergency.

Wartime concern about the availability of oil inevitably influenced the American view of British policies in Saudi Arabia and the Persian Gulf. For the most part, the Americans responded to British activities with the same crisislike alarm with which they viewed their own domestic petroleum situation. Mindful of Britain's self-serving oil diplomacy in Palestine and Mesopotamia, officials had little difficulty in attributing dark motives to Britain's long-standing interests in Saudi Arabia and the gulf. These suspicions were most conspicuous among NE officials charged with the day-to-day tasks of protecting American interests, yet they quickly spread to other agencies. Moreover, to Ickes and Bullitt, long interested in stimulating official interest in foreign reserves, the British bogey provided additional leverage in their campaign to encourage a more active government role in Arabian oil.

Although it is difficult to imagine that any American official, with the possible exception of Wallace Murray, seriously believed that Britain sought to steal the CASOC concession, few were ready to entrust its care to an ambitious ally, let alone to a foreign king. If the United States desired to preserve the American character of the concession, officials believed, then it must create a favorable atmosphere for petroleum development. Maintaining American prestige with Ibn Saud, reducing his dependence on London, and stabilizing Saudi finances all became important elements in securing the concession. Equally pressing was the importance of reaching an oil agreement with Great Britain—an agreement which might not only reduce tensions but also might eliminate the political and economic restrictions blocking the orderly development of Persian Gulf oil. By the end of 1943, despite all the energy and activity of petroleum planning, neither lend-lease nor the PRC had achieved either objective. The Americans thus turned their efforts toward finding new solutions to the problems of securing and developing the nation's stake in Arabian oil.

CHAPTER 4

PRC, PIPELINE, AND PETROLEUM AGREEMENT: ANGLO-AMERICAN RELATIONS IN SAUDI ARABIA, 1944

DURING 1944 the United States continued its efforts to define a national policy toward Middle Eastern oil. The basic problems confronting officials in the new year were those that had dogged the Americans throughout most of 1943—securing and developing American-controlled oil reserves in Saudi Arabia and the Persian Gulf. Specifically, officials sought to reconcile the new importance of this oil with what one report from the Office of Strategic Services (OSS) described as the "century-old policy of regarding Arabia as a British sphere of interest."[1] Despite their skill in securing American investments in Kuwait and Iraq, the oil companies seemed unable to overcome the restrictive agreements on marketing and production which impeded the full development of these oil interests. Nor were officials convinced that the Arabian American Oil Company (ARAMCO, CASOC formally changed its name to ARAMCO on 31 January 1944) operating in a British sphere of influence, could combat the political pressures of an often ambitious American ally.[2] By 1944, the fate of American petroleum interests in Saudi Arabia, policymakers believed, might depend upon the extent and direction of government action.

Official interest in Middle Eastern oil, particularly Saudi reserves, increased with the rising petroleum requirements of a nation geared for world war. Demands of the armed services and war industry for 1944 and 1945 threatened to clear the 5,000,000 barrel mark. "Although Western Hemisphere crude oil supply is adequate to meet estimated demands through 1944," an ANPB study predicted, "there does not exist an adequate margin of safety to relieve U.S. oilfields of possible disproportionate drainage and to provide for the probability of an increased demand in 1945."[3] The report recommended consideration of a limited program of petroleum development in certain "strategic overseas areas, particularly in the Persian Gulf area." Six months later, forecasts were even more pessimistic. Writing to the secretary of the

Joint Staff Planners of the Joint Chiefs of Staff, the ANPB warned that, "the supply of and demand for petroleum products during the remainder of this year and throughout 1945 are in delicate balance. Insufficient reserve capacity exists as insurance against sabotage or catastrophe."[4]

Although the development of Middle Eastern oil for the war effort was still retarded by the lack of adequate refining and transportation facilities, the reserves of Saudi Arabia and the Persian Gulf seemed to offer valuable insurance against the future. Already caught up in the crisis atmosphere of world war, a traditionally oil-hungry military establishment planned for the worst. In an emergency situation petroleum supplies from outside the Western Hemisphere might not be available for military use; in extreme circumstances, supplies from outside the territorial United States could conceivably be cut off. By maximizing the development and flow of Middle Eastern oil to supply world markets formerly supplied by Western wells, petroleum planners believed the United States could husband the more strategically vital reserves of the Western Hemisphere.

This conservation theory, shared by nearly every government agency dealing with foreign oil, provided the basis for the emerging view of petroleum from the Middle East. Moreover, this assumption was based on a growing respect for the unlimited potential of those reserves—a respect which frequently overshadowed the more practical problems of accessibility and security, and underestimated the reaction of domestic petroleum producers who would fight tenaciously against a potential flood of cheap foreign oil. Returning from his PRC mission to the Middle East in early 1944, Everett De Golyer was only one of many who would be greatly impressed by the reserve potential: "It is the opinion of this mission that given reasonable time . . . any single one of these four groups [AIOC, IPC, KOC, ARAMCO] can develop and maintain within its own properties sufficient production to supply world requirements from the Middle East area for many years to come. For the next ten to fifteen years at least, the Middle East area is likely to develop and maintain productive capacity of as much as four times its probable market outlet."[5]

Despite official consensus on the potential importance of Middle Eastern oil, there was considerable disagreement over the means to deal with it. Part of the difficulty lay in the number of agencies involved with petroleum matters and their conflicting lines of authority. In 1944, there were no less than ten government departments dealing directly with Middle East oil and half a dozen more concerned with the related areas of domestic supply, development, and pricing.[6] Bureaucratic confusion only reflected deeper divisions among government agencies. Not only were Harold Ickes and Cordell Hull at odds with one another, but the army and navy often had their own ideas. The situation was further complicated by infighting within the Department of State and by traditional tensions between the federal government and the domestic petroleum industry, particularly the independent producers. The rift between Ickes and Hull focused primarily on the role of government in the development of American-controlled oil reserves. Uneasy over the security of the concession in Saudi Arabia, Ickes seemed determined, despite his later apologies, to secure some form of government participation in Saudi reserves and petroleum facilities. Although much of Ickes's maneuvering was specifically aimed at increasing American bargaining power with the British in the Persian Gulf, he apparently considered some form of government sponsorship the only permanent safeguard for the American concession.

Though sharing Ickes's concern about the welfare of American-owned reserves, the Department of State was wary of the consequences of direct government involvement in the ARAMCO or Gulf Oil concession. Convinced that petroleum matters were intimately tied to the diplomatic complexity of Anglo-American relations in the Middle East, the department saw the necessity of immediate negotiations with Great Britain. Without an understanding with the British, permanent security and the full and orderly development of the oil might only be achieved at the risk of a damaging confrontation with a vital American ally. Equally risky was the potential conflict with the various segments of the domestic petroleum industry. Although neither the State Department nor Ickes were beyond compromise, it appeared by January 1944, that the two were preparing for another sharp round over the most effective means to maintain a strong American position in Arabian oil.

The collapse of PRC-CASOC negotiations only intensified Ickes's efforts to secure Persian Gulf reserves through some form of government sponsorship. Uneasy over British influence in the Gulf, Ickes continued to urge aggressive government action. Writing to Roosevelt in early January 1944, Ickes warned that "the British are overlooking no opportunity to increase their advantage in the Middle East." According to Fred Ohliger of ARAMCO, Ickes reported, "the company he represents cannot deal on equal terms with the British unless the United States has an ownership interest in the American companies doing business in that area."[7] Although Ickes saw the value of petroleum negotiations with the British, he was not yet prepared to abandon PRC's original objective of government participation in the concession without strengthening the American position. Writing to Hull, Ickes noted that the "principal reason" for United States' participation in the ownership of ARAMCO or the company's oil reserves, was to "strengthen the position of the companies and of this Government in those fields. It is the unanimous judgment of the departments which participated in the formulation of the program that American control of these oil reserves is vital to the security of this Nation, and that this control was imperiled so long as the companies did not have the participation, in an ownership capacity, of the United States Government."[8]

Hull was not at all happy with Ickes's response. In fact, the Department of State, then arranging petroleum negotiations with Great Britain, was seriously concerned about the consequences of continued PRC maneuvering with the companies. Not only was Ickes invading the State Department's traditional preserve, but the activities of the PRC threatened to complicate the already intricate character of Anglo-American negotiations. In early January, Hull advised the president that in view of the fact that the proposed discussions with the British temporarily encompassed the role of the PRC, "negotiations of the Petroleum Reserves Corporation looking to governmental participation in companies having foreign reserves should be held in abeyance and I have advised Secretary Ickes accordingly."[9]

Having supported Ickes's more aggressive designs from the outset, however, Roosevelt was eager to pursue negotiations with the companies. In a joint memorandum to Hull and Ickes, the president threw his support, as he had in the past, to his secretary of the interior. Although Roosevelt conceded that the State Department should routinely handle matters of foreign policy, he concluded, "but at the present time I think it vital that we should go ahead with some speed in negotiating with the American companies, in order to find out just where the United States stands before we take the matter up with the British."[10] The following day Secretary of the Navy Knox added his support to the continuance of PRC negotiations. "In the opinion of the Navy, we would be much better equipped to enter into negotiations with the British on this subject if we, like them, owned a direct interest in the oil resources of that region." It might be useful, Knox concluded, "to have some ace up our sleeves ourselves."[11]

Disappointed over the failure of stock purchase, Harold Ickes continued to search for the "ace" which would bolster American bargaining power with the British. Sometime between December 1943 and early January 1944, Ickes began to toy with the idea of a government-sponsored pipeline. The idea of a trans-Arabian pipeline, to be sure, was not Ickes's creation. The oilmen had broached the plan to the Department of State in late 1943.[12] Not only would a pipeline enable ARAMCO to bypass the transit tolls of the Suez Canal, the company argued, it would also provide a link to the prospective markets of Western Europe and the Western Hemisphere. However, unlike ARAMCO's earlier proposal, Ickes's plan called for government sponsorship of the Arabian line. The United States would fund, supervise, and operate the pipeline in addition to contracting with ARAMCO for a billion barrel military reserve in the Persian Gulf.

The new project seemed to offer Ickes and his colleagues all of the advantages of stock purchase without entering into the full partnership which the companies were certain to reject. If the United States could not buy its way into ARAMCO stock, perhaps it could build its way into Arabian oil. "This pipeline," James Byrnes, director of the Office of War Mobilization, wrote to Roosevelt, "will be essential to the proper development of all the Middle East fields and its ownership by the United States will give to our Government a commanding position in the development of these fields."[13]

With the exception of the Department of State, the new pipeline project seemed to offer something for everyone concerned with Arabian oil. To Ickes, the project provided a means to increase the United States' commitment to the security of American-controlled oil reserves and to strengthen the nation's negotiating position with the British.[14] Eager to secure a foothold in the prolific reserves of the Persian Gulf, the military was attracted by the project's provision for the establishment of a billion barrel military reserve. On 25 January the Joint Chiefs of Staff unanimously approved the pipeline plan, reasoning, as Admiral William Leahy put it, that in view of the "inadequacy" of known domestic reserves and the potential of the Middle Eastern fields, "the assurance that a portion of the oil in place will be maintained as a military reserve is of utmost importance to the U.S. Army and Navy."[15] Finally, for the companies, the pipeline offered government support without the risks of full partnership. Moreover, a pipeline linking Kuwait and Saudi Arabia to the eastern Mediterranean would enable ARAMCO and Gulf Oil to reduce the total cost of production and shipping substantially. Determined to reach a working agreement, government and company representatives began negotiating on 18 January. Within a week, a tentative arrangement was formulated.[16]

The "Outline of Principles of a Proposed Agreement," approved by representatives of the Texas Company, SOCAL and Gulf Oil, provided for the construction, operation, and maintenance by the PRC of a pipeline from the Persian Gulf to the Mediterranean. The cost of the project, estimated at 130 to 165 million dollars, was to be amortized through pipeline tolls over a period of twenty-five years. In addition, ARAMCO and Gulf agreed to maintain a billion barrel military reserve for government use. Although the preliminary understanding with the companies appeared to shackle the United States with total responsibility for the pipeline venture, Ickes later confided to the PRC board that the government might not become involved in either the construction or operation of the line provided that an "advantageous agreement" was finally reached with the companies.[17] The primary objective of the pipeline, Ickes realized, was not to involve the government directly in the operation of the project, but to lend official support and approval to American-controlled oil interests in the Persian Gulf. A pipeline, funded by the United States and attached to a plan committing the government to a fifty-year reserve option, was clear evidence of America's permanent interest in Arabian oil. In early February, following Roosevelt's approval of the proposed outline of principles, the PRC released the terms of the pipeline proposal to the press.[18]

Although Ickes had accurately sensed Gulf and ARAMCO's interest in the proposed Arabian pipeline, he underestimated the reaction of the American petroleum industry to his latest PRC maneuver. Release of the details of the pipeline venture immediately mobilized the opposition of all segments of the domestic and foreign oil industry. To the small independent producers and wildcatters, backbone of the domestic industry, the PRC and pipeline were clear manifestations of the influence of big oil and big government. A government-sponsored pipeline, which facilitated the importation of cheap foreign oil into the United States, seemed to confirm the dangers of government interference in the industry. The independents were not alone in their opposition to the pipeline. The campaign against the project was joined by the larger domestic and foreign petroleum producers. In late February, the National Oil Policy Committee of the Petroleum Industry War Council (PIWC), an organization created by Ickes, submitted its preliminary report on national oil policy. Although the study conceded that American companies need "intelligent and sympathetic diplomatic support by the government," it concluded that government participation "should be rigorously avoided in any phase of their operations."[19]

On 1 March, the PIWC, in a separate resolution, focused its attack directly on the pipeline and the PRC. Not only was the project commercially unsound and unrelated to the war effort, but also it threatened to involve the United States in the maze of Middle East and great power politics. The proposed contract with Gulf and ARAMCO, the resolution added, was "against the interest of the people of the United States and all the American oil industry." The committee called for the abrogation of the proposed contract and the dissolution of the Petroleum Reserves Corporation.[20]

The oil industry's attack on the pipeline was supported by certain segments of the Congress. Liberals and isolationists joined with representatives from the oil-producing states in opposition to the project.[21] Moreover, the pipeline venture called into question the legitimate role of the PRC and raised the more crucial issue of a national petroleum policy. Few legislators were prepared to endorse a project whose consequences might affect the entire postwar pattern of domestic and foreign petroleum trade without more careful consideration of the issues involved. A resolution to dissolve the PRC had already been introduced into the Senate. The pipeline project, viewed as the latest of Ickes's PRC schemes, only intensified congressional opposition. In March, the Senate established a special committee to investigate both the pipeline matter and the entire question of petroleum resources. The membership of the committee did not bode well for advocates of the pipeline. Spearheading the investigation were representatives of four important oil-producing states—Tom Connally of Texas, also chairman of the Senate Foreign Relations Committee, E. H. Moore of Oklahoma, Joseph C. O'Mahoney of Wyoming, and John C. Overton of Louisiana. In April, the committee's interim report cautiously concluded that "determination of a sound and long-range national petroleum policy compelled the utmost care and public consideration prior to the commitment on the part of the United States along the lines of the pipeline proposal."[22]

Increasing opposition from Congress and the domestic petroleum industry indicated that Ickes might be forced to abandon his plans for the Arabian pipeline. Moreover, Gulf and ARAMCO had not yet reached final agreement on a proposed contract. In early April, Abe Fortas informed the PRC that Gulf Oil was insisting upon assigning part of its interests in the pipeline to its partner in Kuwait, AIOC. The Texas Company and SOCAL had refused Gulf's request.[23] Continuing pressure by the special Senate committee to force the PRC either to postpone negotiations with the companies, or to give the committee a month's notice before taking any action on pipeline matters, further weakened Ickes's position. In late May, apparently pleased with the progress of the preliminary Anglo-American petroleum talks, Roosevelt advised Ickes to accept the committee's thirty-day proposal.[24]

By June, the last of Ickes's original supports had collapsed. Having conducted a study of the pipeline, the ANPB informed the Joint Chiefs of Staff that although the project was of "military importance" it could not be classified as an "immediate military necessity." [25] Despite Ickes's last-ditch efforts to save the project, the PRC pipeline was dead. With the approach of Cabinet-level petroleum discussions with Great Britain, advocates of a government-sponsored pipeline had reluctantly yielded the initiative in petroleum matters to the Department of State. [26]

Wary of the consequences of direct government involvement in the ARAMCO concession, the Department of State had been cool to Ickes's pipeline venture from the outset. Although the PRC, at the department's insistence, promised to review the question of continued government ownership of the pipeline after the war, officials were nonetheless concerned about the immediate effects of a government-sponsored pipeline in Saudi Arabia. [27] The proposed arrangements with the companies not only made the United States indirectly responsible for the defense of the pipeline, but also threatened to violate the spirit of equal access and economic opportunity promised in the Atlantic Charter. Similarly, the pipeline proposal seemed to provide official American protection for a private oil concession in exchange for preferential price reductions on petroleum. In February, Charles Rayner, the State Department's petroleum adviser, summarized the objections:

> The agreement may be interpreted in some quarters as an exclusive arrangement for the defense of the United States, discriminating against the access of other countries to important oil reserves, qualifying the independence of local states, and burdening the United States with important political responsibilities in Arabia. It has many of the characteristics of "spheres of interest" agreements of the kind objected to by the United States in Morocco (1906), Manchuria (1911), and Mosul (1920). [28]

Equally important was the State Department's concern that the pipeline scheme might interfere with the success of the larger objective —Anglo-American negotiations on Middle Eastern oil. Early in January, Rayner had advised Davies of ARAMCO that although the department favored the idea of a pipeline in principle, there were "certain questions and developments relating to oil in the Middle Eastern area to which a project of this nature must be properly related." B. F. Haley, chief of the Commodities Division, warned: "Adoption of this policy will weaken our position in the forthcoming petroleum conversations with the British, since we are anxious to urge a relaxation of certain restrictive and preferential arrangements not dissimilar to the one under discussion."[29]

The emergence of Ickes's pipeline venture only intensified the department's efforts to initiate petroleum discussions with the British. Anglo-American negotiations, directed toward a comprehensive agreement, seemed to offer a possible diplomatic approach to the problems of securing American interests in Persian Gulf oil. Moreover, the future development of American concessions was dependent upon the elimination of prewar restrictions on production and marketing.

In January 1944, John Loftus, soon to be attached to the policy section of the Department of State's Petroleum Division (PED), outlined an "American policy" toward Middle Eastern petroleum. Despite its potential reserves and productive capacity, the American petroleum economy, Loftus warned, was shifting from a position of net exporter of oil to net importer. In order to insure the "maximum conservation" of strategically vital reserves in the continental United States and Western Hemisphere, it would be necessary to supply former markets with oil from the Eastern Hemisphere and ultimately to import substantial quantities of Middle Eastern oil in the postwar period. Maximizing the flow of crude was dependent upon a relaxation of "existing restrictions." Anglo-American discussions, Loftus concluded, must specifically focus on the cancellation or modification of the Red Line, revision of the Kuwait restrictions, greater intergovernment cooperation in the policies of the IPC, an agreement on expanded production in Qatar, and immediate exploration in Trucial Oman.[30] Rayner expressed a similar line to Cordell Hull. One of the principal objectives of United States foreign oil policy, Rayner concluded, was "removal, by international agreement, of existing impediments to large scale exploitation of Middle East concessions held by United States nationals."[31] By early 1944, many of the State Department's petroleum planners saw Anglo-American negotiations not as the end result of American diplomacy, but as the *sine qua non* of further oil diplomacy in the Middle East.

Although the Department of State had formally invited the British to participate in petroleum discussions in December 1943, it was not until early February that Michael Wright, first secretary of the British Embassy, officially accepted. Wright made it clear to the department that the proposed negotiations might begin with the Middle East, but should not be confined to any single area.[32] Determined to avoid specific commitments the British attempted to widen the framework of the negotiations. Broadening the geographic limits of the discussions might not only enable London to avoid specific situations in Iraq or

Kuwait, but also the expanded coverage might be used as bargaining leverage against America's predominant petroleum position in the Western Hemisphere. The British assumed that unless the Americans were prepared to oppose all preferential arrangements in petroleum, including the preeminent position of American companies in Europe and the Western Hemisphere, they could not wage an effective campaign against British interests in the Middle East. The State Department, however, eager to focus negotiations specifically on the Middle East, was quick to press its point. "This Government," Hull wrote to Lord Halifax, "believes that it may be found desirable to extend the scope of the conversations beyond a discussion of the problems concerning Middle Eastern oil but that a determination of whether that should be done and to what extent can be made best in the light of the progress of the discussions on Middle East oil."[33]

By the middle of February, uneasy over the direction of the proposed petroleum negotiations, the British sought further assurances from the State Department concerning the purpose of the forthcoming discussions. Sensitive to any attempt to revise the existing pattern of oil concessions, Great Britain was justifiably disturbed by the possibility of wide open negotiations with the Americans. In an effort to secure the British position, the Foreign Office began to insist that any discussion of concession rights be confined only to future areas of oil development and not to "existing concession rights."[34] The British were also disturbed by the apparent shift in American negotiating tactics. Although the State Department had originally informed the Foreign Office that discussions might begin on the staff level and only later move to the Cabinet level, Roosevelt now advised the department that all conversations should fall under the nominal supervision of a Cabinet-level group. On 18 February, Edward Stettinius informed Halifax that because the president believed petroleum was of such "extreme importance" to both nations, Cabinet-level discussions were basic to the success of the proposed negotiations. As to concession rights, Stettinius concluded, in view of the proposed "frank and open discussion of all matters of mutual interest . . . ," there was no apparent reason to exclude a discussion of existing concessions.[35]

Uneasy over the import of immediate Cabinet-level discussions covering existing concessions in the Middle East, Great Britain was reluctant to rush into negotiations without conclusive assurances of American intentions. On 20 February, in an effort to clarify the nature of the proposed negotiations and to avoid a "wrangle about oil," Churchill cabled Roosevelt: "There is apprehension in some quarters here that the United States has a desire to deprive us of our oil assets in the

Middle East on which among other things, the whole supply of our Navy depends." Anticipating problems with Parliament, Churchill added that if Great Britain entered into negotiations with the secretary of state, "it will be felt that we are being hustled and may be subjected to pressure."[36] Churchill requested Roosevelt to consider technical staff discussions first. The president, however, apparently disturbed by London's evasive maneuvers, cabled the prime minister with concerns of his own. "You point to the apprehension on your side that the United States desires to deprive you of oil assets in the Middle East." On the other hand, the president added,"I am disturbed about the rumor that the British wish to horn in on Saudi Arabian oil reserves." Turning to the question of petroleum discussions, Roosevelt pressed his original point, "it is my firm conviction that these technical discussions should take place under the guidance of a group at Cabinet level, and I cannot, therefore, change my position in this regard." For good measure Roosevelt added that he desired to preside at the opening session.[37]

There was, however, a compromise which enabled the petroleum discussions to proceed. It is likely that both the United States and Great Britain, in view of the need for particularly close cooperation in the months ahead, were eager to avoid a major diplomatic row over oil. Rumors were already rife in the press that Washington and London were having serious difficulties over oil; neither the prime minister nor the president seemed ready to face the political fallout of a major disagreement between allies. The British nonetheless were determined to exact certain guarantees from the United States before committing themselves to formal discussions. Most important was the assurance that the Americans would not attempt to use the negotiations to alter the existing pattern of concession ownership in the Middle East. Early in March, Roosevelt personally assured Churchill that "we are not making sheep's eyes at your oilfields in Iraq or Iran."[38] The president's guarantee apparently quieted British fears. On 6 March, Roosevelt received a message from Churchill, via Frederick Winant in London, welcoming his assurances. Winant added that the British would dispatch a group of staff experts to be followed by a formal Cabinet negotiating team.[39]

In mid-April, after almost two months of delay, the British and American delegations finally sat down at the conference table in Washington. Although the atmosphere during the discussions was cordial enough, it was clear that both the Americans and British had different objectives in mind. The technical discussions were designed primarily to formulate a general understanding of petroleum matters prior to

Cabinet negotiations, yet the American team, led by Charles Rayner, acting chief of the newly created Petroleum Division, also sought to focus on the specific problems of oil development, particularly in the Middle East.[40] The American negotiators, supported by their industry advisers, recognized that the key problem in the postwar period might not be the shortage of petroleum but rather a potential abundance of oil. It was in the interests of all parties, the Americans believed, to effect the orderly development of these resources within the framework of the Atlantic Charter. Perhaps the greatest violation of these principles were the political and economic restrictions currently impeding the development of Middle Eastern oil. Even more important, without the removal or at least relaxation of these restrictions, the reserves might not be employed to conserve reserves of the Western Hemisphere. The proposed conversations, a State Department agenda concluded in March, should deal with the Open Door "not in terms of abstract principles but with reference to specific phenomena."[41] High on the department's list were the renegotiation of the Kuwait marketing clause and the cancellation of the Red Line restrictions.

To the British, however, already wary of American intentions, the technical discussions were to be purely exploratory in nature. The British team, led by Sir William Brown, former secretary of the Petroleum Division of the British Ministry of Fuel and Power, was instructed by the War Cabinet to make no commitment, least of all in the Middle East.[42] Early in the discussions, the Americans suggested that the proposed joint commission deal with problems arising "particularly but not exclusively in the Middle East."[43] British objections were so vigorous that the American group withdrew its suggestion. Broadening the geographic framework of the negotiations seemed inevitable. Uneasy over the possibility that the Americans might question the validity of existing concessions, the British team was determined to steer discussion away from sensitive areas. So too, the purpose of technical talks, the British believed, was only to formulate general principles which might serve as a basis for the proposed Cabinet-level talks.

The result of the technical discussions clearly reflected this end. Early in May, after two weeks of negotiation, the groups agreed to a nonbinding "Memorandum of Understanding" which proposed a set of principles for the availability, supply, and development of the international petroleum trade. The primary purpose of any future accord, the Americans believed, was to assure ample supplies of petroleum to all nations on an orderly basis. The British, concerned that the United States was not sensitive enough to Great Britain's petroleum needs, could not have agreed more. The accord, whose language was intentionally vague, seemed to contain something for everyone. The British were particularly happy with the pledge to respect all valid concession contracts. The Americans seemed pleased with the idea that petroleum development would not be impeded "by restrictions imposed by either Government or its nationals, inconsistent with the purposes of this Memorandum of Understanding."[44] Finally, both sides pledged themselves to work toward negotiation of an international petroleum agreement.[45]

Although the initialled Memorandum did not include a single mention of the Middle East, the exploratory discussions had taken up the problems of Middle Eastern oil development. The British experts could make no commitments, but they did concede that the Kuwait marketing agreement and Red Line restrictions were "inconsistent" with the principles of the Memorandum of Understanding.[46] Equally important, the British assured the Americans that they would respect all concessions in the area—a pledge which seemed to quiet American concerns about the security of the Saudi concession. Writing to Moose in Jidda following the conclusion of the technical discussions, Hull noted: "If this clause is included in the final agreement, which now appears likely, it is considered that a material contribution will have been made to the protection of the American oil concession and interests in Saudi Arabia."[47] Implementation of the British promises was another matter, yet the technical discussions had done a great deal to allay American suspicions. The Americans now eagerly awaited the proposed Cabinet discussions.

However, much to the dismay of the Americans, the Cabinet negotiations did not begin until late July. The British, apparently uneasy over the terms of the Memorandum of Understanding, were in no hurry to rush into high-level talks in Washington.[48] Yet, after further prodding from the White House and rumors in the press about the collapse of the negotiations, the British named their negotiating team.[49] Finally on 25 July, the two delegations (the American headed by Hull and the British by Lord Beaverbrook, Lord Privy Seal) sat down at the conference table. Early in August representatives of the United States and United Kingdom signed the Anglo-American Petroleum Agreement.

Although the Cabinet-level negotiations had not been as smooth as anticipated, and had nearly collapsed over British demands to secure their foreign exchange position with respect to oil, the agreement was a testament to the importance which the two allies attached to wartime cooperation.[50] The accord was a clear reflection of the ideals of equal access and opportunity embodied in the Atlantic Charter and offered a valuable precedent in the field of postwar economic cooperation. Moreover, the agreement set guidelines for the orderly development of world petroleum resources and laid the basis for a multilateral accord on oil.[51]

The final agreement also addressed the problems of Middle Eastern oil. Although the accord, like the Memorandum of Understanding, did not specifically refer to the Middle East, it was obviously directed toward that area. The fourth "agreed principle" emphasized the importance of "equal opportunity" with respect to the acquisition of exploration and development rights in areas not now under concession, an obvious reference to Britain's use of "special political relationships" to influence the granting of concessions in the Persian Gulf. More important, the accord urged the signatories to respect "all valid concession contracts and lawfully acquired rights." This principle, Loftus later noted, "is designed to put an effective end to the suspicion and mistrust that have beclouded Anglo-American relations in the Middle East in the recent months."[52] Finally, in an apparent reference to marketing and producing restrictions in the area, the sixth principle provided that the exploration and development of petroleum resources "shall not be hampered by restrictions imposed by either Government or its nationals inconsistent with the purpose of the agreement."[53]

Despite the strengths of the agreement, it was difficult to see how general principles, "agreed" or otherwise, might be applied to specific situations, particularly when the accord itself avoided mention of geographic areas.[54] The agreement provided no "legal machinery" nor "powers of compulsion" to enforce its principles. Nor could it be realistically expected to do so given the size and character of the international petroleum trade. How could the "agreed principles" facilitate the removal of the Kuwait marketing restrictions or the impediments of the Red Line agreement? The operating companies were not bound by intergovernment commitments, only by their "own good faith." Although Loftus predicted that the "mere publication of this code of principles will in large part ensure its realization," it was more likely that the conduct of the companies would be determined by the realities of world markets and prices, and that the reaction of the Congress would be shaped by the realities of domestic politics.[55]

Finally, like the Memorandum of Understanding, the agreement was singularly and perhaps intentionally vague. Although no doubt intended to put the Americans and British on record as advocating certain "broad principles" relating to petroleum development, its generality jeopardized its chances for success. The expanded geographic coverage of the agreement and the proposed International Petroleum Commission inevitably aroused the suspicion of congressional watch-dogs. Moreover, the domestic petroleum industry attacked the agreement from every conceivable angle. Not only were independent oil companies suspicious of federal intrusion into the industry, but also some larger companies soon wondered whether the advantages of the accord were worth an "overt conflict" with the independents.[56]

What had begun as an attempt to conclude a limited agreement on Middle Eastern oil had evolved into a bold but vaguely worded accord likely to offend both Congress and the industry. In August, the accord was submitted to the Senate, not as an executive agreement as planned, but as a treaty. It was then referred to the Senate Foreign Relations Committee where it lay under the critical eye of Chairman Connally. In January 1945, rather than risk an open confrontation with Congress, the agreement was withdrawn from the Senate for "renegotiation" with the British.[57]

Although the agreement had not specifically referred to the Middle East, the exploratory and Cabinet discussions enabled the Americans and British to come to a greater understanding with respect to the security of concessions in the area. The Americans were particularly pleased with British assurances of noninterference in Saudi Arabia. Testifying in executive session before the Senate Foreign Relations Committee in August, Charles Rayner noted that the agreement had secured "an understanding on the part of the British to respect our concessions in the Middle East and not to interfere directly or indirectly with those concession rights."[58]

British promises at the conference table had resolved much of the Anglo-American tension over oil, yet the situation in the field continued to arouse American concern. To many of the department's Middle East hands, British motives remained suspect. "I am convinced," Loy Henderson, minister to Iraq, wrote from Baghdad, "that British officials in this area hope to see the whole question of British-American relations in the Near East solved in such a manner similar to that in which they have solved the problem of oil in Iraq. Their idea is that the British Government would remain the dominating foreign power . . . the Americans would be associated in the role of silent partners."[59]

Officials were particularly concerned about the situation in Saudi Arabia. Despite London's assurances of noninterference in the concession, Great Britain continued to exert considerable influence in the internal affairs of the Saudi kingdom. Since 1941, British subsidies to Ibn Saud had comprised nearly 90 percent of the king's requirements.

Equally important, Britain's position in the Persian Gulf together with its support of Ibn Saud's Hashemite rivals afforded considerable leverage with the king. Although the British had no intention of stealing the ARAMCO concession, neither were they willing to concede to the Americans their hard-earned position in Saudi Arabia.

Already sensitive to the paucity of American aid to the king, NEA (in 1944 the Division of Near Eastern Affairs, NE, became the Office of Near Eastern and African Affairs, NEA; the new division was composed of three smaller geographic units—the Division of Near Eastern Affairs, NE; the Division of Middle Eastern Affairs, ME; and the Division of African Affairs, AF) was disturbed by the possible consequences of British control. Without a stable source of revenue and sound financial management, the king might be vulnerable to outside pressure. To the officers of NEA, the problem in Saudi Arabia was clear. Unless the Americans succeeded in increasing their influence and prestige with the king, breaking his dependence on Great Britain, and stabilizing his finances, the concession might never be secure. By 1944, the Arab experts turned their efforts toward strengthening the official American commitment in Saudi Arabia.[60]

With the earlier decision to extend lend-lease aid to Saudi Arabia in February 1943, State and Treasury Department officials had begun to assess the problems of an ailing Saudi economy. Aside from the mismanagement and chaos of Saudi Arabia's finances, the king's most pressing problem was the lack of revenue. With petroleum production at only 21,296 b.p.d. in 1944, oil royalties were not yet sufficient to balance the king's budget. Although in August 1943, the United States had agreed to lend-lease Ibn Saud enough silver to mint 15 million riyals, the king's budget for 1944 threatened to exceed 109 million riyals. By early 1944 it seemed clear that the United States might have to assume a more direct role in Saudi finances. "In view of our vital interest in Saudi Arabian oil," Leonard Parker of NE wrote, "do we wish to permit King Ibn Saud to be obligated to any other government to a greater extent than he has already obligated himself."[61]

In fact, the real problem facing the State Department was not an increase but a planned reduction in Britain's currency commitment to Ibn Saud. Due to the increasing stability in the Middle East and the waste and inefficiency of the Saudi financial system, the British saw little reason to continue pouring gold and sterling into the king's treasury. Already pressed by British Treasury officials to reduce subsidies, the Foreign Office had no intention of paying the price for Saudi fiscal irresponsibility. "It is apparent that the Saudi Arabian Government," the Foreign Office informed Jidda, "have made no effort to cut their coat according to their cloth and that they will spend as much money as His Majesty's Government are prepared to give them. The continued demands for more currency to meet necessary governmental expenditure, when apparently unlimited rials can be found for such luxuries as palaces at El Kharj, make a bad impression, and the extravagance of the royal princes can only be regarded as an abuse of His Majesty's Government's generosity."[62] In mid-January, Alexander Kirk reported from Cairo that the British desired to withhold further gold subsidies until a program of fiscal reform was developed.[63]

The Foreign Office strategy seemed clear. The British would slightly reduce their currency commitments to the Saudis for the first half of 1944 and thereafter reduce assistance to a level consistent with their political and military interests. As for the Americans, it was obvious that London sought their cooperation but had no intention of leaving them the entire field. "We do not know at present how the American mind is working over aid to Ibn Saud," C. W. Baxter, head of the Eastern Department minuted, "and it's possible any reduction in our subsidy might be followed by a spontaneous offer of further American assistance. I should be inclined to recommend that, when the time comes for an approach to America, we should ask them whether they are prepared to bear half the cost of the subsidy in [the] future in they now have considerably altered their ideas about the importance of Saudi Arabia to American interests. And, after all, it's American interests, and not British, who are getting Saudi Arabian oil."[64]

Britain's intended message seemed clear. If the United States indeed claimed a primary economic interest in Arabian oil, then it had best contribute its share to the maintenance of a stable Saudi economy. The department's Middle East hands were quick to see the opportunities of the proposed British reduction. In fact, their response only confirmed Baxter's suspicions. NE suggested that the United States assume total responsibility for subsidies to Ibn Saud. The advantages of such a plan, Parker concluded, were obvious—"Saudi Arabia would no longer be obligated in any way to another foreign power, thus making the American oil concession more secure." It was highly unlikely, however, that the British would withdraw completely from the subsidy program. At best, U.S. Treasury officials believed, the United States and Great Britain might share equally in a joint program of assistance.[65]

State Department efforts to increase American aid to Ibn Saud were spurred by reports of British interference in the internal affairs of Saudi Arabia. Much of the department's concern focused on the activities of

S. R. Jordan, Britain's minister to Saudi Arabia. Jordan, described by Sir Maurice Peterson, undersecretary of state for foreign affairs, as a "big breezy Australian," had joined the Levant Consular Service in 1919 and gathered considerable experience in Arabia, serving as acting agent and consul in Jidda in 1925. Well-liked by Ibn Saud, Jordan had acted as intermediary in the negotiations which eventually led to the surrender of Jidda to the Saudis. A year later at the king's request, he had accompanied Ibn Saud's son, Amir Faisal, to Great Britain. Despite Jordan's reputation, the British minister's recommendations to reform the Saudi economy and reduce British subsidies dampened his popularity both in royal circles and among local officials.[66] Even more important, his views were to bring him into direct conflict with the Americans.

Although Moose had initially welcomed Jordan's plans to eliminate the inefficiency of Saudi finances, by the spring of 1944, the American's view of his colleague had changed substantially. According to "unconfirmed reports," Moose cabled the State Department, Jordan was attempting to extend British influence in Saudi Arabia and to establish a measure of British control. The British minister had reportedly persuaded the king to accept a British economic adviser and possibly a petroleum adviser. Moreover, according to a "reliable informant," Jordan was responsible for the removal of Najib Salha, Saudi director of Mines and Public Works and reportedly an advocate of closer American-Saudi ties.[67] Reports that London planned to increase its food subsidy sixfold further alarmed NEA officials. The State Department instructed Moose to forward the details of Jordan's activities, and concluded that it would "take all appropriate steps to safeguard vital American interests in Saudi Arabia."[68]

Reports from Cairo and Jidda only accelerated NEA's efforts to increase the American commitment to Ibn Saud. Outlining the problem for the State Department's Policy Committee, Paul Alling warned that Ibn Saud's dependence on Great Britain offered the British an opportunity to exact certain *"quids pro quo"* from the king. As oil was Saudi Arabia's only resource, it was likely that any arrangements with them might be made at the expense of this valuable American concession. Not only did the military consider Saudi reserves "essential" to the nation's interests, but also diminishing domestic reserves might force the United States to draw indirectly or directly on Arabian oil. In order to counter British influence and to secure the concession, Alling concluded, the United States might consider assuming 50 percent of the subsidies to Ibn Saud.[69]

Early in April, Hull submitted NEA's recommendations to the president. "It is believed necessary for this Government," the memorandum began, "to extend additional financial and economic assistance to Saudi Arabia in order to safeguard adequately the American national interest in the great petroleum resources of that country." To lessen the danger of the British demanding a *"quid pro quo* in oil," the United States should share the subsidy on an "over-all equal basis" with the British. In view of the urgency of the situation, the department concluded, the necessary funds might be drawn from either lend-lease or the Foreign Economic Administration (FEA) budget. Long an advocate of greater security for American oil interests in Saudi Arabia, Roosevelt gave his immediate approval.[70]

The State Department's growing concern about the welfare of American oil interests in Saudi Arabia was reflected in a series of conversations with the British in April. The discussions, held in London, were part of a larger mission led by Under Secretary of State Stettinius, and were designed to cover a broad range of foreign policy concerns, including a number of Middle Eastern matters.[71] Saudi Arabia, however, was high on the agenda. Although the discussions were expected to be informal and congenial, the State Department was determined to make London aware of the importance of the American stake in Saudi Arabia. Wallace Murray, now director of the Office of Near Eastern and African Affairs, and one of the department's most virulent Anglophobes, was charged with the task.[72]

The British knew exactly what the Americans had in mind—at least in Saudi Arabia. In a brief prepared for the conversations with Murray, the Foreign Office accurately sensed the temper of their American allies. "There is already a tendency for the Americans to suspect that we are trying to exclude them and to oppose the increase in their influence. It would be well therefore to give Mr. Wallace Murray the definite impression that we recognize the growing commercial interest of the Americans in Saudi Arabia and that we have no wish to prevent them from playing a role in Saudi Arabian affairs corresponding to the importance of this interest." At the same time, the memorandum continued, "the Americans must recognize that we have a strong economic, as well as political interest in Saudi Arabia quite apart from our general strategic interest in a territory neighbouring on Palestine, Transjordan, Iraq and vital imperial communications. . . . We must therefore try to make the State Department understand that, while we have no intention of queering their pitch in any way in Saudi Arabia and would welcome their co-operation, and while the development of a major oil industry may alter the economic position in the future,

Saudi Arabia is for the above reasons still more important to us than to them."[73]

Not everyone in the Foreign Office agreed with the directness of the proposed approach. In a note to Sir Maurice Peterson, Neville Butler minuted: "Frankly, I think it would be dangerous to speak to as truculent a nationalist as Wallace Murray quite as bluntly as in the attached extract from your minute. I say dangerous because it would risk defeating what I understand to be our purpose in these talks, namely, to persuade Murray that our policies are necessities for us, and also beneficial to the rest of the world, including the U.S., and therefore deserving of the latter's general support."[74]

Although the British had anticipated difficulties with the Americans, they were pleasantly surprised at how conciliatory Wallace Murray proved to be. "So far the conversations haven't revealed any fundamental difference of policy," Peterson wrote to Anthony Eden on 14 April, "Mr. Murray entirely accepted our assurance that we weren't 'horning in' on Saudi Arabia oil and gave a reciprocal assurance as regards the Anglo-Iranian Oil Company in Persia. . . . In general he has been in a genial mood and has only shown that he has teeth once or twice."[75]

The discussions which covered questions of subsidy and currency plans for Saudi Arabia did indeed result in agreement in principle on a number of troublesome issues. The Americans and British agreed to initiate discussions on a joint assistance program and a joint military mission. More important, the Americans once again accepted British assurances that His Majesty's government had no intention "to undermine or prejudice American oil rights in Saudi Arabia."[76] Still, there remained the knotty problem of the leadership of the military mission, the matter of a financial adviser to the king, and the practical details of implementing the subsidy.[77] Although Stettinius could inform Hull in late April that the talks on Saudi Arabia were moving toward "close American-British cooperation and collaboration," it was clear that there were still differences in both theory and practice as to how the Saudi situation should be handled.[78]

In April, Moose informed the State Department that the British minister was "pursuing a policy calculated to be detrimental to American interests in Saudi Arabia."[79] Not only had Jordan reportedly failed to keep his American colleague abreast of Britain's policy, he had worked for the dismissal of local officials favorable to the United States and withheld pilgrimage revenues from the king. These activities, Moose reported, "look remarkably like attempt to establish British influence here."[80] Nor did the Americans care much for Jordan's personality. William Eddy, special assistant to Moose, observed that Jordan's "emotional instability and lack of breeding, if not incipient insanity, are suggested by the sudden fits of rage when in the presence of strangers he hurls vile epithets at his own career colleagues, epithets too vile to be put on paper."[81] By June, Hull could inform Halifax that according to reports from Jidda, Jordan was doing his "level best to injure the American Government's relations with the King."[82]

Although the Americans seemed convinced that the British minister had embarked on a single-handed campaign to swindle them out of Saudi Arabia, Jordan apparently had no such intention. The minister was determined, however, to bring some order to Saudi financial affairs—an objective which the Americans tirelessly misinterpreted as a British plot to control the Saudi economy. In view of the widespread corruption and mismanagement of Saudi finances, Jordan had repeatedly advised the Foreign Office to discontinue pouring currency into Ibn Saud's seemingly bottomless coffers. London should continue to maintain the king's essential requirements but only on a level necessary to preserve Britain's strategic and political interests in the area. Jordan had little patience for American plans to buy Saudi goodwill through promises of large-scale financial aid. "The United States," the minister wrote to Baxter in May, "have undoubtedly seized the opportunity afforded by our efforts to place this country on a sound economic basis to play mother bountiful to the Saudis and with the encouragement of Abdulla Suleiman, Yusuf Yasin and Nejib, made offers of assistance which have taken away from the King in some measure and totally from Abdulla Suleiman any desire to retrench since the future looks tolerably golden to them."[83]

Equally damaging to British interests, Jordan believed, were American shortsightedness and naiveté in dealing with the Saudis. These attitudes, evidenced by Washington's plans to assist the king at any cost, enabled Ibn Saud to exploit Anglo-American differences and to "make the best of two worlds." The situation was further complicated, the British minister believed, by American hostility toward Britain's "preferential position" in Saudi Arabia. Writing to the Foreign Office, Jordan presented his case:

> We do enjoy Ibn Saud's confidence in a larger measure than the
> United States and this is anathema to them. As usual however
> they have overplayed their hand and aroused suspicions as to their
> good intentions. Frankly I share those suspicions but they may be
> ill-founded. Let us hope so. They have had little experience in

Mohammedan countries and do not yet appreciate the value which Ibn Saud attaches to his religion and to non-interference in his internal affairs. They see a backward country and immediately want to run it on modern lines not realizing that Ibn Saud's strength and prestige in the Moslem world, which is of considerable advantage to us, lies in his insularity and will be undermined and largely neutralized if there is any large infiltration of Americans or for that matter members of any other Christian power in Saudi Arabia. This is why Ibn Saud who really wants to reorganize his country insists on Sunni Moslems as advisers, experts and teachers and it is of course a further sore point with the Americans that we are in a position to supply these while they are not.[84]

Jordan's reports carried considerable weight at Whitehall. Already pressed by the Treasury to reduce its subsidy commitments, the Foreign Office fully supported their minister's efforts to reduce the subsidy.[85] Nor were the British much impressed by Moose's or Murray's reports of Jordan's alleged anti-American activities. "Meanwhile," R. M. A. Hankey minuted in June, "I find the tone of Wallace Murray's complaints definitely disappointing. Some of them could hardly have been made unless the underlying American intention was to prevent us having any influence in Saudi Arabia, and to exercise influence there themselves at almost any reasonable cost. I am convinced it will not pay us to be rattled by this sort of stuff, or by the way in which he 'waves' Mr. Hull and the President at us on every occasion. However we must persevere."[86] Foreign Office views of Moose were equally contemptuous. According to Gerald Hume Pinsent of the British Treasury, Moose seemed to be a "second-rate" man envious of Jordan's abilities and of his close relations with Ibn Saud. William Crofts writing from Cairo confirmed Pinsent's impressions. Though "fairly intelligent and in casual intercourse not disagreeable," Crofts wrote to Peterson, Moose was "a lightweight, poorly equipped for his job."[87]

Difficulties between Moose and Jordan only highlighted the differences in the American and British views of Saudi Arabia. For Great Britain, Saudi Arabia provided a painful exercise in balancing imperial priorities. Pressed by the strains of wartime economy, London anticipated reduction in its currency commitment to the king. Although most Foreign Office officials were not opposed to the United States sharing the subsidy, neither were they prepared to concede their hard-earned influence in political and military matters. Aside from the strategic importance of the Arabian peninsula, the British, with mil-

lions of Muslim subjects under their charge, believed they had a considerable stake in maintaining prestige and influence with Ibn Saud,
guardian of the holy cities.

So too, if the Americans pushed their way into Saudi Arabia without
regard to the king's sensitivities to foreign influence, Ibn Saud's position in the Arab and Muslim world might be weakened. Equally important, a Saudi kingdom, supported by American money and
material, and set loose on a course of modernization and development,
could easily threaten the stability of the Persian Gulf and south Arabia
and weaken Britain's Hashemite clients in Transjordan and Iraq. Although the British sensed that increasing American oil interests might
ultimately result in a predominant American position in Saudi Arabia,
for the present at least they were determined to preserve their influence in the political and military affairs of the Saudi kingdom.[88]

Unfortunately for Whitehall, the State Department no longer believed it possible to separate economic and political influence in Saudi
Arabia. Eager to safeguard the American stake in the king's oil, officials were determined to play the dominant role in the Saudi economy
and to at least maintain some influence in political matters. The Americans did not want to destroy Britain's influence in Saudi Arabia or to
threaten its position in south Arabia and the Persian Gulf. What they
did seek, however, was nothing short of a reversal of traditional roles.
If the United States were to secure and develop a national interest in
Arabian oil, officials believed, then it must abandon its role of junior
partner and assume a dominant position in the economic and political
future of the Saudi kingdom. "Very simply, Saudi Arabian officials do
not understand," Eddy observed in June, "why we do not insist openly
on prior economic leadership in their country just as we concede freely
prior British interest in Palestine, India, Iran." This lack of commitment, "leaves the natives suspicious that we are not serious nor permanent in Arabia."[89]

Formulation of a joint subsidy plan in July 1944 did not quiet NEA's
concern about British influence in Saudi Arabia. The subsidy program
concentrated on the immediate requirements of the king, yet the department's Arab hands were still uneasy over the future of the Saudi
economy.[90] Furthermore, troubled by British plans to appoint a British
subject as financial adviser to Ibn Saud, NEA was even more convinced
that any long-range plans for financial reform or economic aid must
be initiated under American auspices.[91] In July, Murray advised a
meeting of State and Treasury Department representatives that, in
view of "the large economic interests of this country in Saudi Arabia
arising out of the American oil concession," the British alone must not

be permitted to implement banking or currency reform.[92] Pressing the point, Hull had written to Peterson: "The reason it was proposed that the head of any financial mission or that a single financial adviser furnished to the Saudi Arabian Government be an American is that the preponderant interest in Saudi Arabian economy is unquestionably American in character and will presumably remain so for many years to come."[93]

The Foreign Office, however, seemed reluctant to accept American economic predominance. As early as April, Peterson had informed Murray that the British had a "very considerable economic interest" in Saudi Arabia arising largely from the pilgrimage and from Saudi commerce with India.[94] Although Peterson later conceded that the pilgrimage was not "exclusively" a British concern, a large proportion of the pilgrims came from the Commonwealth. Even during the war years, the hajj had yielded 40 million riyals to the king. In comparison, Peterson noted, American petroleum operations produced only 4 million riyals in oil royalties and 10 million in local expenditures.[95]

British arguments only intensified NEA's concern. Moreover, officials were disturbed by Britain's apparent plans to force Ibn Saud to reduce his expenditures and put his finances in order. Moose had already reported that the king was unhappy with the joint supply program and predicted that Ibn Saud might pressure ARAMCO for additional funds.[96] So too, maintaining Saudi goodwill was of even greater importance now that the War Department was actively pursuing plans to survey a location for an airfield in the vicinity of Dhahran.[97] Meeting with Michael Wright of the British Embassy, Wallace Murray bluntly noted that the United States would not see its "vital interests" in Saudi Arabia threatened by a "penny-wise pound-foolish" British policy. As for Minister Jordan, Murray concluded, unless London made plans for his recall, Britain must be prepared to face the consequences of "discarding" Anglo-American cooperation in Saudi Arabia.[98]

The Foreign Office, however, had no intention of sacrificing Jordan to the Americans. Although the State Department's plans to elevate the status of its diplomatic post at Jidda, and to replace Moose with Eddy in the rank of full minister, were designed in part to persuade London to replace Jordan, the British held fast.[99] Indignant over Washington's charges against their minister, Hankey bitterly noted: "We knew the local Americans have been making trouble for Mr. Jordan. But then they have been double-crossing us + Mr. Jordan has rightly brought them to book." Alexander Cadogan, permanent under secretary of state for foreign affairs, added his support. "The Americans have failed to make a case against Mr. Jordan, and it would be unfair to him, and to ourselves, to offer him up as a sacrifice."[100]

Although the British had stood firm in the defense of their minister, London realized that in most matters cooperation with the Americans was far better than competition. "We are endeavouring, as you know," the Foreign Office informed Jordan, "to establish our relations with the Americans in the Middle East, and particularly in Saudi Arabia, on a basis of mutual confidence and co-operation, and rely on you to continue to do your best with your American colleagues."[101] More important, Foreign Office officials seemed to recognize that the United States was eager to secure its oil interests in Saudi Arabia and might as a result overplay its hand with Britain and particularly with the Saudis. There were those in London who believed that British interests in Saudi Arabia might best be protected by dealing with the Americans in a patient, albeit, paternal manner. "American impulsiveness and inexperience in dealing with the Arabs may sometimes lead them to act injudiciously," the Foreign Office observed, "but we must endeavour to persuade and guide them on the right lines, and be patient with their mistakes."[102]

So too, there were those at Whitehall who began to question whether Britain, already financially pressed, should continue to play the leading role in Saudi affairs. In view of the potential of the CASOC concession and the possibility of future oil royalties, British Treasury officials recognized that the American oil companies would eventually become the most important factor in the country's future. Writing to Hankey, William Lawson of the Treasury posed a difficult set of questions:

> Without knowledge of the figures involved, I believe that those oil concessions are of enormous importance—probably as much as the Iranian ones—and therefore the American influence in Saudi Arabia cannot but gain momentum. As the Americans will have a profit earning interest in the country, their outlook on subsidy matters will be on a much grander scale than ours. Are we then to go on competing with the Americans in the development of the country, or at least in ensuring that it enjoys a moderate degree of peace and plenty? Can we really curb the Americans' impetuosity in offering Ibn Saud all sorts of supplies which previously he did without? It seems that the answer depends largely on the Foreign Office's opinion of the advantages which we shall ultimately derive from our interest in Saudi Arabia.[103]

The Treasury's pitch for economy had meanwhile received additional support from an unexpected quarter. Early in September, Stanley Jordan, in a revealing message from Jidda, called for a review of London's entire subsidy commitment to Saudi Arabia. To the British minister, long an advocate of greater economy by Saudi Arabia, the problem was painfully clear. After extended conversations with the new American minister, Eddy, Jordan noted that the Americans were determined to increase their subsidy to the king whatever the cost. "Unless we are to be drawn into this spate of philanthropy," Jordan continued, "I feel that we should put a limit to our financial responsibilities, or indeed cease any subsidy to this country, as soon as our present obligations are liquidated. . . . If the Americans wish to sink millions of dollars in the desert sands of Saudi Arabia I do not think that we would be justified in endeavouring to prevent them from so doing since they will be taking billions out of the same sands in the form of oil, but I see no reason why we should be drawn into this vortex since we have little or nothing to gain from it. The position of a junior partner being towed along in the wake of the Americans is, in my humble opinion, a very undignified one for His Majesty's Government to accept and the political advantages to be gained from fifty/fifty participation in the United States of America's projects appear to be few or none." As for the preservation of His Majesty's political interests, Jordan assured his superiors, that as long as the Empire harbored the majority of the world's Muslims and as long as Britain's influence predominated in other Middle Eastern countries, Ibn Saud would continue to regard Great Britain as the "predominant political factor."[104]

The Foreign Office, however, was not particularly impressed by either the arguments of the Treasury or Jordan. Commenting on the British minister's dispatch, both Hankey and Baxter agreed that it would be unwise at this time to give up Britain's share in the fifty/fifty subsidy. "The next year will be vitally important in the Middle East, as the Palestine question seems certain to come to a head," Hankey minuted, "there will be a definitive settlement to be reached between the French and Syrians and no doubt other essential questions will arise in connection with the peace settlement. It will be of great value to us to have Ibn Saud on our side during these important and formative times."[105]

Foreign Office representatives soon took a similar line with the Treasury. "While we cannot object if the Americans wish to indulge in a policy of squandermania in Saudi Arabia," Thomas Wikeley, former chargé d'affaires at Jidda commented, "it would be politically foolish

and morally reprehensible to withdraw all our support from Ibn Saud
and thereby deliver him bound hand and foot to the no doubt well
intentioned but often ill informed mercies of the Americans."[106]
Nevertheless it was clear that even the Foreign Office had begun to
see the inevitability of a declining British role in Saudi Arabia. In the
event the Americans insisted upon increasing the subsidy or refused to
cooperate jointly, Wikeley recommended that Ibn Saud be informed
that "we continue to wish him well and will provide him during 1945
with assistance on a certain fixed scale regretting that because of our
need for economy we cannot do more but adding that we have no wish
to obstruct any help the United States Government may wish to give
and he to receive."[107]

While the British debated the merits of cutting the subsidy, the
Americans were busy devising means to increase their commitment to
the king. Reports that the British were planning to reduce their support
for 1945 by one-third, and that London was directly interfering with
War Department plans to construct an airdrome at Dhahran,
increased American determination to strengthen its influence with the
king.[108] More important, some officials believed that neither lend-
lease nor joint subsidies were adequate tools to support the king's economy and permanently secure American interests. According to reports
from Jidda, despite Ibn Saud's willingness to establish closer ties with
the United States, he was reluctant to run the risk of alienating Great
Britain without a firm American commitment. "Without arms or
resources," Shaikh Yusuf Yassin, Saudi deputy foreign minister,
informed Eddy, "Saudi Arabia must not reject the hand that measures
its food and drink."[109] Beyond a modest lend-lease program, Washington had shown little official interest in long-term assistance. There
must be some way, Eddy informed the State Department, "in which
Saudi Arabia and America can collaborate alone, on a basis that leads
far beyond [the] end of the war."[110]

Once again NEA had taken the initiative and by early October had
begun to toy with various proposals for extending long-range assistance
to Saudi Arabia. In view of Ibn Saud's projected budget, it was unlikely
that oil royalties alone could meet the king's expenditures. It was clear
—at least in NEA—that the United States should play the key role in
covering the Saudi deficit in the immediate postwar years. In return
for airfield rights, officials believed, the War Department might consider paying Saudi Arabia some $10,000,000. Similarly, the navy might
contract for options on petroleum. In short, the United States, in
order to guarantee a stable economy, would balance Ibn Saud's budget
for the next five years.[111] Writing to Stettinius, Murray left no doubt

about the objectives of NEA's proposals. "In order to retain and develop our position of primacy in Saudi Arabia, we must take immediate and effective steps to provide for the budgetary and economic needs of King Ibn Saud for a few years until oil production and renewal of pilgrim traffic increase the King's revenue to the point where foreign subsidies are no longer necessary."[112] Although NEA's plans for long-range aid to Saudi Arabia were facilitated by the War Department's interest in airfields, it was clear that Arabian oil was the motivating force behind government action. "Both from a long and a short-range point of view," Stimson had informed the secretary of state in October, "the most important military interest in Saudi Arabia is oil."[113]

In November, NEA formally presented its plan of long-range assistance. At the request of Stettinius, Murray outlined the major issues. "The extensive oil deposits of Saudi Arabia, which are among the greatest in the world," Murray began, "are now entirely in American hands." The "fundamental question" is whether the United States recognizes a "national interest" in Arabian oil. If such an interest existed, then it was the responsibility of the United States to support Ibn Saud "in order that Saudi Arabia will not be obliged to lean . . . upon some other country which might eventually secure a quid pro quo in oil." After highlighting the details of a $57,000,000 subsidy plan, Murray concluded: "This would be a relatively small investment on the part of this Government to safeguard our national interest in the oil reserves of Saudi Arabia."[114] Aware of the potential of Saudi reserves, and the importance of securing an airfield, military officials reacted favorably to NEA's proposal. Both Ralph Bard, under secretary of the navy, and R. Keith Kane, the special assistant to the secretary, informed Stettinius and Rayner that the navy was very much interested in the establishment of a reserve in Saudi Arabia. Stettinius suggested that both the War Department and Navy consider approaching the president with details of such a plan.[115]

Although Stettinius seemed to support NEA's proposal, there was significant resistance within the department to the use of government funds to protect ARAMCO's concession. The State Department's economic divisions were clearly uneasy about a subsidy program which might be "unduly preferential" to a single American oil company. Since ARAMCO could anticipate large profits on the sale of low-cost oil, the economic officers argued, the company ought to be willing to raise enough capital to protect its concession. The resources of ARAMCO and its parent companies, Paul McGuire of the State Department's Financial and Monetary Affairs Division (FMA), concluded, were "unquestionably adequate."[116] Moreover, the Petroleum and the British

Commonwealth Divisions were reluctant to admit that diplomacy alone could not secure American petroleum interests. "Is our general diplomacy vis à vis the British and the Saudi Arab Government so bankrupt," Loftus asked, "that it must be supplemented by expenditure of public monies?" Matthew Hickerson of the British Commonwealth Division echoed that line: "I should hate very much to see us try to run a competing show in this regard in Saudi Arabia." [117]

By the end of November, it was clear that NEA's subsidy plan faced other troubles. Not only was the military reluctant to use its funds to subsidize Ibn Saud, but the plan was certain to evoke the opposition of the oil industry, Secretary Ickes, and the Congress. NEA, however, seemed determined to secure long-range assistance for Saudi Arabia, and even suggested a direct request be made for executive or congressional appropriations. [118]

NEA's efforts were undoubtedly facilitated by the navy's timely concern for the security of American oil interests abroad. "It is patently in the Navy's interest," Forrestal wrote to the secretary of state, "that no part of the national wealth, as represented by the present holdings of foreign oil reserves by American nationals, be lost at this time." [119] Although the navy seemed reluctant to spend its own funds in Saudi Arabia, Forrestal urged the State Department to use its offices to protect American concessions abroad, particularly in the Persian Gulf.

In late December, the State Department submitted NEA's subsidy plan to the president. As a result of financial difficulties, heightened by wartime conditions, the Department's memorandum began, Saudi Arabia was faced with substantial deficits. Unless the United States offered financial assistance to Ibn Saud, the memorandum continued, "undoubtedly it will be supplied by some other nation which might thus acquire a dominant position in that country inimical to the welfare of Saudi Arabia and to the national interest of the United States." Although the department emphasized the importance of maintaining a "strong and independent" Saudi Arabia, it was clear that Arabian oil was the motivating force behind the government's efforts to assist Ibn Saud. "The vast oil resources of Saudi Arabia," the memorandum concluded, "now in American hands under a concession held by American nationals, should be safeguarded and developed in order to supplement Western Hemisphere oil reserves as a source of supply." Roosevelt was requested to approve measures to protect the American "national interest" in Saudi Arabia. Foremost on the department's agenda was a plan to request congressional appropriations in order to meet the financial requirements of Saudi Arabia. [120] According to Stettinius, after some "searching questions" regarding Saudi Arabia's need for funds, the president approved the general idea of seeking congressional appropriations.[121]

State Department efforts to assist Ibn Saud not only reflected a growing recognition of the importance of Arabian oil, but also revealed a new determination to safeguard a valuable American interest. Uneasy about the king's financial position and disturbed by British influence, NEA sought to convince higher officers in the State Department that the stability of the Saudi economy was inextricably linked to the security of the ARAMCO concession. Moreover, the department's Middle Eastern hands sensed that permanent security for the concession could not be achieved by piecemeal gestures to Ibn Saud. Without assurances of long-range assistance, Eddy informed Murray, the king would never be freed from the "narrow confines of supply and shipping controls now raised largely by the British who dictate limits to him and to us."[122]

Finally, NEA urged department officials to consider the consequences of remaining Britain's junior partner in Saudi Arabia. Although Murray had informed Stettinius in November that the "King is disposed to play ball with us in everything that pertains to the development of our great oil concession in his country," NEA was still uneasy about the consequences of Ibn Saud's dependence on Great Britain.[123] There was no reason to believe, Murray had earlier noted, that "if we fumble the ball and make a mess of things in Saudi Arabia the British will not be quick to profit by our mistakes."[124] The increasing importance of American petroleum interests in al-Hasa challenged the United States to establish a permanent commitment in Saudi Arabia. By 1945, American officials set out to convince Ibn Saud that the economic, if not the political, future of his kingdom lay with the United States.

CHAPTER 5
A VERY SPECIAL
RELATIONSHIP: THE
UNITED STATES AND
SAUDI ARABIA, 1945

SHORTLY after Pearl Harbor, Admiral Chester W. Nimitz, soon to be commander in chief of the U.S. Pacific Fleet, observed that victory over the Axis would depend upon "beans, bullets, and oil." By 1945, however, Nimitz had shifted his priorities to "oil, bullets, and beans."[1] The admiral's about-face was by no means unwarranted. World War II had dramatically revealed the vital role of oil in modern warfare. Petroleum consumption in World War I paled before the increasing use of oil in the new conflict. At the peak of military operations in Europe alone, the daily gasoline consumption of the United States Army and Air Force was fourteen times the total amount of gasoline shipped to Europe between 1914 and 1918. By 1945, 7 billion barrels of petroleum had been required to support the allied war effort.[2]

The burden of fueling the war inevitably fell upon the United States. With nearly 40 percent of the world's proven reserves and an excess productive capacity of 1,000,000 b.p.d., American sources provided a secure and prolific supply of petroleum. Aligned with the Petroleum Administration for War, the American industry energetically accepted the challenge. By the end of the war, the United States was producing almost 5,000,000 b.p.d. of crude oil out of a total world production of 7,500,000 b.p.d.—over 66 percent of the total. American wells and refineries accounted for almost 6 of the 7 billion barrels of oil consumed by the Allies during the war.[3]

Although the American petroleum industry had successfully met the challenge of fueling a global war, by 1945 it appeared that the United States might well pay a price for its efforts. In 1941, domestic wells were producing more than 3,800,000 b.p.d. By August 1945, production surpassed 5,000,000 b.p.d. Increased production did not necessarily endanger American reserves or productive capacity, yet it did generate increasing concern about the domestic situation, particularly the rate at which the United States had drawn on its own reserves. Had the war continued into the middle of 1946, a PAW official concluded, "it would have required a continued production in the United States above the maximum efficient rate in spite of everything that could be done in foreign areas."[4]

The war alone was not responsible for increasing uneasiness over the domestic oil situation. Prewar surveys seemed to indicate that annual discoveries of new reserves were declining. Although there was considerable disagreement within industry and government circles about the seriousness of the decline, it was clear that since 1937 annual additions to petroleum reserves had been successively decreasing. There had been downward turns in discovery rates before, yet never had they appeared so prolonged in the face of so much exploratory drilling.[5] Moreover, in view of rising civilian and military demand, there was some concern that maximum efficient production might fall below domestic consumption. Combined with unparalleled wartime production, decreasing discovery rates seemed to suggest that there might indeed be a bottom to the national oil barrel.

Uneasiness over domestic reserves did not indicate any immediate fear of petroleum shortages. Proud of their wartime achievements, many in the industry were optimistic about the future. By 1945, the domestic industry claimed twice the number of wells, three times the proven reserves, and five times the production rates of 1918. Confident of the nation's reserve potential, geologists like Wallace Pratt of SONJ believed that proven reserves were at least twice conventional estimates. Decreasing discovery rates, Pratt concluded, might simply be a result of the lack of adequate drilling material and the depressed price of crude. Similarly, Robert Wilson, chairman of the board of Standard Oil of Indiana, noted that in 1918 proven reserves were calculated at only 6,500,000,000 barrels. Present estimates, Wilson confidently observed, exceeded 20,000,000,000 barrels.[6]

In view of the possibility of declining discovery rates and increasing demand, however, government officials, already conditioned by the "worst case" scenarios of the war years, approached the future with considerable caution. Although postwar consumption was not expected to exceed peak wartime levels for at least ten years, domestic demand was certain to surpass prewar figures. Expanding civilian requirements in gasoline, kerosene, and heating oils, government planners believed, were certain to offset wartime increases in production. In short, postwar trends indicated that the United States might be forced to draw upon its own reserves and those of the Western Hemisphere at an unprecedented rate.[7] To some, the consequences of increasing consumption were already unmistakably clear. "Failing a substantial increase in the discovery of new reserves," Charles Rayner informed a Senate subcommittee in June 1945, "the United States, long an exporter on balance, is facing the definite probability of becoming a net importer."[8]

The increasing importance of petroleum during the war inevitably stimulated government interest in foreign oil. Between 1941 and 1945, the Allies received 1,670,000,000 barrels of petroleum products from sources outside of the United States. The majority of this oil was supplied by the wells and refineries of South America and the Caribbean, particularly Venezuela.[9] Nevertheless, the oil of the Middle East had emerged as a significant factor in wartime petroleum planning. Despite the lack of adequate transportation, refining, and production facilities, by 1945 the crude output of Iraq, Iran, Saudi Arabia, and Bahrain was estimated at 194,000,000 barrels—an increase of 52 percent over 1939 production levels. By the end of the war, Middle Eastern oil supplied 7 percent of the total Allied requirements in aviation gasoline, Navy Special, and British Admiralty grade fuel oil.[10]

The new significance of Middle Eastern petroleum, however, was not measured in its contribution to the war effort. In 1945, Venezuelan production alone accounted for almost twice the total output of Iran, Iraq, Saudi Arabia, and Bahrain. Far more important was the potential value of oil reserves in the Middle East. The area's total proven reserves were estimated between 15,000,000,000 and 26,000,000,000 barrels. Unproven estimates for Saudi Arabia alone were thought by some to exceed 100,000,000,000 barrels.[11] New developments in Persian Gulf oil, *The Economist* observed in June 1945, "do not nearly exhaust the potentialities of the region, the oil resources of which are estimated to account for three-tenths of the world's known reserves."[12]

Government petroleum planners were quick to see new possibilities for the development of Middle Eastern oil. In a memorandum prepared for Roosevelt's use at Yalta, the State Department's Petroleum Division echoed an already familiar refrain: "Since there is sufficient Middle Eastern oil to supply world markets for the foreseeable future, this Government should not look upon those distant fields as security reserves but as sources of peacetime supplies for Eastern Hemisphere markets so that oil exports from the Western Hemisphere may be curtailed." The United States, the memorandum concluded, should continue to safeguard Middle Eastern concessions under American control and to encourage companies to expand and develop production.[13] Similarly, Harold Ickes informed Edwin Pauley, American representative on the Allied Reparations Commission, that the oil of Iraq and Saudi Arabia would supply the refineries of southern France as soon as refinery capacity became available.[14] "The development of the vast oil resources of the Middle East is progressing at such a rapid pace," the *New York Times* observed in January 1945, that European requirements might be met without having to draw upon production in the United States or the Caribbean.[15]

Impressed by the enormous potential of Middle Eastern reserves, government agencies, led by the Department of State, continued their efforts to secure the American stake in Arabian oil. The department's campaign focused primarily on the extension of large-scale subsidies to Ibn Saud. Uneasy about the king's budgetary deficits and eager to increase American prestige with the king, NEA's officers were determined to keep Ibn Saud financially solvent until oil production and royalties made him self-sufficient. There was, to be sure, no immediate threat to American oil interests, yet officials continued to justify long-range assistance on the basis of future insurance for the concession. Although the department's economic officers were quick to point out that subsidies for the king should come from the oil companies, NEA continued to emphasize the importance of "official" ties with Saudi Arabia and the dangers of continued inaction. To some the British lion still roared with impunity in Jidda and Riyadh. For others, a new threat had emerged in the form of the Russian bear. Writing to Stettinius, Murray observed that the Russians "would like to expand their influence and gain some sort of long-term foothold, through the concession of a free port or by some other means, upon the shores of the Persian Gulf. This, of course, would place the Russians within a very short distance not only of the oil fields in southern Iran, Iraq, and Kuwait, but also of those in Bahrein and eastern Saudi Arabia."[16]

More important, NEA's officers began to envision a new relationship between the United States and Saudi Arabia which would provide a basis for cooperation well into the postwar period. If the United States were to achieve the elusive security it had been seeking for Arabian oil since 1943, the Arab hands believed, the Americans would not only have to recognize a national interest in Saudi Arabia but also act to preserve it. This might involve securing financial and technical assistance for Ibn Saud as well as pursuing a policy toward the Arab world in general, and the Palestine problem in particular, which would enhance American prestige in the eyes of the Saudis. Not everyone agreed with such an adventurous course. In view of the opposition from domestic petroleum producers, the difficulties involved in postwar foreign aid, and growing support in congressional circles for a Jewish homeland, many officials were wary of the political consequences of creating special ties with Saudi Arabia. Nonetheless there were those in both the State Department and navy who were convinced that the importance of Arabian oil justified the risk. Led by NEA, these officials continued their efforts throughout 1945 to secure long-range assistance for Saudi Arabia. Although their campaign was largely unsuccessful, these officials began to lay the foundation of future economic and military assistance to the Saudis and to create the framework for the special relationship between Saudi Arabia and the United States.

NEA's efforts to support the Saudi economy and to increase American prestige with the king hinged on the problem of how to assist Ibn Saud. Eager to avoid delay and perhaps embarrassment to the king, the State Department had initially sought to bypass congressional funding. Any government program, however, which facilitated the development of Saudi oil was certain to arouse the opposition of the domestic petroleum producers and their supporters in the Congress. Moreover, it would be difficult to convince Congress that subsidies to Saudi Arabia were not directly supporting ARAMCO—all at taxpayers' expense. Earlier plans to expend army and navy funds in exchange for oil reserves had not proved feasible. By early 1945 it seemed clear that official assistance to Saudi Arabia might indeed depend on some form of congressional appropriations.

Meeting with Ickes and Davies of PAW in early January, James Dunn, an assistant secretary of state, outlined the department's position. Dunn played on a familiar theme. Unless the United States made an effort to balance Ibn Saud's budget, "there was every indication the King would turn to the British for assistance." The State Department, Dunn continued, was considering approaching Congress for a loan to cover the king's deficits over the next five years. Ickes, who had no doubt grown wiser as a result of the PRC venture, agreed with the general idea of supporting the king, but warned Dunn of the opposition he might expect from the domestic oil bloc in Congress. Dunn agreed, adding that the department planned to discuss the problem with Senator Connally, powerful chairman of the Senate Foreign Relations Committee, before any definite action was taken.[17]

Although the State Department fully appreciated the difficulties of congressional appropriations, there appeared to be few alternatives. Not only was lend-lease considered a "temporary expedient," but it had not proved entirely satisfactory. More to the point, formal lend-lease funding was due to expire in July. Early in January, Stettinius presented the problem to the president. Referring Roosevelt to the department's earlier request for long-term assistance, Stettinius argued that Ibn Saud ought to be helped on the basis of national interest—"otherwise Saudi Arabia will undoubtedly turn elsewhere with resulting grave long-range effects on our position in that country." [18] Long sympathetic to official efforts to strengthen American influence in Saudi Arabia, Roosevelt approved the department's request to approach Congress. After further discussion among Dunn, William Clayton, and Murray, it was agreed that Assistant Secretary of State Dean Acheson would sound out Senator Connally. [19]

By early 1945, the central problem confronting the State Department was no longer whether the United States ought to aid Ibn Saud, but how such assistance might be channeled. Although the department had requested FEA to continue lend-lease subsidies to Saudi Arabia until the end of fiscal 1946, government officials envisioned a more permanent American commitment. After preliminary discussions with army and navy representatives, Charles Rayner broached a number of plans to Wallace Murray—among them a navy contract for an underground reserve and a direct government loan. Whatever plan was adopted, Rayner was convinced of the need for action:

> A decision must be reached by this Government as to whether or not it is in the national interest to support our economic interests and the interests of American nationals in Arabia as a matter of national policy, or whether we shall indefinitely decline to take such a course of action and face the consequences of a paramount British interest in that area. . . . [T]here is ample evidence to show that the King will turn to the British for assistance if this Government fails to support his financial requirements. [20]

The State Department's efforts to assist Saudi Arabia focused on two levels. Although the campaign to balance the Saudi budget was considered top priority, government officials also sought to provide interim assistance for the king. In late 1944, after discussion with the military, the department had recommended that the War Department undertake "certain improvements" in Saudi Arabia. Early in February 1945, Assistant Secretary of War John McCloy informed the State-War-Navy Coordinating Committee (SWNCC) that the War Department was prepared to sponsor the construction of roads and the enlargement of a military training mission. [21]

Of more immediate importance was the War Department's desire to acquire an airfield at Dhahran near Ras Tanura. The idea of a landing field on the Persian Gulf littoral was not new. In view of the importance of redeploying troops to the Pacific theater, however, the Air Transport Command now considered the base to be of "immediate military necessity." Furthermore, permanent military rights at Dhahran, a War Department memorandum noted, "would serve as a deterrent to other nations which might consider aggression toward Saudi Arabia and her vast oil reserves in which American interests now hold a predominant concession."[22] To the Department of State, construction of an airfield at Dhahran seemed to offer another opportunity to increase the American commitment in Saudi Arabia.

In February, the issue of aid to Saudi Arabia was referred to SWNCC's newly created ad hoc committee. The committee's report left little doubt as to the motivation behind SWNCC's handling of financial aid to the king:

> The most important economic fact in connection with Saudi
> Arabia is the presence in that country of rich oil resources pres-
> ently under concession to American companies. Although the
> War Department has an interest in Saudi Arabia because of its
> geographical location athwart the most direct air route to the East,
> it is the oil of Saudi Arabia which makes that country of particular
> importance to the armed services.[23]

Although the committee noted that the only "permanent solution" to Saudi Arabia's financial problems was the development of the country's oil reserves, it concluded that the United States should consider direct financial aid until oil royalties increased the king's revenue. Moreover, financial assistance ought to be considered with the intention of working out a solution based on oil, perhaps the purchase of underground reserves by the United States. Finally, the ad hoc committee recommended that the State Department prepare estimates of Saudi requirements, consider methods of financial aid, and discuss the problem informally with the Chairman of the Senate Foreign Relations Committee.[24]

Increasing official interest in Saudi Arabia was reflected in Roosevelt's meeting with Ibn Saud at Great Bitter Lake in mid-February. Returning from conversations with Churchill and Stalin at Yalta, the president made arrangements to meet with King Farouk of Egypt, Haile Selaisse of Ethiopia, and Ibn Saud. The exact origin of Roosevelt's rendezvous with Ibn Saud is not clear. Early in February, the State Department received a message from the president's naval aide indicating Roosevelt's desire to meet with the monarchs near Ismailia in the Suez Canal on 10 February. That day the department informed Cairo, Addis Ababa, and Jidda instructing the American diplomatic staffs to make the necessary arrangements.[25]

The idea of a presidential meeting with Ibn Saud, however, had been germinating in the department for some time. On 20 December 1944, Murray reminded Hull that Roosevelt had expressed an interest in visiting Ibn Saud and added that the king expected the president to call should he be in the area. Three days later Stettinius informed Murray that Roosevelt was "entirely sympathetic" to the idea of a visit and planned to get in touch with the king.[26] By mid-January the president had already solicited suggestions on how to raise the subject of Palestine during his proposed meeting with the Saudi king.[27]

The historic meeting between Ibn Saud and Roosevelt was filled with the pomp and panoply befitting a king of Saudi Arabia. Transported from Jidda on an American destroyer, U.S.S. *Murphy*, the king and the royal party sailed north through the Red Sea toward the Gulf of Suez and finally entered the Great Bitter Lake north of the city of Suez. Although William Eddy had encouraged the king to restrict his retainers to a maximum of twelve, it was clear that Ibn Saud had no intention of scrimping where his image was concerned. The royal entourage consisted of no less than forty-eight—including Bedouin bodyguards, coffee-servers, and Majid Ibn Khataila, the court astrologer.[28]

The visit was not all pomp and ceremony, however, and contained its share of humor. During the voyage from Jidda, Eddy had his hands full trying to stop the king's servants from making coffee on charcoal burners near the ship's explosives and rerouting the ship's crew who were continuously walking in front of the king's party while in prayer. To Eddy's dismay, two of the king's sons insisted on attending a showing of a night movie which starred Lucille Ball scantily clad, running through a men's dormitory at a college. According to the minister, news of this "orgy" never reached Ibn Saud.[29] Eddy was apparently not the only nervous American aboard. The commander of the *Murphy*, having misjudged his approach to the presidential cruiser, accidently struck the bow of the *Quincy*.[30]

Finally, at 10:00 A.M. on 14 February, accompanied by three Saudi Amirs, Yusuf Yassin, foreign minister, and Abdullah Sulaiman, powerful minister of finance, the king boarded the U.S.S. *Quincy* for preliminary discussions with the president. After lunch, conversations continued until midafternoon among Roosevelt, Ibn Saud, and Yassin, with Eddy serving as interpreter. At 3:30 P.M., after exchanging final pleasantries and sipping Arab coffee at the king's request, the royal party again boarded the U.S.S. *Murphy* for the journey to Port Said. The king and the president, Eddy noted, were together for at least five "very intense hours."[31]

Roosevelt's motives in meeting with Ibn Saud at Great Bitter Lake are not entirely clear. On 5 February, Eddy had informed the department that Ibn Saud was pleased to accept Roosevelt's invitation for "confidential talk on political and economic matters."[32] The president seemed particularly interested in seeking Ibn Saud's assistance in resolving the problem of Palestine. Why Roosevelt believed he could use personal diplomacy to persuade the king to support the case of thousands of Jewish refugees or the idea of a Jewish homeland in Palestine is not clear. The president had been repeatedly warned by his own experts that Ibn Saud would never compromise on Palestine.[33] Barely a month before his meeting with the Saudi king, Stettinius had informed the president that in a recent statement Ibn Saud had indicated a willingness to die in defense of the rights of Palestinian Arabs.[34] Roosevelt clearly overestimated his own personal charm and misjudged the strength of the king's convictions. Instead of flexibility on Palestine, Ibn Saud revealed his determination to oppose a Jewish homeland. In fact, if there were any concessions, they came from the president. Roosevelt assured the king that he would do nothing to aid the Jews against the Arabs or make any move hostile to the Arab people.[35]

It is also unclear whether the conversations aboard the *Quincy* touched on the subjects of oil development or financial aid. Although Admiral Leahy who was traveling with the president indicated that Roosevelt and Ibn Saud had a "long talk" about Saudi oil, the official minutes of the conversation, initialled by the president and the king, are conspicuously silent on the subject. As for financial assistance, Eddy, in his account of the meeting, insists that Ibn Saud never raised the matter. As a guest aboard the presidential cruiser, the king was prevented by Arab custom from initiating topics of conversation. More important, Ibn Saud, Eddy believed, came seeking friends not funds.[36]

Eddy's reports to the department, however, indicate that the king did his best to familiarize the president with his situation. The British, Ibn Saud informed Roosevelt, had always implied that American interests in Saudi Arabia were transitory, based on a temporary wartime "joint partnership." The security and economic stability of Saudi Arabia, London repeatedly told the king, were bound up with British foreign policy. According to Eddy, Roosevelt replied that plans for the postwar period envisioned a decline of such spheres of influence in favor of the Open Door. The king was pleased with the prospect, but seemed to suggest that he expected British pressure to continue. If Roosevelt missed Ibn Saud's message it was remarkably clear to Eddy. The king's fear of Great Britain, he concluded, "is no doubt well-grounded and will be dispelled when and if the United States gives material substance to plans for long range economic and political accords with Saudi Arabia to open up the Open Door."[37]

Although Roosevelt presumably assured Ibn Saud of America's permanent interest in Saudi Arabia, it is unlikely that the president committed the United States to specific programs of assistance. In January, Roosevelt had indeed approved the State Department's plan to approach Congress for aid, yet programs for long-range subsidies were still in the preliminary stage. Moreover, the department had already informed the king that a comprehensive aid package had been tentatively prepared, pending legislative approval. Still, the meeting at Great Bitter Lake represented more than the president's fascination with the "colorful panoply" of Middle Eastern monarchs.[38]

Roosevelt's conversations with the Saudi king seemed to reflect the United States' growing awareness of its interests in Saudi Arabia—if not the entire Middle East. Similarly, for Ibn Saud the meeting held great significance. For the first time since the formal establishment of his kingdom, Ibn Saud had journeyed beyond his borders in search of an ally to support the economic and perhaps even the political independence of Saudi Arabia. Shortly after Roosevelt's return, Herbert Feis noted: "I assume that the President's talk with Ibn Saud will speed up events—that is advance the plans for the pipeline construction (perhaps accompanied by some form of financial assistance either lend-lease or Import-Export Bank). It seems fairly certain that we are on the verge of establishing important new centers of permanent economic interest in Saudi Arabia reaching out through adjoining countries."[39] Perhaps C. L. Sulzburger's analysis in the *New York Times* was even more penetrating. Writing shortly after Roosevelt's return from Great Bitter Lake, the columnist observed, "American interest in this area is strongly centered on two subjects of intense national interest to Americans—oil and air bases. The immense oil deposits in Saudi Arabia alone make that country more important to American diplomacy than almost any other smaller nation. As one observer phrased it, 'except for the Philippine Islands Saudi Arabia may well prove to be the most interesting foreign area, to the United States, in this century.' "[40]

Determined to gain approval for long-term assistance to Saudi Arabia before the end of 1945, the Department of State continued to act on SWNCC's recommendations. Early in March, SWNCC approved the ad hoc committee's suggestions for a military mission, airfield, and road construction. The Joint Chiefs of Staff had also approved the acquisition and construction of an airfield at Dhahran provided the

British withdrew their earlier objections.[41] Far more important, however, was the question of long-range subsidies. Inflation, the small size of oil royalties, and a three-year drought, officials argued, had placed severe strains on the king's revenues. His expenditures for the next five years alone were expected to exceed $135,000,000, leaving a deficit of some $45,000,000. Disturbed by the prospect of chronic economic instability in Saudi Arabia, the department sought nothing less than to balance Ibn Saud's postwar budget. Official plans, however, involved the expenditure of large sums of public money. In view of potential opposition from Congress and the domestic oil industry, the department was well advised to proceed with extreme caution. SWNCC's ad hoc committee again recommended that Dean Acheson sound out certain members of Congress before taking any definite action.[42]

Early in March, accompanied by representatives of the army and navy, Acheson presented the government's case to selected congressional leaders. SWNCC's strategy was simple. Instead of mounting a direct frontal assault on the hard-core opponents of aid to the Saudis, the State Department sought informally to broach a number of plans to more sympathetic members of Congress.[43] The collection of dignitaries at the 8 March meeting was indeed impressive, though hardly representative of the congressional view on foreign oil—Sam Rayburn, Speaker of the House, John W. McCormack, majority floor leader, Carl Vinson, chairman of the House Naval Affairs Committee, and Patrick Drewry, ranking majority member of that committee. Sensing that he was in friendly territory, Acheson moved directly to the point. Saudi Arabia required a total of $50,000,000 over the next five years to cover its deficits. If Ibn Saud's financial difficulties were not resolved, there was a "possible danger" to the concession. As far as Congress was concerned, Acheson noted, the Department of State was hesitant to run the risks of seeking formal appropriations. A much better approach might be an "understanding" with the Senate and House Appropriations Committees to appropriate funds through the Department of State. The representatives seemed impressed by Acheson's presentation. Not only did Rayburn conclude that it was "highly desirable" to aid the king, but Vinson even suggested an amendment to the Elk Hills Reserve Act authorizing the secretary of the navy to obtain overseas oil reserves for "secret and strategic purposes."[44]

Despite the favorable reactions of Vinson and Rayburn, it was clear that the department's problems with Congress were only beginning. Vinson represented the "pro-reserve" group on the Hill. It was unlikely that congressional spokesmen for the domestic petroleum industry would have anything to do with government efforts to secure foreign oil reserves. Led by Senators Tom Connally of Texas and E. H. Moore of Oklahoma, and allied with staunch conservatives like Owen Brewster of Maine, who questioned the very principle of government involvement in the industry, the domestic oil bloc was certain to oppose long-term subsidies to Ibn Saud. The State Department's declaration of an alleged "national interest" in Saudi Arabian oil was no password which would magically open the doors of congressional appropriations, particularly for representatives who believed that the nation's petroleum future lay within its borders. Moreover, neither Congress nor the industry had fully recovered from the PRC venture. Any plan which even remotely resembled stock purchase or a government pipeline might even arouse the opposition of Ickes who, according to Charles Rayner, "will not wish to burn his fingers again."[45]

The NEA and SWNCC campaign seemed hampered not only by congressional opposition, but also by resistance within the Department of State. Led by Emilio Collado, director of the department's Office of Financial and Development Policy (OFD), many of the department's economists and financial experts had opposed NEA's subsidy plans from the beginning. Uneasy about possible reaction in Congress, Collado believed government subsidies to Ibn Saud were "shortsighted" and destined to fail.[46]

In late March, Collado presented OFD's position to William Clayton. The ARAMCO concession, he began, was in no immediate danger. Neither the British nor the Russians had the desire or capability to steal American oil interests. As for Ibn Saud, Collado argued, he would never risk losing American interest in Arab problems or Arabian oil. The interest of the department's political officers, Collado continued, "is the result of a strange conglomeration of neuroses and misconceptions." They suffer from an "inferiority complex" vis à vis the British as a result of being continuously outsmarted by London. Arabian oil, Collado noted, "was the greatest opportunity they have ever had to stimulate interest in the Middle East and U.S. backing against their long-time adversaries." Finally, Collado concluded, the political officers never raised the question of ARAMCO's ability to help the king out of his financial predicament.[47]

The Collado memorandum seems to have raised serious doubts in Clayton's office about subsidies. In February, Collado had already advised Clayton that the political arguments for subsidizing Ibn Saud were "weak." No amount of financial aid could stop Great Britain or the Soviet Union if they were indeed determined to exert pressure on the king. Early in April, Clayton wrote to Dunn expressing additional reservations. Although Clayton conceded that Arabian oil is of "great importance" to the United States, he questioned the methods being considered to secure foreign reserves. Neither a loan nor an underground reserves plan would be acceptable to Congress or to the petroleum industry. Clayton also warned Dunn of the danger of being drawn into a political controversy between Connally, who opposed government sponsorship of oil reserves, and Vinson and Ralph Bard, who sought to acquire government-owned reserves. SOCAL and the Texas company, Clayton concluded, ought to fund the king. The money required to support Ibn Saud through 1950 could be easily recovered from future oil royalties.[48]

Disturbed by reports from Saudi Arabia and by the arguments of the economists, NEA intensified its efforts to secure interim and long-range financial assistance for the king. By April, Eddy's reports from Jidda indicated the possibility of serious food shortages. The Saudis had already appealed for an increase in foodstuffs for 1945. The problem was complicated by locust infestation in the Najd which was reported by both British and American observers to be "serious and extensive."[49] The department had also learned that London planned to reduce its share of the joint subsidy program to £1,250,000—50 percent of the 1944 subsidy.

The Americans were not prepared to court the risks of London's austerity program. The department, Joseph Grew had informed Eddy, was prepared to ask the Foreign Economic Administration (FEA) to fund the king's entire subsidy requirements for 1945 "with or without British participation."[50] Although NEA was somewhat relieved to learn that Britain would not stand in the way of increased American aid, officials realized that the responsibility for funding the king now lay primarily with the United States. Failure to act quickly might have a detrimental effect on American prestige and undermine Washington's credibility. Eddy, however, knew he could not satisfy the king with American promises. "Troubled, indignant, convinced delay is unnecessary," Eddy informed the department in April, "he is entitled now to statement of our intentions re: his normal supply and budgetary needs."[51]

Long-range assistance to Saudi Arabia seemed bogged down in congressional and interdepartmental opposition. Furthermore, neither the State Department nor the British Foreign Office had yet formulated the king's subsidy grants for 1945. Although the State Department had received assurances that FEA would earmark $12,060,000 in lend-lease aid for 1945, NEA was determined to secure more permanent assistance.[52] In an apparent attempt to soften the opposition to long-term funding, Loy Henderson, recently appointed director of NEA, forwarded a memorandum to Collado. The paper, drafted by Moose, was predictably anti-British and outlined four aims of "varying importance and urgency" in connection with assistance to Saudi Arabia. Heading NEA's list of priorities was continued American control over Arabian oil. The concession faced a "potential" threat from the Soviet Union and the more immediate problem of British designs. Great Britain, it was noted, did not seek actual ownership of reserves but control of Saudi oil. This control could be achieved by increasing London's influence over Ibn Saud and thus indirectly pressuring ARAMCO to accept unfavorable marketing arrangements or even British partners. Furthermore there was "much evidence" that Britain had already tried to establish control over Saudi Arabia. Financial assistance to the king, the memorandum concluded, might be handled through special congressional funding or by an Export-Import (EXIM) Bank loan.[53]

By the beginning of May it was clear to State Department officials that the prospects for long-range aid in 1945 were not good. To guarantee the king's minimum requirements for 1945 and to provide for contingency aid in 1946, the department had approached FEA for lend-lease funds.[54] So too, the department was actively exploring the prospects of a $5,000,000 Export-Import Bank development loan to the Saudis. Despite the obstacles, SWNCC continued to lay the groundwork for future assistance. On 17 May, Acheson, George Brownell, and Ralph Bard held a meeting with Senate leaders. The State Department was apparently still not ready for a confrontation with Senator Connally and selected instead Senate majority leader, Alben W. Barkley, Walter F. George, chairman of the Senate Committee on Finance, and David I. Walsh, chairman of the Senate Committee on Naval Affairs.

Again playing the role of public relations man, Acheson carefully presented the department's position. Producing a map of the concession areas complete with production figures, Acheson pointed out that the United States had an important stake in protecting national interests in Arabian oil. To remedy Ibn Saud's financial difficulties, Acheson outlined the familiar plans of loans and reserves. The Senators agreed that the United States had a "vital interest" in Saudi Arabia, but concurred that an outright grant to Ibn Saud would never receive congressional approval and an unsecured loan would meet with considerable difficulty. They also advised that any plan should be implemented with as little need for legislation as possible and certainly with no specific mention of the area involved. The Senators agreed that some action was necessary and suggested that SWNCC work on two plans, an EXIM Bank loan and an arrangement for purchasing oil in the ground. Under Secretary of the Navy Bard added that it might also be desirable to obtain the approval of the new president, and offered to arrange a meeting.[55]

On 12 April, with the sudden death of Franklin Roosevelt, Harry Truman assumed the responsibilities and challenges of his new office. President Truman was already quite familiar with the problems of petroleum. As a young man, he had even tried his hand in the oil business. Later as chairman of the Senate Special Committee Investigating the National Defense Program, Truman had been exposed to the problems of fuel oil and gasoline distribution and shortage.[56] Whether the new president had any particular exposure to Middle Eastern oil is not clear, yet it quickly became apparent that the matter would not escape his attention. Writing to Truman in early May, Ickes brought the question of foreign oil reserves right to the White House door. After describing the "indispensability" of oil in modern warfare, Ickes voiced a now familiar refrain: "It seems to me that we ought to consider the possibility of available oil reserves in different parts of the world where they might be urgently needed in the event of another global war. Least of all ought to be overlooked the tremendous possibilities in the Middle East, particularly in Saudi Arabia and Bahrein, where our nationals already have valuable interests."[57]

On 23 May, Joseph Grew, acting secretary of state, presented the president with the particulars of the Saudi situation. After reviewing the king's financial difficulties, Grew referred to the meetings with House and Senate leaders. "All agreed that, because of Saudi Arabia's strategic position in relation to the Pacific War, and even more importantly, because of its vast oil resources now under concession to American nationals the United States has a vital interest in the stability of Saudi Arabia." To guarantee this stability, the representatives had concurred in the need for appropriations to assist Ibn Saud. All had indicated a "distinct preference" for some arrangement related to securing Saudi reserves for future use of the United States Army and Navy. Grew recommended that Truman approve the general objectives and methods of the State Department's approach.[58]

Later that week, Bard and Acheson met with the president to discuss the situation in Saudi Arabia. Although Truman had been briefed by his naval aide, Acheson, again equipped with his map of the Middle East, described the concessions and their production potential. The president was informed of the financial requirements of the king and of Roosevelt's decision to seek congressional appropriations. Truman was apparently impressed by Acheson's well-rehearsed presentation.

He approved the idea of approaching Congress and even offered to speak with Senator Joseph O'Mahoney, chairman of the Senate Committee Investigating Petroleum Resources and a member of the Senate Appropriations Committee. The following day the president formally approved the Grew memorandum.[59]

Despite its determination to implement long-range assistance to Saudi Arabia, the Department of State had proceeded cautiously in its approach to the problem of postwar subsidies. The idea of balancing Ibn Saud's budget was an unprecedented maneuver. Suspicious of both government intervention in the oil industry and support for foreign oil operations, Congress was sure to limit the possible options in funding the king. So too, NEA was forced to fight a rearguard action against the department's own economic officers who questioned both the feasibility and desirability of subsidizing Ibn Saud. From the beginning, the Department of State, joined by the armed services, had attempted to convince their critics of the necessity of supporting Saudi Arabia. "We have all felt," Ralph Bard concluded, "that we had to sell the financing of Saudi Arabia to Congress and the President in principle, and after that had been done, discuss all the details of a definite program with the companies. . . ."[60] By the end of May, supported by the president, officials once again tackled the knotty problem of assisting Ibn Saud.

Writing to Bard in June, Carl McGowan of the Navy Department summarized the status of the Saudi problem. "There has been a sharp conflict within the State Department between the political people of the Near East Division . . . and the economists of Clayton's office . . . with respect to both the desirability and feasibility of doing something for Saudi Arabia." The conflict, McGowan noted, had been resolved by the "higher powers" in favor of aiding Ibn Saud.[61] Despite agreement in principle, however, government officials had not yet discovered a satisfactory method of channeling long-term aid to Saudi Arabia. Part of the problem resulted from the conflicting plans and ideas proposed by the navy and State Department. By June, government efforts seemed to focus on three major approaches—a direct loan, an EXIM Bank loan, and the purchase of oil reserves.

The major problem in funding the king, however, was the possible difficulty with Congress and the oil industry. Preliminary discussions with congressional leaders revealed a preference for an exchange—American dollars for Saudi oil—yet it was clear that any reserve plan would require formal legislation accompanied by lengthy legislative debates. The proposal also bore an uncomfortable resemblance to the disastrous pipeline-reserve scheme of 1944. An outright grant to Saudi

Arabia in 1945 was simply out of the question. Moreover, as Grew observed, a long-range financial aid package for Ibn Saud was "without precedent in United States history."[62] Even the EXIM Bank loan appeared to be snagged on the problems of loan security and dollar exchange.

Although Grew might assure Eddy that there was "practically unanimous agreement" among government officials on the necessity of aiding the Saudis, it was clear that long-range aid might not materialize until early 1946—if at all. Eddy was instructed to assure the king that the delay reflected methods, not objectives, and that the president had given his personal approval.[63] Promises, however, would not improve American prestige. Further delay, Eddy cautioned, only increased Ibn Saud's doubts as to whether the "machinery of American government will permit long range commitments to Saudi Arabia." Even more damaging Eddy warned was the possibility that the Saudis would "bleed" ARAMCO for loans. "To have the king continue to extort loans from them," the American minister concluded, "will contribute to the decline of the relative prestige of our government."[64]

The department's efforts to increase American influence in Saudi Arabia were not only hampered by the obstacles of long-range assistance. SWNCC's plans for the acquisition of a military airfield at Dhahran and the dispatch of a military training mission were also facing serious problems. The matter of the Dhahran airbase was of primary concern. Acting upon SWNCC's recommendation, the Joint Chiefs of Staff had approved the construction of an airfield on the basis of military necessity. The redeployment of troops to the Far East required a landing and servicing station midway between Cairo and Karachi. After receiving British approval in April, the State Department opened preliminary negotiations with Ibn Saud. By May, Eddy had informed the department that Ibn Saud would agree to the airfield provided that its control pass immediately to Saudi Arabia after the war. Although the department was anxious to negotiate postwar commercial rights, Eddy advised that it might be unwise to push the king at this time.[65]

The problem at hand, however, was not Ibn Saud's demands, but the War Department's apparent reassessment of the Dhahran project. In June, the Army Air Force advised SWNCC that events after the JCS decision together with changes in redeployment planning "have resulted in a substantial diminution of the military necessity for this airfield." Because the war might be over before the project was completed, Lauris Norstad, assistant chief of Air Staff Plans, concluded, it might be best not to justify construction on the basis of military security alone.[66] Apparently uneasy over the War Department's reevaluation, the State Department hurried to present its views to SWNCC. After outlining the importance of Arabian oil, air rights, and the stability of the Persian Gulf, the department's representatives concluded: "The effect of now cancelling the airport . . . would be to strain to the limit Saudi Arabian confidence in the U.S. This confidence has been sorely tried in the last two years by our seeming inability to follow through." The memorandum noted that the airport project was only one phase of the department's overall aid program for Saudi Arabia. Finally, in a direct appeal for aid, the State Department dramatically concluded: "Each passing day of continued inactivity weakens the King's position and may force him to the conclusion that the powerful U.S. is either prevented by political subordination to Great Britain or by lack of interest in Saudi Arabian oil resources, from lending the slight assistance needed so urgently now. U.S.-Saudi Arabian relations are living on borrowed time."[67]

The department's presentation was convincing. SWNCC considered the Dhahran matter and decided to request President Truman to approve the decision to build the airfield at the War Department's expense.[68] On 26 June, Grew presented SWNCC's position to the White House. Despite the decreasing military necessity for the airfield, the State Department considered construction of the Dhahran base to be in the national interest. Heading the list of national priorities in Saudi Arabia was Arabian oil.

> The Saudi Arabian oil fields, which promise to be among the most valuable in the world, are now under concession to an American company. The continuance of that concession in American hands holds out the best prospect that the oil of Saudi Arabia will be developed commercially with the greatest rapidity and upon the largest scale, producing revenues which will contribute to the betterment of the economic condition of Saudi Arabia and, in consequence, to its political stability. The manifestation of American interests in Saudi Arabia in addition to oil will tend to strengthen the political integrity of Saudi Arabia externally and, hence, to provide conditions under which an early expansion of the costly development of the oil concession can be proceeded with. The immediate construction by this country of an airfield at Dhahran, to be used for military purposes initially but destined for an ultimate civil utilization, would be a strong showing of American interest.

Grew recommended that the president authorize the secretary of war to construct the Dhahran field at War Department expense.[69] Later that day, Admiral Leahy informed the State Department that Truman had approved construction of the airfield.[70]

Although Washington and London had since 1944 been cooperating on the problem of coordinating subsidies, NEA continued to push for a greater American commitment in Saudi Arabia.[71] Reports from Jidda continued to emphasize the importance of increasing American influence with the king. In July, Eddy surprised the department with the news that Ibn Saud had decided to decline the proposed American military mission. In view of the fact that the king had been urging the United States for over two years to render military aid, Grew attributed Ibn Saud's new attitude to British pressure.[72] Eddy could not have agreed more. Although he conceded that Ibn Saud's reluctance to accept American military personnel may have been partly a result of his sensitivity to criticism by traditional religious elements, Eddy was convinced that British pressure was the decisive factor. "[The] British oppose and will oppose any U.S. activity in Saudi Arabia which gives even the appearance of political or military precedence." The only way to match British influence, Eddy concluded, was for the United States to implement a program of long-range financial aid and to conclude an agreement with London recognizing the "primary interest" of the United States in the Saudi economy.[73]

With the end of the war against Japan, the prospects of long-range economic aid to Saudi Arabia seemed even less likely. In fact, the State Department was immediately faced with the termination of lend-lease aid. Perhaps even more important, American interest in Arabian oil and airfields was based on wartime exigencies. In view of the decreasing military necessity of financing Ibn Saud and constructing the Dhahran airfield, Richard Sanger wrote to Loy Henderson, the United States would have to determine whether it still considered its interests in Saudi Arabia "vital."[74] To NEA's officers, the answer had never been in doubt. NEA was not willing to run the risks of disappointing Ibn Saud over airfields or financial aid. Writing to Willard Thorp, Henderson concluded:

> Our failure to carry out our promise would not only result in the economic collapse of Saudi Arabia . . . but would also cause Saudi Arabia . . . to lose confidence in the trustworthiness of our promises. The feeling against the United States would undoubtedly be so strong that our economic interests in Saudi Arabia, including the oil concession, . . . would be endangered. The known oil reserves . . . approximate five billion barrels and probable reserves are believed to be three or four times that amount. They

are the only substantial reserves of oil completely under United States control outside of the Western Hemisphere.[75]

NEA's arguments again proved convincing. Late in August, Truman informed the director of the Office of War Mobilization and Reconversion (OWMR) that Saudi Arabia was eligible for continued lend-lease assistance throughout 1945.[76]

Although the question of extended lend-lease to the king had been temporarily resolved, the State Department again faced the problem of the Dhahran airfield. In early August, agreement had finally been reached with Ibn Saud over postwar use of the airfield. According to Eddy, the agreement was characterized by marked concessions on the part of the king and provided for operation of the base by the United States for a three-year period after the war. Ibn Saud had insisted upon ownership of the base, yet had agreed not to turn the facilities over to his own subjects or to a third power.[77] In August, however, the War Department again questioned the necessity of constructing the field. The military's arguments were extremely persuasive. The rapid conclusion of the war and plans to inactivate the India-Burma theater indicated that by the time the airfield could be completed it would be of "doubtful military usefulness." The War Department advised the State Department to assume full responsibility for the base "entirely as an implementation of United States national interest."[78]

Eager to avoid any breach of commitment or agreement with Ibn Saud, the newly created SWNCC Subcommittee for the Near and Middle East, which seemed to reflect the State Department's views, mustered its arguments in support of the Dhahran field. Although the subcommittee conceded that Dhahran was no longer a military necessity, it was still important in order to "consolidate and expand general U.S. interests in Saudi Arabia." Heading the list of American interests was Arabian oil. Saudi Arabia, the subcommittee's memorandum noted, possessed reserves estimated at 5,000,000,000 barrels—one-fourth the total reserves in the United States. "The world oil center of gravity is shifting to the Middle East where American enterprise has been entrusted with the exploitation of one of the greatest oil fields. It is in our national interest to see that this vital resource remains in American hands, where it is most likely to be developed on a scale which will cause a considerable lessening of the drain upon the Western Hemisphere reserves." Sensitive to the importance of increasing American influence and prestige in Saudi Arabia, the subcommittee added that "evaluation of the airfield project cannot be based wholly on questions of utility as an airfield. There are ramifications in the realm of U.S.-Saudi relations that make this issue complex." The sub-committee recommended that the president authorize the War Department to construct the airfield at War Department expense.[79]

The subcommittee, however, was only in the business of making recommendations. In September, the Dhahran matter was discussed at the full meeting of SWNCC. The committee—Henderson and Mat-thews of the State Department, Gates for the Navy, and McCloy and Hilldring of the War Department—agreed that Dhahran was indeed in the national interest. "Although there is no immediate military interest," SWNCC's military representatives concluded, "there is a long-range military interest in protecting the oil reserves, having a foothold in a strategic area, and having some military officers familiar with the area."[80]

Funding the proposed airfield still presented problems. Congressional appropriations might be too time-consuming. The War Department had also informed SWNCC that it could not legally expend its own funds without express approval of the president and Congress. After further discussion by the Near East subcommittee, it was decided that the secretary of state should request the president to authorize completion of the Dhahran base. On 28 September, Truman formally approved the continued construction of the airfield by the War Department at its own expense.[81]

By the fall of 1945, the larger question of long-range financial aid to Saudi Arabia had still not been resolved. With lend-lease due to expire in December 1945, the State Department was determined to assure the king of American support in the immediate postwar period. Eddy's reports continued to suggest that a permanent American commitment was necessary to prevent the British from closing the "open door" in Saudi Arabia.[82] The prospects for aid, however, did not look good. Fred Vinson of OWMR, Truman's designated representative in matters of Saudi aid, had been appointed secretary of the Treasury and had apparently left the matter "undecided." In addition, the navy seemed reluctant to support an assistance program which might entangle it with Congress.[83] It was clear that any further initiative would have to come from the Department of State.

By October, in an attempt to bypass the necessity of congressional approval, the Department of State had shifted its tactics to the negotiation of a long-term development loan for Saudi Arabia. On 16 October, John L. Sullivan, assistant secretary of the Navy for Air, informed James Forrestal that the State Department was now trying to implement a "straight-out loan" to Saudi Arabia without any "tie-up" to oil reserves. "The feeling over there," Sullivan continued, "is that if it is going to be possible to make loans of hundreds of millions of dollars to countries like Czechoslovakia, it will be perfectly possible to secure approval of a loan of the much smaller amount (estimated at approximately $30,000,000) which will be necessary to take care of Saudi Arabia's financial deficits over the next five years."[84] The loan plan offered several immediate advantages. Not only had the department already received tentative approval for a smaller development loan for the Saudis, but also EXIM Bank funding might be obtained before the end of the year. Moreover, ARAMCO officials had agreed that if "political considerations" made the reserve plan undesirable, the company would consider the loan proposal.[85]

On 19 October, the Office of Financial and Development Policy, supported by NEA, presented the department's new proposal to Wayne C. Taylor, president of the EXIM Bank. In view of the American national interest in Arabian oil, the memorandum noted, it was necessary to support Ibn Saud financially until oil royalties made the country self-sufficient. Although Collado's office continued to oppose War and Navy Department plans to purchase Saudi oil or to set up underground reserves for military use, there was now no reason why Saudi Arabia was not a good risk for an EXIM Bank loan. There was even a "fair chance" that ten years from now, if not sooner, the United States would have to import Arabian oil to supplement domestic supplies. In fact if the experts were correct, it was pointed out, Arabian oil production might reach 100,000,000 barrels a year by 1955, bringing Saudi Arabia surplus revenue of at least $3,000,000 per year.[86] According to the proposed plan, the United States would advance Ibn Saud $25,000,000 over the next five years. Amortization of the loan, to be repaid in oil royalties, would begin in 1955 and would continue for ten years. As for congressional approval, it was believed that Saudi Arabia was a good enough credit risk for a twenty-year loan so that the bank could advance funds as part of its regular lending program.[87]

By December the loan was on the verge of completion. The EXIM Bank board, however, was not scheduled to meet until early January 1946. In response to Eddy's pleas for something definite before the end of the year, the bank agreed to permit Ibn Saud to see part of the draft agreement. The terms of the loan differed substantially from the original plan proposed by OFD or NEA. Although the bank agreed to establish a $25,000,000 line of credit, it now specified that $5,000,000 had to be used for development projects approved by the bank and $20,000,000 for the purchase of American products. Moreover, each advance to the king had to be accompanied by a Saudi promissory note.[88]

The king's preliminary reaction to the loan package was not favorable. Not only had the loan been cut from the $50,000,000 aid plan initially envisioned by the department, but also the duration of the loan had been reduced from five to two and one-half years. "The Dept. will understand," Eddy concluded in late December, "that delays and whittling down of amount of loan and its duration from 5 years to shortest period, necessitated by technicalities, are not convincing to SAG who fear that hostile elements and my own ineffectiveness are interfering with consummation of long-promised budgetary help."[89] Finally, early in January 1946, the department informed Eddy that the EXIM Bank had formally approved the $25,000,000 line of credit to Saudi Arabia.[90]

During 1945, the Department of State had endeavored to formulate a consistent policy toward Saudi Arabia. What had originally begun as a loosely defined wartime interest in oil and airfields now seemed to require a definite postwar policy. Troubled by the lack of American influence with the king, the department's Middle Eastern hands, with the support of the military, were determined to secure American interests on a more permanent basis. Although Saudi Arabia's strategic location was an important element in American planning, Arabian oil was clearly the motivating force behind official efforts to support the Saudi economy. In a draft of a memorandum to Truman, Gordon Merriam noted:

> In Saudi Arabia, where the oil resources constitute a stupendous source of strategic power, and one of the greatest material prizes of world history, a concession covering this oil is nominally in American control. It will undoubtedly be lost to the United States unless this Government is able to demonstrate in a practical way its recognition of this concession as of national interest by acceding to the reasonable requests of King Ibn Saud that he be assisted temporarily in his economic and financial difficulties until the exploitation of the concession on a practical commercial basis begins to bring substantial royalties to Saudi Arabia.[91]

Even the department's financial officers, long-time opponents of NEA's methods, finally conceded that there was enough of an American interest in Arabian oil to warrant an EXIM bank loan to the Saudis.

Similarly, the armed services, particularly the navy, were interested in guaranteeing the future safety of American oil reserves in the Persian Gulf. Saudi oil might not only be used to conserve Western Hemisphere reserves, but also the prospect of increasing naval operations in the postwar period seemed to justify the procurement of a large reserve abroad. The navy, to be sure, was never interested in the establishment of a billion barrel underground reserve as an end in itself. As previously mentioned, Persian Gulf petroleum was simply too remote and unpredictable a factor to be relied upon in times of emergency. Far more important was the navy's interest in assuring the United States of a "tangible stake in the continuity and future safety of the concession" and conversely denying Arabian oil to a hostile power.[92] OSS and military intelligence reports had already begun to speculate on the king's health and the possibilities of a succession crisis upon Ibn Saud's death.[93] Writing to the secretary of state regarding the importance of aid to Saudi Arabia, James Forrestal, already one of the government's foremost advocates of Middle Eastern oil, concluded: "Because of my firm conviction that within the next twenty-five years the United States is going to be faced with very sharply declining oil reserves and because oil and all of its byproducts are the foundations of the ability to fight a modern war, I consider this to be one of the most important problems of the government. I don't care which American company or companies develop the Arabian reserves, but I think most emphatically that it should be *American.*"[94]

The government's campaign to assist the king had focused on the importance of increasing American prestige in Saudi Arabia. Although maintaining the stability of the country was vital to the security of American petroleum interests, it is unlikely that even NEA's officers feared the imminent economic or political collapse of the Saudi kingdom. Government officials must also have realized that neither ARAMCO nor the parent companies would have purposely jeopardized their own concession. Had the government not managed to provide subsidies, the oil companies would surely have seen to the essential needs of the king.

Far more essential to American policy was the importance of convincing Ibn Saud that the United States could indeed establish a permanent commitment in Saudi Arabia, independent of Great Britain —a commitment which would carry the official American-Saudi relationship well beyond the end of the war. Both Eddy's telegrams and military intelligence reports indicated that the king was anxious to decrease his dependence on Great Britain and enter into a closer relationship with the Americans. Although Washington obviously overestimated Ibn Saud's dissatisfaction with London, there is little doubt that the king sought to encourage American aid, particularly financial support. With the gradual reduction in the British subsidy, the king searched for another source of funds. The Americans seemed willing benefactors. Promises of American aid, however, were not strong enough inducements to risk jeopardizing existing arrangements with London. "It is obvious that he awaits clear evidence that the United States will act independently of British controls and dictation," Eddy had reported, "before he will risk a suicidal move in that direction himself."[95]

So too, the British appeared to have great influence over the policies of the king's Hashemite rivals in Transjordan and Iraq—strategically situated on Saudi Arabia's borders. The British, Ibn Saud realized, not only had the potential to create serious problems in the Hijaz, traditional stronghold of Hashemite loyalties, but could conceivably block the king's plans for expansion on the peninsula—or even threaten his independence. The United States, because of its wealth, prestige, and its stake in the oil concession, might offer a counterweight to British power.

The king had no illusions about his situation. Britain was, at least for the time being, the dominant power in his world and that of his Arab neighbors. He had no intention of alienating London even with the support of the Americans. Nor was Ibn Saud prepared to compromise his position with his Wahhabi followers by permitting the Americans to flood his country with their military and economic advisers. Moreover, in view of increasing American support for a Jewish homeland in Palestine, the king could not afford to become too closely identified with Washington. Still, the king apparently believed that for a small power trying to survive in a world of great power diplomacy, the United States could be a valuable ally—offering financial and even diplomatic support.

The Americans eagerly embraced the prospects of the new partnership. NEA's officials came to believe that hammering out a Saudi Arabian policy which was totally independent of British subsidies or joint assistance programs, represented the ultimate test of American intentions toward the Saudi kingdom. In this sense, the EXIM Bank loan, however insufficient, was much more than a simple monetary transaction—it was as Eddy believed, "a political commitment of long standing."[96]

Although officials had exerted great effort to subsidize Ibn Saud's postwar needs, by the end of 1945 it was clear that direct long-range aid was simply not possible. The final loan was, at best, a poor substitute for the larger development plans originally envisioned by the State Department's officers. Despite NEA's efforts, the case for assuming Ibn Saud's budgetary deficits was not strong enough to overcome the political and legal obstacles involved in aiding the king.

Despite high-level State Department and White House interest, fears of British intrigue and economic instability in Saudi Arabia were, for the most part, confined to a small group of area specialists and military officials. Still impressed by the sheer size of Saudi reserves and eager to maintain American influence with the king, these officials urged their superiors to secure American interests on a more permanent basis.

For the most part NEA's officers, both in Washington and in the field, exaggerated the threat to the oil concession and overestimated the importance of providing an official bankroll for Ibn Saud. In 1945 neither Britain nor the Soviet Union had the capacity or inclination to make a determined grab for Saudi oil. Similarly, the Saudi economy, though badly managed and hardpressed, was far from total collapse. Pilgrimage revenues were again on the increase and it is more than likely that the Saudis could have managed on a much less grand budget than Ibn Saud had proposed. Still, many officials seemed to accept almost without question that the primary responsibility for bailing out Ibn Saud lay with Washington rather than with the companies. Although this view was no doubt part of the department's campaign to create closer ties with Saudi Arabia, officials seemed reluctant to press ARAMCO to make any contribution at all. Some like Eddy, who would later join the ARAMCO organization, argued that American prestige would inevitably suffer if Ibn Saud were permitted to "bleed" the company for funds. Others in NEA automatically assumed that the companies' financial resources were inadequate to support the king. As late as April, Clayton expressed his surprise that ARAMCO had not even been consulted about official plans to balance Ibn Saud's budget.[97]

It would be unfair, however, to be too critical of State Department policies. To NEA officials charged with the responsibility of looking after an oil concession of enormous potential, the absence of a more active American role in Saudi Arabia no doubt seemed a threat to their ability to safeguard American interests. Officials may be criticized for their almost hysterical view of British designs and for their failure to press the oil companies to attend to the requirements of the king, but they cannot be faulted for their desire to strengthen Saudi-American ties. They were, after all, planning for the future in an effort to create a basis for friendship and cooperation between the two countries which would outlast the king's death. However awkward their methods or unrealistic their expectations, State Department officials recognized that Saudi Arabia and its oil might become of great strategic and economic importance to the United States. Had the concession been jeopardized or American access to Saudi reserves imperiled in any way, the department would certainly have been taken to task for its lack of foresight in not protecting American interests.

The government's inability to translate concern into actual policy in Saudi Arabia also reflected the lack of politically or legally acceptable methods with which to fund the king. Lend-lease was never intended as a postwar tool. In the closing months of the war against Japan, it was highly unlikely that the Department of State could have convinced FEA or Truman, to continue to manipulate wartime legislation for post-war objectives. So too, government action was severely limited by both Congress and the domestic petroleum industry, already suspicious of State Department sympathy and support for foreign oil interests.

More fundamental to the failure of efforts to subsidize the king was Washington's view of Middle Eastern oil and its relationship to foreign policy. Despite the increasing importance of petroleum, interest in Arabian oil had emerged as a wartime concern—to be used primarily as a potential source of military supply. Saudi oil might become vital to the conservation of Western Hemisphere reserves and to the supply of Eastern Hemisphere markets, yet by and large these arguments were based on future developments and long-range forecasts. For the present, it appeared that the domestic industry, with its wartime accomplishments under its belt, could handle the nation's petroleum requirements. In short, formulating postwar policy in Saudi Arabia based on a wartime interest in petroleum was simply not within the grasp of policymakers. In a draft memorandum to President Truman, requesting the establishment of a fund to carry out American strategic and political objectives in the Middle East, Gordon Merriam expressed a widely felt frustration:

> For nearly a year we have known that some money—about ten million a year for the next five years—would be necessary to obtain an economic stability in that country sufficient to give a reasonable security to American interest in the vast Arabian oil fields. This project, together with subsidiary projects, has been shunted around month after month in the Government departments while the interested officials were trying to determine whether the Export-Import Bank could safely make a loan, or whether legislation should be sought, involving the risk that it might become a football for special, short-sighted interests. . . . This is an outstanding example of the fact that we lack money for long-range, general political and strategic use for the purpose of winning the peace in that crucial part of the world.

Merriam's pitch for a special fund went the way of so many of the department's projects for aiding the king. Writing to Henderson, Acheson simply noted, "I have talked with the Secretary who believes that this cannot be done at present."[98]

CHAPTER 6
POSTWAR DEVELOPMENTS: COMPANIES, CARTELS, AND COMMUNISM, 1946–1947

AMERICAN policy toward Saudi Arabian oil between 1941 and 1945 had emerged and developed as a direct response to the exigencies of world war. With victories over Germany and Japan much of the urgency which had characterized the United States' oil diplomacy disappeared. In view of increasing oil production and improving Anglo-American relations in Saudi Arabia, there was little need to implement specific measures to support the Saudi economy or to safeguard Arabian reserves.[1] The Department of State was more than sympathetic to Ibn Saud's requests for technical and financial aid, yet it was becoming increasingly clear to many government officials that the future of the concession depended primarily on ARAMCO's relations with the king and its ability to develop Saudi oil. In short, by 1946, the focus of American oil diplomacy in the Middle East had shifted from official attempts to secure Saudi reserves to private commercial efforts to develop the potential of Arabian oil. Although the increasing fear of Soviet expansion and the rising tensions of the Palestine problem would soon draw attention to the difficulty of securing Middle Eastern reserves, for the time being the Department of State simply left Arabian oil to the companies.

The end of the war challenged policymakers to take a hard look at the balance sheet on Middle Eastern petroleum. Wartime oil diplomacy had often been inconsistent and uncoordinated, yet it had focused on the general objective of securing and developing Arabian crude as a potential source of military and peacetime supply. The immediate postwar advantages of Saudi oil seemed less clear. Although Persian Gulf oil might ultimately supply the markets of Europe and the Far East, many petroleum experts cautioned against too rapid a development of the area's reserves. In view of Europe's prewar reliance on coal and the lack of adequate refining and tanker capacity, some government planners believed it might be three to five years before the European market could handle an increasing flow of Persian Gulf crude. Similarly, the large-scale destruction of European industrial and transportation facilities seemed to indicate a short-term decline in Eastern Hemisphere demand. Finally, there was no pressing need to develop Middle Eastern crude as a source of military resupply. "The probable need of Middle Eastern oil as an emergency reserve," Herbert Feis observed, after the war, "seemed less clear than it did in 1943. Its military usefulness also appeared less clear. The subject was tending to reduce itself to ordinary economic dimensions."[2]

The immediate postwar relationship between Middle Eastern oil and the United States' petroleum economy seemed equally uncertain. Although postwar consumption was expected to increase rapidly, the domestic industry was confident that it could supply the nation's petroleum requirements without a heavy reliance on foreign crude. Given a competitive price structure and freedom from regulatory controls, the industry was optimistic about the future. Testifying before a Senate committee in October 1945, Robert E. Wilson of Standard Oil of Indiana observed that "under favorable conditions for crude production the ability of our domestic industry to produce crude will probably for the next five years—and possibly for the next ten years—nearly equal the lower range of probable demand and will make possible a substantially self-contained domestic industry if that should be deemed desirable."[3] Similarly, domestic oil interests and their supporters in Congress were certain to oppose any official policy of encouraging large-scale imports of foreign oil, particularly the cheaper crude of the Persian Gulf. Middle Eastern petroleum might eventually be used to conserve Western Hemisphere reserves or even to supplement domestic production, yet these trends were clearly viewed as distant developments. "I do not believe," Wilson informed the Senate Special Committee Investigating Petroleum Resources, "we will need to go outside of South America for this twenty year period. If you were talking 40 or 50 years ahead, we might have to go to the Eastern Hemisphere to keep our crude supplies."[4]

State Department and military petroleum experts were considerably more cautious about the future. Decreasing military requirements were expected to be almost entirely offset by increasing civilian consumption. Moreover, it was estimated that postwar military demand would exceed prewar levels. By the end of 1946, the demand for motor gasoline alone was expected to exceed 1,641,000 b.p.d. In 1946, oil and gas, for the first time, would comprise more of the nation's total energy picture than coal.[5] Could domestic reserves alone, government officials wondered, continue to generate enough petroleum to meet anticipated demand? To the government's experts, particularly those interested in stimulating interest in Middle Eastern oil, the answer seemed clear. No less than five studies, Charles Rayner informed a Senate committee in June 1945, indicated that the United States might be forced to import between 100,000 and 500,000 b.p.d. to maintain anticipated levels of postwar consumption. John Loftus's predictions were even more startling. Within twenty years, he declared on an NBC radio program in August 1946, the United States might conceivably import 50 percent of its petroleum needs.[6]

Although time would not until much later confirm the predictions of the government's experts, Middle Eastern oil could not but occupy a significant position in the long-range petroleum forecast. With proven reserves of at least 16,000,000,000 barrels and an estimated capacity of billions more, Persian Gulf oil seemed to offer a rich source of supply for civilian as well as military requirements. "Certain foreign areas, particularly in the Middle East," Ralph Davies observed in November 1945, "appear to contain more oil per 1,000 square miles than most of the productive parts of the United States. . . . For the sake of the American economy and of future American security, nothing should be left undone to promote full participation by American interests in the development of these areas."[7]

Similarly, military planners, though cautious in their approach, continued to view Persian Gulf oil as a valuable strategic advantage. In a draft memorandum to the secretary of state in August 1945, the navy had concluded: "From the point of view of the Army and Navy, . . . a strategic benefit will be realized if the oil of Saudi Arabia can be gotten into large-scale peacetime production as rapidly as possible. The effect of such peacetime utilization will be that the pressure upon oil resources in the Western Hemisphere will be correspondingly lessened, and the oil of Saudi Arabia will go to meet needs . . . which might otherwise be satisfied from Western Hemisphere resources."[8] Almost a year later, Colonel G. H. Vogel of the ANPB noted that the navy was receiving almost half of its fuel oil requirements from the refineries of Bahrain and Ras Tanura.[9]

Despite the end of the war, the State Department's petroleum and Middle East experts continued to follow the development of Arabian oil with great interest. The security of the Saudi concession was no longer of immediate concern, yet the commercial development of Persian Gulf crude might require the department's services. By 1945, ARAMCO representatives were seriously involved in planning and negotiating the construction of a trans-Arabian pipeline from their fields to the Mediterranean. The success of the venture depended upon securing transit rights through at least three Middle Eastern countries— some like Syria and Lebanon enjoying recently acquired independence, others like Transjordan and Palestine still under British control. In view of chronic instability in the area and increasing tensions over the Palestine problem, the department might be called upon to facilitate negotiations or even to protect American interests.

Middle Eastern oil was also still entangled in a web of interlocking agreements which retarded petroleum development from Egypt to Kuwait and made a mockery of the principles of the Atlantic Charter and Open Door. As early as 1943, Gulf Oil representatives had already informed the department of the company's desire to break out of its Kuwait agreement with the AIOC. Similarly, representatives of Socony-Vacuum and SONJ had expressed their dissatisfaction with operating conditions in Iraq.[10]

The end of the war may have altered the focus of official oil diplomacy, yet the State Department's postwar objectives toward Middle Eastern oil remained largely the same. In January 1946, John Loftus, now chief of the department's Petroleum Division, outlined an American policy toward foreign oil. United States' efforts, Loftus began, ought to concentrate on exploiting the oil as a means of conserving Western Hemisphere reserves and supplying the future demands of the Eastern Hemisphere. To effect the full development of Middle Eastern oil, it was necessary to remove restrictions on production and marketing. Finally, the United States must strive to assure the producing countries "maximum economic benefits."[11] Loftus had long argued that the only permanent security for American oil interests lay in equitable dealings with the host countries. In view of the companies' postwar development plans, it was particularly important to ensure that contractual arrangements with local governments were "fair and just." Arrangements which gave one company or companies exclusive rights to a concession or enabled companies to restrict production might seriously jeopardize relations with the host countries. The only way the United States might maintain a "secure and durable" position, Loftus later concluded, was to "ensure that American commercial interests deal with local governments in such a way as to guarantee goodwill and reciprocal benefits."[12]

Loftus's assumptions were essentially sound, yet it was difficult to see precisely how the Department of State could force the oil companies to deal "fairly" with local governments or to abandon the advantages of their own business arrangements. Although it was very unlikely that the companies, particularly ARAMCO, would do anything that would alienate the host governments, the companies would take whatever steps were necessary to ensure their competitive positions in producing or marketing. Moreover, government efforts to "open up" existing concessions or to encourage more companies to participate in Middle Eastern oil development might clash with the interests of those companies dominating the area's oil. The State Department might encourage the companies to grant more generous terms to host countries, as it did in the case of ARAMCO's pipeline agreement with Transjordan, and air its own ideas on international oil, yet it could not hope to influence the more important intercompany arrangements of the postwar years. Moreover, many State Department officials saw advantages for the United States in the companies' new joint ventures. The department's relationship with the companies seemed to reflect the changing pattern of postwar developments. In short, the immediate postwar years, 1945 to 1949, witnessed the declining influence of official oil diplomacy and the reemergence of the companies' efforts to develop and control the flow of Middle Eastern crude.

Postwar efforts to secure and develop Arabian oil as a potential source of supply for Eastern Hemisphere markets focused on the development of the trans-Arabian pipeline. Although the proposed facility was a private venture sponsored entirely by ARAMCO and the parent companies, the Department of State followed the company's efforts with great interest. Not only might the trans-Arabian line provide the future link between Persian Gulf oil and world markets, but also it might enhance the position of American petroleum interests throughout the Middle East. Extensive pipeline and refining facilities in Saudi Arabia, Transjordan, Palestine, and Lebanon might facilitate the economic development of the entire area. By guaranteeing local states the "reciprocal benefits" of petroleum development, department officials believed, American concessions might be more firmly secured. Eager to support the project as a private venture, the department had facilitated ARAMCO's requests for travel permits and air transport for the dispatch of a pipeline survey team.[13]

Although the Department of State may have viewed the pipeline as an integral part of its plans for Middle Eastern oil development, to ARAMCO the trans-Arabian line represented its future stake in Saudi petroleum. Unless the company could find a cheap and expedient method of transporting Persian Gulf crude to the Mediterranean, it could not hope to supply the potential markets of Europe, let alone compete with its European or American rivals. The advantages of a 1,000-mile pipeline linking the Persian Gulf and Mediterranean were enormous. Not only might such a facility shorten the distance between ARAMCO's fields and European markets by some 3,500 miles, but it might reduce the need for tankers in a period of anticipated shortage.

Furthermore, a trans-Arabian line would enable the company to eliminate a Suez Canal toll of between $.13 and $.18 per barrel—a possible
savings of $15,000 to $30,000 per tanker cargo. In view of the potential
of Saudi reserves ARAMCO could only realize that a pipeline would be
the key to controlling the flow of a large part of the world's oil. By late
1945, the company had conducted numerous surveys and had already
begun negotiations for transit rights with British authorities in Palestine and Transjordan.[14]

By early 1946, ARAMCO had succeeded in negotiating a transit agreement with British mandatory authorities in Palestine, yet the company
still faced the prospect of negotiations with Transjordan, Lebanon,
and possibly Syria. Although both the Foreign Office and British military seem to have accepted the inevitability of the pipeline and even
supported it for strategic purposes, it was clear that London would
not leave the field entirely to the Americans.[15] Discussions between
ARAMCO representatives and Foreign Office officials had revealed that
the British were particularly sensitive to the possible location of the
pipeline terminus and to the issue of transit fees to local states.[16] In the
interests of military security, the British Chiefs of Staff had suggested
that the company not use Haifa or the Bay of Acre area as the pipeline's Mediterranean outlet. The area already contained IPC's refineries
and the Kirkuk to Haifa pipeline terminus. Similarly, in view of plans
to construct a 160,000 b.p.d. IPC-AIOC pipeline, parallel to the Kirkuk
line, it might be unwise to concentrate another strategic facility in the
same area. British military officials proposed that if the company
planned to terminate the pipeline in Palestine, it might consider some
point further to the south.

In view of the fact that ARAMCO had apparently not yet decided on
an exact location for the pipeline terminus, the matter was not of
pressing concern. More important to the actual progress of the pipeline negotiations was the problem of compensation to local states. In
the course of ARAMCO's discussions with the Colonial Office, the company had learned that the Amir Abdullah, ruler of Transjordan, desired a transit fee for the right to construct a pipeline across his
country. Abdullah's request was a significant departure from past practice. According to previous IPC contracts, local states were paid a fixed
"security fee" in exchange for protecting the company's facilities.
Transjordan now sought compensation not merely for expenses connected with the pipeline but for the actual right of transit. The British
Colonial Office was strongly opposed to establishing such a precedent.
Allowing local states to demand compensation for the right of transit
might ultimately prejudice British-controlled IPC or AIOC pipeline sys-

tems. Transit countries might also demand direct payment for the actual amount of oil flowing through the pipeline. The British informed the Americans that these were "minor points," yet it was clear that they might easily delay the progress of the negotiations.[17]

Although ARAMCO seemed willing to conform to the British view on transit compensation, the Petroleum Division seemed determined to protect the company's rights with or without its support. To Loftus the problem of transit rights was far more than a crusade of principle; it went to the very heart of the problem confronting American petroleum interests in the Middle East. The "security of our oil investments in the Near East, the protection against hostile internal and external forces and the goodwill of our American companies," Loftus wrote to Henderson and Merriam in February 1946, "will be much enhanced if the various countries in that area participate directly in the economic benefits resulting from the development of local oil resources."[18] In the case of Transjordan, Loftus noted earlier, ARAMCO should be encouraged to break the pattern of IPC contracts and to grant more favorable terms to Abdullah.[19] In short, Loftus was asking the companies to surrender a possible advantage for what he was sure were long-term benefits.

The company, however, was far more concerned about the immediate success of the negotiations and their competitive position than about future relations with the Jordanians. In view of the Colonial Office's "unalterable" opposition to a transit fee or tax, ARAMCO officials informed Loftus, the British could deny the company the already limited access it had to Abdullah. ARAMCO suggested that it would rather accede to the wishes of the British and later, after Transjordan received its formal independence, renegotiate the contract on "more favorable terms." Loftus was not enthusiastic about the company's proposal. Writing to Loy Henderson and Gordon Merriam, he observed with some sarcasm: "Incidentally, with reference to the company's program for modifying the concession terms at a later date I do not know of any oil concession anywhere in the world the terms of which have been voluntarily liberalized by an oil company."[20]

Although ARAMCO was uneasy about the prospect of irritating the British, the company was not opposed to the payment of a "reasonable" transit tax provided it did not discriminate against the marketing of Arabian oil. Prompted by the Petroleum Division, NEA officers took the matter up with their superiors. If the British succeeded in pressuring Abdullah into accepting inequitable compensation for transit rights, Henderson informed Secretary of State Byrnes and William Clayton in March, it might be detrimental to the "long-run stability of the American economic position in the Near and Middle East. . . ." Henderson recommended that the State Department discuss the matter with the Colonial Office and advise the American companies in Iraq to bring whatever pressure they could on the IPC.[21]

The department seemed prepared to act on NEA's recommendations. In March, Byrnes instructed the American chargé in London to advise the Colonial Office that "whatever may be [the] historical precedents, Transjordan is entitled to receive determinate and proportionate compensation for transit privileges granted to company in any pipeline concession."[22] It seemed that the Colonial Office had little choice but to comply with the department's request. As the mandatory power administering Transjordan, Britain was legally bound not to discriminate against the nationals of any foreign state and to promote the full development of the area's natural resources. The Americans were quick to push this point. "Unless Brit Govt wishes to waive its rights as Mandatory," the department informed the American Embassy in London, "it is obligated to assist Aramco to obtain concession on terms not less favorable to Aramco than IPC terms if such are the terms Aramco wants." This would not, the department concluded, prevent the company from voluntarily offering a "non-generalized benefit" to Transjordan in excess of IPC terms.[23] In May, the companies began negotiating directly with British and Jordanian officials in Amman. By early August, after months of what the American minister in Jerusalem termed the "more or less normal oriental course and unavoidable delays," the pipeline convention was signed in Amman. The fourth article of the contract provided for the payment of £60,000 Palestinian to the government of Transjordan for each year ARAMCO's oil passed through the line.[24]

Although the State Department had become directly involved in ARAMCO's negotiations with the British, it was clear that the diplomats had little influence on the companies' postwar plans to divide Middle Eastern oil. In the case of transit rights, officials had been confronted with a prospective violation by another government of an international accord on the administration of mandates. Oil company affairs, however, were shrouded in the secrecy of half a century of interlocking private agreements. There were no international codes governing the conduct of the major oil companies and little evidence of intercompany activities. In the absence of effective and well-coordinated antitrust legislation, the government lacked leverage to sway the decisions of an international cartel. Moreover, there were those officials in the State Department who seemed willing to subordinate the antitrust implications of the companies' joint ventures to the advantages of the proposed arrangements—advantages which might strengthen the American petroleum position abroad and enhance the "national security." In short, the Department of State approached the question of the companies' postwar arrangements largely as an interested observer. The government's petroleum and international trade experts had definite plans for eliminating and rearranging prewar marketing and production restrictions, yet there was little, if anything, they could do about them. As private agreements, the fate of the Red Line and "As Is" accords as well as the new joint ventures lay primarily in the hands of the oil companies themselves.

By 1946, it seemed, at least temporarily, that the major oil companies involved in the Middle East might be in the process of voluntarily dismantling many of their prewar marketing and producing arrangements. To the American companies participating in the IPC, the Group Agreement of 1928, with its emphasis on self-denial, had become a useless and confining arrangement—not only preventing them from obtaining new concessions within the Red Line, but also from buying into existing concessions. The war appeared to offer Socony-Vacuum and SONJ a legal opportunity to escape their IPC commitment. With the German occupation of France and the establishment of Vichy, the British Alien Property Custodian had sequestered both the French and Gulbenkian shares in the IPC. Since the IPC shares were now technically "enemy property," the Group Agreement was no longer considered valid under British law and could not be resumed without complete renegotiation. Although the American companies realized that Gulbenkian and the French might contest the matter in a potentially embarrassing court battle, they were determined to break through the "thick Red Line." In August 1946, representatives of Socony-Vacuum and SONJ informed the Department of State that they were seriously considering "renegotiating" a new Group Agreement without the restrictive clauses of the 1928 accord.[25]

The companies' plans to abrogate the Group Agreement, however, only marked the beginning of a set of arrangements designed to adjust production and marketing accords to the new realities of the postwar period. Between the two world wars, the major companies involved in the IPC, Royal Dutch-Shell, AIOC, Socony-Vacuum, and SONJ had sought to stabilize the international petroleum market by a complex set of production and marketing agreements. By 1945, the IPC members were confronted with an unprecedented threat to the stability of the old order—ARAMCO's control of Arabian oil. Although SONJ, AIOC, and Royal Dutch-Shell had long been aware of the competitive potential of Arabian crude, by 1945 it was clear that ARAMCO's oil might soon be pouring into world markets. If ARAMCO, as an outsider to the IPC family, were permitted to develop the vast potential of Saudi crude, the company could easily disrupt if not destroy the stability of the international petroleum market.[26]

Perhaps the American members of the IPC were most keenly aware of the rapidly changing circumstances of the postwar period. With only a minority interest in the oil of Iraq and no claim to the rich fields of Iran, Socony-Vacuum and SONJ were seriously disturbed by the potential of Persian Gulf crude. By 1946, ARAMCO was already selling crude for $.90 a barrel when the lowest available price at the U.S. Gulf was $1.28. Moreover, in 1946 both SOCAL and the Texas company estimated that the actual cost of producing Arabian crude was $.33 a barrel. Unless the companies could somehow control or share in Arabian oil, their ability to market competitively in Europe or the Far East might be severely restricted. SONJ thus began seriously to explore the possibility of purchasing a substantial interest in ARAMCO. "A deal through which Jersey would obtain a substantial interest in Saudi Arabia," a company source noted, "would not only have the advantage of providing additional supplies to Jersey . . . but would have the further advantage of easing the pressure that would otherwise come from Caltex in their efforts to expand their outlets."[27]

By June 1946, discussions between ARAMCO, SONJ, and Socony-Vacuum were already underway. Although some in ARAMCO argued against the proposed sale of one-third of company stock, the deal seemed to offer immediate advantages to the company. The arrangement provided the capital necessary to finance the proposed $100,000,000 trans-Arabian pipeline, enabled ARAMCO to distribute the risks of any future investments, and furnished the capital necessary to guarantee the investment in the future.

Equally important was the problem of marketing. According to an ARAMCO source, the new American minister to Saudi Arabia, J. Rives Childs, informed the State Department that the company believed its marketing outlets were not yet sufficient to handle the potential of Saudi crude. Rather than compete with the well-developed marketing facilities of Socony-Vacuum and SONJ, ARAMCO no doubt believed it was wiser to cooperate. Moreover, in view of the pressure which might be expected from Ibn Saud to increase production, ARAMCO thought it wise to assure itself secure markets.[28]

By late 1946, the only remaining obstacle to the transaction was the Group Agreement which prohibited IPC members from buying into existing concessions within the Red Line. It is not surprising that Socony-Vacuum's and SONJ's efforts to escape the IPC accord coincided with their consideration of the ARAMCO deal. Writing to Laurence Levi in July 1946, Harold Sheets of Socony-Vacuum confided: "I took Charlie Rayner into my confidence . . . and I disclosed to him the nature, extent and present status of our negotiations with ARAMCO, with particular emphasis on the Red Line problem. . . . I urged Rayner to get Byrne's [sic] and Acheson's support for asking British Government to join with U.S.A. in bringing about the elimination of the Red Line restrictions and Kuwait restrictions as soon as possible." [29]

The Department of State had assured the companies that it would support their efforts to renegotiate the Group Agreement on a nonrestrictive basis, yet official diplomacy could do little to alter the existing terms of a private agreement. [30] In November 1946, Loftus and Rayner met with British representatives for informal discussion on a wide range of petroleum matters. The Americans made it quite clear that the United States considered the Group Agreement and Kuwait marketing accord entirely incompatible with the spirit of the Anglo-American Petroleum Agreement. British officials agreed, yet noted that the IPC members had freely accepted the conditions of the Group Agreement and were therefore responsible for its renegotiation. [31]

In view of the legal complications of the accord and the necessity of dealing with both Gulbenkian and the French, the ultimate fate of the Red Line lay primarily in the English courts and IPC board rooms. In November, the Department of State informed its chargé in London that although it hoped the American IPC members would succeed in eliminating the restrictions of the Group Agreement, "the Department . . . does not feel that it is competent to or could appropriately enter into a discussion of whether or not the inter-company agreement is *de facto* void at the present time." [32] Determined to clear the way for their entry into ARAMCO, however, SONJ and Socony-Vacuum had decided to act. Early in January 1947, company representatives formally notified Clayton, Loftus, and Rayner that they considered the Group Agreement legally void and no longer felt bound by its terms. [33]

Although the State Department's petroleum experts were pleased with the prospect of eliminating the Red Line restrictions, by 1947, government officials were forced to confront a new set of commercial arrangements. The new oil deals, centered on the two relatively untapped sources of Middle Eastern crude, have been variously interpreted: by some as cartel control over crude oil and world markets; and by others as a sound attempt to provide the money and markets necessary to produce Middle Eastern oil. In Saudi Arabia, the entry of SONJ and Socony-Vacuum into ARAMCO assured four American companies control of Saudi crude. SOCAL and the Texas company secured markets for their oil and money for their pipeline. In return SONJ and Socony-Vacuum bought into Arabian oil, shifting their source of crude from the fields of Iraq to Saudi Arabia. To quiet the AIOC fear of a united American front in Arabian oil, SONJ entered into a series of long-term contracts with AIOC to purchase oil from Iran and Kuwait and to join with the British company in building a pipeline from Abadan to the Mediterranean. In Kuwait, Gulf Oil and Shell planned to enter into a set of agreements designed to control Kuwait crude and to eliminate excess competition between the two partners. The Department of State could not ignore the obvious implications of the new arrangements. In January, Leslie A. Webb, formerly with the department and then with the Atlantic Refining Company, informed Loftus that the smaller companies, Sun Oil, Atlantic, and Phillips, believed they were being "ruthlessly and effectively frozen out of the world oil markets" by the new oil deals.[34]

State Department reaction to the proposed transactions was mixed. Although the agreements seemed to guarantee a handful of companies virtual control of a third of the world's oil, the arrangements also seemed to offer the United States substantial advantages. In February 1947, Robert Eakens, assistant chief of the Petroleum Division (PED), forwarded to Clair Wilcox, director of the Office of International Trade Policy, (ITP), a study prepared by ITP and PED on the "projected inter-company arrangements." After summarizing the proposed transactions, the study noted:

> They have the cumulative effect of preserving the balance of power as among the major oil companies in the world market in approximately its historical pattern. They range in duration from 10 years in case of Gulf-Shell deal to 60 years in ARAMCO deal. They therefore tend to immobilize for a long time the competitive status quo in international oil trade. Consequently they tend to determine the distribution pattern for virtually all of the oil likely to move into Eastern Hemisphere markets within the next 20 years. . . .

The department, however, the study continued, "cannot and should not oppose" the arrangements. Not only do the proposed deals serve the "national interest" by hastening the development of Middle Eastern oil and its entry into world markets, but they "facilitate the development of extensive American holdings in the Middle East." Even the SONJ-AIOC transaction might benefit United States' interests by permitting SONJ to supply Eastern Hemisphere markets from Middle Eastern oil—leaving the company in a stronger position to supply Western

Hemisphere markets with Western Hemisphere oil. Finally, the study concluded, *"taken separately"* each deal might be considered a "reasonable commercial transaction," inspired by the desire of the marketers to adjust their crude supplies to market outlets.[35]

Although the ITP-PED reaction to the oil deals was not shared by all of the State Department's trade and petroleum planners, it did represent a view which would become increasingly popular in the postwar years. Eager to acquire American oil holdings and uneasy about the increasing tensions of an emerging cold war world, officials in the Department of State often seemed willing to subordinate antitrust considerations to what they believed to be the higher priorities of national security. Whatever their drawbacks, the Middle Eastern oil deals seemed to provide greater long-term security for American companies in the area and a broader base for their operations at a time when American interests abroad seemed particularly vulnerable. Despite their commitment to the principles of free trade and their opposition, at least in theory, to international cartels, many State Department officials were reluctant to oppose openly arrangements which might strengthen American access to and control over strategically valuable Middle Eastern reserves.

Regardless of the possible advantages of the accords, however, the department's trade and petroleum specialists agreed that the government could not "unreservedly approve" the arrangements. The transactions, the study continued, "facilitate the emergence or continuance of market and price policies incompatible with general United States trade objectives." The government might not only be accused of perpetuating the status quo in oil but also compromising the United States' avowed determination to oppose international cartels. Moreover, the government's policy of cooperating with the British in oil matters was vulnerable on the grounds that it fostered new monopolies. Since the Department of State could not give blanket approval or disapproval to the transactions, Eakens concluded, perhaps the "no objection" formula might be employed. The oil companies involved, however, should be informed of the department's misgivings.[36]

State Department officials were clearly aware of the full impact of the proposed oil deals. The department, however, was apparently not interested in blocking the objectives of the deals, only in eliminating their "immediate and obvious, as well as possible long run, disadvantages."[37] Writing to Clayton in late February, Paul Nitze, of ITP, proposed a possible alternative. Under Nitze's plan, Socony-Vacuum would purchase SONJ's interest in the IPC and then withdraw from the ARAMCO deal and possibly from the SONJ-Socony-Vacuum-AIOC arrangement. Socony-Vacuum would then become the only American member of the IPC, leaving three instead of four American companies in Saudi oil. Not only might such an arrangement "simplify and perhaps arrest the trend toward multiplication of the interlocking arrangements between and among the oil companies engaged in the international oil trade," but also it might help in meeting the criticism of the deals by Congress and other American companies. Finally, Nitze suggested that the State Department might consider a plan under which SONJ would offer its share in the IPC to a group of American companies interested in participating in Middle Eastern oil.[38]

Although the department broached Nitze's plan to Socony-Vacuum and SONJ, the companies were clearly not interested in sacrificing their interest in the IPC. According to Orville Harden of SONJ the only commercial justification for the company's desire to participate in both IPC and ARAMCO was its desire to increase its "spread in ownership" of Middle Eastern oil.[39] Nitze's solution might have succeeded before the companies became convinced that the Red Line was invalid under English law, but by March, Socony-Vacuum and SONJ were negotiating in London with Gulbenkian and the French for revision of the Group Agreement. Moreover, the companies had already made plans to close the ARAMCO deal. Even had the Department of State wanted to alter the arrangements, the diplomats had little chance of influencing the actions of the American companies. The fate of the staff report on the proposed deals seemed to reflect the basic problem confronting the department. In view of the fact that it was probably too late to revise the companies' transactions, Eakens wrote to Wilcox, it might not even be practical to submit the study to the secretary's staff committee. Commenting on his own proposals to decentralize control of Middle Eastern oil, Eakens concluded that this program was not intended as "a goal to be attained within a specified time period of one or two years, nor as a policy of which the petroleum companies necessarily would be informed."[40]

During the early years of the war, American policy toward Middle Eastern and particularly Saudi oil was shaped by the familiar themes of military supply, conservation, and the development of relations with the British. By 1945, however, new factors were gradually emerging which would permanently influence American thinking and strategy. The now familiar sound of Anglo-American bickering in Saudi Arabia was beginning to give way to the more distant and ominous rumbling of Soviet-Allied tension in the Middle East. Russian activity in Iran in late 1944 and Soviet diplomatic pressure on Turkey in 1945 seemed to raise serious questions regarding Russian intentions toward the entire Middle Eastern area. Writing to Roosevelt as early as December 1944, Stettinius noted: "The Russians are showing a growing interest in the Arab world and are quite plainly anxious to expand their influence in the area, particularly toward the Persian Gulf. Such expansion would of course, be in the direction of the oil fields in Saudi Arabia and Bahrein as well as those in Iran, Iraq and Kuwait."[41] Similarly, reports from Moscow seemed to indicate that the Soviet Union, through its recently established diplomatic missions in the area and its large Muslim population, was seeking greater influence in the Arab world. The aims of these Russian diplomatic missions, Averell Harriman, American ambassador in the Soviet Union, informed the State Department, "would appear clear, namely to create an atmosphere of friendship for the Soviet Union in the Arab world, to break down existing suspicions of and hostility to Soviet Communist doctrine, and to obtain Arab support in furthering any specific Soviet objective which may develop."[42] Although a department report on American economic policy in the Middle East in May 1945 suggested that Soviet policy was essentially defensive, Gordon Merriam cautiously noted that, "in view of our oil interests in Iraq, Kuwait, Bahrein, Saudi Arabia, and Qatar, it is of importance to us, as well as to the British to keep any possibly disturbing influence out of the Gulf."[43]

The gradual but increasing uneasiness over Russian objectives in the Middle East was heightened by the problem of Palestine. Although State Department officials had perceived a possible conflict between American support for a Jewish homeland and the security of United States' interests in the Middle East since the 1930s, it was not until World War II that the Palestine issue began to emerge as a serious factor in American domestic and foreign policy. Moved by the horrors of the Nazi genocide and committed to past Democratic party platforms, both Roosevelt and Truman issued statements supporting Jewish immigration into Palestine and endorsing the idea of a homeland for the Jewish people.

Although the Roosevelt administration had shown interest in the question of refugees and the president had personally expressed sympathy for the idea of a Jewish homeland, Roosevelt was clearly ambivalent about the extent to which the United States should become committed to supporting Zionist objectives. The Department of State had warned the president about the risks and dangers of such a course. Even Zionist activities in the United States, Joseph Grew wrote to Roosevelt before his trip to Yalta, "will remain the gravest threat to friendly relations between the United States and the countries of the

Near East."[44] Roosevelt's meeting with Ibn Saud only seemed to impress upon the president the Arab determination to resist a Jewish homeland. In fact, Roosevelt apparently agreed with the State Department's view that a Jewish state could only be established and maintained by force. A week before his death, in a letter to Ibn Saud, the president once again reassured the king that he would take no action hostile to the Arab people.[45]

Although the Department of State had some success in impressing upon Roosevelt the dangers of the Palestine problem, it had a much more difficult time with his successor. Fascinated by the Arabs and long aware of the strategic importance of the Middle East, Roosevelt had vacillated considerably on the Palestine issue—assuaging, to some degree, the concerns of both the Arabs and his own State Department. Harry Truman, however, seemed less willing to cater to either group, particularly to the "striped-pants boys" at State. Moreover, since 1941, the Palestine problem had remained subordinate to wartime priorities. With the end of the war against Germany and the liberation of concentration camps like Buchenwald, the world was forced for the first time to confront the Nazi horrors. Although domestic political considerations would eventually influence the new president's thinking, Truman initially acted far more out of sympathy for the survivors and on his conviction that the United States could assist Jewish refugees and still attend to its own interests in the Middle East. By the fall of 1946, Truman had supported the entry of 100,000 refugees into Palestine and, to the dismay of both the State Department and British, officially endorsed the partition of Palestine.

Disturbed by what they perceived to be the pro-Zionist leanings of both Congress and the White House, and particularly sensitive to the pledge Roosevelt had made to Ibn Saud at Great Bitter Lake, the department's Arab experts continued to warn of the possible dangers of a partisan approach to the Palestine question. Writing to Secretary of State Byrnes in August, Loy Henderson, an implacable foe of a Jewish state in Palestine, noted that active U.S. support of Zionism would have a "strongly adverse effect" on American interests throughout the Near and Middle East. Reflecting the views of the majority of NEA's officers, Henderson, now the office's director, concluded: "We believe it would be lamost inevitable that the long-established American cultural, educational and religious institutions in the Near East would be placed in a difficult position and might be forced to suspend their activities; that American trade would probably be boycotted; that American economic interests, including our oil concessions in Saudi Arabia and in other Arab countries would be jeopardized."[46] Finally, William Eddy, whose anti-Zionism was even more intense than Henderson's, informed him in October 1945, that if the Saudis believed that the Americans are "flirting with a Palestine policy friendly to political Zionism and therefore (in Arab opinion) hostile to the Arabs, United States enterprises will be seriously handicapped." Although Ibn Saud had never mentioned sanctions against ARAMCO, Faisal had hinted that the king would not permit a trans-Arabian pipeline to terminate in a Jewish-controlled area. These were "small straws in the wind," Eddy noted, yet they were "indications" of the attitude Saudi Arabia might assume if the United States pursued a pro-Zionist course.[47]

Throughout 1946, as tensions between the United States and the Soviet Union continued to increase, officials began to attach new importance to the security of American and British interests in the Near and Middle East. Although the Americans continued to view Western Europe as the area of primary importance in any potential struggle with the Soviets, the Middle East was rapidly emerging as a crucial factor in postwar strategic planning. Not only did the area contain almost one-third of the world's known petroleum reserves, but it possessed supply lines, communications facilities, and air bases vital for defense of much of the British Empire. In view of the United States' reluctance to assume a stronger military role in the area, the maintenance of the British position in the eastern Mediterranean and Persian Gulf was considered essential to the preservation of American interests.[48] Writing to Clark Clifford, special counsel to the president, Robert Patterson, secretary of war, observed that Soviet activities directed toward weakening the British in the Middle East "threaten to create a vacuum into which Soviet political and military influence may move."[49]

Soviet maneuvering in Turkey and Iran only seemed to confirm official suspicions of Russian intentions. To the Americans, Russian policy appeared unchanged since the time of Peter the Great. Not only did the Soviets seem eager to gain control over the Bosporus and Dardanelles, but they appeared determined to push their quest for warm water from the Mediterranean to the Persian Gulf. Although many military planners believed that the Soviets primarily sought to construct a defensive perimeter in Iran in order to keep the Allies at bay, they were disturbed by the new aggressiveness of Soviet policy. The Soviet delay in removing its troops from northern Iran only increased Washington's fear of Russian plans to dominate the entire area. "Present Soviet maneuvers to control North Iran," a navy intelligence source noted in January 1946, were designed to push the "front" farther away from the Soviet oil areas of Baku, Batum, and Grozny and closer to the "enemy's" oil in Mosul and the Persian Gulf.[50] Permanent Soviet control of the Iranian province of Azerbaijan, the Joint Chiefs informed SWNCC, would constitute "a permanent penetration" into Iran and allow movement of Soviet forces near the oil fields of Iraq.[51]

By July, the Joint Chiefs of Staff had concluded that the Soviets sought nothing less than to bring Greece, Turkey, and Iran within their orbit. Toward that end, the JCS noted, the Russians had attempted diplomatically to gain control of the Dardanelles, the Dodecanese, and Tripolitania, and to undermine the British position in Greece, Egypt, and the Middle East.[52] In October, the State Department added its own caveat. In a memorandum prepared in the Office of Near Eastern and African Affairs and approved by Byrnes, Acheson, and Henderson, NEA concluded: "A Russion-dominated Turkey would open the floodgates for a Soviet advance into Syria, Lebanon, Iraq, Palestine, Transjordan, Egypt and the Arabian Peninsula, all of which are at present still relatively free from Russian activities and direct Russian pressure. . . . It would also dangerously, perhaps fatally, expose Greece and Iran."[53]

One of the State Department's most vocal opponents of Soviet expansion in the Near and Middle East was Loy W. Henderson, the Arkansas-born diplomat who would shape many of NEA's attitudes and policies in the postwar years. Henderson, whose career had carried him from chargé in Moscow to assistant chief of the Division of European Affairs, had earned quite a reputation for baiting the Russian bear. In fact, during the 1943 State Department "purge," Henderson was "exiled" to Baghdad as minister to Iraq, presumably for the intensity of his anti-Soviet views.[54] Nevertheless, by March 1945, he had returned from the field to head the Office of Near Eastern and African Affairs. There is little doubt that Henderson was picked for the job because of his experience in dealing with the Russians—qualifications which his superiors believed would put him in good stead for dealing with the Soviets in Turkey, Greece, and Iran.

Henderson brought new commitment and dedication to NEA. He not only continued the anti-Soviet orientation of his predecessor Wallace Murray (who had since become ambassador to Iran) but carried it to new heights. For Henderson, Soviet expansionism was an inescapable and harsh reality of the postwar world. There was no point in babying the Soviets nor even maintaining the fiction of international cooperation as long as Moscow pursued its expansionist designs. This was particularly true, Henderson believed, in areas where the Russians had long-standing objectives—like the Near East. "The Soviet Union seems to be determined," Henderson wrote to Acheson, "to break down the structure which Great Britain has maintained so that Russian power and influence can sweep unimpeded across Turkey and through the Dardanelles into the Mediterranean, and across Iran and through the Persian Gulf into the Indian Ocean."[55]

Recognizing the Soviet threat, however, was only part of the challenge. It was imperative, Henderson believed, that the United States begin to pursue a policy in the entire Middle East area more attuned to its own strategic and economic interests—and those of its allies. Although Henderson hoped to strengthen the United Nations he also looked with contempt upon naive concepts of international cooperation. Here he and his NEA colleagues had waged a running battle with Clayton's economists over the importance of using Export-Import Bank loans to further American political objectives throughout the Middle East. Similarly, Henderson urged that the United States work to maintain its prestige and influence in the Arab world. Fundamental in this regard was his unfailing opposition to United States' support for political Zionism—a support Henderson passionately believed would not only destroy American influence and interests and throw the Arabs into the arms of the Soviets, but also ultimately endanger the peace of the postwar world.

The threat of Soviet penetration into the eastern Mediterranean and Middle East inevitably focused the attention of the diplomats and generals on the security of American and British petroleum interests throughout the area. Although military planners were the first to concede that access to Middle Eastern oil might be restricted in the event of war, they believed it imperative to secure and develop Persian Gulf petroleum as a potential source of supply for counteroffensive action and to deny it to the enemy. The JCS had already estimated that the Soviet Union did not produce enough oil within its own borders to fight a major war. With proven reserves perhaps equal to those of the United States, Middle Eastern oil fields were certain to become a primary Soviet objective in any future conflict. The plan of the Soviet Union, an army intelligence report noted in May 1946, was to "choke off" American and British oil reserves in Iran, Iraq, and Saudi Arabia and ultimately to establish joint companies designed to control the area's wells and refineries.[56] Writing to SWNCC regarding the strategic importance of Iran, the JCS concentrated heavily on oil:

Loss of the Iraq and Saudi Arabia sources to the United States and her allies would mean that in case of war they would fight an oil-starved war. Conversely, denial of these sources to the USSR would force her to fight an oil-starved war. However, due to Russia's geographic position, great land mass, and superior manpower potential, any lack of oil limiting air action by the United States and her allies or hampering their transportation ability or their war production would be of great advantage to the USSR. It is therefore to the strategic interest of the United States to keep Soviet influence and Soviet armed forces removed as far as possible from oil resources in Iran, Iraq, and the Near and Middle East.[57]

By the fall of 1946, however, increasing American involvement in the Palestine question seemed to present a potential threat to the security of American interests and influence throughout the Middle East. Troubled by Truman's support for increased immigration to Palestine and his official endorsement of a Jewish homeland, State Department and military officials continued to point out the dangers of American support for any plan to partition Palestine. Not only would the creation of an independent Jewish homeland lead to chronic instability in the area, they argued, but also it would directly strengthen Soviet influence among the Arabs. In May 1946, Bedell Smith, ambassador in Moscow, informed the department that once the United States adopted an official pro-Zionist policy the Soviets would exploit the Palestine issue fully—particularly to capitalize on Arab dissatisfaction and to "seize every opportunity to expand Soviet influence in the Near East."[58] Writing to SWNCC regarding the Anglo-American Committee of Inquiry's recent report on Palestine, the JCS reached similar conclusions. Any attempt to implement the report by force might prejudice British and American interests throughout the Middle East. The Soviet Union might replace Allied influence and power in an area in which the United States has a "vital security interest."[59] Finally, in a memorandum to Acheson in October, Henderson warned of the consequences of American support for the establishment of a Jewish state in Palestine: "Vigorous advocacy of this extreme program will cause a serious deterioration in our over-all relations with the British and with the Arab and Moslem World. . . . Already the almost childlike confidence which these people have hitherto displayed toward the United States," Henderson concluded, "is giving way to suspicion and dislike, a development which may lead the Arab and Moslem World to look elsewhere than toward the West for support."[60]

This belief, that the Palestine problem threatened American interests and influence throughout the Middle East, caused the Department of State particular concern about the development of American-Saudi relations. Since the 1930s Ibn Saud had expressed his opposition to American support for Zionist activities. Now in light of Roosevelt's pledge at Great Bitter Lake and Truman's personal support for Jewish immigration and a homeland, Saudi protests became more frequent and decidedly less friendly in tone. The harshest words and threats, however, rarely came directly from Ibn Saud, but through the king's second son and foreign minister, Amir Faisal. Although there is little doubt that Faisal himself was bitterly opposed to American policy on Palestine, Ibn Saud, in an effort to maintain complete cordiality with an American president, used his son to air his views. "I personally still hope that your Govt," Faisal remarked to Eddy, "will not sacrifice the good will and the considerable investment of the American people in the Middle East in favor of Zionism. Surely the mutual best interests in this area of 140,000,000 Americans and of 45,000,000 Arabs will prevail against the special pleading of almost 5,000,000 Jewish lobbyists. It is precisely America's total interest in the Middle East that would be sacrificed." [61]

Although NEA's officers both in Washington and in the field still believed that Ibn Saud drew a "clear distinction" between official American policy on Palestine and his relations with the oil companies, no one could be certain that the king's profound hatred of Zionism or pressure from his Arab brothers would not ultimately lead him to take action against the ARAMCO concession. It is still very much an "open question," Parker T. Hart, American vice-consul at Dhahran, informed the department, whether Ibn Saud might eventually act against American oil interests. [62]

It was clear to most department officials, however, that Ibn Saud planned no immediate action. Increasing oil royalties and the king's fear of Soviet influence in the area indicated that he would exercise "the greatest possible degree of moderation" in determining Arab policy toward the United States. It was doubtful, J. Rives Childs informed the department in January 1947, that "any" course the United States pursued regarding Palestine would result in cancellation of the ARAMCO concession. A pro-Zionist American policy, however, might directly weaken the king's influence in the Arab world and strengthen the extremist elements. "We might find that in [the] end," Childs concluded, "we would have compromised our influence among the Arab masses and undermined [the] strength of our best friend, [the] Saudi family." [63]

By early 1947, government officials were becoming increasingly concerned about the security of American and British interests in the eastern Mediterranean and Middle East. Many of the strategic concerns of the war years, which had temporarily subsided after the defeat of Germany and Japan, had now reemerged in the cold war atmosphere of the postwar period. The increasing preoccupation with national security, perhaps the most fundamental theme of American foreign policy in the postwar period, was reflected in the State Department's attitude toward the oil companies' new joint ventures and toward the problem of Palestine. In both cases State Department and military planners continued to emphasize the importance of strengthening American oil interests in the area and maintaining American prestige within the Arab world. Implicit in each situation and indeed in the entire issue of national security was the now vital importance of the Middle Eastern area and its place in a hot or cold war with the Soviets. "As to the importance of a stable Middle East, friendly to the Western Powers," the JCS observed, "it is obvious that this area is the buffer between Russia and the British Mediterranean life line. If the peoples of the Middle East turn to Russia, this would have the same impact in many respects as would military conquest on this area by the Soviets." [64]

The strategic importance of the Middle East inevitably focused attention on the area's petroleum. Certainly, Middle Eastern oil was not the only American concern in the area. In the event the Soviet Union penetrated into the Persian Gulf or succeeded in establishing its influence in Iran or Iraq, the security of American-controlled oil reserves would become entirely academic. Continued access to Middle Eastern oil, particularly Saudi oil, was the most visible and tangible American interest. With known reserves at least equal to those of the United States, and unproven estimates of several hundred billion barrels, the oil constituted a prize of enormous strategic and political potential. Determined to redefine the American postwar strategic interest in the Middle East and to highlight the importance of the area, officials at all levels began to use Arabian oil as a common reference point in their presentations. In short, Saudi Arabian oil—the all-American enterprise—offered both a convenient and impressive foundation on which officials could begin to build a more active American role in Middle Eastern affairs. Although the postwar advantages of Middle Eastern crude were yet unproven, State Department and military officials continued to urge the administration to protect a potentially valuable interest. Warning of the possible dangers of American involvement in the Palestine question, a JCS memorandum reflected the renewed interest in Middle Eastern petroleum: "For very serious consideration from a military point of view is control of the oil of the Middle East. This is probably the one large undeveloped reserve in a world which may come to the limits of its oil resources within this generation without having developed any substitute. A great part of our military strength, as well as our standard of living, is based on oil."[65]

CHAPTER 7
PALESTINE AND PIPELINE:
SAUDI ARABIAN OIL AND
COLD WAR, 1947–1948

DURING the immediate postwar years, the Americans continued their efforts to secure their interest in the oil of Saudi Arabia and the Persian Gulf. There was little need, however, to pursue the stopgap aid programs which had characterized the war years. The two problems which had dogged officials during the war— Ibn Saud's lack of money and Britain's influence with the king—now seemed to have dissipated or become less pressing. By 1946, Saudi crude production, while still undeveloped, exceeded 164,000 b.p.d., reportedly adding $20,000,000 in royalties to the king's coffers.[1] Similarly, greater Anglo-American cooperation throughout the Middle East had quieted any lingering concerns about British intentions toward the ARAMCO concession. "In the economic field, British oil interests are so extensive and the possibilities for the free development of U.S. oil interests are so extensive," a State Department memorandum noted in 1947, "that there is little logical basis for political conflict with the British in the development of oil in these Arab lands."[2] In fact by November 1947, after a series of talks at the Pentagon, British and American representatives had even pledged to support their mutual interests in Saudi Arabia.[3] For the most part, postwar petroleum policy focused on the development of facilities to market Saudi Arabian crude and on the maintenance of American influence and prestige with Ibn Saud.

The postwar years, as mentioned earlier, soon revealed new and more dangerous challenges. The emergence of the Soviet Union as a world power raised new fears of Russian expansion into the eastern Mediterranean and Middle East. Similarly, the United States' increasing involvement in the Palestine question aroused concern about the security of American petroleum interests throughout the area. Although neither Soviet activities nor the Palestine problem presented any immediate threat to American petroleum reserves, officials were clearly uneasy about the future. Writing to Loy Henderson in February 1947, Acheson predicted that the coming year was likely to be "a bad year in Palestine and the Middle East, with increasing violence and grave danger to our interests in that area."[4]

Although the war had introduced the Americans to the strategic importance of Middle Eastern oil, air bases, and communications facilities, the emerging cold war fundamentally altered their attitudes and policies toward the area. In the year following the defeat of Japan, Soviet policy toward the Balkans and Eastern Europe and Moscow's pressure on Turkey and Iran challenged the Truman administration to reassess its view of Russian intentions. "We have here a political force," George Kennan wrote from Moscow in a celebrated telegram, "committed fanatically to the belief that with [the] US there can be no permanent modus vivendi, that it is desirable and necessary that the internal harmony of our society be disrupted . . . if Soviet power is to be secure."[5] Soviet delay in withdrawing troops from Iran and the administration's apparent desire to "get tough with the Russians" only hardened Washington's view of Moscow. By the summer of 1946, government officials, convinced that Soviet policy was motivated more by ideology than security, were no longer prepared to accommodate an "ally" whose policy appeared to rest on a course of world conquest (see also pp. 166–69). "The ultimate objective of the Soviet Union," the Joint Chief of Staff bluntly informed Clark Clifford in July, "is to dominate the world through Communist party organizations whose first loyalty is to the Comintern."[6]

Although the Soviet Union, shattered by four years of war, was in no position to launch a determined campaign of world conquest, Moscow's presence in Iran and pressure on Turkey and the Bosporus and Dardanelles convinced the Americans that the Russians might indeed be softening the area for an eventual push southward. In view of the Soviet Union's vast land mass and superior manpower potential, military planners were already concerned that Soviet penetration of Turkey and Iran might expose the entire Middle East to attack. In the event of Soviet-initiated hostilities, Chester Nimitz cautioned Forrestal, the Near and Middle East were likely to become the "initial focus of the infection."[7] To old cold warriors like Henderson and newer converts like Forrestal, Moscow's probing represented only the latest phase of an historic quest for warm water—a quest which might even carry the Soviets to the shores of the Persian Gulf. The Soviets, to be sure, a State Department memorandum suggested, had not yet revealed any "direct interest" in the area, yet access to the Persian Gulf was one of Moscow's "unexpressed objectives."[8]

The general uneasiness over Soviet intentions was heightened by the prospect of British troop withdrawals from the eastern Mediterranean—a development the State Department had anticipated since the fall of 1946. Suffering from severe economic dislocation and under increasing domestic political pressure to reduce commitments in the area, Britain might not be able to support its own position indefinitely, let alone protect the interests of its allies. Although British troops in Greece were never intended to withstand a determined Soviet attack, they offered considerable evidence of the West's determination to resist external aggression. Moreover, the State Department's Near Eastern experts argued that the stability of Greece, already weakened by a shattered economy, was being gradually undermined by a "well-organized and armed Communist-dominated minority" backed by Moscow and her satellites. Sudden withdrawal might not only weaken Britain's influence in Greece, but ultimately undermine Western influence throughout the eastern Mediterranean and Middle East.[9]

By early 1947, events in the eastern Mediterranean area seemed to confirm American fears. In February, Great Britain formally notified the Department of State that it could no longer carry the burden of economic and military support for Greece and Turkey.[10] To the department's policy planners, the announcement offered an excellent opportunity to alert the American public to the dangers of communism and to the importance of defining a policy based on containment. So too Britain's withdrawal seemed to leave Washington with few options. Either the government must accept the responsibility to be abandoned by Britain, or as Henderson warned, "face the consequences of a widespread collapse of resistance to Soviet pressure throughout the Near and Middle East and large parts of Western Europe not yet under Soviet domination."[11] Similarly, department officials sensed that withdrawal from Greece and Turkey were only part of the larger problem resulting from a "change in Great Britain's strength." Study should be given, Acheson wrote to Patterson in early March, to other situations which might require "analogous financial, technical and military aid on our part."[12]

In the hectic weeks following Britain's announcement, the State Department's special committees hammered out the framework of a policy based on "the support [of] free peoples who are attempting to resist subjugation from armed minorities or from outside forces."[13] The language of the Truman Doctrine seemed to give policymakers a mandate to check the spread of communism on a global scale, yet State Department planners focused immediate attention on Greece and Turkey.[14] Not only were these areas, a SWNCC committee noted, "directly threatened" by "Soviet-Communist infiltration," but also they held the key to the security of Anglo-American interests throughout the Middle East. "Soviet-Communist domination of Greece," the committee concluded, "would threaten the stability of the entire Near Eastern area and would endanger American strategic and economic interests in that area."[15]

Although containment soon emerged as the cornerstone of American policy in the eastern Mediterranean and Middle East, policymakers were becoming increasingly aware of the importance of maintaining Western influence in areas not immediately threatened by "Soviet-Communist infiltration." Countries like Iraq and Saudi Arabia possessed vast petroleum reserves and refining facilities, and contained air and communications links vital to Allied planning in the event of conflict with the Soviets. Moreover, much of the Near and Middle East, the Joint Chiefs noted, offered possibilities for "direct contact with our ideological enemies." In view of the increasing strategic importance of the entire area, the JCS repeatedly cautioned against "orienting" the peoples of the Middle East away from the Western powers.[16]

Increasing American involvement in the Palestine question, however, seemed to undermine American influence throughout the area. To those State Department and military planners who were determined to shape a new consensus regarding the strategic importance of the Middle East, American support for a Jewish homeland was an error of catastrophic proportion. Washington's identification with Zionist objectives, the Arab hands argued, would arouse the undying opposition of the Arab and Muslim world. Equally dangerous, instability in Palestine might make the area more vulnerable to Soviet influence. By 1947, the Palestine problem was becoming increasingly more complex. In February, unable to find a compromise plan acceptable to both Jews and Arabs, Great Britain announced its intention to return the mandate to the United Nations. The situation seemed particularly troublesome to the United States. With the focus of the Palestine question shifting to the UN it was more than likely that the Americans would be called upon to play a major role in the resolution of the problem. In short, the United States might soon be forced to make or support a decision which could adversely affect its influence and interests throughout the Middle East.[17]

The increasing importance of the Middle East and its new role in cold war strategy inevitably aroused official interest in the oil of Saudi Arabia and the Persian Gulf. In view of the indispensability of petroleum to national security and the vast size of Persian Gulf reserves, Middle Eastern oil quickly emerged as one of the more visible elements in strategic planning. One of the six "specific objectives" which might "enhance" the national security of the United States, a JCS committee concluded, was the continued availability of Middle Eastern oil.[18] "In general, the War Department feels," Kenneth C. Royall, secretary of war, noted, "that . . . the use of mid-east oil to reduce exports from the U.S. and to augment our domestic supply should be encouraged within the limits necessary to prevent an undue strain upon our domestic production."[19]

Military planners were well aware of the risks of utilizing Middle Eastern oil. "Petroleum from the Middle East," the ANPB noted, "could make a major contribution toward fulfilling the U.S. requirements in event of a war emergency if that oil were available."[20] In view of the Soviet Union's proximity to the oil fields of Iran and Iraq and the uncertainties of tanker and pipeline transport, unrestricted access to the oil was problematic. To some, Persian Gulf oil was even a liability. In the event of conflict with the Soviets, the army's *Intelligence Review* noted, "Middle East oil would be of negligible if not negative strategic value to the United States."[21] From a strictly strategic point of view, the problem confronting military planners was clear. Although the value of Middle Eastern oil might prove critical in a wartime situation, it simply could not be guaranteed as a source of oil for campaign operations or resupply.

Although the military advantages of Middle Eastern oil were yet undetermined, its economic potential emerged as an important element in postwar planning. Nowhere was this fact more apparent than in plans for the reconstruction of the European economy. With Europe facing the prospect of severe coal shortages, postwar planners sought to encourage the conversion from coal to oil.[22] Coal was expected to remain the mainstay of Europe's energy base for some time, yet petroleum offered a vital source of fuel which might prove "essential" to the complete recovery of European industrial and transportation sectors.[23] By 1951, planners estimated that total petroleum requirements for participating Marshall Plan countries would exceed 76,760,000 metric tons—consumption in 1938 had totaled 36,224,000 tons.[24] Writing to Clifford in September 1947, C. H. Bonesteel, special assistant to the under secretary of state, observed: "This, together with the increasing demands for petroleum products resulting from the mechanization of agriculture, the expansion of industry and the growth of road transport presents a formidable problem to all participating countries, for this whole area has no natural resources of oil."[25]

The petroleum resources of the Middle East seemed to offer a natural source of supply for the European Recovery Program (ERP). Caribbean crude, to be sure, might be the main source for European requirements during the early years of the ERP. Still, the importance of conserving Western Hemisphere reserves and the costs of shipping Venezuelan crude indicated that exports to the Middle East from the Caribbean area would decrease rapidly. Moreover, rising oil consumption in the United States seemed to suggest that there would be little surplus crude available for export. "The European Recovery Program," Oscar Chapman, acting secretary of the interior, observed, "was most carefully designed to relieve the present drain on American petroleum supplies and to result in most of Europe's requirements being met from the Middle East." [26]

Postwar trends were dramatically clear. In 1946, the Western Hemisphere had supplied 77 percent of Europe's petroleum needs, with the Middle East accounting for the balance. By 1951, Middle Eastern sources were expected to supply over 80 percent of European needs. Although Europe's refining capacity would have to be increased to handle the anticipated flow of crude, the relationship between Middle Eastern oil and European markets was already unmistakable. "Should Middle East oil not be available on the basis as now estimated," Robert Eakens concluded, "a full review of the energy requirements under the program would be required." [27]

Despite its potential importance for European recovery, Arabian oil was not the overriding American concern in the Middle East. For the most part, oil interests were shadowed by Washington's preoccupation with containment. In the event the Soviet Union succeeded in weakening the British position in the eastern Mediterranean, penetrating the northern tier, or establishing its own influence in the Persian Gulf, access to Middle Eastern oil reserves would become entirely academic. Similarly, the security of American oil interests, particularly in Saudi Arabia, seemed inextricably linked to maintaining the United States' prestige and influence in the Arab world—a task which was becoming increasingly more difficult in view of American policy on Palestine. Still, the oil of Saudi Arabia and the Middle East had emerged as a prominent American interest in its own right. With proved reserves of at least 27,000,000,000 barrels and unproven estimates of billions more, Middle Eastern oil represented a tangible interest of enormous potential. [28]

Even more important, at a time when American officials were nervously weighing the prospects and pitfalls of a more active role in Middle Eastern affairs, the American stake in Arabian oil offered both continuity with past policy and direction for the future. Faced with the uncertainty of Soviet intentions, the possibility of British withdrawal from Palestine, and the unpredictability of a president who seemed committed to supporting Zionist objectives, State Department and military officials sought to define an American policy more attuned to what they believed to be the strategic realities of the postwar world. Convinced of the importance of the Middle East, these officials searched for a way to highlight their concerns. By 1947 Arabian oil seemed to provide just such an opportunity—offering both the means and motivation to reshape American attitudes and policies toward the Middle East.

The American approach to Saudi oil was based on two general considerations. First, eager to conserve domestic reserves and to develop Arabian crude as an alternative source of energy for European recovery, officials sought to facilitate the construction of ARAMCO's trans-Arabian pipeline (TAPLINE). Second, officials, particularly in the Department of State, urged the administration to consider the consequences of American support for the partition of Palestine and the establishment of a Jewish state. Not only might a pro-Zionist policy weaken American influence in Saudi Arabia, but also it might strengthen the Soviet position in the Arab world. Although by 1947 sanctions against the ARAMCO concession seemed remote and Soviet penetration into the Persian Gulf even less likely, officials once again began to conjure up "worst case" scenarios of the war years. By late 1947, Palestine and pipeline had begun to merge in a nightmarish vision of the future. In the event Palestine exploded into full-scale war between Arabs and Jews, TAPLINE and European recovery, if not the entire American position in the Arab world, might be threatened.

By 1947, substantial increases in postwar consumption and anticipated requirements of the ERP focused attention on the development of Middle Eastern crude.[29] Officials were particularly concerned about the progress of ARAMCO's trans-Arabian pipeline. Although TAPLINE was a company project, the pipeline appeared to offer the United States strategic and economic advantages. Not only would the successful completion of ARAMCO's 300,000 b.p.d. pipeline offer Europe a valuable source of energy, but also it would help to conserve the more strategically vital reserves of the Western Hemisphere. By the summer of 1947, however, the ARAMCO project faced serious obstacles. Although the company had successfully concluded an agreement with Saudi Arabia in July, Syria proved to be a much tougher negotiator, demanding high transit fees and a pipeline terminus on the Syrian coast.[30] Moreover, in view of export controls on steel, the Commerce Department had postponed its decision to grant ARAMCO export licenses for steel pipe and tubing.[31]

Eager to begin construction of the Saudi section of the line before winter, the company presented its case to the Department of State. Although ARAMCO had altered its presentation to fit the changing circumstances of 1947, company strategy had not really changed since Davies and Rodgers had descended upon Washington looking for lend-lease aid. Determined to gain the department's assistance in securing steel pipe for TAPLINE, the oilmen set out to convince officials that the interests of their companies were closely aligned with if not identical to American strategic objectives in the Middle East. It was neither a bold nor innovative strategy, yet it was designed to fit the arguments and assumptions of officials already attuned to the problems of cold war and national security. By facilitating the development of Saudi crude, the oilmen argued with considerable justification, the United States might not only bring economic prosperity to Europe but also simultaneously conserve its own reserves. Similarly, the influx of American capital and technology would help to stabilize the Middle East as well as strengthen it against Soviet influence. The oil companies could neither directly control policy nor dominate policymakers, but they could attempt to shape and influence the climate in which decisions were made.

Meeting with department officials in late July, ARAMCO representatives, led by the articulate, British-born company Vice-President James Terry Duce, laid down their case for export licenses for steel pipe and tubing. Use of steel for TAPLINE, Duce began, is "far superior" to any conceivable use within the United States. Not only had domestic productive capacity reached its maximum efficient rate of production, but given increasing demand for petroleum products, the Middle East offered the only large-scale source of supply. Finally, a pipeline, Duce concluded, would reduce the need for ocean tankers in a period of anticipated shortage.[32]

Duce's arguments were well tailored to fit the department's thinking and carefully designed to coincide with top-level strategic and economic planning. In a follow-up presentation in early August, Duce noted that by 1949 European fuel oil and gasoline requirements might total 800,000 b.p.d. If TAPLINE were completed, Arabian crude could supply Europe with 300,000 b.p.d. reducing considerably the amount of oil exported from the United States and the Caribbean. As a result of the "Truman Plan," Duce continued, the petroleum requirements of the armed forces of Greece and Turkey might have to be met from the Middle East, particularly since Romanian oil had fallen into Russian hands. Finally, the oilman assured officials that TAPLINE "fits in very well . . . with the Marshall Plan and other plans for the rehabilitation of European manufacturing establishments."[33]

State Department Arab experts and petroleum specialists seemed impressed by Duce's arguments. In anticipation of the Commerce Department's intention to review the granting of export licenses in September, department officials began to mobilize support. In late August, NE's officers presented a memorandum to Loy Henderson outlining the political importance of the TAPLINE project. Failure to grant ARAMCO licenses, the memorandum noted, might be "misinterpreted" by the Arabs, Greece, and Turkey as a sign of an American retreat to an "isolationist foreign policy." Together with an adverse American policy on Palestine, NE concluded, such a failure "might well provoke the Arab League into implementing the decisions . . . to boycott all American enterprises." Moreover, completion of TAPLINE might not only "directly" aid the Marshall Plan, but "large quantities of oil should facilitate the increased industrialization of the Near East which would thereby support the Truman Plan by strengthening the economies of these countries and thus rendering them less vulnerable to totalitarianism, of whatever form."[34] Early in September, the department's petroleum experts added their support for the project. Echoing ARAMCO's arguments sometimes word for word, Malvin Hoffman of the Petroleum Division (PED) observed that TAPLINE would indeed conserve tankers as well as domestic reserves.[35]

Support for TAPLINE was not confined to lower-level officials in the Department of State. By the fall of 1947, the importance of conserving domestic oil and developing foreign sources had begun to attract the attention of other government agencies. Already concerned about possible shortages in its fuel oil stocks, the navy urged the expansion of Persian Gulf output. Writing to the JCS, the ANPB noted that TAPLINE's 300,000 b.p.d. capacity might reduce the demand from Western Hemisphere sources by 50 percent.[36] Similarly, Max Ball of the Department of Interior's Oil and Gas Division, a reluctant advocate of exporting steel, informed Secretary of the Interior Julius Krug that "by 1951, it is believed that construction of TAPLINE will decrease the demand on U.S. oil more than the same amount of steel would increase U.S. oil supplies."[37] Finally, having been approached by W. S. S. Rodgers, ARAMCO's director and board chairman of the Texas Company, to "do a little more to get that pipe," Secretary of Defense Forrestal, perhaps the government's leading champion of Arabian oil, assured the oilman that he had already spoken with Secretary of Commerce Averell Harriman, and would "look into the matter further."[38]

Increasing domestic demand and the continuing shortage of tankers highlighted the advantages of constructing the pipeline. Officials were particularly aware of the transportation problem. By 1949, it was estimated that the demand for tankers might exceed availability by 457 ships. Failure to construct TAPLINE or build additional tankers, Max Ball noted, might result in a "serious shortage" of petroleum.[39] Early in September, upon the recommendation of NEA and ITP, Robert Lovett, under secretary of state, advised the Commerce Department that the construction of TAPLINE was in the "national interest." Lovett concluded:

> As Middle East oil becomes increasingly available, the general economy of the Near and Middle East areas can be expected to rise and thus render them less vulnerable to outside pressures. Delay in the construction of the line might result in serious economic and political repercussions in the area, with an extremely adverse effect upon the United States' position there. Furthermore, additional Middle East oil will be needed for the reconstruction of the European countries that are cooperating with the United States in the implementation of the Marshall Plan.[40]

Aware of the increasing interest in TAPLINE, the Commerce Department called a preliminary meeting attended by more than a dozen government agencies, among them the Departments of State, Interior, and Defense. According to State Department sources, the Commerce Department was in favor of granting the export licenses and had scheduled the meeting for the purpose of "lining up support." Although the Agriculture Department abstained from voting and the Offices of International Trade and Domestic Transport opposed the licenses, it was clear, Richard Sanger of NEA later noted, that the meeting was "overwhelmingly in favor" of ARAMCO's request.[41] Secretary of Commerce Harriman did not attend but was believed to favor the project. It was agreed that the matter would now be referred to the Commerce Department's special advisory committee for final consideration.[42]

Although TAPLINE had considerable support among a number of government agencies, some officials doubted the importance of granting ARAMCO's request. Acutely aware of domestic shortages of steel, the Office of Defense Transport wondered whether the steel might be more wisely used for domestic purposes—in farm machinery and railway cars. The Interior Department had supported the licenses but was seriously concerned about the effects of steel shortages on domestic oil producers.[43] Moreover, wary of the effects of steel exports on American industry, the Senate Special Committee on Small Business was likely to oppose large shipments abroad.

The State Department was aware that the case for TAPLINE was not entirely convincing. In an effort to demonstrate the advantages of the project, the department sought to highlight its political importance. At the advisory committee meeting, the department's officers pointed to TAPLINE's role in the stability of the Middle East and its relationship to Greece and Turkey and other countries on the "periphery of the Soviet sphere of influence."[44] Finally, writing to Lovett, Henderson noted that political factors might be "decisive" in the issuance of ARAMCO's licenses. Delay in constructing TAPLINE, Henderson concluded, would not only seriously strain the American position in Saudi Arabia, but also might be construed by the Arabs as a part of "our 'unfriendly' Palestine policy."[45]

By the end of September, ARAMCO's request for export licenses had received Cabinet and final Commerce Department approval. Although the amount of steel requested by the company had been cut, it was clear that TAPLINE had wide support among administration officials. Writing to Secretary of State Marshall in support of the project, Paul Nitze noted that, as a net importer of oil, the United States must develop foreign petroleum. Moreover, Middle Eastern oil must be developed to meet world demand, particularly for the rehabilitation of Western Europe.[46] "Until there were indications of new fields of substantial magnitude in the Western Hemisphere," Forrestal informed the Senate Committee on Small Business, "I said pipe for the Arabian pipeline should have precedence over pipe for similar projects in this country."[47] Similarly, Lovett noted that no fields in South America can offer "the same possibility of prompt and sizeable development as do the fields of Saudi Arabia."[48]

Political considerations also influenced official thinking. State Department support for TAPLINE was clearly influenced by the recent American commitment in Greece and Turkey, the Marshall Plan, and by the new importance of the Middle East in cold war planning. Determined to strengthen the entire area against communist propaganda and influence, the department saw the advantages of exporting American capital and expertise. Moreover, TAPLINE might make a substantial contribution to the stability and economic prosperity of Western Europe and simultaneously strengthen the position of American companies operating in the Middle East. Ever attuned to the political climate in Washington, ARAMCO quickly saw which way the wind was blowing. Writing to Harriman in support of the company's requests, James Terry Duce noted that the Russians were eager to expand their influence in the Middle East and had already begun to send instructions to their "supporters" in Saudi Arabia. The United States, Duce warned, should not permit the oil of the area to fall into Russian hands.[49]

Likewise, the pipeline seemed to provide a means of regaining any American influence and prestige which might be lost as a result of the Palestine problem. The consideration of ARAMCO's request for export licenses coincided with the publication of the United Nations Special Committee on Palestine (UNSCOP) report recommending partition. Disturbed by the implications of the report and aware that the United States might be compelled to support its conclusions, department officials apparently saw TAPLINE as a way of countering the negative effects of the administration's Palestine policy. In this respect, the companies were only especially valuable allies, offering "unofficial" assistance and support for the American position in Saudi Arabia at a time when the Saudis were particularly upset by "official" United States policy. The Arab world, Henderson wrote to Lovett recommending TAPLINE, was already "exercised" over the trend of American actions. "A beneficent economic policy in the Near East," he concluded, "is one of the few means we have of offsetting, in some degree, the effects of our Palestine policy."[50]

By the fall of 1947, the Palestine question was rapidly emerging as a crucial consideration in the development of American policy toward the Middle East. The United States had no legal or historical responsibility for the disposition of the Palestine mandate, yet both the Roosevelt and Truman administrations had become intimately involved in the fate of the "much too Promised Land." Responding to a curious mixture of humanitarian concern and domestic political considerations, the Truman White House had taken up the issues of Jewish immigration and homeland.[51] Despite the opposition of State Department and British officials, between 1945 and 1947 Truman had expressed support for increased Jewish immigration to Palestine and for the idea of a Jewish homeland. The president's policy, to be sure, was not entirely his own. Previous congressional resolutions and party platforms together with current public opinion seemed to commit policymakers to support the idea of a Jewish homeland. Although Truman was personally moved by the horrors of the Nazi genocide and eager to alleviate the suffering of the survivors, he had no illusions about the constraints and pitfalls of the Palestine problem. In a memorandum to David Niles in May 1947, the president, already annoyed by Zionist lobbying, such as that by Rabbi Abba Hillel Silver, observed: "We could have settled this Palestine thing if U.S. politics had been kept out of it. Terror and Silver are the contributing causes of some, if not all, of our troubles. I surely wish God almighty would give the Children of Israel an Isaiah, the Christians a St. Paul and the sons of Ishmael a peep at the Golden Rule. Maybe He will decide to do that."[52]

Truman's homespun advice, however, provided little comfort to State Department officials committed to protecting the national interest in the Middle East. To the Arab hands and cold warriors, the "official" association with political Zionism seemed nothing short of a "major blunder in statesmanship." Not only would the creation of a Jewish state in Palestine jeopardize the stability of the Middle East, William Yale of NE noted, it "might even threaten world security." Similarly, William Eddy, passionately anti-Zionist, concluded that implementation of the UNSCOP plan for partition is an endorsement of a "theocratic sovereign state characteristic of the Dark Ages."[53]

American support for the partition plan also seemed damaging to the United States' position in the Arab World. Although the State Department was uneasy over the security of American petroleum interests in the area, officials were far more concerned about increasing Soviet interest in the Palestine question. Moscow's preferred solution, Ambassador Bedell Smith informed the department in August, was a binational state which would be predominantly Arab. Such a state, the Soviets believed, would lead to weakness, internal conflict, and eventual communist penetration and party control.[54] Bill Eddy could not have agreed more. American support for partition, he warned, might force the Arab League, "for the sake of survival," to align itself with the Russians.[55]

Fear of partition and its relation to cold war strategy was not confined to the department's Arab experts. Speaking to the United States Delegation to the United Nations in September, Secretary of State Marshall noted that: "Adoption of the majority report . . . would mean very violent Arab reaction. To be consistent with the integrity of its position, the United States should avoid actively arousing the Arabs and precipitating their 'rapprochement' with the Soviet Union in the first week or ten days of the General Assembly."[56] During a luncheon meeting of the Cabinet in late September, Forrestal also lobbied for a more realistic handling of the Palestine issue. It was important, the secretary of defense informed Truman, to "lift the Jewish-Palestine question out of politics and to be more aware of the security needs of the United States."[57]

Despite the State Department's objections to partition and the diplomats' determination to avoid committing the United States to its defense, officials had little choice but to support UNSCOP's majority report. Already publicly committed to the support of a Jewish homeland and aware that failure to endorse the recommendations of an established United Nations committee might damage the credibility of the organization, Truman overrode the objections of his State Department. On 11 October, Herschel V. Johnson, United States deputy representative on the UN Security Council, announced that the United States supported the "basic principles" of the majority report.[58]

Although the State Department had no alternative but to support partition publicly, officials were quick to register their opposition in private. In late September, Loy Henderson submitted a memorandum to Marshall which signaled the opening round in the State Department's campaign to force revision of the partition plan. Henderson was not alone in his opposition. The views expressed in this memorandum, Henderson began, "are also those of nearly every member of the Foreign Service or of the Department who has worked to any appreciable extent on Near Eastern problems." Henderson's presentation rested squarely on the importance of maintaining stability in the Middle East and its relation to American strategic interests. The attitude which the United States assumed toward the Palestine problem, Henderson continued, "may greatly influence the extent of success or of failure of some of our efforts to promote world stability and to prevent further Soviet penetration into important areas free as yet from Soviet domination." Specifically, advocacy of partition "would be certain to undermine our relations with the Arab, and to a lesser extent with the Moslem world." The United States not only needed "Arab cooperation" in maintaining the British presence as a "stabilizing power" in the eastern Mediterranean, Henderson concluded, but also in preventing "violent Arab nationalists uprisings" against the French in North Africa.[59]

Middle Eastern oil was also a part though not the focus of Henderson's presentation. During the next few years, he noted, the United States would rely "heavily" on the "resources" of the area not only for its own use but for the reconstruction of Europe. In a draft of the memorandum forwarded to Dean Rusk, director of the Office of Special Political Affairs, Henderson emphasized the importance of safeguarding the American stake in Persian Gulf oil:

> We shall need Arab friendship if we are to retain our petroleum position in the Arab world. During the next few years we are planning to obtain huge quantities of oil from Iraq, Bahrein, Kuweit and Saudi Arabia, not only for our use but for the recon-

struction of Europe. Furthermore we are intending to transport oil from Persia, Iraq, and Saudi Arabia across a number of Arab countries by pipelines to Mediterranean ports. Already, partly as a result of our policies regarding Palestine the attitude of Saudi Arabia towards the United States has changed sharply and its demands on the oil companies are becoming more and more truculent and extravagant.

Finally, Henderson noted that, although the Arabs "have in general no use for communism," the establishment of a Jewish State in Palestine might force them "to consider the United States as their foremost enemy and enter into at least temporary cooperation with the Soviet Union against us just as we cooperated with the Russians during the war years against common enemies."[60]

The State Department was not the only agency concerned about the danger of the proposed partition plan. Military planners had also repeatedly cautioned against jeopardizing American influence in the Middle East. If, as a result of American support for partition, the peoples of the area turned to the Soviet Union, the Joint Chiefs informed the secretary of defense in October, it would have the "same impact in many respects" as military conquest of the Middle East by the Russians. It was Middle Eastern petroleum, however, which provided the central focus of JCS concern. "The most serious of all possible consequences, from a military point of view," the JCS noted, "is that implementation of a decision to partition Palestine would gravely prejudice access by the United States to the oil of Iran, Iraq and Saudi Arabia." In the event of war, the JCS continued, the loss of Iraqi and Saudi sources would force the United States to fight "an oil-starved war." "Conversely, denial of these sources to our most probable opponent, . . . the USSR, would force her to fight an oil-starved war." It is therefore of "great strategic importance," the Joint Chiefs concluded, that the United States maintain the "goodwill" of the Arab and Moslem states.[61]

Although there was little evidence that United States' interests were immediately threatened by American endorsement of UNSCOP's majority report, officials nervously anticipated the General Assembly's upcoming vote on partition. Reports from Saudi Arabia indicated that while Ibn Saud might not take "economic reprisals" against American oil interests, relations with Riyadh had "deteriorated." According to reports from Jidda, the Saudi deputy foreign minister had indicated that if that United States wished to maintain the "unquestioned friendship" of Saudi Arabia, it must alter its position on Palestine.[62] Simi-

larly, in a personal letter to Truman, Ibn Saud warned that United
States support for partition would "without doubt" result in a "death-
blow" to American interests in Arab countries.[63] Reports from Damascus were equally gloomy. In view of American support for partition, it
was likely that the TAPLINE pipeline convention would not be submitted
to the Syrian Parliament for final ratification. According to British
sources, the Iraqis were apparently prepared to sever relations with
Washington.[64] Finally, the political committee of the Arab League had
reportedly already considered the possibility of recommending the
cancellation of all British and American concessions in the Arab
world.[65]

Arab dissatisfaction with American policy inevitably stimulated official concern about Soviet intentions toward Palestine. State Department officials had little doubt that the Soviets would readily exploit
any loss of American or British influence in the area. Moscow's unexpected decision to support partition seemed to indicate a new and
dangerous Soviet strategy. According to Smith, the Kremlin now
believed that the chaos and tension resulting from partition might
"soften up" the area for Soviet penetration.[66] Implementation of partition would not only facilitate British withdrawal, but also would create an environment conducive to covert infiltration by communist
indoctrinated emigrants from Eastern Europe. According to information from Romania, Zionist agents were even collaborating with the
Soviets to facilitate the immigration of communist provocateurs.
Although the department was not inclined to put much faith in these
reports, officials were deeply disturbed by the Soviets' desire to exploit
the partition issue.[67] The possible scenarios seemed ominous. The
United States, Henderson and Rusk informed Marshall in November,
should discourage the implementation of partition by force. Such a
move if supported by the Security Council, might permit the Soviets
to use their own troops, thus "affording an opportunity to the USSR to
infiltrate militarily as well as politically into the Middle East."[68]

The General Assembly's endorsement of partition in November
deepened official concern about the security of American interests
throughout the Middle East. Immediate reaction in the Arab world
seemed to confirm the department's worst fears. In Damascus a "well-
organized" mob of some 2,000 stormed the American legation and tore
down the American flag. Similarly, in Baghdad, the office of the
United States Information Service was attacked.[69] Still, reaction from
the Saudis was considerably milder than some officials had anticipated.
Although Childs warned that "Iraq and fire-eating Arab states may
press for precipitate or violent action," it was clear that Saudi Arabia

sought to avoid being drawn into conflict with the United States.[70] Ibn Saud had assured Childs that his hatred of Zionism was as intense as that of Iraq or Transjordan, yet the king, Childs informed the department, is a "realist" and "recognizes that his immediate economic interests are bound up with the United States." The Americans might hear "alarming noises" over Palestine, a well-informed Saudi official noted, but they should not be interpreted as a basic change in Saudi Arabia's attitude toward the United State.[71] According to H. St. John Philby, a former confidant of the king, Ibn Saud had informed the Iraqis that when they were willing to advance him $300,000,000 for lost oil royalties, he would consider "more attentive plans" for economic warfare against the United States.[72] Finally, in an audience with Childs within a week of the UN vote on partition, Ibn Saud had simply remarked: "Although the other Arab states may bring pressure to bear on me I do not anticipate that a situation will arise whereby I shall be drawn into conflict with friendly western powers over this question."[73]

Saudi reaction seemed reassuring for the present, yet the Arab hands held to the conviction that United States' support for a Jewish state would ultimately undermine American interests and influence. NEA's officers were wholeheartedly convinced that the Arab world would never accept partition and, as the Iraqi Foreign Minister, Fadhil Jamali claimed, "would die in defense of their rights." Any attempt to implement partition by force, Rusk and Henderson had already informed Marshall, would do "irreparable damage" to American relations with the Arabs.[74] Moreover, officials at all levels agreed that any direct American contribution in men, money, or arms which facilitated the establishment of a Jewish state would surely lead to the loss of bases and oil concessions. Already as a result of American support for partition, the American chargé in Damascus informed the department, Syria would not ratify the ARAMCO pipeline convention at the present session of Parliament.[75]

By December most State Department officials involved in Middle Eastern affairs were firmly convinced that partition was an unworkable and dangerous solution. Eager to prevent a war in Palestine that could only jeopardize American interests, the officials anxiously sought alternative solutions. Writing to Henderson, Gordon Merriam boldly proposed that in order to "restore the situation following the recent shambles in New York and in order to forestall disaster to the U.N. and U.S. interests," the department should urge the president to admit publicly that he was satisfied that "undue pressure" had been brought upon United Nations delegates to support partition and that the United States did not feel the United Nations had the right to enforce a political settlement upon Palestine without the "free consent of the majority of both of the Palestinian communities."[76] A more subtle approach, however, had already been initiated by the National Security Council (NSC). Upon NSC recommendation, the State Department was instructed to prepare a study on "priority basis" of partition and its relation to American security interests. By late December despite the lack of coordinated policy, State Department intentions were clear. Among other things, the department's preliminary recommendations to the NSC emphasized the "impossibility" of implementing the partition of Palestine.[77]

Official reaction to partition if not to the entire Palestine question reflected the Americans' increasing awareness of their strategic interests in the Middle East. In this sense, the Palestine problem serves as a kind of barometer to measure State and Defense Department sensitivity on a broad range of strategic concerns—not the least of which was the importance of Saudi Arabian oil. The Americans overestimated the threat of Soviet expansion into Iraq and the Persian Gulf and overreacted to Arab threats against United States' interests. Reports from Jidda indicated that Ibn Saud would not take direct action against the oil concession. In fact, it was clear even after the November vote on partition, that the king would go to great lengths to protect ARAMCO's interests—a fact which the Arab experts conveniently omitted in communications to their superiors. Nonetheless, with rare exception, State Department officials sincerely believed that American endorsement of partition would ultimately jeopardize the United States' interests throughout the Middle East. Cancellation of oil concessions was not likely, yet all-out war in Palestine (a condition the department argued which would inevitably follow attempts to partition the country) would disrupt petroleum development, hinder TAPLINE, and thus interfere with European recovery. Similarly, a United States-supported UN decision to implement partition by force might open up the area to Soviet penetration and even push the reluctant Saudis into more aggressive action.

To the State Department's Arab hands and cold warriors, American policy was an error of catastrophic proportion. At best, officials conceded, endorsement of Zionist objectives was a result of misguided humanitarianism; at worst, it was a product of narrow-minded political concerns. Neither motivation, Henderson and Forrestal argued, should interfere with the protection of the nation's interest in Middle Eastern oil.

Arabian oil was not the dominant element in strategic planning. The importance of securing Saudi oil was encompassed by an even greater strategic priority—containing Soviet influence in the eastern Mediterranean and Middle East. So, too, access to Middle East reserves was far too unpredictable a factor to be relied upon in an emergency situation, let alone in a full-scale war with the Soviets. Still, the advantages of preserving access to the rich wells of al Hasa and the Persian Gulf highlighted the value of maintaining a stable Middle East and a friendly Arab world. By 1948 the State Department frantically searched for allies and arguments in its fight against partition. Arabian oil seemed to provide officials with just such opportunities—a means to demonstrate the risks of supporting the UN decision and a motivation for adopting a policy more attuned to what they believed to be the new strategic realities of the postwar world.

In the new year, 1948, the situation in Palestine continued to deteriorate. The guerrilla war between Jewish and Arab organizations continued to escalate, reprisal by reprisal. The activities of the Haganah, once considered a Jewish defense group, began to resemble the methods of the more violent Irgun Zvai Leumi. Equally disturbing were reports of large-scale infiltration of Arab irregulars from neighboring states. According to Central Intelligence Agency estimates, over 8,000 volunteers, "ununiformed and armed," had entered Palestine from Syria, Lebanon, Iraq, and Transjordan.[78] By February, it was unmistakably clear that the Arabs intended to oppose the establishment of a Jewish state by force. Equally serious was Britain's intention to withdraw its troops in May—a development which threatened to plunge the Holy Land into chaos.

In Washington, State Department and military officials at all levels nervously assessed the impact of partition on American interests. The Palestine situation, Major General Alfred Gruenther of the Joint Staff informed Forrestal in January, "had pretty well 'spiked' any consideration of any military operations in the Middle East and had pretty well disposed of the idea that the United States would continue to have access to the Middle East oil."[79] Robert McClintock of the State Department's Special Political Affairs Division predicted that American participation in enforcing partition might ultimately result in the "undying animosity" of the Arabs and the loss of Middle Eastern oil and airfields. The participation of Russian troops in such enforcement measures, on the other hand, might lead to "Soviet-Communist" military infiltration of the area.[80] Finally, despite Ibn Saud's desire to preserve American-Saudi ties, relations with Saudi Arabia were becoming considerably less cordial. American support of partition, Childs informed the department, has "accentuated King's doubt" as to whether he could find a stable political partner in the United States. Foreign Minister Faisal had even informed Childs that had he exerted the decisive influence on Saudi policy, he would have broken relations with the United States.[81]

Determined to maintain American influence in Saudi Arabia, State Department officials sought to counter the negative effects of official Palestine policy with promises of diplomatic and economic support for Ibn Saud. Prompted by NEA, the department had been more than sympathetic to the king's fears of British-controlled Hashemite ambitions in Saudi Arabia and had repeatedly assured Ibn Saud of the United States' "unqualified" support for his country's territorial integrity and political independence.[82] Equally important, NEA had supported the king's request for larger Export-Import Bank loans and lobbied for funds to upgrade the facilities of the Dhahran airfield. Still, the Palestine question was clouding relations with the king and might even affect specific American interests. The matter of continued tenancy of the Dhahran airfield was a case in point. "If our support Palestine partition were not the excessive incubus it is in all our dealings with SAG," Childs wrote from Jidda, "I would feel very hopeful in being able persuade king to request us to remain at Dhahran after March 1949."[83] Already under pressure from the Iraqis and Jordanians for his tolerance of Washington's Palestine policy, it was inevitable that Ibn Saud would raise the ante on the Dhahran airfield. The United States could count on using the airfield, Fuad Bey Hamza, one of the king's closest advisers, informed Childs in February, if the question of military aid to Saudi Arabia was handled "satisfactorily."[84]

Convinced that American support for partition might not only jeopardize the United States' interests in Saudi Arabia but also throughout the Middle East, the State Department began to advocate a fundamental reconsideration of American support for the plan. In January, the department's Policy Planning Staff (PPS) completed a study of partition and its relation to American "security interests" in the eastern Mediterranean and Middle East. Although the PPS's primary concern focused on the importance of preventing Soviet forces from entering Palestine, the report, which was forwarded to Marshall, also pointed out the value of maintaining access to Middle Eastern oil. United States' support of partition, the PPS argued, might retard the development of Middle Eastern petroleum, thus presenting a "serious threat" to the overall success of the Marshall Plan. The PPS study did not recommend immediate abandonment of partition, yet it did suggest that "when and if" events "conclusively" demonstrated that there was "no reasonable prospect for success" of partition without the use of force, the United States might recommend that the matter be referred back to the UN General Assembly.[85] The thrust of PPS recommendations was clear. Forwarding the report to Lovett, Dean Rusk observed that the study was nothing short of "a reversal of the Palestine policy supported by the United States in the recent General Assembly."[86]

The State Department's approach rapidly gained the support of other high-level policy planners. In February, the staff of the National Security Council circulated a draft paper on Palestine to the Departments of State, Army, Navy, and Air Force. The study, apparently based on much of PPS's groundwork, emphasized the direct relationship between Palestine and American strategic interests. "The United States," the report began, "on the basis of high motives and in consideration of conditions existing at the time," voted to support the partition of Palestine. Although the NSC report conceded the United States could not "without cause" fail to fulfill this "moral obligation," it concluded that the "most impelling cause" for a change in American policy would be "demonstration of the incompatibility of our present position with the security of our own nation."[87]

The NSC draft sought to provide such a demonstration. NSC's strategic assumptions rested squarely on the importance of containing Soviet influence and maintaining access to Middle Eastern oil reserves. Although the report noted that the "greatest threat to the security of the United States and to international peace is the USSR and its aggressive program of Communist expansion," it cautioned against jeopardizing American oil interests. First, the NSC staff believed that "unrestricted access" to Middle Eastern oil was "essential" to the economy of the United States and to the economic recovery of Europe under the ERP. Second, it assumed that in the event of war, the oil and "certain strategic areas" of the Middle East "will figure prominently in the successful prosecution of such a war." Finally, the report added that "a friendly or at least neutral attitude" by the Arab peoples toward the United States is "requisite" to the protection of these interests. American support for partition, the NSC staff concluded, jeopardized the nation's strategic objectives. Not only might it "alienate the Moslem world" but it might provide a "vehicle for Soviet expansion into an area vital to our security interests."[88]

The military members of the NSC staff seemed even more sensitive to the dangers of partition than their State Department colleagues. The representatives of the army, navy, and air force called for an immediate repudiation of partition and proposed that the General Assembly convene to reconsider the Palestine question.[89] The reasons for the military's sensitivity were reflected in a study done by the Joint

Strategic Survey Committee (JSSC) and forwarded to the JCS on the same day the NSC staff presented its report. After reaffirming the "critical strategic importance" of the Near and Middle East, the committee noted that American support for partition had resulted in a "serious deterioration" of American influence in the area. According to CIA reports, the Arabs would fight against "any force, or combination of forces," which attempted to set up a Jewish state. Similarly, any attempt to implement partition using American troops or equipment might also result in the "implacable hatred" of the Arab world. The effects on American interests, particularly petroleum, would be dangerous. "In consequence," the JSSC noted, "access by the United States to the strategic base areas . . . and to the oil of Iran, Iraq and Saudi Arabia would, in all probability, be possible only by force." Because of the "critical importance" of Middle Eastern oil to the future security of the United States, the memorandum concluded, the risk of implementing partition by force was "extremely grave."[90]

By early March, supported by the strategic arguments of NSC and JCS planners, State Department officials intensified their own efforts to find another solution to the Palestine problem. In the place of partition, officials now proposed a temporary United Nations trusteeship. The idea was not new, nor was it intended as a permanent solution, yet it seemed to offer several immediate advantages. Not only might trusteeship offer a salutary step toward restoring American influence in the Arab World, but also it might provide some stability in the wake of Britain's proposed withdrawal.[91] The department's arguments were apparently convincing. On 19 March, with the approval of Secretary Marshall, the United States introduced a resolution in the Security Council calling for a temporary trusteeship over Palestine.[92] To the Arab experts trusteeship was no panacea, yet it was a step in the right direction. "It seems clear," Merriam wrote to Henderson, "that although there are many doubts about trusteeship, no one has anything better to offer and that in turning away from partition, the U.S. avoided plunging into a deep abyss."[93]

Official efforts to abandon partition were unquestionably motivated by strategic considerations. In view of the mounting tension in Palestine and Iraq's recent rejection of a treaty with Great Britain, Ambassador Smith informed the department, the Kremlin now considered the Middle East "softer" than originally estimated.[94] In the event the UN decision had to be implemented by force, officials believed, the Soviets might request that their troops or those of their satellites be stationed in the area. In short, Palestine appeared to offer Moscow a means to undermine Western influence in the Eastern Levant. The ultimate consequences of American support for partition seemed painfully clear. "If we do not effect a fairly radical reversal of the trend of our policy to date," the Policy Planning Staff wrote to Marshall and Lovett, "we will end up either in the position of being ourselves militarily responsible for the protection of the Jewish population in Palestine against the declared hostility of the Arab world, or of sharing that responsibility with the Russians and thus assisting at their installation as one of the military powers of the area. In either case, the clarity and efficiency of a sound national policy for that area will be shattered."[95]

The importance of containing Soviet influence seemed to provide sufficient justification for abandoning partition, yet officials were also anxious about the fate of American oil interests. The State Department was not immediately concerned about cancellation of the ARAMCO concession. Ibn Saud's reaction to partition had been relatively moderate. It was also clear that unless the United States actively took part in enforcing the General Assembly's decision, the king might be expected to exercise considerable restraint. Officials were, however, disturbed by the possible effects of the Palestine situation on the development of Middle East oil. Already the Arab League had agreed that no petroleum facilities or concessions would be negotiated until the situation in Palestine had been "clarified." Even more important, full-scale war between Jews and Arabs could delay TAPLINE and retard the flow of Persian Gulf oil to the Mediterranean and to world markets. The effects on the European Recovery Program might be particularly severe. "There must be access and assured access to those Middle Eastern oil fields," Harriman informed a congressional committee, "if Europe is to secure the energy fuel which we cannot afford to divert permanently." Lewis Douglas, ambassador to Great Britain, expressed his own concerns to the House Committee on Interstate and Foreign Commerce. Any "impairment of this Middle East proposed supply," he observed, would require a complete review of the energy requirements of the ERP.[96]

For State Department planners, however, the link between European recovery and Middle Eastern oil depended upon the successful completion of ARAMCO's 300,000 b.p.d. trans-Arabian pipeline. By early 1948, the status of TAPLINE was at best uncertain. The company had set up construction camps in Saudi Arabia but had not yet laid pipe. Eager to press the company for better terms and angered by American support for partition, the Syrians had refused to submit the pipeline concession for ratification. Although ARAMCO had decided to begin preliminary work in Saudi Arabia, the company was worried about the future. If hostility toward the United States continued, and the Syrians did not ratify the agreement, Duce bluntly informed department representatives in January, there would be no pipeline. There was no point, Duce continued, in playing the Arabs against one another by threatening to terminate the pipeline in Egypt instead of Lebanon. Anti-Zionism he concluded was a "people's movement."[97] In a letter to Henderson, the ARAMCO vice-president went a step further. "To those who say that the Arabian stake in oil is so great that there is no possibility of the concession being cancelled, the reply is a simple one—such people have not considered the passions to which such populaces are subject."[98]

State Department officials were already fully aware of the possible consequences of abandoning the pipeline project. If TAPLINE were abandoned, the Near East Division wrote to Rusk early in January, "the European recovery program will be seriously handicapped because of the acute tanker shortage, and the impracticability of constructing sufficient tanker tonnage." Not only might the United States have to locate alternate sources of oil for Europe, but also it was conceivable that rationing of domestic supplies might have to be considered.[99] In view of the importance attached to conserving Western Hemisphere reserves and the lack of indigenous European sources, Middle Eastern crude offered the only available source of petroleum for European recovery. "If the Middle Eastern supplies are cut off," the chairman of the Senate Foreign Relations Committee asked Secretary of the Interior Julius Krug, "have you not so totally disrupted the European economy that this Plan or no other Plan would sustain?" Krug agreed, adding that "we would be in for something far more serious than merely sending this specified quantity of aid to Europe."[100] Finally, in a letter to an official of SONJ, Secretary of State Marshall urged that in the interests of European recovery the company not abandon its plans to construct a pipeline from Kuwait to the eastern Mediterranean.[101]

However, Palestine was not the only obstacle confronting advocates of TAPLINE. By February, the project once again faced the problem of securing export licenses for steel pipe and tubing. Although administration officials, particularly in the State Department, had been able to mobilize support for ARAMCO's earlier requests, circumstances had changed. In view of the deteriorating situation in the Middle East and the tight situation in steel, exporting large amounts of material abroad might not be a sound policy. There was also some doubt whether the military would continue to support the construction of a pipeline whose success depended on stability in Palestine.

The increasing uncertainty about the future of TAPLINE was reflected in a study prepared by the petroleum staff of the National Security Resources Board (NSRB). In late February, the NSRB, an agency created by the National Security Act to advise the president on matters of military, civilian, and industrial mobilization, addressed the problem of ARAMCO's export licenses. From a "national security resources viewpoint," the NSRB memorandum began, the construction of the pipeline is not justified and should not be supported. The United States could not depend on a petroleum facility which was vulnerable to "enemy action." From a "world-wide economic and 'cold war' point of view," however, TAPLINE should be supported. "Under the Marshall Plan," NSRB staff noted, "we will assume the responsibility for Western European recovery and economy and the completion of this pipeline will make more oil available and probably for a lower price than a like expenditure of funds and materials can produce in the United States." Finally, from an "economic and political viewpoint" completion of the pipeline will "reduce the heavy drain on Western Hemisphere oil resources" and replace Venezuelan oil in supporting European recovery —provided of course the oil companies made Middle Eastern oil available at reasonable prices. Although the petroleum staff recommended that the company's request for pipe be supported, it also advised that the secretary of defense be informed of NSRB's reservations.[102]

Early in March, the Department of State, aware that support for TAPLINE might be fading, rallied to support ARAMCO's request for export licenses. The department's petroleum specialists conceded that Middle Eastern oil might not be available in a "serious emergency," yet they insisted that TAPLINE would increase the flow of Persian Gulf oil to European markets and reduce the need for tankers. To NEA's officers the pipeline represented a commitment to the Saudis as well as a means of reviving Washington's sagging influence in the Arab world. The only difficulty with the project, officials conceded, was the situation in Palestine. Writing to Assistant Secretary Thorp, Robert Eakens, chief of PED, noted that Palestine must be prevented from developing into a situation that would upset the stability of the Middle East. "This Government," Eakens concluded, "is working toward that end in the hope of achieving a peaceful settlement and is of the opinion that the problem will not prove to be a serious obstacle to the flow of oil from the Middle East to Western Europe and to other areas where it is so desperately needed."[103]

As in the past the TAPLINE project generated considerable interest among administration officials. The State and Commerce Departments, principal advocates of the project, however, were disturbed by rumors that the military establishment, particularly Secretary of Defense Forrestal, had lost interest in the project. Forrestal was clearly more interested in maintaining access to Persian Gulf oil than in ARAMCO's pipeline. Navy officials had also indicated that the services had become too much involved in the TAPLINE project. Finally, increasing tension in Palestine and the prospect of all-out war in the area, indicated that steel for tankers might prove to be a sounder investment. The arguments against continuation of the pipeline were becoming harder to counter. The "principal justification" for granting the licenses to date had been "national security considerations." If these were withdrawn, State Department officials believed, an entirely new and less defensible position might have to be formulated. In short, according to Defense Department sources, officials in the Departments of Commerce and State were "extremely concerned" that Forrestal might withdraw his support for the pipeline.[104]

Forrestal supported ARAMCO's second quarter requests for steel pipe, yet military planners had indeed begun to reexamine the possibilities of access to and availability of Middle Eastern oil.[105] Responding to Forrestal's request for a study of the "Military and Strategic Value to our National Security of Middle East Oil Developments," the Joint Chiefs presented their conclusions in mid-March.[106] The JCS study reflected the increasing uncertainty surrounding the American view of the area's oil. Although the report noted that the potential military and strategic value of these petroleum reserves will become "altogether critical" under major war conditions, "it follows that the risk of their loss will increase under the same conditions." As a result, the JCS observed, it was necessary to evaluate continuously the "general criteria" which might preclude American access. Among the most important, the military planners believed, were Soviet control of Greece, Italy, Gibraltar, and the Mediterranean pipeline terminal area, or direct Soviet or Arab action. As for TAPLINE, export licenses for steel should be granted but "periodically examined." Middle Eastern oil developments should be continued, the Joint Chiefs concluded, "until the necessity of their stoppage is unmistakable."[107]

Although the Commerce Department agreed to grant ARAMCO export licenses for a limited amount of steel pipe, the future of the pipeline was uncertain.[108] By April, observers were predicting full-scale fighting in Palestine in the wake of Britain's withdrawal. The problems of securing the oil now seemed even more acute. Middle Eastern oil might be beneficial to the United States, an Army Intelligence report noted, "*if* this area could be securely held, *if* production were not disrupted by war, and *if* the petroleum produced could be transported to points where it was needed."[109] Finally, writing to Forrestal in early

April, the Joint Chiefs noted that "due to the weakness of the United States general reserve, at least for the next twelve months, the Allies cannot expect to hold the Middle East oil against a determined attack by the USSR." Immediate and detailed plans, the JCS added, should be developed for the "timely and proper abandonment (plugging) of oil producing wells in the Middle East."[110]

The deteriorating situation in Palestine seemed to confirm the military's worst fears. Events rushed toward an almost inevitable conclusion. In view of the failure of the United Nations' trusteeship proposals and Britain's intended withdrawal, it was clear that Arabs and Jews would take matters into their own hands. "There is an apparent possibility," a CIA report noted in April, "that, in default of positive UN action, anarchy may ensue in Palestine after 15 May, with dire consequences throughout the Middle East."[111] Determined to make partition a reality, the Jewish Agency announced its intention to establish a Jewish State. The Arabs responded accordingly, threatening to invade Palestine and put an end to Zionist ambitions. Finally, on 14 May, David Ben Gurion, former chairman of the Executive of the Jewish Agency and soon to be prime minister, formally announced that at 6:00 P.M. the State of Israel would come into existence. Eleven minutes later, President Truman extended de facto recognition to the new Jewish state.[112]

Despite its increasing importance, the oil of Saudi Arabia and the Middle East played little, it any, role in Truman's final consideration of the Palestine problem. It is possible that without State and Defense Department lobbying for the importance of Saudi oil Truman might have gone further in his support of Israel, yet this seems unlikely given the president's desire to minimize U.S. involvement in the Palestine question. White House support for partition and eventual recognition of Israel was rooted in a curious mixture of moral, political, and cold war considerations. Truman was certainly aware of the strategic concerns of his State Department and defense establishment. He was apparently not impressed, however, by the "arguments of the diplomats," and seemed to believe that he could still support a Jewish homeland, protect his own political future, and safeguard American national interests in the Middle East.[113] In fact, in view of the reality of a Jewish state and Moscow's plans to recognize it, Truman apparently believed that prompt U.S. recognition was quite compatible with American national interests. Truman's personal advisers, David Niles and Clark Clifford, supported this argument and provided an effective counter to State and Defense Department concerns about oil. In fact, Niles had informed Truman that he should not be prevented from supporting Jewish claims because of the fear of alienating Ibn Saud. "You know that President Roosevelt said to some of us privately he could do anything that needed to be done with Ibn Saud with a few million dollars."[114]

The view that Washington could buy off the Saudis also found its way into Clark Clifford's arguments. Writing to Truman in support of partition in March, Clifford noted, "there are those who say that such a course of action will not get us oil if we back up the United Nations partition plan. The fact of the matter is the Arab States must have oil royalties or go broke." Ninety percent of Saudi Arabia's revenue, he continued, comes from American oil royalties. Moreover, Ibn Saud "has publicly and repeatedly" refused even to threaten the United States with cancellation of the concession. In short, "military necessity, political and economic self-preservation," Clifford concluded, "will compel the Arabs to sell their oil to the United States. Their need of the United States is greater than our need of them."[115]

Truman no doubt appreciated his advisers' straightforward "common sense" approach to the problem. If the president had not succumbed to the pressure of his own State Department, it was unlikely that he would be intimidated by the Saudis. Truman must also have realized the difficulties of maintaining assured access to Saudi oil even under the best of circumstances. Although Persian Gulf sources offered a valuable supply of petroleum for European recovery, the area's resources might simply not be available in times of instability, let alone in the event of a determined enemy attack. From the standpoint of our national security, Senator Owen Brewster of Maine noted, "the oil reserves of the Middle East are not worth a tinker's dam. This is the testimony of every competent and responsible military authority. . . . [s]acrificing our honor in Palestine for the unattainable oil of Arabia is not only dishonourable—it is stupid."[116] More important, Middle Eastern oil played a relatively small role in supplying the nation's own energy requirements. By March 1948, the United States was importing approximately 450,000 b.p.d. of foreign crude—about 8 percent of its total domestic production. Imports of crude oil from Saudi Arabia in 1948 averaged a mere 29,300 b.p.d.[117]

Finally, Saudi Arabia's moderate reaction to American Palestine policy further downplayed the importance of the oil factor. From partition to recognition, Ibn Saud continued to exercise extreme caution in his relations with Washington. Exchanges between the king and the president, with rare exception, remained exceptionally cordial and even Amir Faisal kept his diatribes to a minimum. Moreover, both in private conversation and in Arab League councils, the king continued to draw a distinction between official American policy and that of the companies. In fact, in late May, Duce informed Henderson that Ibn Saud considered ARAMCO personnel to be members of his own household.[118]

Ibn Saud, to be sure, was deeply disturbed by the direction of American policy. The news of Truman's de facto recognition, Childs cabled the department on 15 May, "has profoundly shocked Saudi Arabs." The U.S. minister even suggested that the United States might now be "invited" to evacuate the Dhahran air base.[119] In the weeks immediately following recognition, Saudi-American relations were considerably strained. Reports from Jidda even indicated that the king might impose sanctions. It was clear, however, that Ibn Saud's "economic horizons" were considerably broader than "the boundaries of the Palestine Question."[120] Ibn Saud did allow the unused portion of a $15,000,000 Export-Import Bank loan to lapse in symbolic protest over American policy, but he was not prepared to go much further.[121] Unless the United States unilaterally lifted its arms embargo or sent troops to Palestine, the king would continue to resist Arab League pressure for economic sanctions against American oil interests.

Ibn Saud was also eager to retain the United States as a potential political ally against a variety of potentially hostile elements. The king's hatred of Zionism was only surpassed by his fear of Bolshevism. Wary of the prospect of increasing Soviet influence in the Middle East, the king sought closer ties with the United States.[122] Uneasy over the traditional Saudi-Hashemite rivalry and convinced that Britain might "egg on Hashemites to adventures in western Saudi Arabia," Ibn Saud also saw the United States as a valuable counterweight to Britain's support of Transjordan's "territorial ambitions."[123] The king had received assurances that the United States would "unqualifiedly" support the territorial integrity and political independence of Saudi Arabia and by 1948 had even hinted that he would favor a formal treaty.[124] Under these circumstances, it was clear that Ibn Saud would be reluctant to jeopardize his ties with the Americans. In fact by the fall of 1948, the questions of military aid and the Dhahran airfield had replaced Palestine as the most pressing problem in Saudi-American relations.

If Saudi Arabian oil had little, if any, effect on White House consideration of the Palestine issue, by 1948 it had emerged to shape State Department and military views of the Middle East. Impressed by the size and potential of the area's petroleum reserves, officials continued to emphasize the importance of maintaining Western access to this rich resource. Eager to secure the American interest in the king's oil, NEA's Arab hands urged their superiors to maintain and increase American influence and prestige with Ibn Saud. Saudi-American relations suddenly assumed new importance and generated new challenges. The days of lend-leasing trucks and silver riyals had yielded to Ibn Saud's requests for large-scale military assistance and diplomatic support. So too, the Palestine problem and attendant arms embargo hindered American efforts to meet the king's requests and to strengthen Saudi-American ties. Still, by the end of 1948, there was little doubt that relations between the two countries would steadily improve. If ties between Washington and Riyadh were not broken over Palestine, Childs informed the department in December, "one can only imagine the extent of relations in a normal period."[125]

It was the emerging cold war atmosphere of the postwar years, however, that stimulated official interest in Saudi oil and strengthened American ties with Ibn Saud's desert kingdom. "The oil resources lying within the Saudi Arabian peninsula," JCS planners concluded in May, "are of major importance to the United States and her Allies both in peace and in the prosecution of war against the USSR."[126] Although strategic planners were fully aware of the logistical problems involved in securing Arabian oil, these reserves assumed an important role in contingency planning. Both the "emergency" and the 1952 war plans, the Joint Logistics Plans Committee informed the JCS, "envisage a major effort to regain or retain the Persian Gulf oil by the second year of warfare." In the event the Allies could not immediately secure Saudi or Persian Gulf oil, military planners were determined to deny them to the Soviet Union.[127]

Officials also began to attach new importance to continuing American control of the Dhahran airfield. For the State Department, the question of the airfield was of immediate concern. The agreement covering United States' rights at Dhahran was due to expire on 15 March 1949, and officials were anxious to renew the accord in order to maintain American influence with the king. Military planners also had a stake in the air base. Although the air force did not consider Dhahran "vital" to American interests, the JCS informed Marshall in November that "our world-wide strategic position would be greatly improved if, in the event of war, the means could be developed to defend successfully and to conduct sustained air operations from Dhahran Air Base."[128] In short, Dhahran provided further evidence of the increasing strategic value of the entire area. "Saudi Arabia is strategically the most important nation in the Arabian Peninsula," the Joint Strategic Survey

Committee wrote to the JCS, "and the Arabian Peninsula is the most important area in the Middle East-Mediterranean region."[129]

Finally, there were the economic advantages of securing Saudi reserves. Concerned by the projected patterns of domestic consumption, government officials urged the development of sources in the Middle East. Although this oil supplied only a fraction of total world requirements in 1948, loss or impairment of Arabian oil, the State Department's petroleum experts argued, might "create extremely serious consequences," particularly for the European Recovery Program. Moreover, if the United States were forced to "underwrite" Europe's petroleum needs, in addition to meeting its own requirements, widespread rationing of gasoline and fuel oil might have to be considered. To the department's petroleum and trade analysts and experts on Middle Eastern affairs, the importance of Arabian oil was undeniable. Writing to the Office of United Nations Affairs in May 1948, the assistant chief of PED cautioned against adopting a policy which might jeopardize "what is probably the richest economic prize in the world in the field of foreign investment, i.e. Saudi Arabian oil."[130]

CHAPTER 8
THE SEARCH FOR SECURITY

WRITING to Clemenceau in late 1919, Henri Berenger, French Commissioner-General for Fuel, bluntly noted that "who has oil has Empire."[1] The French, to be sure, were not alone in their conviction that petroleum was a key ingredient of national power. Following World War I, the British, French, and Dutch laid claim to the already fabled oil wealth of the Eastern Hemisphere. Only the United States seemed slow to respond. Confident of the nation's petroleum resources and reluctant to engage in a scramble for oil in the Middle East, the Americans entered the field well behind the Europeans. Nonetheless, American attitudes were quickly changing. Impressed by the growing importance of oil in their war and peacetime economy and disturbed by their allies attempts to corner the oil wealth of the Mesopotamian Basin, industry and government representatives began to express new interest in the oil resources of the Middle East. Between 1920 and 1939, American oilmen, supported by the Department of State, laid the foundation of United States' interest in Middle Eastern oil.

Although the Great War had stimulated the United States' interest, it was World War II that shaped American attitudes toward the Middle East and fundamentally altered the official view of the area's oil. The war represented an important watershed separating attitudes from action and challenging the nation to move from isolation to involvement in Middle Eastern affaris. The United States still continued to defer to Great Britain's experience and influence in most military and political matters, yet the Americans could not ignore the responsibilities of their new wartime role. The presence of American troops in North Africa and the Persian Gulf together with an increasing flow of lend-lease supplies broadened American contact and influence throughout the area. The ideals of the Atlantic Charter and United Nations, embodied in the personal diplomacy of Franklin Roosevelt, further enhanced American prestige.

More important, the war radically altered the United States' view of its interests in Middle Eastern oil. The shift involved more than a change in attitude. Disturbed by dramatic increases in wartime consumption and uneasy about the possibility of decreasing domestic reserves, representatives of the Departments of State, War, and Navy urged their superiors to take steps to safeguard the nation's interest in the area's reserves. In short, the war had transformed the commercial importance of the area's oil into a potential source of national power. By 1943, determined to secure the reserves of Saudi Arabia and the Persian Gulf as a potential source of military resupply and eager to develop them for postwar use, the Americans sought for the first time to formulate a national policy toward Middle Eastern oil.

Although American oilmen had gained entry into the reserves of Iraq, Bahrain, and Kuwait, it was the oil of Saudi Arabia which fundamentally altered the course of American diplomacy and changed the relationship with Saudi Arabia. Unlike the ventures in Iraq or Kuwait, the ARAMCO concession was an all-American enterprise—unfettered by the restrictive agreements with IPC or AIOC and free at least from the formal restraints of Bahrain's treaty relationship with Great Britain. The Americans were determined to keep it that way. Wary of Britain's economic leverage with Ibn Saud, the Department of State, led by NEA and NE, sought to reduce the king's dependence on British subsidies and create new economic and political ties with the Saudis. Although the Americans had no desire to destroy British influence on the peninsula or in the gulf, in Saudi Arabia they sought nothing less than a reversal of traditional roles. No longer would the United States be content to remain Britain's junior partner, but it would now demand primacy in the economic sphere and at least an equal voice in political matters which might affect the fate of the concession.

Between 1939 and 1943, the United States' involvement in Saudi Arabia and the Middle East was defined primarily by the needs of its Allies. Eager to support the British position and to maintain a flow of supplies to the Soviet Union, the Americans established supply and communications links between the Red Sea and Persian Gulf. More important, the Americans began to take notice of the strategic and political advantages of expanding their influence in Saudi Arabia. Official interest, to be sure, was initially confined to the State Department's Middle Eastern hands. Veterans of service in Cairo, Baghdad, and Damascus, these men were particularly impressed by the geographic and political importance of Saudi Arabia and its king. Determined to maintain and increase Allied prestige, the State Department urged the Roosevelt administration to consider financial subsidies to Ibn Saud. Despite the favorable reaction of the Departments of State, Navy, and the White House, the United States, still formally neutral, was not yet prepared to undertake the risks and responsibilities in an area where British interests were predominant.

During the early years of the war, American interest in Saudi Arabia focused primarily on the geographic importance of the peninsula and on the political significance of Ibn Saud's position as guardian of the holy cities. Impressed by the king's independence and convinced of the importance of his prestige and influence within the Muslim world, the Arab experts began to attach special significance to a closer relationship with Saudi Arabia. As the United States prepared for the responsibilities of fighting a two-front war, officials also became increasingly aware of the potential value of the king's oil. Finally, the War Department was also taking a greater interest in the possibilities of overflight rights and landing bases on the Arabian peninsula.

Official interest in ARAMCO's concession was intensified by the company's own representatives. Broadening the channels of communication they had opened in the 1930s, the oilmen, some of whom were former State Department officials, continued to educate the department about the value of Arabian oil and the need for government support. There appeared to be nothing illicit nor collusive in such relationships. Although the oilmen played upon the department's fears of declining reserves and British intrigue, such tactics seemed well within the limits of special-interest lobbying. As for those oilmen like Duce, Davies, and Thornburg, who actually held government positions, the line between company and government loyalties was more hazy. There is little doubt that oilmen like Thornburg brought to Washington both the general outlook of their industry and the specific ideas and proposals of their companies.

For the most part, government officials, particularly sensitive to charges of catering to the companies, exercised great caution in their dealings with the oilmen. Although the companies provided an important source of information on Ibn Saud and his Arabia and no doubt helped to arouse official interest in the king's oil, by 1943 Washington had already begun to grasp the importance of securing the nation's stake in Arabian oil. Eager to protect an interest of enormous potential, the State Department was generally receptive to the company's requests for support. In short, despite the wartime conflicts and tensions between the oilmen and government, their relationship appeared mutually satisfactory. To ARAMCO, the government seemed a valuable ally in its efforts to protect the concession. The State Department, on the other hand, while recognizing the company's prime motive in exploiting the concession, saw ARAMCO as a means of securing the national interest in Arabian oil.

By early 1943, American policy toward Saudi Arabia had undergone significant changes. What had begun as an Allied interest in oil, supply routes, and air bases was now transformed into an intense national concern. Reports of increasing British influence in Saudi Arabia, reinforced by traditional Anglo-American tensions over oil, disturbed many State Department officials. At the same time concern about a downward trend in the discovery of new reserves challenged the Americans to consider acquiring control over petroleum reserves abroad. The United States was not running out of oil nor was the integrity of the ARAMCO concession threatened by Great Britain. Already caught up in the crisis atmosphere of global war, however, the Americans were not prepared to take any chances with a potentially valuable enterprise. This time the State Department found support for its requests to strengthen the American commitment to Ibn Saud. Roosevelt's decision to extend lend-lease to Saudi Arabia, in February 1943, thus initiated a series of policies designed to maintain American influence with the king and to secure what officials already believed to be a valuable national interest.

For the next two years, the Departments of State, War, and Navy, PAW, and the White House struggled with the problems of security and development for American oil interests. Despite differences in method, officials seemed to agree that Saudi Arabian oil was too important a commodity to be left entirely to the companies, to the British, or to the Saudis. In June 1943, the Petroleum Reserves Corporation, the first of a series of ill-fated programs designed to lend the official seal of approval to the ARAMCO concession, was launched. PRC was quickly followed by the pipeline fiasco, motivated partly by Ickes's desire to increase American negotiating strength with the British, but interpreted by the domestic producers as direct federal intrusion into the industry.

Equally important, the United States was no longer prepared to permit the British to dictate in matters of Saudi Arabian or Persian Gulf oil. Between 1943 and 1945 the Americans entered into discussions with the British designed to secure their interests, facilitate the removal of restrictions on the concessions, and bring about a more orderly development of the world's oil. Finally, in an effort to strengthen the official commitment in Saudi Arabia, increase American prestige with Ibn Saud, and find a basis of cooperation that might extend well beyond the end of the war, State Department and military officials toyed with a variety of programs to subsidize and improve the Saudi economy. Although the prospect of congressional opposition prevented the government from balancing the king's postwar budget, by 1945 the foundation of future American economic and military aid programs to the Saudi kingdom had been laid.

In the immediate postwar years, 1945 to 1949, the official interest in

Saudi oil continued, though in different ways and under changing circumstances. At the outset there was little reason for government to involve itself directly in company business. Eager to develop marketing facilities, neglected on account of the war, the companies laid their own plans for the commercial development of Saudi crude. More important, the circumstances which originally challenged the United States to pursue an aggressive course in Arabian oil had changed. Anglo-American bickering in Saudi Arabia had ceased and an ailing Saudi economy was recuperating in the wake of increasing oil royalties. Official interest in Saudi Arabian oil remained, yet there was little need for aggressive government action. The State Department continued to support development loans to Saudi Arabia and to facilitate the negotiation of transit rights for the trans-Arabian pipeline.

Although the postwar development of Saudi oil was primarily a record of the private efforts of the companies, by 1947 Arabian oil was once again becoming a source of official concern. The problems of war quickly merged into those of cold war, changing the nation's perceptions of its friends, its enemies, and its security needs. This sudden reorientation challenged the Americans to redefine the nation's interests in the eastern Mediterranean and Middle East according to a new set of strategic criteria. As Soviet power seemed to grow in the wake of weakening British influence, Americans inherited new roles and interests in the Middle East. Containment of Soviet influence quickly emerged as the basis of the American response, yet access to the oil of Iran, Iraq, and Saudi Arabia occupied a prominent place in strategic planning. The tactical advantages of Middle Eastern oil were still not clear. The JCS even had grave doubts whether Iranian or even Saudi oil could be held in the event of a determined Soviet attack. Yet most strategic planners agreed that Persian Gulf oil must be denied to the enemy and eventually regained if the West were to wage a successful war against the Soviet Union. In a hot war with the Soviets, Saudi oil was too vulnerable to be of immediate use, yet in a cold war Arabian oil might be employed to conserve Western Hemisphere reserves. Postwar planners also saw the new relationship between European recovery and the development of an accessible source of supply. The success of the Marshall Plan so vital to strengthening Western Europe against Soviet influence would in part depend on the availability of Saudi oil.

Soviet penetration into the Persian Gulf, let alone into Western Europe, was still only a potential consideration. Of more immediate danger, officials believed, was the explosiveness of the Palestine problem and its consequences for American interests. To NEA's area specialists, State Department policy planners, and Defense Department officials, Palestine presented an insidious situation, prefectly suited to Moscow's objectives in the Middle East. Not only might partition accelerate British withdrawal from the eastern Mediterranean, but also the United States' endorsement of the plan might damage its influence in the Arab world. Finally, full-scale war in Palestine threatened to disrupt the development of Persian Gulf oil and might even lead to the introduction of Soviet forces in the area.

Although Ibn Saud's oil played no part in Truman's decision to support partition or to recognize the State of Israel, the Palestine problem itself provided an effective barometer to measure the degree of American interest in Middle Eastern and particularly Arabian oil. As the Truman administration was drawn deeper into its relationship with political Zionism, officials registered their opposition to partition and warned of its dangers for American interests. Determined to revise American support for the plan, State Department and military officials emphasized the importance of safeguarding Western access to Middle Eastern petroleum. With proven reserves almost equal to those of the United States, comprising nearly 40 percent of world reserves, Middle Eastern oil held enormous potential. Eager to maintain American influence in the oil-bearing areas, the State Department urged the administration to consider the risks of a policy which could alienate the Arab world.

The Americans seemed particularly uneasy about the situation in Saudi Arabia. Although it was unlikely that Ibn Saud would take direct action against the ARAMCO concession, the State Department continued to insist that American support for a Jewish state would ultimately destroy American influence in Saudi Arabia, weaken Ibn Saud's position in the Arab world, and make him more vulnerable to the demands of the more extremist elements in Iraq and Syria. The view that Saudi Arabia was a moderate Arab state whose interests in the Middle East roughly paralleled those of the United States would become increasingly popular in the postwar period. The image of Saudi moderation combined with petroleum resources thus challenged the State Department to be particularly sensitive to the king's reaction to events in Palestine and increasingly receptive to any ideas which might boost American prestige.

The State Department's response to the Palestine question was determined by a desire to preserve American influence and Western strategic interests in the eastern Mediterranean and Middle East. Although the written record can offer only a partial insight into the motives of the Department's officers, it is likely that some of NEA's

Arab hands may have mixed their anti-Zionism with anti-Semitism. Truman seemed to believe so. "There were some men in the State Department who held the view that the Balfour Declaration could not be carried out without offense to the Arabs . . . I am sorry to say that there were some among them who were also inclined to be anti-Semetic."[2] In any event, men like William Eddy, having invested years of study in language and area skills had a deep emotional stake in the Arab world and would have opposed a Jewish state in Palestine under any circumstances. For the most part, however, there seemed to be nothing sinister in State Department opposition to partition. From the Secretary of State to the Policy Planning Staff, officials were simply more sensitive to the necessity of assuaging the Arabs than placating American Jewry or the survivors of Nazi atrocities. Similarly, Secretary of Defense Forrestal, outraged by the apparent subordination of national interest to domestic politics, fought vigorously against partition. With the exception of some of NEA's Arab experts, State Department opposition to partition and recognition was more a result of a cautious Realpolitik than any particular emotional commitment to the Arabs or hostility to the Jews. "As for the emotion of the Arabs," Robert McClintock noted, "I do not care a dried camel's hump. It is, however, important to the interests of this country that these fanatical and over-wrought people do not injure our strategic interests through reprisals against our oil investments and through the recision of our air base rights in that area."[3] The Americans may have misjudged the extent of Soviet capabilities and intentions in the Middle East and overreacted to Arab threats of immediate action against American oil interests, yet these were largely errors in judgment, not entirely unexpected during a period of considerable uncertainty and confusion abroad. Eager to maintain a stable Middle East and to preserve American interests and prestige, officials opposed partition and urged the Truman administration to adopt a policy more attuned to what they believed to be the changing strategic realities of a postwar world.

What lay behind increasing American interest in Saudi Arabia and sent a half-dozen government agencies scurrying to develop a consistent policy toward Arabian oil was the importance of securing the American interest. The concept of security was not always easy to define and varied according to the changing circumstances of the war and postwar years. More important, because the "threats" to the concession were difficult to substantiate, the Americans were never quite sure how best to protect their interests. During the war, the official response to Arabian oil was shaped by the possibility of shrinking domestic reserves and by vague reports of British designs on the concession—factors which were not only difficult to define but also even harder to accommodate in actual policy. The problems of convincing large segments of the domestic petroleum industry, its supporters in Congress, and skeptical State Department economists that the United States was either running out of oil or faced with a serious challenge from its closest ally, were self-evident. Even by 1948, the threat of Soviet penetration into the Persian Gulf or Ibn Saud's cancelling ARAMCO's concession over Palestine was not considered likely.

Although the search for security led some officials to propose actual government involvement in ARAMCO's concession, it was clear that, for most, security for Saudi oil involved maintaining free and unrestricted American access to the reserves. In view of the constraints on official action the companies became the key players in promoting and enhancing American influence in Saudi Arabia. Supporting ARAMCO's requests for steel pipe and tempering opposition to the new joint ventures all became part of a larger community of interest linking the State Department to the companies. Finally, the companies provided a vehicle to maintain American prestige in Saudi Arabia at a time when official influence was waning as a result of the Palestine situation.

Yet Washington still had a crucial role to play. Maintaining access to Saudi oil entailed far more than supporting export licenses for steel. Because the concession was so inextricably linked to the maintenance of the Saudi regime in general and the welfare of Ibn Saud in particular, the Americans felt new responsibilities for strengthening their ties with Saudi Arabia and the king. Meeting Saudi requests for greater economic and military aid, maintaining the air base at Dhahran, and pursuing a Palestine policy more acceptable to the Arab world thus became important elements in keeping the all-American enterprise in Saudi Arabia permanently American in character. Security for Saudi oil thus challenged the United States to create nothing less than a special relationship with Saudi Arabia, which would provide a permanent basis for mutual cooperation and goodwill.

Official efforts to develop a national policy toward Middle Eastern oil or even to channel greater assistance to Saudi Arabia, were frustrated by a variety of domestic and political restraints. Not only were the State Department, PAW, and the military services hindered by bureaucratic bickering within their own ranks, they were limited by opposition from independent and large producers who were determined to keep cheap foreign oil out of the United States and the government out of the oil industry. Opposition to PRC, pipeline, and the petroleum agreement, the three government-initiated projects of the war years, was sufficient proof of the industry's determination to curb federal meddling in its affairs. Similarly, the failure of the State Department's campaign to subsidize Ibn Saud's postwar economy was partly a result of opposition from congressional representatives of the oil-producing states. Finally, try as they might, the State and Defense Departments could not alter or reverse a Palestine policy which had been taken out of their hands by a president committed to balancing political realities with humanitarian considerations.

Nonetheless by 1948, the oil of Saudi Arabia had emerged to play an important role in the formation of American attitudes and policies toward the Middle East. Arabian oil was only part of the American stake in the area, yet it challenged the United States to shed its traditional role of noninvolvement and enter a world of great power and regional politics. The transition, to be sure, held greater significance for the future, yet it represented an important stage in the development of American policy in both global and regional contexts. Increasing American interest in Saudi Arabia revealed how rapidly Washington's view of the nation's strategic needs had expanded. Saudi Arabia neither shared a border with the Soviet Union nor constituted a front-line buffer zone in the Middle East's strategic northern tier. Similarly, Saudi reserves were distant and vulnerable, particularly in time of war. Still, in the uncertainties of an emerging cold war world they represented a potentially valuable economic and strategic weapon which could not be ignored.

Finally, the emerging interest in Arabian oil laid the foundation of a new and special relationship with Saudi Arabia. Military and economic aid to the Saudis during the 1970s would dwarf the aid programs of the earlier years, yet the basic policy—strengthening the Saudi kingdom, maintaining American influence, and above all preserving access to the immense oil reserves—had its roots in the 1940s. Similarly, the view that Saudi Arabia and the United States shared common objectives in the Middle East and could begin to build on these mutual interests had its origins in the war and postwar years. The Americans came to believe that Saudi Arabia, tied to the United States by oil revenues, economic aid, and a shared anticommunist ethic, represented a potential force of modernization, moderation, and stability in the Arab world. The strategic importance of Saudi Arabia, together with the increasing value of the country's oil, challenged policymakers to strengthen the Saudi kingdom and keep it firmly aligned with the west. Specifically, the Americans continued to search for a way to provide long-term assistance to Ibn Saud—assistance which had eluded them since the 1940s. In an effort to cement U.S.–Saudi ties, the Department of State continued to support ARAMCO's requests for steel pipe for TAPLINE until the project's completion in 1950, and to provide limited technical and military aid to the Saudi government. This was hardly sufficient, however, to assuage Ibn Saud's increasing desire for funds and a greater share of ARAMCO's profits.

It was not until the fall of 1950 that the State Department found a solution to the problem of aid to the king. Caught up in the hardening cold war atmosphere which followed the outbreak of the Korean War, officials grew increasingly concerned about Soviet influence in the Middle East. In an effort to maintain American prestige with the Saudis and to head off a serious rift between the companies and the king, the Department of State began to support an arrangement between ARAMCO and Ibn Saud which took advantage of a 1918 tax law exempting income taxes paid out to a foreign government against taxes paid to the federal government. The plan, which was developed by ARAMCO in response to the king's growing appetite for funds, enabled ARAMCO to transfer to Ibn Saud as revenue the taxes that it paid to Washington. The "King's Tax" seemed to contain something for everyone. The company was relieved of much of the burden of supporting Saudi Arabia; the king was assured a lucrative and steady source of income; and the State Department succeeded in bolstering the Saudi kingdom. The "Golden Gimmick" was in fact the culmination of almost a decade of official efforts to find a way to support Ibn Saud without the necessity of congressional approval or direct foreign aid.[4]

As currents of nationalism and pan-Arabism swept the Middle East during the 1950s and 1960s, the United States–Saudi relationship came under greater strain. The golden age of American-Saudi ties under Ibn Saud yielded to the more unpredictable tenure of his eldest son Saud. Moreover, the United States faced the impossible task of reconciling its special relationships with Israel and Saudi Arabia. Although Saud's brother and successor, Faisal, drew closer to the United States in an effort to strengthen his kingdom against the radicalism and socialism of his Arab neighbors, he was also the first Saudi leader to use oil as a weapon to protest American support of Israel. It thus became clear that the Saudis could no longer prevent the Palestine problem from complicating their relations with the Americans. With the assassination of Faisal in 1975 and the accession of King Khalid and Prince Fahd, the dilemma of reconciling Saudi Arabia's national interests with its commitment and responsibility to the Arab world continued to place even greater strain on the U.S.–Saudi relationship. Finally, and inevitably, the Saudis began to demand a greater and greater share of the oil profits and production—demands that would put them on the road to total control of the concession. The origins of these problems and policies, however, lay in an earlier period. The years between 1939 and 1949 not only witnessed the development of an American national interest in Saudi Arabia and its oil but also left a complex legacy of involvement and responsibility in the Middle East which challenges the United States to this day.

ABBREVIATIONS

AF	Divison of African Affairs
AIOC	Anglo-Iranian Oil Company
ANPB	Army-Navy Petroleum Board
APOC	Anglo-Persian Oil Company
ARAMCO	Arabian American Oil Company
BAPCO	Bahrain Petroleum Company
CALTEX	California-Texas Oil Company
CASOC	California Arabian Standard Oil Company
CIPP	Committee on International Petroleum Policy
ERP	European Recovery Program
EXIM	Export-Import Bank
FEA	Foreign Economic Administration
FMA	Financial and Monetary Affairs Division
IPC	Iraq Petroleum Company
ITP	Office of International Trade Policy
JCS	Joint Chiefs of Staff
JSSC	Joint Strategic Survey Committee
KOC	Kuwait Oil Company
ME	Division of Middle Eastern Affairs
MER	maximum efficient rate of production
MESC	Middle East Supply Center
NE	Division of Near Eastern Affairs
NEA	Office of Near Eastern and African Affairs
NSC	National Security Council
NSRB	National Security Resources Board
OFD	Office of Financial and Development Policy
OSS	Office of Strategic Services
OWMR	Office of War Mobilization and Reconversion
PAW	Petroleum Administration for War
PED	Petroleum Division (of State Department)
PIWC	Petroleum Industry War Council
PPS	Policy Planning Staff
PRC	Petroleum Reserves Corporation
RFC	Reconstruction Finance Corporation
SANACC	State-Army-Navy-Air Force Coordinating Committee
SOCAL	Standard Oil of California
SOCONY	Standard Oil of New York
SONJ	Standard Oil of New Jersey
SWNCC	State-War-Navy Coordinating Committee
TAPLINE	Trans-Arabian Pipeline
TPC	Turkish Petroleum Company
UNSCOP	United Nations Special Committee on Palestine
WPB	War Production Board

NOTES

Chapter 1

1. During the eighteenth and nineteenth centuries the Americans were more active in the eastern Mediterranean and North Africa than in the Arab east. In 1786, the United States signed a treaty with Morocco—the nation's first agreement with a non-European power. Under Jefferson, the Americans waged an undeclared naval war with the Barbary States—Algiers, Tunis, and Tripoli—over freedom of passage. Throughout the nineteenth century American merchants were involved in trade with the Ottomans. (In 1830, the United States signed a commercial agreement with the Porte.) The Americans even carried on some trade with the Yemen. In 1833 the United States negotiated a treaty of Amity and Commerce with the Sultan of Muscat. American missionaries were also active throughout the Ottoman Empire—establishing missions in Syria, Iraq, Egypt, and Arabia. Still, in comparison with American interest and involvement in Latin America and the Far East during the nineteenth century, activity in the Middle East was marginal. For the development of American commercial and naval activity in the Mediterranean area during the nineteenth century, see James A. Field, Jr., *America and the Mediterranean World, 1776–1882*. For early contacts with the Arabian peninsula, see Joseph J. Malone, "America and the Arabian Peninsula: The First Two Hundred Years," pp. 406–24. On the role of missionaries and philanthropists, see Joseph L. Grabill, *Protestant Diplomacy and the Near East* and Robert L. Daniel, *American Philanthropy in the Near East, 1820–1960*. The best and most comprehensive account of American interests in the Ottoman Empire, Iran, and the Arab East before 1939 is John A. DeNovo, *American Interests and Policies in the Middle East, 1900–1939*. See also A. L. Tibawi, *American Interests in Syria, 1800–1901*. For a concise overview of early American contact with the Middle East, see Robert W. Stookey, *America and the Arab States*, pp. 1–28.

2. For surveys of United States policy toward Turkey and the Arab provinces during and after World War I, see DeNovo, *American Interests and Policies in the Middle East*, chap. 4; Laurence Evans, *United States Policy and the Partition of Turkey, 1914–1924*; Roger R. Trask, *The United States Response to Turkish Nationalism and Reform 1914–1939*; and Harry N. Howard, *Turkey, The Straits and U.S. Policy*, chaps. 2, 3. See also Harry N. Howard, *The King-Crane Commission*.

3. H. St. John Bridger Philby, *Arabian Jubilee*, p. 179.

4. In 1940 Saudi Arabia produced 13,866 b.p.d.; in 1945, 58,386 b.p.d.; in 1948, 390,309 b.p.d.; in 1950, 546,703 b.p.d.; and in 1959,

1,095,399 b.p.d. (Roy Lebkicher, George Rentz, and Max Steineke, *ARAMCO Handbook*, p. 171). In 1938, production from Iran alone accounted for 215,000 b.p.d. (ibid., p. 113).

5. For a brief account of Drake's discovery, see Harold F. Williamson, Ralph L. Andreano, Arnold R. Daum, and Gilbert C. Klose, *The American Petroleum Industry*, 1:77–81.

6. American Petroleum Institute, *Petroleum Facts and Figures*, 1950, pp. 450–51.

7. Ibid., p. 452. New York and Ohio also produced small quantities of oil that year.

8. Mira Wilkins, *The Emergence of Multinational Enterprise*, p. 82.

9. Fanning, *American Oil Operations Abroad*, pp. 257–58. See also *Petroleum Facts and Figures*, 1950, pp. 445–49.

10. Harold F. Williamson et al., *American Petroleum Industry*, 2:190, 169–70.

11. *Petroleum Facts and Figures*, 1950, pp. 444, 450.

12. Stephen Longrigg, *Oil in the Middle East*, p. 16.

13. U.S., Congress, Senate, Special Subcommittee Investigating Petroleum Resources, *American Petroleum Interests in Foreign Countries* (hereafter cited as *American Petroleum Interests*), Hearings before a Special Committee Investigating Petroleum Resources, 79th Cong., 1st sess., 1946, p. 184.

14. On the role of oil in World War I, see Williamson et al., *American Petroleum Industry*, 2:261–64. See also Longrigg, *Oil in the Middle East*, pp. 33–34.

15. Marian Kent, *Oil and Empire*, p. 6. See also *Petroleum Facts and Figures*, 1950, p. 444.

16. Ibid., p. 182.

17. Williamson et al., *American Petroleum Industry*, 2:295. For a concise discussion of the postwar oil scare, see Gerald Nash, *United States Oil Policy, 1890–1964*, pp. 43–48 and John A. DeNovo, "The Movement for an Aggressive American Oil Policy Abroad, 1918–1920," p. 868.

18. Standard of New Jersey felt particularly pressed to acquire sources of crude. In 1918 the company produced only 16 percent of its own oil. See Henrietta M. Larson, ed., *History of Standard Oil Company (New Jersey)*, 2:278. See also Mira Wilkins, *The Maturing of Multinational Enterprise*, pp. 113–22.

19. Larson, *History of Standard Oil Company*, 2:88.

20. *Petroleum Facts and Figures*, 1950, p. 444. See also Robert B. Krueger, *The United States and International Oil*, p. 43. For a brief discussion of developments in Mexican oil, see Leonard Fanning, *Foreign Oil and the Free World*, pp. 24–31. See also Nash, *United States Oil Policy*, pp. 68–71. Developments in Venezuelan oil are covered in Edwin Lieuwen, *Petroleum in Venezuela*.

21. On American interest in the oil of the Dutch East Indies, see

Irvine H. Anderson, Jr., *The Standard-Vacuum Oil Company and United States East Asian Policy, 1933–1941*, pp. 27–30; Wilkins, *The Maturing of Multinational Enterprise*, p. 121; Nash, *United States Oil Policy*, pp. 60–68; and Larson, *History of Standard Oil Company*, 2:91–94.

22. For a concise treatment of the geology and geography of Middle Eastern oil, see Longrigg, *Oil in the Middle East*, pp. 1–15.

23. For developments in Persian oil before 1914, see L. P. Elwell-Sutton, *Persian Oil*, chap. 2.

24. On the origins of the TPC, see Benjamin Shwadran, *The Middle East, Oil and the Great Powers*, pp. 195–97. See also U.S., Congress, Senate, Committee on Foreign Relations, *Multinational Corporations and United States Foreign Policy* (hereafter cited as *Multinational Corporations*), Hearings before a Subcommittee on Multinational Corporations of the Senate Committee on Foreign Relations, 93rd Cong., 2d sess., 1974, pt. 8, pp. 495–97. See also William Richard Smyser, "The Formation of the Iraq Petroleum Company, 1888–1928."

25. A detailed examination of the negotiations which led to the "Foreign Office Agreement" can be found in Kent, *Oil and Empire*, chaps. 4, 5.

26. By 1920 Persia was producing 12,230,000 barrels out of a total 13,272,000 for the entire Middle East (*Petroleum Facts and Figures*, 1950, pp. 447, 448). For Churchill's account of the new importance of oil, see Winston S. Churchill, *The World Crisis*, pp. 78–82.

27. Longrigg, *Oil in the Middle East*, p. 48.

28. For the relationship between Britain's petroleum interests and territorial desiderata, see Kent, *Oil and Empire*, chap. 7. For details of the San Remo accord, see Shwadran, *The Middle East, Oil and the Great Powers*, pp. 198–201, and Kent, *Oil and Empire*, pp. 140–50.

29. DeNovo, *American Interests and Policies in the Middle East*, pp. 169–73. See also Shwadran, *The Middle East, Oil and the Great Powers*, p. 403. For a brief discussion of American interest in oil concessions in Palestine, see Frank Manuel, *The Realities of American-Palestine Relations*, pp. 267–72 and Shwadran, *The Middle East, Oil and the Great Powers*, pp. 449–52.

30. For American reaction to the San Remo accord, see Evans, *United States Policy and the Partition of Turkey, 1914–1924*, pp. 300–308.

31. Preliminary exchanges between Colby and Curzon can be found in U.S. Department of State, *Foreign Relations of the United States* 1920, 2: 663–67. (Hereafter cited as *FRUS*.) See also *FRUS* 1921, 2: 80–105. The most complete account of official efforts on behalf of the companies can be found in DeNovo, *American Interests and Policies in the Middle East*, pp. 176–91. See also U.S., Congress, Senate, A Study Prepared for the Special Committee Investigating Petroleum Resources, *Diplomatic Protection of American Petroleum Interests in*

Mesopotamia, the Netherlands East Indies and Mexico, S. Doc., 43, 79th Cong., 1st sess., 1945, pp. 1–30. See also Michael J. Hogan, *Informal Entente*, pp. 179–85.

32. Shwadran, *The Middle East, Oil and the Great Powers*, pp. 237–38.

33. The idea of a self-denying clause had been carried over from both the original TPC accord of 1912 and the Foreign Office Agreement of 1914. With only a financial interest in the TPC, Gulbenkian sought a way to protect his investment in the company from his oil producing partners. Stocking, *Middle East Oil*, pp. 43, 57. See also Shwadran, *The Middle East, Oil and the Great Powers*, p. 196.

34. *Multinational Corporations*, pt. 7, p. 47. For Gulbenkian's role in the agreement, see Ralph Hewins, *Mr. Five Per Cent*, chap. 17, and Nubar Gulbenkian, *Portrait in Oil*, pp. 81–100. Brief but colorful accounts of the events leading to the accord can be found in Leonard Moseley, *Power Play*, pp. 46–50 and Anthony Sampson, *The Seven Sisters*, pp. 66–70. For details of the actual agreement, see U.S., Congress, Senate, Subcommittee on Monopoly of the Select Committee on Small Business, *The International Petroleum Cartel* (hereafter cited as *Petroleum Cartel*), Staff Report of the Federal Trade Commission, 82nd Cong., 2d sess., 1952, pp. 198–219. See also *Multinational Corporations*, pt. 7, pp. 46–51.

35. See the prepared statement of David I. Haberman, *Multinational Corporations*, pt. 7, p. 47. For entertaining descriptions of the Achnacarry meeting, see Sampson, *The Seven Sisters*, pp. 71–74, and Moseley, *Power Play*, pp. 89–90.

36. The motives and implications of the agreements, particularly the Red Line accord, remain a subject of considerable debate. Raymond F. Mikesell and Hollis B. Chenery, in *Arabian Oil*, note that the Red Line "is an outstanding example of a restrictive combination for the control of a large portion of the world's oil supply by a group of companies which together dominate the world market for this commodity" (p. 45). John M. Blair, in *The Control of Oil*, notes that "by means of a web of cartel arrangements set up in most of the world's consuming countries," the major international companies gained control of most of the world's markets (p. 28). For a different approach, see Neil H. Jacoby, *Multinational Oil*. Jacoby argues that the conditions of producing abroad, the gradual growth of demand, and the nature of government controls "inevitably produced an oligopolistic type of market structure"—a structure, Jacoby adds, that does not per se "carry any implication of overt or tacit collusion among the supplying firms" (p. 5 and p. 11, n.3, respectively). As for the "As Is" Agreement, Jacoby notes, restraints on markets and efforts to stabilize prices during a period of economic depression "are not improbable consequences of an oligopolistic industrial structure" (p. 30). Longrigg, who was at one time employed by the Iraq Petroleum Company (TPC be-

came IPC in 1929), wisely skirts the issue. "The Red Line Agreement, variously assessed as a sad case of wrongful cartelization or as an enlightened example of international cooperation and fair sharing, was to hold the field for twenty years and in large measure determined the pattern and tempo of oil development over a great part of the Middle East" (Longrigg, *Middle East Oil*, p. 70.)

37. *Petroleum Facts and Figures*, 1950, p. 449.

38. Lieuwen, *Petroleum in Venezuela*, p. 40.

39. For developments in Iranian oil between the wars, see DeNovo, *American Interests and Policies in the Middle East*, pp. 283–86, and George Lenczowski, *Russia and the West in Iran, 1914–1948*, pp. 75–86.

40. For surveys of the geography and topography of Saudi Arabia and the Arabian peninsula see Karl Twitchell, *Saudi Arabia*, pp. 13–16; David Long, *Saudi Arabia*, pp. 5–8; Louise E. Sweet, "The Arabian Peninsula," pp. 202–6; Norman C. Walpole et al., *Area Handbook for Saudi Arabia*, pp. 11–16; and Richard H. Sanger, *The Arabian Peninsula*, pp. 41–44.

41. Shwadran, *The Middle East, Oil and the Great Powers*, p. 390. See also Stocking, *Middle East Oil*, pp. 73–75.

42. Shwadran, *The Middle East, Oil and the Great Powers*, p. 391.

43. For documentation on the State Department's activities on behalf of Gulf Oil, see *FRUS* 1929, 3: 80–82.

44. For detailed personal accounts of the negotiations for the Kuwait concession, see Archibald H. T. Chisholm, *The First Kuwait Oil Concession Agreement* and Thomas E. Ward, *Negotiations for Oil Concessions in Bahrain, El Hasa (Saudi Arabia), The Neutral Zone, Qatar and Kuwait*, chaps. 5, 11. Ward was Holmes syndicate's New York representative. Chisholm was APOC's chief field negotiator.

45. See *FRUS* 1932, 2: 1–2, 14–16.

46. A detailed account of negotiations in Kuwait between 1932 and 1934 can be found in Chisholm, *The First Kuwait Oil Concession*, chap. 3. For details of the Gulf-APOC agreement, see Stocking, *Middle East Oil*, pp. 114–17, and *Petroleum Cartel*, pp. 124–34.

47. See memorandum by John A. Loftus, 19 May 1944, Folder: "Policy—Historical Review of the U.S. Foreign Oil Policy," Box 1, Miscellaneous Files of the Former Petroleum Division in the Office of International Trade Policy (ITP-PED), 1943–1949 (hereafter cited as *PED Records*), Record Group 59 (RG 59), National Archives (NA).

48. Sampson, *The Seven Sisters*, p. 89.

49. Both Twitchell and Philby played important roles in the development of American interests in Saudi Arabia. Twitchell not only helped to establish preliminary contacts with Ibn Saud, but also he provided an important source of information on Arabia in the years before the establishment of diplomatic ties in 1940. For Twitchell's account of his role, see Twitchell, *Saudi Arabia*, pp. 147–51. For

Philby's description of his role in the negotiation of the concession, see Philby, *Arabian Oil Ventures*, pp. 73–116. See also Philby, *Arabian Jubilee*, pp. 175–83, and Elizabeth Monroe, *Philby of Arabia*, pp. 201–4.

50. The doctrine of Wahhabism espoused conformity to the practices of early Islam, accepting as its only law the Sharia or divine canon as established during the first three centuries of Islam. The movement aimed at ridding Islam of all innovations such as veneration of saints, pilgrimages to their tombs, and the use of alcohol, and tobacco. The Wahhabis, a name given to them by outsiders, referred to themselves as Muwahhidun or unitarians, as a result of their absolutist notion of the unity of God. For an excellent discussion of Wahhabi doctrine, see George Rentz, "Wahhabism and Saudi Arabia," pp. 54–66. See also P. M. Holt, *Egypt and the Fertile Crescent 1516–1922*, pp. 149–55 and R. Bayly Winder, *Saudi Arabia in the Nineteenth Century*, pp. 8–15.

51. For a brief survey of the rise of the house of Saud, see Holt, *Egypt and the Fertile Crescent 1516–1922*, pp. 149–55. See also Gary Troeller, *The Birth of Saudi Arabia*, pp. 13–20, and Sheikh Mohammad Iqbal, *Emergence of Saudi Arabia*, chaps. 1, 2, 3.

52. Holt, *Egypt and the Fertile Crescent*, pp. 154–55.

53. For a detailed survey of Saudi fortunes in the nineteenth century, see Winder, *Saudi Arabia in the Nineteenth Century*. Although during the 1930s Ibn Saud would negotiate treaties of nonaggression with both Transjordan and Iraq, he remained suspicious of their Hashemite leaders. The king was particularly concerned about the possibility that Britain might encourage Hashemite ambitions at the expense of Saudi territory. This distrust of the Hashemites resulted in Saudi Arabia's closer alliance with Egypt between 1945 and 1956 and in its opposition to any proposals to include Syria in a Hashemite-controlled union. It was not until the mid-1950s that Saudi Arabia, in view of its growing fear of Nasser, began to see the advantages of closer ties with the Hashemite kings. In September 1956 King Saud, who had succeeded his father in late 1953, met with King Faisal of Iraq. The Saudi-Iraqi rapprochement continued with Saud's meeting with Abdul Ilah, Iraqi Crown Prince, in Washington in February 1957. The Saudis also reportedly provided Jordan's King Hussein with diplomatic and financial support during an attempted coup by leftist-leaning military officers in April 1957.

54. On the factors governing Anglo-Saudi relations during the war and immediate postwar years, see Troeller, *The Birth of Saudi Arabia*, chaps. 3, 4. Britain's decision to support Sharif Hussein against the Ottomans relegated Ibn Saud to a minor role during the early years of the war and even resulted in an Ottoman-Saudi treaty in 1914. In 1915, however, in an effort to ensure that Ibn Saud would not attack Hussein and pledge at least nominal loyalty to the British war effort, London concluded a treaty with the king. In exchange for promises of aid

against the Rashidis and a pledge to protect the independence of Ibn Saud, the British received the king's assurances that he would not attack Britain's allies or support its enemies. The treaty, which also prohibited Ibn Saud from dealing directly with foreign powers, was replaced in 1927 by an Anglo-Saudi treaty signed at Jidda. By this agreement the British formally recognized Saudi independence and renounced the protectorate provisions of the earlier accord.

55. Background on Ibn Saud and his rise to power can be found in David Howarth, *The Desert King*; Sanger, *The Arabian Peninsula*, pp. 27–40; Philby, *Saudi Arabia*, chaps. 9, 10, 11; and Troeller, *The Birth of Saudi Arabia*, pp. 20–65.

56. There is little doubt that Wahhabism shaped Ibn Saud's world view, yet he was not consumed by the religious fanaticism of many of his followers. It is significant that Ibn Saud's father did not pass on to his son the title and office of Imam, thus freeing him from some of the religious constraints. (Troeller, *The Birth of Saudi Arabia*, p. 20.) At the Uqair conference in 1921 at which Ibn Saud hosted Sir Percy Cox, Britain's high commissioner for Iraq, he provided his guests with cigars and whiskey—both prohibited by Wahhabi doctrine (Howarth, *The Desert King*, p. 138). The British political agent in Bahrain, H. R. P. Dickson, recollected that during a visit to Ibn Saud's camp he received after dark several tins of "superb English cigarettes." (H. R. P. Dickson, *Kuwait and Her Neighbors*, p. 249.) See also Philby, *Saudi Arabia*, pp. 304–5.

57. Despite his commitment to Islam and his desire to maintain his influence in the Muslim world, Ibn Saud put great faith in the notion of Wataniyyah or national independence. Although soon after his conquest of the Hijaz he convened an Islamic conference at Mecca to determine the fate of the holy cities, he rejected the proposal of Indian Muslims to turn the Hijaz into an Islamic protectorate. Having recovered his ancestral lands, maintaining them against the "designs" of both the British and their Hashemite clients became the king's primary objective in the years before World War II. Although determined to increase his patrimony, Ibn Saud often had to curb his own expansionist ambitions and those of his followers in order to avoid direct conflict with Great Britain—a conflict which he felt might conceivably jeopardize his own independence.

58. During the 1920s the number of pilgrims had averaged about 100,000 per year with one peak year of 130,000. By 1938 the number had declined to 63,800 (George Kirk, *The Middle East in the War*, pp. 335–36). See also Howarth, *The Desert King*, pp. 220–21, and D. Van Der Meulen, *The Wells of Ibn Saud*, p. 134.

59. Howarth, *The Desert King*, p. 198; Philby, *Arabian Jubilee*, p. 81; and Philby, *Saudi Arabia*, p. 295.

60. Fox to secretary of state, 28 June 1933, 890F.797/3, State Department Decimal File, RG 59 (hereafter cited with decimal number and date).

61. For accounts of the negotiations, see Shwadran, *The Middle East, Oil and the Great Powers*, pp. 303–4; Philby, *Arabian Oil Ventures*, pp. 73–116; and Twitchell, *Saudi Arabia*, pp. 148–52.

62. Philby, *Saudi Arabia*, p. 331. See also Howarth, *The Desert King*, p. 229.

63. Quoted in Ward, *Negotiations for Oil Concessions*, p. 48.

64. Ibn Saud's motivation in granting the 1933 concession to the Americans remains a subject of considerable debate. Shwadran claims that the king's suspicion of British control played no part in his decision to deal with the Americans (*The Middle East, Oil and the Great Powers*, pp. 310–11, n.11). Philby noted, in fact, that the king had a preference for granting the concession to a British firm (Philby, *Arabian Oil Ventures*, pp. 88, 125–27). Fritz Grobba, German minister to Iraq, even claims that Ibn Saud offered the concession to the Germans if they would match the American bid (Fritz Grobba, *Männer und Mächte im Orient*, pp. 94–95). According to Richard Sanger of the Department of State, however, the king liked the idea of having his economy tied to a country "as large, as powerful, as distant, as skilled in the techniques of oil production, and as little interested in imperialism as the United States" (Sanger, *The Arabian Peninsula*, p. 101). See also Howarth, *The Desert King*, pp. 233–34. Philby claims to have favored the Americans as well because their "record at that time was entirely free of any imperialistic implications" (*Arabian Oil Ventures*, p. 86).

65. Although Ibn Saud would be deeply disturbed by United States policy toward Palestine, he would not allow this issue to jeopardize American-Saudi ties (see chap. 7). For discussion of the king's view of the United States and Britain, see Philby, *Saudi Arabia*, pp. 335–37; Van Der Meulen, *The Wells of Ibn Saud*, p. 134; and D. C. Watt, "The Foreign Policy of Ibn Saud, 1936–1939," pp. 152–60.

66. Memorandum by Leonard Parker of the Division of Near Eastern Affairs, 7 Dec. 1944, 711.90F/12–744, RG 59. (All decimal file references to follow are to be found in RG 59.) See also Morris to secretary of state, 23 Mar. 1937, 125.0090F JEDDA/18.

67. In a letter of 26 January 1911, from Evan Young, the first chief of the Division of Near Eastern Affairs, to the chief clerk of the Department of State, Young noted: "The special familiarity of the officers of the Division with conditions in the Near East, acquired by previous service in that portion of the world and by careful study of the current literature concerning those countries, enables the Division to give more personal and efficient attention to important questions which may arise than would otherwise be possible." (Wallace S. Murray, "The Division of Near Eastern Affairs," pp. 16–18.) Young, who had entered the foreign service in 1905, had only served as consul in Turkey before his appointment as chief in 1909. As late as 1944 NE could claim only three Near Eastern language specialists. Not since 1935 had

the division been able to detail a single officer for Arabic language study.

68. *Register of the Department of State*, 28 Dec. 1909, p. 18.

69. Ibid., 1 Oct. 1939, p. 13.

70. J. Rives Childs, *Foreign Service Farewell*, pp. 101–2. For background on the division, see Phillip J. Baram, *The Department of State in the Middle East 1919–1945*, pp. 66–86, and Graham H. Stuart, *The Department of State*, pp. 216–17, 365–66. See also Natalia Summers, "Outline of the Functions of the Offices of the Department of State, 1789–1943," Internal Reference Aid, RG 59.

71. Stuart, *The Department of State*, p. 295.

72. Murray also served as one of the department's four advisers on political relations and was a member of the policy committee. On 20 Feb. 1945, he was appointed ambassador to Iran.

73. Biographic information on Murray, Alling, and Merriam can be found in the *Biographic Register of the Department of State 1945*. See also the obituary of Paul Alling, *Washington Post*, 19 January 1949, p. 2B, and the obituary of Wallace Murray, *New York Times*, 28 April 1965, p. 45.

74. The United States recognized the "Kingdom of the Hejaz and Nejd and Its Dependencies" in May 1931. In November, Saudi Arabia and the United States signed a provisional agreement regarding diplomatic and consular representation, juridical protection, commerce, and navigation. In June 1939, Washington decided to accredit the American minister in Egypt to Saudi Arabia as well.

75. J. Loder Park to secretary of state, 8 July 1925, 890F.00/5.

76. Alling to Shaw, 28 Oct. 1928, 890F.01/11. Alling also predicted that American economic relations with the Hijaz would increase as a result of Ibn Saud's "progressive tendencies." See also Clayson W. Aldridge to the secretary of state, 23 Jan. 1928, 890F.00/8. For an excellent discussion of American perceptions of Ibn Saud and his Arabia, see Malcolm C. Peck, "Saudi Arabia in United States Foreign Policy to 1958," pp. 33–44. In 1944, an Office of Strategic Services (OSS) report described Ibn Saud as "a tall and handsome man, endowed with great personal charm"—"a son of the desert" possessing all the "true Arab qualities: valor and generosity, pride and a strong sense of freedom." ("The Position of Saudi Arabia within the Arab World," 4 Feb. 1944, R + A No. 1652, Records of the Office of Strategic Services [hereafter cited as *OSS Records*], RG 226.)

77. Murray to Stimson, 14 Jan. 1931, 890F.01/24.

78. Writing to Stimson to request an appointment for Rihani, Murray noted that he was "without a doubt the most distinguished authority in this country on Arabia" (13 Jan. 1931, 890F.01/21). For Rihani's own account of his experiences in Arabia, see Ameen Rihani, *Ibn Sa'oud of Arabia*.

79. In November 1932, H. S. Villard of the Division of Near Eastern

Affairs, after a conversation with Twitchell, noted that "Twitchell impressed me as a man of obvious integrity and sincerity. He has a fund of valuable knowledge about Saudi Arabia and a collection of photographs which he is willing to show the Department at any time." (Memorandum of conversation with Twitchell, 1 Nov. 1932, 890F.6363/10.)

80. In a letter to President Roosevelt, Crane described Ibn Saud as "the most important man who has appeared in Arabia since the time of Mohammed" (21 Jan. 1939, 890F.001/Ibn Saud/23). In his response to Crane, the president requested additional information on the king.

81. Loomis, a SOCAL vice-president, had served as an assistant secretary of state. Patchin, one of SOCAL's directors, had been appointed chief of the State Department's Division of Information and had served as assistant to the department's counselor.

82. For documentation on the decision to extend recognition to the Saudi kingdom, see *FRUS 1931*, 2: 547–54.

83. Loomis to Stimson, 25 Oct. 1932, 890F.6363 Standard Oil Company/1. Stimson to Loomis, 26 Oct. 1932, 890F.6363 Standard Oil Company/2.

84. Merriam to secretary of state, 22 Apr. 1932, 890F.51/10. See also Merriam to secretary of state, 10 June 1933, 890F.6363 Standard Oil Company/15. Merriam, of course, was wrong. In 1923 Ibn Saud had granted Holmes, acting on behalf of the Eastern and General Syndicate, an option for a concession in al-Hasa. By 1928, having failed to interest other companies in the concession or to develop the area on its own, the group lost its option. See Shwadran, *The Middle East, Oil and the Great Powers*, pp. 301–2, and Philby, *Arabian Oil Ventures*, pp. 53–69.

85. Murray to Twitchell, 26 June 1933, 890F.6363 Standard Oil Company/14.

86. In a memorandum to Hull, Murray recommended that in view of "growing American interests" in Saudi Arabia, the possibility of an increasing number of American citizens in the area, and the "continued appeals" of American business, the department might investigate the desirability of establishing a consular office in Jidda (22 July 1936, 125.0090F JEDDA/10). See also Hull to Moffett, 24 July 1936, 125.0090F JEDDA/9.

87. For the full text of Morris's dispatch, see Morris to the secretary of state, 23 Mar. 1937, 125.0090F JEDDA/18. See also Murray to Hull, 7 May 1937, 125.0090F JEDDA/22.

88. In his May memorandum to Hull, Murray had noted that American interests do not warrant official representation in Jidda "unless the Department wishes to give unusual support to the efforts of the Standard to extend its existing oil rights in the area" (125.0090F JEDDA/22). See also Murray to the American Embassy in London, 8 June 1933, 890F.6363 Standard Oil Company/65 and memorandum of

conversation among Feis, Welles, and Moffett, 12 July 1937, 890F.6363 Standard Oil Company/93.

89. Moffett, a personal friend of Franklin Roosevelt, would figure prominently in CASOC's attempts to gain diplomatic support for its Saudi concession.

90. Memorandum of conversation among Murray, Moffett, and Wahba, 5 July 1938, 890F.6363 Standard Oil Company/102. See also memorandum of conversation between Loomis and Murray, 13 May 1938, 890F.6363 Standard Oil Company/98.

91. Memorandum of conversation between Loomis and Alling, 18 Jan. 1939, 890F.6363 Standard Oil Company/105.

92. Murray to Hull and Welles, 27 Jan. 1939, 124.90F/6.

93. In January 1939, Grobba was accredited to Jidda, making Germany the first state to establish representation in Saudi Arabia without a direct interest in the pilgrimage. Britain, France, Holland, Turkey, and Egypt could all claim association, however indirect, with the pilgrimage to the holy cities. Ibn Saud's dealings with Nazi Germany before 1939 were motivated largely by the king's desire to acquire arms, support for Saudi territorial claims, and political backing on the Palestine question. Ibn Saud would not, however, compromise his relationship with Great Britain. Although Khalid al-Hud al-Qarqani, an adviser to the king, met with Hitler and Ribbentrop in Berlin in May 1939 and concluded an arms agreement in July, the king would not permit Germany to establish a diplomatic mission in Jidda. According to one source, Ibn Saud informed Fritz Grobba that the Germans could open a legation whenever they occupied Suez (Gerald DeGaury, *Faisal*, p. 65). For concise treatment of Saudi Arabia's policy toward Germany, see Lukasz Hirszowicz, *The Third Reich and the Arab East*, pp. 47–61, 68–69. According to Hirszowicz, Saudi "ruling circles" displayed "complete reserve" toward the war (p. 101). Great Britain's East African offensive in early 1941, the liquidation of Italy's colonial empire, and British control of the Red Sea "all helped to prevent the Saudis abandoning the watchful, waiting attitude" (p. 101).

94. Murray to Messersmith, 20 Mar. 1939, 124.90F/6.

95. Loomis to Messersmith, 25 Apr. 1939, 124.90F/8. See also Loomis to Hull, 25 Apr. 1939, 124.90F/7.

96. Messersmith to Loomis, 1 May 1939, ibid.

97. Loomis to Welles, 1 June 1939, 124.90F/12.

98. Knabenshue to Hull, 21 June 1939, *FRUS* 1939, 4: 827.

99. Hull to Fish, 24 May 1939, ibid., pp. 824–25. CASOC's field manager, William Lenahan, later reported that the Japanese had offered Ibn Saud $1,648,000, large yearly rentals, and 20 percent of production for a concession (Murray to Berle, Messersmith, and Welles, 2 Aug. 1939, 890F.6363 Standard Oil Company/118). Much has been made of the Japanese visit to Jidda. According to D. C. Watt, the Japanese decision to dispatch a diplomatic representative was probably moti-

vated by a desire to imitate the German example rather than by serious thoughts about an oil concession ("The Foreign Policy of Ibn Saud 1936–1939," pp. 157–60).

100. Knabenshue to Hull, 22 June 1939, 124.90F/14.

101. Hull to Roosevelt, 30 June 1939, *FRUS* 1939, 4: 827–28. Roosevelt noted in the margin of Hull's memorandum, "O.K., excellent idea." See also Hull to Roosevelt, 30 June 1939, OF (Official File) 3500, Roosevelt Papers. Fish was confirmed as minister to Saudi Arabia on 3 August 1939 and presented his credentials to the king on 4 February 1940.

102. *American Petroleum Interests*, p. 163.

103. Shoshana Klebanoff, *Middle East Oil and U.S. Foreign Policy*, p. 10.

Chapter 2

1. In April 1941, Rashid Ali al-Kilani, a former Iraqi prime minister, together with four colonels known as the Golden Square, attempted an unsuccessful coup against the British-supported government in Iraq. The movement was more nationalist and anti-British than pro-Axis, but the conspirators received money and military equipment from Berlin. For a detailed account of the coup and Germany's role, see Hirszowicz, *The Third Reich and the Arab East*, pp. 134–72.

2. Cordell Hull, *Memoirs*, 2:1498.

3. Saudi crude production began in 1938 with a total output of 1,357 b.p.d. By 1941, production according to CASOC's own figures totaled 11,809 b.p.d. However, in his testimony before a Senate committee, James Moffett claimed that Saudi wells could have yielded between 100,000 and 200,000 b.p.d. in 1941 [U.S., Congress, Senate, Special Committee Investigating the National Defense Program, *Petroleum Arrangements with Saudi Arabia* (hereafter cited as *Petroleum Arrangements with Saudi Arabia*), pt. 41, 80th Cong., 1st sess., 1948, p. 24714.] By the middle of 1942, CASOC's American staff was reduced to less than 100 employees. The company's main activity was producing and shipping 12,000 to 15,000 b.p.d. to the Bahrain refinery (Lebkicher et al., *ARAMCO Handbook*, p. 145.) In Iraq, production dropped from 30,791,000 barrels in 1939 to 19,726,000 in 1942 (*Petroleum Facts and Figures*, 1950, p. 448).

4. In June 1941, Knabenshue wrote from Baghdad: "It is my considered opinion that most of the Iraqi Army and Iraqi people are anti-British and that if the Germans make an appreciable thrust in this direction the Iraqi Army will arise against the British unless the British maintain here a force adequate to stop a German thrust and at the same time keep Iraqis under control." (Knabenshue to secretary of state, 5 June 1941, *FRUS* 1941, 3: 512–13.) Although Ibn Saud would

not associate himself with the Rashid Ali movement, he did provide refuge to several of the Rashid Ali conspirators. After the war Rashid Ali himself lived for a time in Saudi Arabia.

5. In 1940, the United States produced 1,353,214,000 barrels of crude oil—almost 63 percent of the world's oil (*Petroleum Facts and Figures*, 1950, pp. 444–49). See also Louis E. Frechtling, "Oil and the War," p. 73.

6. Fish to secretary of state, 6 Mar. 1940, 811.503190F/9. Murray forwarded Fish's report to the secretary of state, the under secretary, and three assistant secretaries.

7. Hare to secretary of state, 11 Apr. 1940, 890F.6363 Standard Oil Company/121.

8. See Kirk, *The Middle East in the War*, pp. 355–56. In 1929, Ibn Saud's total revenue from pilgrimage and customs duties exceeded 4,000,000 gold sovereigns; by 1939, it had dropped to 1,000,000. That same year CASOC paid out almost $800,000 in royalties (Committee Investigating the National Defense Program, OP-38 Gas & Oil, Box 839, Arabian American Oil Company, Records of the United States Senate, RG 46).

9. Murray to Welles, Long, and Berle, 25 Sept. 1940, 890F.796/3. See also Fish to secretary of state, 9 Mar. 1940, 890F.001/53.

10. Fish to secretary of state, 11 Nov. 1940, 890F.00/56.

11. Patchin to Murray, 24 Dec. 1940, 890F.6363 Standard Oil Company/123.

12. Memorandum of conversation between Duce and Alling, 27 Dec. 1940, 890F.6363 Standard Oil Company/126.

13. *Petroleum Arrangements with Saudi Arabia*, p. 24804. According to W. S. S. Rodgers of the Texas Company, advances to the king before 1939 had not exceeded $330,000 in any given year. In 1939, advances topped $1,700,000 and in 1940, over $3,500,000 above both royalties and rent (ibid., p. 25051).

14. Davies to Ohliger, 7 Jan. 1941, ibid., p. 25389.

15. Lenahan to Davies, 1 Apr. 1941, ibid., p. 25391. Refusal to meet the king's latest requests, Lenahan informed Davies, would provoke "another crisis" in relations between the company and the government.

16. Davies to Ohliger, 2 Apr. 1941, ibid., p. 25392.

17. Both Rodgers and Moffett would later claim before a Senate committee that CASOC's main objective in approaching Washington for assistance in April 1941 was to obtain "insurance" for the concession. Although neither oilman believed that Britain would attempt to force a transfer of the concession, they seemed to believe that increasing British influence might seriously prejudice operating conditions for an American company. See ibid., pp. 24805, 24741.

18. Ibid., p. 24743.

19. See William Hassett to Stephen Early, 8 Aug. 1939, OF 2101,

Roosevelt Papers. Roosevelt and Moffett were more than casual acquaintances and had maintained contact since Roosevelt's term as governor of New York. Early, the president's staff assistant, observed "the President likes Jimmy and Jim loves him." Early to Watson, 6 May 1939, PPF (President's Personal File) 2800, Roosevelt Papers. According to Moffett, Roosevelt sought his advice "on any question of oil." (*Petroleum Arrangements with Saudi Arabia*, p. 24710.) Harold Ickes noted in November 1939, "Jimmy, of course is just a play boy, although he has been a rather generous contributor, and for years he was tremendously set up because he was able to go in to see the President practically whenever he wanted to." (Harold L. Ickes, *The Secret Diary of Harold L. Ickes*, 3:62.)

20. Much of the evidence for contact between CASOC and government officials throughout 1941 is drawn from statements and cables of company representatives presented before a special Senate committee investigating the national defense program in 1947 and 1948. The difficulty with oral testimony, particularly six years after the actual events, is obvious. In the case of James Moffett, a central figure in the 1941 affair, the credibility issue is even more complex. In January 1947, Moffett brought a $6,000,000 suit against the Arabian American Oil Company charging that the company had never compensated him for services he had rendered in 1941. Still, if used carefully and checked against State Department documents, the testimony of Moffett, and his colleagues, and the companies' cables provide the best available information on the oilmen's activities before 1945.

21. *Petroleum Arrangements with Saudi Arabia*, p. 24809. See also PSF (President's Secretary File) Diplomatic, Box 68, Folder: Saudi Arabia, Roosevelt Papers.

22. Moffett to Roosevelt, 16 Apr. 1941, *FRUS* 3: 624–25. According to Moffett, while vacationing in South Carolina, he received a telegram from the White House which expressed Roosevelt's interest in receiving a memorandum on finished oil products [Memorandum of 23 June 1948 "Arabian American Oil Company James A. Moffett Suit, Moffett's Story" (hereafter cited as *Moffett's Story*) Folder: 1947–49 Arabian Am. Oil Co. Case, Box 31, Landis Papers.]

23. Moffett to Roosevelt, 16 Apr. 1941, *FRUS* 1941, 3: 624–25.

24. Ibid., pp. 625–27. The oilmen also proposed that the State Department request the British to increase their yearly subsidies to the king. The company cautioned, however, that any advances from London should be made on political or military grounds and should not involve any transfer or supply of Saudi oil.

25. Murray to Hull, 21 Apr. 1941, *FRUS* 1941, 3: 627–29.

26. Ibid., p. 629. The timing of the companies' approach to Washington could not have been better. The Rashid Ali coup had occurred on 1 April. Although by mid-May the British had restored order in

Iraq, by June, with Hitler's invasion of the Soviet Union and push toward the Caucasus, London and Washington were increasingly concerned about the possibilities of German penetration into the Fertile Crescent. Moffett's proposal was no doubt seen as a way to ensure the support of Saudi Arabia and strengthen Allied influence in the Persian Gulf. By August, as the Roosevelt administration weighed the possibilities of aiding the king, Russian and British troops had invaded and occupied Iran.

27. Roosevelt to Knox, 30 Apr. 1941, PSF, Diplomatic, Box 68, Folder: Saudi Arabia, Roosevelt Papers. The idea that the navy might be interested in Moffett's plan was first broached by Murray in his memorandum to Hull. Roosevelt's experience as assistant secretary of the navy might also have predisposed him to sound out Knox.

28. Memorandum of conversation between Alling and Thornburg, 29 Apr. 1941, *FRUS* 1941, 3: 629–32.

29. "Notes on Washington, D.C. Visit, 8 May 1941," *Petroleum Arrangements with Saudi Arabia*, p. 25478. CASOC's campaign to educate State Department officials about the situation in Saudi Arabia had intensified in the fall of 1940. Moffett later recollected, "I don't recall that I was attempting to make any real representation to the State Department. The other boys were handling that end." *Moffett's Story*, Landis Papers. According to Rodgers's recollection, the "first approach" the company made to the United States government was in April 1941. The oilman added that "there may have been some informal talks by some of our people with the State Department, but they were not authorized by the board of ARAMCO." (*Petroleum Arrangements with Saudi Arabia*, p. 24806.)

30. Memorandum of conversation between Hull and Halifax, 7 May 1941, *FRUS* 1941, 3: 632. According to Moffett, he had discussed the question of financial aid to Ibn Saud with Hull at a dinner party on 6 May. Moffett recalled that Hull "took the position as always that this was a matter within the British sphere of influence." (*Moffett's Story*, Landis Papers.)

31. Memorandum of telephone conversation, 13 May 1941, *FRUS* 1941, 3: 633–34. Moffett indicated that he and his colleagues would attempt to persuade the British to take some action.

32. Stonehewer-Bird to Foreign Office, 20 May 1941, E2414/155/25. F.O. 371:27265. See also Foreign Office to C. G. L. Syers, 24 May 1941, E 2414/155/25 F.O. 371:27265. Records of the British Foreign Office, General Correspondence, Political (Eastern). Hereafter cited with file and index number.

33. Murray to Berle and Hull, 29 May 1941, 890F. 51/21. According to CASOC officials, the British had already granted Ibn Saud £800,000 between January 1940 and May 1941. See also memorandum of conversation between Alling and Hamilton, 3 June 1941, 890F.51/32.

34. Murray to Hull, 10 May 1941, *FRUS* 1941, 3: 632–33. Murray had even considered the possibility of channeling Red Cross supplies to Saudi Arabia (Murray to Berle, 3 May 1941, ibid., pp. 603–4).

35. Murray to Berle, 16 May 1941, 890F.51/31. The Reconstruction Finance Corporation (RFC) was originally created by the Hoover administration to lend federal money to banks and other institutions. Under Roosevelt and the RFC's new head, Jesse Jones, the agency became more investment minded. Its subsidiaries ranged from federal mortgage agencies to the Commodity Credit Corporation and the Export-Import Bank. (William E. Leuchtenburg, *Franklin D. Roosevelt and the New Deal*, pp. 71–72.)

36. Davies to Ohliger, 20 May 1941, *Petroleum Arrangements with Saudi Arabia*, p. 25420.

37. See *Moffett's Story*, Landis Papers. According to Thornburg, Knox had informed Moffett that his proposal was "purely a political matter" in which the navy was not presently interested (memorandum of conversation between Thornburg and Alling, 15 May 1941, *FRUS* 1941, 3: 634–35).

38. Knox to Roosevelt, 20 May 1941, ibid., pp. 635–36. According to Knox, the gasoline produced in Saudi Arabia had a very low octane number and the diesel fuel oil had too high a sulphur content. W. John Kenney, later under secretary of the navy, noted that the sulphur content, the tanker shortage, and the problems of supply made the Moffett proposal "unattractive." (Kenny to Forrestal, 26 Mar. 1947, Box 1, Kenney Papers.) For a detailed navy study of the quality of CASOC's products, see Stuart to Knox, 17 May 1941, Committee Investigating the National Defense Program, Op.-38, Gas & Oil, Box 837 Arabian Amer. Oil, Records of the United States Senate, RG 46.

39. Murray to Hull and Berle, 29 May 1941, *FRUS* 1941, 3: 636–37.

40. Memorandum of conversation between Alling and Hamilton, 3 June 1941, 890F.51/32. On 20 June, Butler informed Murray and Alling that Ibn Saud was in "desperate need" of financial aid and expressed the hope that the United States might find a way to assist the king. (Memorandum of conversation, 20 June 1941, 890F.61A/4.)

41. Hopkins to Jones, 14 June 1941, PSF, Diplomatic, Box 68, Folder: Saudi Arabia, Roosevelt Papers. See also *Petroleum Arrangements with Saudi Arabia*, p. 25415.

42. Memorandum of a telephone conversation between Alling and Hamilton, 18 June 1941, *FRUS* 1941, 3: 638.

43. Memorandum of a telephone conversation between Alling and Hamilton, 19 June 1941, ibid., p. 638. CASOC had also been in touch with Jones about the possibility of a loan to Saudi Arabia either through lend-lease or the Reconstruction Finance Corporation (*Moffett's Story*, Landis Papers).

44. In a conversation with Alling on 15 May, Thornburg noted that

CASOC had mentioned to the king the possibility of sending a formal message to the president requesting financial aid. Alling indicated the matter should receive further study before Ibn Saud should submit such a request. NE seemed attuned to the dangers of disappointing the king or compromising his influence and prestige by submitting a formal request which might be rejected (*FRUS* 1941, 3: 634–35).

45. Kirk to secretary of state, 26 June 1941, 890F.51/22. In a memorandum to Berle and Welles, Murray noted, "this Division is thoroughly in accord with Mr. Kirk's views." (Murray to Berle and Welles, 2 July 1941, 890F.51/33.)

46. Davies to Lenahan, 25 June 1941, *Petroleum Arrangements with Saudi Arabia*, p. 25422.

47. Jones to Hull, 6 Aug. 1941, *FRUS* 1941, 3: 642–43.

48. Davies to Lenahan, 14 July 1941, *Petroleum Arrangements with Saudi Arabia*, p. 25422.

49. Roosevelt to Jones, 18 July 1941, *FRUS* 1941, 3: 643. According to Alling, Jones had shown Butler a "brief memorandum" indicating that financial aid to Ibn Saud was a British responsibility and that Saudi Arabia was " 'a long way from the United States.' " Butler thought the memo was initialled by the president (memorandum of conversation, 29 July 1941, 890F.51/36). Communication between the Department of State and Roosevelt did not seem particularly good. According to Murray, there was some doubt as to whether the president had even been informed of the king's formal request for aid (Murray to Welles, 27 Sept. 1941, *FRUS* 1941, 3: 650–51).

50. Stoner to Thornburg, 2 Oct. 1941, *Petroleum Arrangements with Saudi Arabia*, p. 25445. See also Colquitt to Hare, 13 Dec. 1948, 890F.51/12–1348.

51. Memorandum of conversation among Davies, Hamilton, Murray, and Jernegan, 7 Aug. 1941, *FRUS* 1941, 3: 643–45. Murray was still very much interested in obtaining financial aid for Saudi Arabia. NE's chief advised the oilmen to present the proposal "first and foremost" as a "sound commercial operation" based on some form of collateral. Writing to Berle, Murray added, "I personally feel that it would be all to the good if this loan could go through provided it is handled as a commercial operation and not as a 'political loan.' " (Murray to Berle, 8 Aug., 890F.51/38.)

52. Jones to Hopkins, 22 July 1941, PSF, Diplomatic, Box 68, Folder: Saudi Arabia, Roosevelt Papers. See also Jones to Hull, 6 Aug. 1941, *FRUS* 1941, 3: 642–43. Phillips was the British Treasury's representative in the United States.

53. Memorandum of conversation among Alling, Davies, and Hamilton, 24 July 1941, *FRUS* 1941, 3: 640–41.

54. Colquitt to Hare, 13 Dec. 1948, 890F.51/12-1348. On 28 October, Davies informed Lebkicher that the president had "formally ex-

pressed to British Ambassador through Jones his desire that British supply King with necessary funds." (Davies to Lebkicher, 25 Oct. 1941, *Petroleum Arrangements with Saudi Arabia*, p. 25430.)

55. There is no evidence yet available in either the files of the Reconstruction Finance Corporation or the Department of State which conclusively proves that Jones stipulated in the RFC loan package that the British fund Ibn Saud. When the agreement was signed on 21 July there was no mention of a separate $10,000,000 sum. Just prior to the conclusion of the loan, Jones claims, he spoke to Halifax and Phillips, among others, about British advances to Ibn Saud. Jones also showed Phillips Roosevelt's brief note of 18 July expressing his hope that the British would take care of the king (Jones to Hull, 6 Aug. 1941, *FRUS* 1941, 3: 642–43). According to Hamilton of CASOC, Jones left Moffett and Rodgers with the same general impression (memorandum of conversation, 7 Aug. 1941, ibid., pp. 643–44). According to Moffett, in a meeting with Jones on 10 September, the oilman learned that Jones had "specifically" told the British to support the king with funds from the RFC loan. Moffett also recollected, however, that in a 9 October letter from Jones, the Federal Loan Administrator indicated that he had "suggested" rather than "stipulated" that Britain fund Ibn Saud. According to Moffett, "Uncle Jesse didn't want to put 'stipulate' in for some reason and he did say that they had 'suggested.'" (*Moffett's Story*, Landis Papers.) There is a possibility that a memorandum from the British Embassy to Richard Sanger on 7 December 1948 (890F.51/ 12-748) holds the answer to any specific arrangements made between Britain and the United States. The author, having requested this document under the Freedom of Information Act, was informed that it is exempt from declassification because it contains classified material furnished by a foreign government and held on the basis that it be kept in confidence (letter of 26 August 1976 from Milton O. Gustafson, Chief, Diplomatic Branch, Civil Archives Division, to the author). On 7 February 1977, after an additional appeal, the Department of State informed the author that his appeal had been denied on the grounds that the document in question contains "properly classified information furnished by a foreign government and held by the United States on the understanding that it be kept in confidence." (Letter of 7 February 1977 from William D. Blair, Jr., Deputy Assistant Secretary of State for Public Affairs to the author.)

56. Hull to Kirk, 22 Aug. 1941, *FRUS* 1941, 3: 645–46.

57. Kirk to Hull, 30 Aug. 1941, ibid., pp. 647–48. The Department informed the minister in Egypt on 10 September that the decision was in fact based on the "actual merits" of the case. It was the president's view, the department added, that aid to Saudi Arabia "would take us too far afield and that the British have more reason than ourselves to look after its financial needs." (Hull to Kirk, 10 Sept. 1941, ibid., pp. 648–49.)

58. See *Moffett's Story*, Landis Papers, and Jones to Moffett, 9 Oct. 1941, *Petroleum Arrangements with Saudi Arabia*, p. 25371.

59. Thornburg to Stoner, 29 Sept. 1941, ibid., pp. 25444–45.

60. Lebkicher to Davies, 16 Oct. 1941, ibid., pp. 25428–29.

61. Alling to Berle, 23 Sept. 1941, 890F.51/40. According to Twitchell, Ibn Saud had inquired about the prospect of obtaining American assistance in developing water and agricultural resources in 1940 (Twitchell, *Saudi Arabia*, pp. 165–70). During 1941, Twitchell discussed the possibility of sending an American mission staffed by representatives of the Departments of State and Interior. Although State Department officials were favorable to the idea, they apparently decided to defer the matter until the question of financial aid had been resolved. The oilmen had mixed feelings about the project as well. "Twitchell's intentions are good—and he is very straightforward about everything he does—such as giving everyone copies of his letters—" Thornburg wrote to Stoner, "but I don't see any good coming out of getting another man into our part of the picture. And, of course, his interests are not ours." (Thornburg to Stoner, 29 Sept. 1941, *Petroleum Arrangements with Saudi Arabia*, pp. 25444–45.) For Twitchell's contacts with the Departments of State and Interior, see *FRUS* 1941, 3: 651–59.

62. Alling to Welles, 27 Sept. 1941, ibid., pp. 650–51.

63. Hull to Kirk, 26 Sept. 1941, ibid., pp. 658–59.

64. Alling to Reed, 16 Oct. 1941, 890F.24/9.

65. Alling to Berle, 23 Sept. 1941, 890F.51/40.

66. Alling to Reed, 16 Oct. 1941, 890F.24/10.

67. Thornburg to Stoner, 29 Sept. 1941, *Petroleum Arrangements with Saudi Arabia*, p. 25444. According to a Department of State press release of 6 August, announcing Thornburg's appointment: "The vital role played by oil in the present war and in our own national-defense efforts has given it a weight in shaping many State Department policies that warrants a specialist within that Department who is acquainted with the oil problems of various foreign countries." (*Department of State Bulletin*, 9 Aug. 1941, p. 117.) Thornburg, who first served in the Office of the Adviser on International Economic Affairs and then as head of the Office of the Petroleum Adviser, left his position in June of 1943, presumably when the department learned he was drawing a salary from SOCAL. Whether Thornburg was "planted" in the State Department, as Senator Owen Brewster later claimed, is difficult to determine. As Thornburg's correspondence with Stoner makes clear, he no doubt saw a definite distinction between the interests of the oil companies and those of the government. Like so many of the oilmen who would serve in official positions during the war, however, Thornburg saw the necessity and inevitability of cooperation with government, particularly in foreign areas. As did many company representatives who served in the Petroleum Administration for War

(PAW), he acted as a conduit through which government was exposed to and influenced by the ideas of the oil industry. Writing to Assistant Secretary of State Dean Acheson in May 1942, Thornburg observed that although a great deal of information on oil could be gained from other Government departments, "even more important are the ideas of other men, and not only in other Government departments, but men outside the Government." (Thornburg to Acheson, 18 May 1942, 800.6363/690-1/2.) For Senator Brewster's comments, see *Petroleum Arrangements with Saudi Arabia*, p. 25262. For a discussion of oilmen in government service, see Robert Engler, *The Politics of Oil*, pp. 281–82.

68. Ferris to Thornburg, 24 Nov. 1941, "A Study of the Foreign Oil Policy of the United States," Folder: Policy-Historical Review of U.S. Foreign Oil Policy, Box 1, *PED Records*. See also Thornburg to Acheson, 21 Jan. 1942, 800.6363/690-1/2.

69. Davies to Lebkicher, 9 Oct. 1941, *Petroleum Arrangements with Saudi Arabia*, p. 25427.

70. "In view of large US advances to British," Davies informed Lebkicher, "necessary funds should be available." (Ibid., p. 25427.)

71. Lebkicher to Davies, 28 Nov. 1941, ibid., p. 25435. According to Lebkicher, the British minister at Jidda believed that an American adviser would be preferable in order to "manifest disinterested attitude and obviate claims that British have control of country."

72. Memorandum of conversation among Alling, Duce, and Davies, 27 Nov. 1941, 890F.51/45.

73. Merriam to Hull, 25 Nov. 1941, 890F.00/74. What quid pro quo CASOC feared is not clear, yet in view of the fact that the company had only developed a fraction of the total concession, it is possible that the oilmen were concerned that Ibn Saud might decide or be persuaded to divide or transfer part of the concession to British companies. However imaginative and independent the oilmen proved to be in obtaining and developing the concession, they knew that its fate rested solely on Ibn Saud. Keeping the king happy was viewed as the key to maintaining access to and control over his oil. This attitude not only became the basis of the companies' policy toward Saudi Arabia but soon provided the foundation of the American approach as well—particularly in the years before the king could reap the benefits of large production royalties.

74. Murray to Charles Bunn, 17 Dec. 1941, 890F.6363/35.

75. For a brief discussion of the strategic importance of the Middle East, see Michael Howard, *The Mediterranean Strategy in the Second World War*, p. 16. On the origins of the American supply missions, see T. H. Vail Motter, *The Persian Corridor and Aid to Russia*, pp. 3–18.

76. Memorandum of conversation by Merriam, 2 Jan. 1942, 890F.61A/21-1/2. By February, the Army Air Forces were already considering securing transit and landing rights to shorten the ferrying

distance for short-range aircraft between Khartoum and Karachi. On the War Department's interest in obtaining overflight and landing rights, see *FRUS* 1942, 4: 567–75.

77. Hull to Ickes, 12 Jan. 1942, 890F.51/44.

78. Welles to Roosevelt, 12 Feb. 1942, *FRUS* 1942, 4: 562–63. The State Department believed that Ibn Saud might request a "suitable quid pro quo" for granting permission for transit or landing rights. An agricultural mission might facilitate the War Department's request for such privileges. See Hull to Kirk, 6 Feb. 1942, ibid., pp. 567–69 and letter from Louis G. Gimbel Jr., Intelligence, Air Corps Ferrying Command, to the Commanding General, Air Corps Ferrying Command, 4 Feb. 1942, 890F.7962/3.

79. Welles to Murray, 12 Feb., *FRUS* 1942, 4: 559.

80. Murray to Welles, 13 Feb. 1942, 124.90F/24. On 1 May, the Americans opened their legation in Jidda. Moose who had been assigned to Paris in 1930 to learn Arabic and undertake Near Eastern studies at l'Ecole Libre des Sciences Politiques and l'Ecole Nationale des Langues Orientales Vivantes, was appointed consul and second secretary at Jidda.

81. Welles to Kirk, 26 Feb. 1942, *FRUS* 1942, 4: 564. The agricultural mission, composed of Twitchell and representatives of the Departments of Interior and Agriculture, was authorized to investigate the agricultural and "related" resources of Saudi Arabia, conduct experiments, and offer counsel to the Saudi government. The mission arrived in Saudi Arabia in May and completed its investigation in December 1942.

82. See Martin W. Wilmington, *The Middle East Supply Centre*, p. 59.

83. Vail Motter, *The Persian Corridor and Aid to Russia*, p. 6.

84. Winant to Acheson, 17 Apr. 1942, *FRUS* 1942, 4: 9.

85. For a discussion of American policy toward Syria before 1942, see Baram, *The Department of State in the Middle East*, pp. 123–26.

86. Kirk to secretary of state, 16 Feb. 1942, *FRUS* 1942, 4: 72–73.

87. In Iran, production declined from 78,151,000 barrels in 1939 to 50,777,000 in 1941 (*Petroleum Facts and Figures*, 1950, p. 448).

88. Ibid., p. 448. By 1945, Iraq was producing 35,112,000 barrels and Iran 130,526,000 barrels.

89. Ibid., pp. 444–452. In Qatar, drilling operations began in 1938; by 1940 production averaged 4,000 b.p.d. In Kuwait, drilling was stopped in July 1942 as a war measure and resumed in August 1946 (Shwadran, *The Middle East, Oil and the Great Powers*, pp. 431, 410). For details of the petroleum situation in the Middle East during the early years of the war, see "A Brief Summary of ME Petroleum," 27 June 1943, Report No. 40923, Records of the OSS.

90. By 1942, Britain and the United States were planning to increase refinery capacity at Abadan. By 1943, steps were taken to expand the

refineries at Haifa and Bahrain, and to construct a refinery at Ras Tanura. By 1945, refinery capacity for the entire Middle East had increased 43 percent—at Abadan more than 100 percent (Vail Motter, *The Persian Corridor And Aid to Russia*, pp. 291–93).

91. Ickes to Roosevelt, 1 Dec. 1941, File 1-188 Preparedness, Petroleum Administrator File, Central File, Office of the Secretary, Records of the Office of the Secretary of the Interior, RG 48. (Hereafter cited as File 1-188 Preparedness, *Interior Records*.) For additional correspondence between Ickes and Roosevelt on the question of oil reserves, see OF56-Oil 1939–1941, Roosevelt Papers.

92. See "Importance of Middle East Oil Industry to the United Nations," July 1942, Board of Economic Warefare/Office of Economic Warfare Analysis, Inter Divisional Oil Committee, Report No. 22012 (A00199), Records of the OSS. For a popular wartime account of Germany's interest in oil and the new importance of Middle East oil, see Robert Baker, *Oil, Blood, and Sand*.

93. See U.S., Congress, Senate, Special Senate Subcommittee Investigating Petroleum Resources, *Wartime Petroleum Policy Under the Petroleum Administration For War* (hereafter cited as *Wartime Petroleum Policy*), *Hearings before a Special Committee Investigating Petroleum Resources*, 79th Cong., 1st sess., 1945, pp. 6, 64.

94. It is estimated that out of the 7 billion barrels of oil used to fuel the allied war effort, 6 billion were supplied by the United States (John W. Frey and H. Chandler Ide, *A History of the Petroleum Administration for War: 1941–1945*, p. 1). Between 1941 and 1945 the United States produced about 65 percent of the world's crude oil.

95. See Williamson et al., *American Petroleum Industry*, 2:763–64.

96. U.S., Congress, House, Committee on Interstate and Foreign Commerce, *Petroleum Investigation (Gasoline and Rubber)* (hereafter cited as *Petroleum Investigation*), *Hearings before a Subcommittee of the House Committee on Interstate and Foreign Commerce*, 77th Cong., 2d sess., 1942, p. 16.

97. Drilling rates for 1942 were expected to decline because of scarcities of material (*Petroleum Investigation*, pp. 52–53).

98. U.S., Congress, House, *Petroleum Investigation—Petroleum Products for National Defense, Report of the Special Subcommittee on Petroleum Investigation of the Committee on Interstate and Foreign Commerce*, House Report 2274, 77th Cong., 2d sess., 31 Dec. 1942, p. 4.

99. "Importance of Middle East Oil Industry to United Nations," July 1942, Report No. 22012 (A00199), Records of the OSS.

100. Memorandum of conversation, 12 Jan. 1942, ASF International Division File, 679 Pipeline, Oil, Iran, Records of Headquarters, Army Service Forces, RG 160.

101. Until Thornburg's appointment in July 1941, petroleum planning in the Department of State was not centralized. International

petroleum questions were handled by the various political and economic divisions within the department. For the origins of the department's petroleum planning organization, see memorandum prepared by G. M. Richardson Dougall, Oct. 1944, Folder: Petroleum General, Records of Harley A. Notter, 1939–1945 (hereafter cited as *Notter Files*), RG 59.

102. Thornburg to Alling, 6 Apr. 1942, Folder: Middle East-General, Box 4, *PED Records*.

103. Memorandum by Thornburg, 23 Nov. 1942, Folder: Foreign Oil Policy, 1942, Box 1, *PED Records*. Thornburg's views represent a curious mixture of petroleum realpolitik and economic nationalism. He seemed to envision great areas of cooperation between government and oilmen—to the advantage of both.

104. Murray to Berle and Acheson, 15 Dec. 1942, 890F.24/20. In a memorandum to Stimson in March, Welles had raised the idea of lend-lease to Saudi Arabia. There was no mention of petroleum (Welles to Stimson, 23 Mar. 1942, 890F.7962/3). See also Winant to Acheson, 5 Mar. 1942, Folder: #1 Iraq, Records of the Office of Assistant Secretary and Under Secretary of State Dean Acheson, 1941–48, 1950, RG 59. Winant had recommended that Iran, Iraq, and Saudi Arabia be declared vital to the defense of the United States and thus eligible for lend-lease aid.

105. In the fall of 1942, the ANPB was created to inform and advise the Joint Chiefs of Staff on various petroleum problems. See the 4th meeting of the Potentials Committee of the Army-Navy Petroleum Board, 18 Dec. 1942, ANPB 26 (4–9–43), CCS 463.7, Records of the Office of the Joint Chiefs of Staff, RG 218. (Hereafter cited as *JCS Records*.)

106. Both Berle and Murray seem to have toyed with the idea of seeking Ibn Saud's assistance in preventing Arab massacres of Jews in the event the Germans invaded Palestine. In a memorandum to Berle in May 1941, Murray noted that the president might appeal to the king's "sense of chivalry" in persuading him to use his influence to prevent widespread violence (Murray to Berle, 3 May 1941, *FRUS 1941*, 3: 603–4). By 1942, Murray seems to have abandoned the thought of using Ibn Saud's influence to solve any aspect of the problem of Palestine. Not only was the British plan to make Ibn Saud the " 'boss of bosses' " in the Arab world a weak one, Murray wrote to Welles, but it was unlikely that the king would accept any arrangement on Palestine favorable to the Zionists (Murray to Welles, 17 Dec. 1942, *FRUS 1942*, 4: 553–56).

Chapter 3

1. *Wartime Petroleum Policy*, p. 4. See also Vail Motter, *The Persian Corridor and Aid to Russia*, p. 284. On 2 December 1942, the Office of Petroleum Coordinator for National Defense (which until 20 April 1942 had been the Office of Petroleum Coordinator for War), under the direction of Harold Ickes, became the Petroleum Administration for War (PAW).

2. Persian Gulf Oil (Iran, Iraq, Bahrain, Saudi Arabia) also supplied the civilian requirements of India, the Middle East, and most of Africa, the Air Transport Command, the 20th U.S. Air Force, and the Africa-Middle Eastern Service Command. Large quantities of aviation gasoline were also shipped via the Persian corridor to Soviet air units. ("Middle East Oil: A Vital Military Factor," 21 Dec. 1945, prepared by the Military Intelligence Service, XL 32531, Records of the OSS.) A copy of this report can also be found in Folder: Middle East General, Box 4 *PED Records*. See also ANPB to secretary of the navy, 19 Mar. 1947, General Correspondence, James Forrestal 36-1-30 (hereafter cited as *James Forrestal, General Correspondence*), General Records of the Department of the Navy, 1798-1947, RG 80. Of the 33,000 b.p.d. refined by facilities at Bahrain, CASOC officials informed Merriam, 13,000 b.p.d. came from Saudi Arabia (memorandum of conversation by Merriam, 12 Feb. 1943, 890G.6363/417).

3. Everett De Golyer, a leading petroleum geologist and assistant deputy petroleum administrator for war, estimated that since 1938 the United States had used 3 percent of its total reserves annually as a result of new discoveries not being able to keep pace with rising consumption [U.S., Congress, House, Committee on Naval Affairs, *Investigation of the Progress of the War Effort (Petroleum Investigation, Volume 3), Hearings before a Subcommittee of the Committee on Naval Affairs*, 78th Cong., 1st sess., pp. 1433, 2111-16]. For a projection of civilian and military demand, see Davies to Knox, 2 Oct. 1943, ANPB 41/1 (10-27-43), CCS 463.7, *JCS Records*. See also O'Brien to Elliot, 27 Oct. 1943, Folder: Foreign Oil Policy, Central Files, General Classified Files (Part 2), Records of the Office of War Mobilization and Reconversion, RG 250 (hereafter cited as *OWMR Records*).

4. See Blair Bolles, "Oil: An Economic Key to Peace." The wartime concern that American domestic reserves were in a state of decline abated considerably in the immediate postwar years. Although there was new concern about increasing domestic consumption, domestic reserves actually increased by almost a billion barrels per year during the next decade. Moreover, the increase in production paralleled the rise in proven reserves. As a result, the "reserve-production ratio" remained stable (Blair, *The Control of Oil*, p. 6). At the end of 1945, the United States had an estimated 282,000,000,000 barrels of "oil in

place;" of this amount 41,000,000,000 barrels had been produced while 241,000,000,000 remained. Twenty billion barrels or 8 percent were considered "proven reserves." Proved reserves are those considered recoverable "under existing economic and operating conditions." (M. A. Adelman, *The World Petroleum Market*, p. 26.)

5. For many of NE's officials, the British lion still roared with impunity from Aden to Kuwait. Only in Saudi Arabia had American oilmen been able to acquire even a small measure of influence. Already disturbed by the lack of American influence throughout the Middle East, many of the Arab hands were concerned about the fate of an oil concession surrounded by British-controlled areas. Writing to Welles in December 1942, Murray observed, "the Arabian Peninsula is already entirely surrounded by areas under British control. Along the Arabian Gulf we have the Arab sheikhdoms in close treaty relation with Great Britain. Along the entire western coast of the Red Sea all the areas are under British control. Along the Gulf of Aden the British are entrenched in the Aden Protectorate and in the Hadhramaut." (*FRUS* 1942, 4: 553–56.)

6. Some of NE's most vocal critics would come from the department's Division of Financial and Monetary Affairs (FMA). Officials like Emilio Collado and Paul McGuire seemed to believe that Murray and his colleagues were suffering from an "inferiority complex" vis à vis the British and were using the British bogey to enhance the American position in Arabian oil. (Collado to Clayton, 27 Mar. 1945, 890F.6363/ 3-2745.) Similarly, European specialists like John D. Hickerson, later chief of the Division of British Commonwealth Affairs (BC), were not anxious to compete with the British in the Middle East (Hickerson to Dunn, 2 Dec. 1944, 890F.51A/12-244). Even John Loftus, later head of the Department's Petroleum Division and a proponent of a more active policy toward Arabian oil, urged a bilateral rather than a unilateral approach in securing the American stake in Arabian oil. [Loftus to Sappington, 18 Oct. 1944, Folder: memos re: petroleum 1943–44 (with index), Box 1, *PED Records*.]

7. Harry Hawkins to the economic adviser, 4 Mar. 1943, Folder: International Petroleum Policy Committee—memoranda 1943, Box 19, *PED Records*. See also minutes of the 9th meeting of the CIPP, 9 Mar. 1943, Folder: International Petroleum Policy Committee—Minutes of Meetings, ibid.

8. Berle seems to have taken a great interest in Arabian oil and in protecting American reserves from Great Britain. For Berle's views on relations with the British, see Martin Weil, *A Pretty Good Club*, p. 111. For Berle's interest in Saudi Arabia, see Beatrice Bishop Berle and Travis Beal Jacobs, *Navigating the Rapids, 1918–1971*, pp. 387–90. Writing in March 1943, Harold Caccia of the Foreign Office observed, "I understand from Mr. Jebb that Mr. Berle has oil on the brain: hence

no doubt any special interest of the State Dept. in Saudi Arabia."
(Campbell to Foreign Office, 23 Mar. 1943, E2035/784/65 F.O.
371:34965.)

9. Berle to Hull, Welles, Feis, and Thornburg, 6 Jan. 1943, Folder:
US Foreign Oil Policy Thru 1943, Box 1 *PED Records*.

10. Berle to Hull and Welles, 9 Jan. 1943, 800.6363/1-943. Berle's
memorandum concerned an earlier conversation with Feis regarding
the coordination of departmental petroleum planning.

11. For the most part, British maneuvering in Saudi Arabia during
early 1943 was a product of the oilmens' fertile imagination. British
efforts to eliminate the locust problem in Saudi Arabia, however, were
quite real. All signs seemed to indicate a major invasion of locusts in
1943 and 1944. Under the direction of the Middle East Supply Center
(MESC) and the Anti-Locust Research Centre in London, the British
organized a number of major expeditions to root out the insects in
their breeding grounds. The expeditions, covering areas of Iran, Iraq,
Yemen, Eritrea, and Saudi Arabia, were often accompanied by British
military units (Kirk, *The Middle East in the War*, p. 184 and Wilmington, *The Middle East Supply Centre*, pp. 122–26). According to CASOC
representatives, London was using the mission in Saudi Arabia as a
scheme to "get in and get their hands on the concession." (*Petroleum
Arrangements with Saudi Arabia*, p. 24830.)

12. Acheson to Stettinius, 9 Jan. 1943, *FRUS* 1943, 4: 854–55. Iraq
had been declared eligible for lend-lease aid on 1 May 1941; Turkey on
7 Nov. 1941; Egypt on 11 Nov. 1941; Iran on 10 Mar. 1942; and Ethiopia on 7 Dec. 1942.

13. Stettinius to Acheson, 12 Jan. 1943, ibid., p. 855.

14. Why the department's request for lend-lease aid omitted reference to Arabian oil is not clear. NE's December memorandum to Berle
and Acheson had singled out the oil factor as partial justification for
extending lend-lease aid to Saudi Arabia. Nonetheless, NE's thoughts
were definitely on oil. Writing to John Ross, chief of the department's
Division of Personnel regarding the assignment of a petroleum expert
to NE, Alling referred to the long-range problems of the "vast oil resources" in the Near East, particularly in Saudi Arabia, Iraq, Iran, and
Afghanistan. "To indicate the importance of this subject," Alling concluded, "I should mention that our information indicates that 42 percent of the known petroleum reserves of the world are located in that
small area." [Alling to Ross, 13 Jan. 1943, Miscellaneous Files of the
Division of Near Eastern Affairs (NE).]

15. See memorandum of conversation by Feis, 11 Jan. 1943, and
revised memorandum of petroleum policy study group, meeting of 11
Jan., Folder: International Petroleum Policy Committee—Minutes of
Meetings 1943, Box 19, *PED Records*. The committee was first called
the Foreign Oil Policy Committee and met under the chairmanship of
Feis with Thornburg as co-chairman. Composed of representatives of

the various geographic units, the committee sought to combine regional expertise and centralized planning.

16. Feis noted during the committee's first meeting that its primary task was to conduct a study of the questions facing the United States in the field of petroleum "with a view towards indicating and carrying out steps that might be necessary to give effect to them." (Ibid.)

17. The committee was established to focus on problems relating to foreign petroleum, yet it spent a great deal of time on Arabian oil. Although the second meeting was scheduled for 18 January, the committee apparently did not meet again until 10 February. At that time attention was focused exclusively on Saudi Arabia.

18. "Forecast of Emerging Problems with Reference to the Foreign Petroleum Policy of the United States Government as regards the Near East and Africa," 14 Jan. 1943, Folder: Study Group-Petroleum Policy, Box 19, *PED Records*.

19. Kirk to secretary of state, 14 Jan. 1943, 890F.515/1.

20. Kirk to secretary of state, 18 Jan. 1943, *FRUS* 1943, 4: 856–57. The minister also noted that after observing the method by which American aid to Saudi Arabia had been "channelized" through the British, "I have gained impression that we have thereby lost considerable prestige in the eyes of Saudi Arabians who have been given increasingly to feel that the British were their only friends in need."

21. Hull to Kirk, 27 Jan. 1943, ibid., pp. 857–58.

22. According to the oilmen, sterling bloc controls would have required the company to handle its transactions in pounds. CASOC was concerned that it might not be able to exchange pounds for dollars to meet dollar obligations.

23. Owen to Davies, 1 Feb. 1943, 890F.51/52B. The British had reportedly offered to mint 5,000,000 riyals, supply 100,000 gold sovereigns, and guarantee Ibn Saud £225,000 per month in sterling credit to purchase supplies through the United Kingdom Commercial Corporation.

24. *Petroleum Arrangements with Saudi Arabia*, p. 24830.

25. Ibid., pp. 25232–33.

26. Ibid., pp. 25385–87, 25218–19.

27. Ibid., pp. 24854–56. According to Ickes, sometime after 8 February a conference on the subject of Arabian oil was held. The meeting was attended by Ickes, Marshall, Patterson, and Forrestal (ibid., p. 25239).

28. Through contacts with Thornburg and Ralph Davies, SOCAL executives met with Feis, Murray, and Alling. Thornburg also arranged a meeting between Welles and Rodgers. (Thornburg to Welles, 3 Feb. 1943, 800.6363/1105.) See also Feis to Thornburg, 8 Feb. 1943, Folder: Study Group-Petroleum Policy, Box 19, *PED Records*.

29. Minutes of the 2d meeting of the CIPP, 10 Feb. 1943, Folder: International Petroleum Policy Committee—Minutes of Meetings

1943, Box 19, *PED Records*. See also memorandum by Leonard Parker, "Suggested Policy and Action with Reference to Petroleum Installations Erected Abroad in Connection with Military Operations," 9 Feb. 1943, Folder: Study Group-Petroleum Policy, Box 19 *PED Records*.

30. Minutes of the 2d meeting of the CIPP, 10 Feb. 1943. Folder: International Petroleum Policy Committee—Minutes of Meetings 1943, Box 19, *PED Records*.

31. The committee also suggested that further study be given to any "direct or indirect action" which might be required to safeguard the oil concession in Saudi Arabia. "This is a reference," the committee minutes noted, "to the personal nature of the government of the country which reposes in the person of the King and the possible complications that may result on his death." (Ibid.)

32. The oilmen seemed convinced that the State Department, particularly the Division of Near Eastern Affairs, would be receptive to their needs. According to Rodgers: "Well, we had no trouble explaining our story to those gentlemen in the Middle East or Near East Division . . . they were very sympathetic. I think they saw our problem." (*Petroleum Arrangements with Saudi Arabia*, p. 24856.)

33. Memorandum of conversation by Feis, 11 Feb. 1943, Folder: International Petroleum Policy Committee—memoranda 1943, Box 19, *PED Records*. Again the oilmen expressed their concern that the government of Saudi Arabia was "an entirely personal one," and thus vulnerable to "abrupt change and hazard."

34. Ibid. See also memorandum of conversation, 12 Feb. 1943, "Petroleum Reserves—Saudi Arabia," Army-Navy Petroleum Board, Entry 40, Rear Admiral A. F. Carter, USNR, Reading (Spindle) File, July 1942–Nov. 1946, Records of the Inter Service Agencies, RG 334.

35. Feis's comments on his meeting with the oilmen were attached to the memorandum of the conversation. The remaining points on Feis's proposed agenda included: the question of American participation in the British bank scheme; the strengthening of the diplomatic staff at Jidda; consideration of CASOC's stock purchase proposal; consideration of the contract reserves plan; and investigation of the construction of a high octane plant. (Ibid.)

36. Minutes of the 3rd meeting of the CIPP, 15 Feb. 1943, Folder: International Petroleum Policy Committee—Minutes of Meetings 1943, Box 19, *PED Records*. On the questions of American participation in the banking plan and strengthening the diplomatic staff at Jidda, the committee recommended further study. CASOC's proposal to have the United States acquire a financial interest in the company was "left open for further consideration." Thornburg agreed to prepare a memorandum on the possibility of contracts for oil reserves.

37. *Petroleum Arrangements with Saudi Arabia*, p. 25233. Accord-

ing to Ickes, the president was "very much interested" in Middle Eastern oil (ibid., p. 25233).

38. Roosevelt to Stettinius, 18 Feb. 1943, *FRUS 1943*, 4: 859. Of the Middle Eastern countries that received lend-lease aid by the end of 1943, the case of Saudi Arabia was the most peculiar. Iran, Iraq, and Egypt provided bases for allied troops and had declared war on the Axis—only Saudi Arabia and Turkey were formally neutral. Lend-lease aid to Turkey seemed far more justifiable from the standpoint of the war effort than Saudi Arabia, which did not officially declare war on the Axis powers until March 1945, two months before the end of the war in Europe. Saudi Arabia also received credit lend-lease as opposed to cash reimbursable aid. Similarly, there were no precise stipulations for repayment. [Wright to Austin, 30 Nov. 1943, "Lend-Lease Policy in the ME," Entry 445, Subject File of the Director, 1943–1944, Box 2771, Records of the Foreign Economic Administration, RG 169 (hereafter cited as *FEA Records*).] Lend-lease assistance to Saudi Arabia between 1943 and 1945 totaled approximately $18,000,000. An additional $15,000,000 in silver was furnished to the Saudis by the U.S. Treasury with precise terms for repayment.

39. By early 1943, the view that American domestic reserves were gradually declining was shared by many State Department and PAW officials. Petroleum planners overreacted to the seriousness of the problem, yet their response is understandable given the crisis atmosphere of the war years. Concern about the availability of oil was not, for the most part, a result of irresponsible cries of shortage or of fabricated rumors of an oil crisis. Confronted with an unprecedented demand for petroleum, officials sought to evaluate the strengths and limitations of American reserves and productive capacity.

40. Minutes of the 5th meeting of the CIPP, 22 Feb. 1943, Folder: International Petroleum Policy Committee—Minutes of Meetings 1943, Box 19, *PED Records*.

41. The committee proposed that the board of directors of the corporation consist of representatives from the Departments of State, War, Navy, and Interior, with State's representative as chairman. The committee also mentioned the possibility of contracting for reserves in the Netherlands East Indies (ibid.). Thornburg had first broached the idea of contract options and the establishment of an "American Holding Company" in a memorandum prepared for the committee on 16 February. The holding company would seek to acquire "sizeable governmental reserves" in large producing areas of the world. ("Memorandum for discussion concerning the advisability and means of United States Government acquiring rights *to oil in Saudi Arabia*, for *current delivery or reserve*," 16 Feb. 1943, Folder: Saudi Arabia Oil, Box 6, *PED Records*.) Not all officials agreed with the idea of the corporation. Both Harry Hawkins, chief of the Division of Commercial Policy and Agree-

ments (CP) and Philip Bonsal, chief of the Division of the American Republics (ARA) wondered whether such a bold response would not set off an international race for oil. (Minutes of the 9th meeting of the CIPP, Folder: International Petroleum Policy Committee—Minutes of Meetings 1943, Box 19, *PED Records*.)

42. Late in February, Kirk informed the department that it was of the "utmost importance" to link lend-lease aid with "concrete proposals" for immediate aid. The American minister recommended shipment of sixty trucks as a token of American assistance. (Kirk to secretary of state, 26 Feb. 1943, *FRUS* 1943, 4: 860–62.) In March, Welles informed Kirk that the trucks could be made available under direct lend-lease (Welles to Kirk, 11 Mar. 1943, ibid., pp. 862–64). Much of the urgency in channeling aid to the king resulted from the State Department's view that Saudi Arabia was in desperate need of food, textiles, and transportation equipment. Unlike Iran, Iraq, or Egypt, which derived considerable revenue from the presence of American and British military units, Saudi Arabia was dependent on income from the pilgrimage, the oil companies, and the British.

43. Sappington to Acheson, 3 Mar. 1943, Folder: International Petroleum Policy Committee—memoranda 1943, Box 19, *PED Records*.

44. See CIPP memorandum to Hull, 22 Mar. 1943, Folder: Petroleum Reserves Corporation Activities Feb. 22–July 2, 1943, Box 1, *PED Records*. See also 800.6363/3-2243.

45. The memorandum also noted the preference of the Division of Commercial Policy and Agreements for an international agreement on petroleum. It was apparently the view of the CIPP, however, that such an agreement would be difficult to achieve, because, among other things, it would have to include assurances by producing countries against restrictions on exports of petroleum. Even with an agreement, the committee believed, in the event of the king's death, the situation would remain "uncertain." The possibility of domestic shortages and the likelihood that PAW or some other agency might press for action on oil reserves also seemed to make the options idea an attractive one. (Minutes of the 10th meeting of the CIPP, 15 Mar. 1943, Folder: International Petroleum Policy Committee—Minutes of Meetings 1943, Box 19, *PED Records*.)

46. See Feis to Knox, Ickes, and Stimson, 31 Mar. 1943, Folder: International Petroleum Policy Committee—Memoranda 1943, Box 2, *PED Records*. For Hull's account of the origins of the memorandum, see Hull, *Memoirs*, 2:1517–18.

47. Stimson to Hull, 19 Apr. 1943, Folder: Petroleum Reserve Corporation Activities Feb. 22–July 2, 1943, Box 1, *PED Records*. Forwarding NE's recommendation to elevate the chargé at Jidda to the status of minister resident, Hull informed the president: "In view of the rapid decline of the oil resources of the United States, the War and Navy Departments are interested in obtaining military and naval re-

serves in the ground in Saudi Arabia." Hull also called Roosevelt's attention to the fact that Saudi Arabia contained "one of the largest oil reserves in the world." (Hull to Roosevelt, 30 Mar. 1943, *FRUS* 1943, 4: 831–32.) The president approved Hull's recommendation on 3 April. On 18 July, Moose presented his credentials as minister resident.

48. The ANPB presented its report on Middle Eastern oil developments to the Joint Chiefs of Staff on 30 April 1943. In early August at their 99th meeting, the JCS discussed plans to construct a 100,000 b.p.d. refinery in Saudi Arabia to produce 20,000 b.p.d. of Grade 130 aviation fuel [ANPB 26/1 (4–9–43), CCS 463.7, *JCS Records*].

49. For a different view of petroleum "shortages," see Clay to Somervell, ANPB 26, 4 May 1943, (4–9–43), CCS 463.7, Section 1, *JCS Records*.

50. See "Crude Supplies for the United States," 31 May 1943, JCS 342 (5–31–43), CCS 463.7, *JCS Records*. In May, Knox responded favorably to the PRC plan and agreed with the importance of safeguarding American oil reserves with or without an international agreement. Knox to Hull, 24 May 1943, Folder: Petroleum Reserve Corporation Activities, Feb. 22–July 2, 1943, Box 1, *PED Records*.

51. In a draft of a letter to Roosevelt in June 1943, Bullitt reflected the navy's concern and added new urgency to the task of acquiring foreign reserves. "Increased demand for our armed forces and essential industry during the remainder of 1943 and 1944," Bullitt noted, "make it certain that *before the end of 1944 we shall run short from 128,000 to 746,000 barrels a day.*" Bullitt continued: "We cannot squeeze out of our own soil enough petroleum for our war needs." [Bullitt to Roosevelt, June 1943, U.S., Congress, Senate, Subcommittee on Multinationals of the Committee on Foreign Relations, *A Documentary History of the Petroleum Reserves Corporation 1943–1944* (hereafter cited as *A Documentary History of the PRC*), 93rd Cong., 2d sess., 1974, pp. 3–6.]

52. See the 91st meeting of the JCS, 8 June 1943, JCS 342/1 (5–31–43), CCS 463.7, *JCS Records*. Horne raised the problems of British intentions toward the concession and whether the United States ought to inform London of its proposed plans. General George Marshall argued that it might be best to keep Britain informed—in order "to go in with clean hands." Admiral William Leahy noted that according to some experts, Saudi fields were considered to be "the only remaining great oil fields in the world." Leahy later recollected that "in the event of another war in Europe possession or access to these Near Eastern oil supplies was practically essential to any successful campaign by the Americans." (William Leahy, *I Was There*, p. 184.)

53. JCS to Roosevelt, 8 June 1943, *FRUS* 1943, 4: 921. On 11 June, Leahy wrote that the president had directed him to discuss the JCS recommendation to obtain an interest in the Saudi oil fields with the secretary of state (ibid., pp. 921–22).

54. Feis to Hull, 11 June 1943, 890F.6363/79. Feis added that the secretary of state believed that if a PRC was created, the department should hold the chairmanship with veto power over all major actions. Ickes disagreed. Feis did not use the term "nationalization" but advised Ickes and Knox that the Saudis might "place those resources in their own governmental possession with refusal to permit either private or public American interest to participate."

55. Hull to Roosevelt, 14 June 1943, *FRUS* 1943, 4: 922–24.

56. Bullitt to Roosevelt, June 1943, *A Documentary History of the PRC*, pp. 3–6.

57. The Special Committee on Petroleum was composed of representatives of the Departments of State, War, and Navy and PAW. See minutes of the first meeting of the committee, 15 June 1943, 811.6363/6-1543.

58. Secretaries' letter to Roosevelt, 26 June 1943, *FRUS* 1943, 4: 924. See also enclosure "Recommendations as to Petroleum Reserves," ibid., pp. 925–30, and Jones to Hull, 11 July 1943, ibid., p. 932. The PRC board was composed of the secretaries of the Departments of State, War, Navy, and Interior and the director of the Office of Economic Warfare. Although the corporation's bylaws stated that it should not undertake any major projects without the prior consent of the secretary of state, Hull was nonetheless dissatisfied with the direction of the PRC. He declined the chairmanship of the corporation. Although the secretary of state attended the first meeting of the board of directors, he would in the future send either Feis, Murray, or Stettinius as his personal representative. The PRC appointed a Texas attorney, Alvin J. Wirtz, as its chief negotiator with the companies.

59. Feis to Bonsal, 15 June 1943, 800.6363/1235.

60. On wartime relations between Roosevelt and the Department of State, see Hull, *Memoirs* 2:1109–11, and George F. Kennan, *Memoirs 1925–1950*, pp. 172–74.

61. Hurley to Roosevelt, 9 June 1943, PSF, Subject File: Patrick Hurley, Box 153, Roosevelt Papers.

62. It seems clear, in a memorandum from Feis to Hull of 3 July, that Roosevelt, although presented with two alternatives—contract options and stock purchase—leaned toward the latter. According to Feis, the president had broached the idea of offering Ibn Saud a permanent oil reserve for the development of Saudi Arabia. Feis concluded: "It was evident that he thought some such gesture on our part would predispose Ibn Saud to the sale of the concession and also have an extremely healthy influence throughout the Arab world." (Feis to Hull, 3 July 1943, 890F.6363/52.)

63. Berle to Hull, 24 Mar. 1943, 800.6363/1145.

64. Early in August, Feis observed that acquisition of 100 percent of CASOC stock might be too financially demanding (Feis to Hull, 4 Aug. 1943, 890F.6363/62).

65. Minutes of the 1 Sept. 1943 meeting of the PRC, Minutes of the PRC, 9 August 1943–12 May 1944, epitome of events delivered to Abe Fortas, File No. 99, Refinery File, Records of the Reconstruction Finance Corporation, RG 234. (Hereafter cited as *PRC Minutes*.)

66. Ickes may have miscalculated and limited his leverage with the companies by tying the refinery to stock purchase. Aware that the military was interested in the refinery, the oil companies must have realized that if the refinery were constructed in the Persian Gulf, the United States would have no alternative but to purchase crude from CASOC or Gulf Oil. It is possible that the oilmen came to believe that refusing to part with their stock did not preclude them from making a profitable deal with the government—for a refinery or even a pipeline. See also Feis to Hull, 26 July 1943, *FRUS 1943*, 4: 933–34, and memorandum by Feis, 3 Sept., ibid., pp. 937–38. For the JCS view of the project, see JCS 281/2 (4–9–43), CCS 463.7, *JCS Records*.

67. Feis to Hull, 9 Sept. 1943, 890F.6363/66. By early September it was becoming clear even to the most committed PRC member that CASOC was not about to part with all of its stock. At the PRC board meeting of 1 September even Ickes admitted that preliminary negotiations with the companies had led him to believe that purchasing 100 percent of the company's stock was not possible.

68. Meeting of 13 Sept. 1943, *PRC Minutes*. See also *A Documentary History of the PRC*, pp. 26–28.

69. Feis to Hull, 25 Sept. 1943, 890F.6363/70.

70. Ickes had been talking with J. F. Drake, president of Gulf Oil, not only about a possible refinery in Kuwait but also about acquisition of stock in the Gulf Exploration Company—the 50 percent owner of the Kuwait Oil Company. According to Ickes, Gulf was prepared to enter into arrangements with the PRC, but Drake's price of "several hundred millions of dollars" seemed somewhat "excessive." See *PRC Minutes* of 13 and 28 September. According to Feis, Ickes's negotiations with Gulf offered a means to make Texas and SOCAL "more amenable to a reasonable adjustment with the Government." Feis to Hull, 16 Sept. 1943, 890F.6363/69.

71. *PRC Minutes* of 28 Sept. 1943. According to the proposed arrangements, the joint government and company board would consist of two representatives from the Texas Company, two from SOCAL, and three from the PRC. If the deal were finalized, Feis wrote to Hull, CASOC planned to change its name to the "American-Arabian Company." Although Feis felt that such a title might offend Ibn Saud, the company representatives believed otherwise on the basis of "local information" (Feis to Hull, 25 Sept. 1943, 890F.6363/70).

72. De Golyer had already informed the PRC board that Saudi reserves "will amount to many billions of barrels." (*PRC Minutes*, 28 Sept. 1943.)

73. *PRC Minutes*, 14 Oct. 1943.

74. Ibid. According to Ickes, Rodgers wanted the government to assume an additional $40,000,000 worth of expenses for the refinery plan (*Petroleum Arrangements with Saudi Arabia*, p. 25242).

75. As might be expected, Ickes and Rodgers both blamed each other for the collapse of the negotiations. According to Ickes, "apparently the Texas Co. was prepared to pull a different card from a different deck everytime that it appeared we were about to get together." Ickes added that SOCAL also "went through the motions." (Ibid.) According to Rodgers, Ickes simply informed him that the "deal is all off." The oilman later recalled, "I have done a lot of trading in my day, but I never had anything like that happen before." (Ibid., p. 24868.)

76. *PRC Minutes*, 3 Nov. 1943. The PRC board also agreed to withdraw proposals for construction of a refinery in Saudi Arabia.

77. Feis, *Seen From E.A.*, pp. 129–30.

78. Sheets to Feis, 27 Dec. 1943, Folder: 1943–1947, Box 29, Feis Papers.

79. *Petroleum Arrangements with Saudi Arabia*, p. 25241. With the beginning of lend-lease and the conclusion of a U.S. Treasury agreement in October to supply silver to Saudi Arabia, the oilmen were probably less willing to part with their stock. What the companies had been seeking from the beginning was security for their concession. If it could be obtained through a government commitment in aid or through official assistance in stabilizing the king's finances, so much the better. Moreover, failure to part with their stock would not preclude the oilmen from negotiating other kinds of profitable government-company ventures.

80. Hull, *Memoirs*, 2:1518.

81. Feis, *Seen From E.A.*, p. 135.

82. The idea of an international or bilateral agreement on oil can be traced back at least as early as Ferris's study on foreign oil policy in late 1941 (see Ch. 2 n.68). During the early meetings of the CIPP, Thornburg, Hawkins, Feis, and Bonsal had raised the matter on numerous occasions. The Special Committee on Petroleum had also discussed the idea of an accord with Britain in June 1943. The committee was chaired by Feis and composed of representatives of the Departments of State, War, and Navy and PAW. On 13 Sept., Feis informed the PRC board that the State Department would submit a draft of a possible agreement with the British (PRC Minutes, 13 Sept. 1943).

83. See meetings of 21 and 28 Sept. 1943, Folder: Special Committee on Petroleum (Minutes), Box 28, *PED Records*.

84. Thornburg to Feis, 26 May 1943, Folder: International Petroleum Policy Committee—memoranda 1943, Box 19, *PED Records*.

85. Bullitt to Roosevelt, June 1943, *A Documentary History of the PRC*, pp. 3–6.

86. Memorandum of conversation by Parker, 15 July 1943, *FRUS* 1943, 4: 875–76.

87. Moose to secretary of state, 24 July 1943, ibid., pp. 879–80. See also Kirk to secretary of state, 28 July 1943, ibid., p. 882.

88. Memorandum of conversation between State and Treasury Department representatives, 11 Aug. 1943, 890F.51/8-1143. In July, John W. Gunter of the U.S. Treasury was sent to investigate financial conditions in Iran, Saudi Arabia, and Turkey. Gunter's reports from Saudi Arabia confirmed the seriousness of the king's situation, particularly with respect to shortages of silver (Kirk to secretary of state, 17 Aug. 1943, FRUS 1943, 4: 889–91).

89. Memorandum of conversation by Feis, 17 Sept. 1943, ibid., pp. 902–3.

90. Eden to Halifax, 8 Aug. 1943, E4462/2551/65 F.O. 371:34975. In response to Ibn Saud's requests for military equipment under lend-lease, the War Department dispatched a military mission under the command of Major General Ralph Royce, Commanding General, U.S. Forces, Middle East. The mission arrived in Saudi Arabia in December 1943 to study and collect information on Saudi military requirements. For documentation on the Royce mission, see FRUS 1943, 4: 904, 917–18.

91. Eden to Halifax, 8 Aug. 1943, E4462/2551/65 F.O. 371:34975.

92. Memorandum from Eden to War Cabinet, 12 July 1943, W.P. (43) 301 CAB:66(39). Eden informed Halifax that reports indicate that the "unco-operative attitude of the State Department is almost entirely due to the influence of Mr. Wallace Murray, the Political Adviser for Middle Eastern Affairs." Eden suggested that the Foreign Office could either arrange for a meeting with Murray in hopes of "overcoming his suspicions and prejudices" or talk to Murray's superiors in the hope of "neutralising his anti-British tendencies, at least in matters of major importance."

93. Minutes of the War Cabinet, 14 July 1943, CAB 65/35.

94. Eden to War Cabinet, 12 July 1943, W.P. (43) 301 CAB:66 (39).

95. Kirk to secretary of state, 13 Oct. 1943, 890F.6363/75.

96. Alling to Sappington, 6 Nov. 1943, 890F.6363/86.

97. British Embassy to the Department of State, 30 Oct. 1943, FRUS 1943, 4: 6–7.

98. This was no coincidence. In its meeting of 14 July, the War Cabinet discussed the subject of Anglo-American interests in Middle Eastern oil. In response to a suggestion by the Home Secretary that the Cabinet consider approaching Roosevelt in order to defuse any tensions over oil, Churchill replied, "there was no good reason for raising the far-reaching issues involved by those oil questions at the present time, and doubted if it was in our interests to do so." (Minutes of the War Cabinet, 14 July 1943, CAB 65/35.)

99. Murray to Stettinius, 6 Nov. 1943, FRUS 1943, 4: 8–10.

100. Halifax had initially requested that Murray join Harold B. Hoskins, Roosevelt's personal representative, for discussions in London.

The State Department believed that discussions should be held in Washington and a detailed agenda prepared in advance. Although the British tentatively agreed on the question of preparing an agenda, they continued to insist that the discussions be held in London. For documentation on the proposed Anglo-American negotiations, see *FRUS 1943*, 4: 6–18.

101. Memorandum by Murray, 24 Nov. 1943, ibid., pp. 943–47.

102. Wright to Patterson and Stimson, 30 Nov. 1943, 800.6363/1455. On 11 December, Patterson approved the memorandum; on 13 December it received Stimson's endorsement. Early in January 1944, Stettinius informed Wright that the State Department's views were generally in accord with his draft (Stettinius to Wright, 3 Jan. 1944, ibid.).

103. Sappington to Murray, 1 Dec. 1943, 890F.6363/92½.

104. Hull to Halifax, 2 Dec. 1943, *FRUS 1943*, 4: 947.

105. Hull to Roosevelt, 8 Dec. 1943, ibid., p. 948. The president approved Hull's plan for the American negotiating team—two representatives from the State Department, one of whom would serve as chairman, and a third member to be chosen by Ickes.

106. Memorandum by Murray, 14 Dec. 1943, ibid., pp. 949–50.

107. Ickes to Forrestal, 19 May 1944, Folder: Petroleum Administration, Box 159, Patterson Papers.

108. Ickes to Roosevelt, 27 Dec. 1943, PSF, Folder: State Dept. January–September 1944, Box 91, Roosevelt Papers.

109. "Oil—In Search of a Policy," *Time*, 27 Dec. 1943, pp. 77–78.

Chapter 4

1. "Conflicts and Agreements of Interest of the United Nations in the Near East," 10 Jan. 1944, Report No. 1206, *Records of the OSS*.

2. In January 1944, CASOC changed its name to the Arabian American Oil Company (ARAMCO). According to Feis, the company had planned to change its name to the "American-Arabian Company" in the event the stock deal was consummated (Feis to Hull, 25 Sept. 1943, 890F.6363/70).

3. Davies to Knox, 2 Oct. 1943, ANPB 41/1 (10–27–43), CCS 463.7, *JCS Records*. See also Report of the ANPB, 30 July 1943, JCS 281 (4–9–43), CCS 463.7, *JCS Records*.

4. Memorandum by ANPB, 5 June 1944, (6–5–44) CCS 463.7, *JCS Records*.

5. For highlights of De Golyer's report, see *PRC Minutes*, 27 Jan. 1944. Ickes forwarded a copy of the report to Roosevelt (Ickes to Roosevelt, 4 Feb. 1944, "Board of Economic Warfare," OF 4226-D, Roosevelt Papers). According to the report, the "proved" reserves of Iraq, Kuwait, Saudi Arabia, Bahrain, Iran, and Qatar totaled 16,500,000,000

barrels. Reserves that were proved but not yet fully explored totaled 27,000,000,000. Of this amount, Kuwait had 9,000,000,000; Iran had 6,000,000,000 to 7,000,000,000; Iraq had 5,000,000,000; Saudi Arabia had 4,000,000,000 to 5,000,000,000; and Qatar had 1,000,000,000. Estimates of Saudi reserves would increase considerably during the war and immediate postwar years. De Golyer put proven reserves at 2,000,000,000 and unproven at 4,000,000,000 to 5,000,000,000; the president of the Trans-Arabian Pipeline Company estimated proved reserves at 7,000,000,000 in 1948; W. S. S. Rodgers estimated 4,000,000,000 to 5,000,000,000 as a conservative total for the same year and 20,000,000,000 barrels as a nonconservative estimate; Secretary of Defense Forrestal calculated reserves at 30,000,000,000 barrels; and in 1950, the American Petroleum Institute put the total at 9,000,000,000 barrels. (Shwadran, *The Middle East, Oil and the Great Powers*, p. 355, and *Petroleum Facts and Figures*, 1950, p. 443.)

6. The Departments of State, Interior, Commerce, War, Navy, and Economic Warfare, the JCS, Foreign Economic Administration, PAW, War Production Board, and OWMR all dealt directly or indirectly with Middle Eastern petroleum.

7. Ickes to Roosevelt, 4 Jan. 1944, PSF, Folder: Saudi Arabian Pipeline, Box 68, Roosevelt Papers.

8. Ickes to Hull, 7 Jan. 1944, *FRUS* 1944, 5: 13–15. On 5 January, Hull had written to Ickes requesting the postponement of PRC's negotiations with the companies (ibid., pp. 10–11).

9. Hull to Roosevelt, 8 Jan. 1944, ibid., pp. 15–16.

10. Roosevelt to Hull, Ickes, 10 Jan. 1944, ibid. p. 16. The president concluded, "I feel that time is important—because after the war the American position will be greatly weaker than it is today. Can't we agree on a policy and on the method of putting it into effect?"

11. Knox to Hull, 11 Jan. 1944, 800.6363/1437.

12. Davies to Murray, 27 Dec. 1943, *FRUS* 1944, 5: 8–9. See also memorandum of conversation among Alling, Murray, and Thornburg, 4 Dec. 1943, 800.6363/1397½. The idea of a trans-Arabian line had been broached as early as 1940. In February 1943 the ANPB was considering such a project (memorandum of conversation, 12 Feb. 1943, 890G.6363/417). It seems that Commodore A. F. Carter, a former oilman himself and executive officer of the ANPB, suggested the idea of the pipeline to Ickes in early January. (memorandum by Carter, 17 Jan. 1944, *FRUS* 1944, 5: 17–20.)

13. Byrnes to Roosevelt, 17 Jan. 1944 OF 56, Folder: Oil, 1943–44, Box 4, Roosevelt Papers.

14. Ickes later claimed that the pipeline scheme was never intended as anything more than a means to an end. "I have never tried to misrepresent or exaggerate the importance of PRC. To me it has always been a means to an end, a threat that would persuade the British that it was highly expedient for them to seriously engage in conversations

about Mid-Eastern oil." (Ickes to Forrestal, 19 May 1944, Folder: Petroleum Administration, Box 159, Patterson Papers.)

15. See 143rd meeting of the JCS, 25 Jan. 1944, JCS 281/16 (4–9–43), Section 3, CCS 463.7, *JCS Records*. See also Leahy to Knox and Stimson, 25 Jan. 1944, Folder: 44(1) JCS Correspondence 1944, Naval History Division, Washington Navy Yard.

16. *PRC Minutes*, 27 Jan. 1944.

17. Ibid.

18. See draft of statement on the pipeline, 28 Jan. 1944, 800.6363/1–2944, and *PRC Minutes*, 5 Feb. 1944. Knox later summed up the attractiveness of the pipeline proposal. "In order to conserve a very large volume of oil for possible use in an emergency, we make a pipeline for oil transportation there. That is about the size of it. We do not go in for oil ownership." (U.S., Congress, House, Committee on Appropriations, *Hearings on Navy Department Appropriations Bill for 1945*, 78th Cong., 2d sess., 1944, p. 1139.)

19. *A Documentary History of the PRC*, p. 79.

20. Ibid., pp. 84–85.

21. Feis, *Seen From E.A.*, pp. 152–55.

22. *PRC Minutes*, 27 Jan. 1944. In late January, Senators Moore and Brewster introduced a resolution into the Senate calling for the dissolution of the PRC. On 13 March, the Senate established the Special Committee Investigating Petroleum Resources under the chairmanship of Senator Francis Maloney of Connecticut. Between 31 March and 13 June, the committee held eleven executive sessions regarding the proposed pipeline. (*FRUS* 1944, 5: 34 n.5.) The committee continued its work under the chairmanship of Joseph C. O'Mahoney of Wyoming and submitted its final report in January 1947. For the text of the committee's interim report, see U.S., Congress, Senate, Special Committee Investigating Petroleum Resources, *Investigation of Petroleum Resources in Relation to the National Welfare, Intermediate Report No. 179*, 79th Cong., 2d sess., 1945. For the final report, see U.S. Congress, Senate, Special Committee Investigating Petroleum Resources, *Investigation of Petroleum Resources in Relation to the National Welfare*, Final Report No. 9, 80th Cong., 1st sess., 1947.

23. *PRC Minutes*, 3 April and 12 May 1944.

24. Ickes to Roosevelt, 29 May 1944, PSF, Folder: Saudi Arabian Pipeline, Box 68, Roosevelt Papers. See also *PRC Minutes*, 12 May 1944. On the president's decision, see memorandum of conversation among Roosevelt, Maloney, Ickes, and Stettinius, 1 June 1944, 890F.6363/6-144.

25. ANPB memorandum to JCS, 17 June 1944, 26/16 (4–9–43), Section 3, CCS 463.7 *JCS Records*. On 8 June, Ickes wrote to Forrestal requesting that the navy support his application to the WPB for materials for construction of the pipeline. Forrestal forwarded Ickes's re-

quest to the JCS who turned it over to the ANPB for study. The ANPB report concluded that the pipeline was of "military importance" because it would make Persian Gulf oil available in the postwar period; it noted that the pipeline was not at this time of "immediate military necessity." See also, "The Relation of the Proposed Saudi Arabian Pipeline to United States Interests in Middle Eastern Oil," 5 May 1944, R&A Report No. 109155, *OSS Records*.

26. In late June, the Department of State informed Moose in Jidda that as a result of an "informal understanding within this Government," no further action would be taken on a government-sponsored pipeline pending Cabinet-level discussions with Great Britain and any hearings which the Senate Special Committee might wish to hold. (Hull to Moose, 27 June 1944, *FRUS 1944*, 5: 33–34.)

27. Rayner to Hull, 29 Jan. 1944, ibid., pp. 21–22. See *PRC Minutes*, 5 Feb. 1944. According to Sappington, the State Department supported the project because the PRC had advanced it on an "urgent basis"—as a war measure. Initially, the pipeline had the support of the army, navy, and the JCS (Sappington to Rayner, 12 May 1944, Folder: Petroleum Reserve Corporation Activities Jan. 1–July 1, 1944, Box 1, *PED Records*).

28. Memorandum by Rayner, 15 Feb. 1944, ibid.

29. Rayner to Davies, 7 Jan. 1944, *FRUS 1944*, 5: 12–13, and Haley to Rayner, 3 Feb. 1944, 800.6363/1505 respectively.

30. "United States Petroleum Policy in the Middle East," 13 Jan. 1944, Folder: US Foreign Oil Policy Thru 1944, Box 1, *PED Records*. Many of Loftus's conclusions and assumptions were later incorporated into a memorandum entitled "Foreign Petroleum Policy of the United States" (11 Apr. 1944) which was prepared by an interdivisional Petroleum Committee of the Department of State (*FRUS 1944*, 5: 27–33). Departmental order 1345, 27 Mar. 1944 established a Petroleum Division (PED) under the charge of the Office of Economic Affairs. Rayner became acting chief with Sappington the assistant chief.

31. Rayner to Hull, 5 Feb. 1944, 800.6363/2-544.

32. Memorandum of conversation between Wright and Stettinius, 7 Feb. 1944, 800.6363/1482. Early in January, the United States' ambassador in the United Kingdom, John Winant, informed the department that the Foreign Office, having learned that Churchill and Roosevelt did not deal with oil problems at conferences in Cairo or Tehran, was now "actively" considering the State Department's invitation. (Winant to Hull, 3 Jan. 1944, *FRUS 1943*, 4: 952.)

33. Hull to Halifax, 10 Feb. 1944, *FRUS 1944*, 3: 94–95. Among the tentative subjects for discussion, Hull listed existing impediments to production, pricing and marketing problems, and concession rights. The latter point was the most sensitive to the British and seemed to explain London's reluctance to engage in discussions on Middle Eastern oil. See also Halifax to Hull, 7 Feb. 1944, ibid., p. 94.

34. Memorandum of conversation by Rayner, 18 Feb. 1944, ibid., pp. 98–99.

35. Memorandum of conversation by Rayner, 18 Feb. 1944, ibid., pp. 99–100.

36. Churchill to Roosevelt, 20 Feb. 1944, ibid., pp. 100–101.

37. Stettinius to Winant, 22 Feb. 1944, ibid., pp. 101–2. The president's message was transmitted through the Department of State to the American ambassador in London.

38. Ibid., p. 103 n.10. On 4 March, Churchill responded directly to the president's earlier message: "Thank you very much for your assurances about no sheeps eyes at our oil fields in Iran and Iraq. Let me reciprocate by giving you fullest assurance that we have no thought of trying to horn in on your interests or property in Saudi Arabia." (Churchill to Roosevelt, 4 Mar. 1944, ibid., p. 103.)

39. Winant to Roosevelt, 6 Mar. 1944, ibid., pp. 104–5.

40. The technical discussions began in Washington on 18 April. The American team of experts consisted of Rayner, Alling, and Leroy Stinebower of the State Department; Ralph Davies, George Walden, and C. S. Snodgrass of PAW; and General Howard Peckham and Commodore A. F. Carter of the War and Navy Departments. In an effort to gain the support and counsel of the oil industry, government officials had invited a group of oilmen to Washington prior to the opening of the technical talks. The industry advisers included John A. Brown, president of Socony-Vacuum; W. Alton Jones, president of Cities Service Oil Company; W. S. S. Rodgers, president of the Texas Oil Corporation; Alvin Jacobsen, president of the Amerada Petroleum Corporation; and Colonel J. Frank Drake, president of the Gulf Oil Corporation. [See meetings of 12 and 13 April, Folder: Petroleum Discussion with the British (except Joint Minutes), Box 3, *PED Records.*]

41. Preliminary Agenda, 18 Mar. 1944, File: Oil [Wildcatting, etc.], Box 12, Hickerson Files, Records of the Office of European Affairs, RG 59. See also Agenda of 17 Mar., Folder: Memorandum of Understanding with the U.K. [1944], Box 17, *PED Records.*

42. The British were in no particular hurry to initiate discussions. Not until 30 March, three weeks after the Americans released the names of their negotiating team, did the British forward the names of their experts to the Department of State (*FRUS* 1944, 3: 106–10). The British team included Brown, F. C. Starling, and V. S. Butler of the Petroleum Department; J. H. Le Rougetel of the Foreign Office; Sir W. Fraser of Anglo-Iranian Oil Company; Sir F. Godber of Royal Dutch-Shell; F. Harmer of the Treasury; and Commodore A. W. Clarke of the navy.

43. Memorandum by Stinebower, 25 Apr. 1944, 800.6363/1628. The British pressed the Americans not only to respect all valid concession contracts but also to support them as well (Hull to Roosevelt, 4 May 1944, *FRUS* 1944, 3: 111–12).

44. For the text of the Draft Memorandum of Understanding, see ibid., pp. 112–15. For a record of the minutes of the technical discussions, see Folder: Petroleum Discussions with the British (except Joint Minutes), and Folder: Petroleum Discussions with the British Joint Minutes, Box 3, *PED Reocrds*.

45. In addition to negotiation of a multilateral petroleum agreement, the United States and Great Britain agreed to establish a Joint Petroleum Commission, which would consider petroleum-related problems and make recommendations.

46. See Minutes, Joint Session No. X, Anglo-American Exploratory Discussions on Petroleum, 3 May 1944, 800.6363/1671.

47. Hull to Moose, 11 May 1944, *FRUS 1944*, 5: 698–99.

48. Memorandum by Rayner, 16 June 1944, *FRUS 1944*, 3: 117–18.

49. Roosevelt to Churchill, 7 June 1944, ibid., p. 117. See also Hull to Winant, 24 June 1944, ibid., p. 118. The British delegation was composed of Beaverbrook; Richard Law, minister of state; Ben Smith, minister resident in Washington; Ralph Assheton, financial secretary to the Treasury; and Geoffry Lloyd, parliamentary secretary to the Ministry of Fuel and Power. The American group was initially led by Hull. Due to Hull's illness, Ickes, as vice-chairman, replaced him. The remainder of the negotiating team consisted of Forrestal, now secretary of the navy; Patterson; Leo Crowley, foreign economic administrator; Davies; and Rayner.

50. For the minutes of the Joint Subcommittee meetings and Plenary Sessions—25 July to 3 Aug.—see Folder: Petroleum Discussions with the British Joint Minutes, Box 3, *PED Records*. For discussion of the problem of foreign exchange, see Joint Subcommittee Session III, 28 July 1944, ibid. The British, anticipating an adverse foreign exchange balance in the postwar period, sought to reserve the right to take certain measures to correct the situation. One of the ways this might be accomplished was to decide the sources from which its oil might be drawn—sterling or nonsterling. Arguing that such a prerogative would contradict the notions of equal access and orderly development of international oil, the Americans refused to agree. A compromise was eventually proposed which would refer any exchange problems to the Joint Commission—before either side took action.

51. For the text of the agreement, see Folder: "Anglo-American Oil Agreement—1945," Box 4, *PED Records*.

52. John Loftus, "The Anglo-American Petroleum Agreement," 14 Sept. 1944 (Black Binder), Box 3, *PED Records*. Loftus, a Johns Hopkins-trained economist, had served with the Board of Economic Warfare. With the establishment of the Petroleum Division in 1944, he became chief of its policy branch.

53. Ibid.

54. According to Loftus, one of the main objectives of the agreement—the protection of American reserves by removing restrictions

on oil development in the Middle East—was not "emphasized or even discussed in public statements" out of concern that such an emphasis might be politically detrimental to the acceptance of the agreement by Congress. [Loftus to Wilcox, 10 Jan. 1946, Folder: Policy (Foreign Policy Problems), Box 8, *PED Records.*]

55. Loftus, "The Anglo-American Petroleum Agreement," 14 Sept. 1944 (Black Binder), Box 3, *PED Records.*

56. The agreement encountered even more resistance than the PRC pipeline scheme. Opposition in Congress was widespread—from representatives of the oil-producing states opposing government intervention to those legislators who believed that the agreement risked too much and offered too little in the way of advantages for domestic producers. On 16 August, in a meeting between State Department representatives and a group of twelve senators, including Connally, only Claude Pepper of Florida expressed no major objection to the accord. (Memorandum of conversation among Long, Rayner, and the senators, 16 Aug. 1944, 800.6363/8-1644.) See also Sappington to Rayner, 30 Oct. 1944, Folder: U.S.-Foreign Oil Policy Thru 1944, Box 1, *PED Records.* Many in the petroleum industry, particularly the independent oil producers, argued that the agreement was so loosely worded that it could be interpreted as granting power to the federal government to control the domestic oil industry. The smaller companies were also concerned that the agreement's reference to the "orderly conduct" of the international petroleum trade might create an organized oil cartel.

57. By the fall of 1944, the State Department realized that the agreement had little chance of success in its present form. Connally had already indicated that hearings on the accord would not even begin until after the November elections, and in December he publicly claimed that it was unlikely that the accord would ever be ratified. The agreement was renegotiated with the British in the fall of 1945 and sent to the Senate in November 1945. In July 1947, after a series of hearings, the Senate Foreign Relations Committee recommended the agreement to the Senate. The agreement was never ratified.

58. Memorandum by Rayner, 17 Aug. 1944, 800.6363/8-1744.

59. Henderson to secretary of state, 17 Apr. 1944, 800.6363/1601.

60. For a detailed comparison of British and American aid to Saudi Arabia, 1941 to 1944, see Moose to secretary of state, 12 Jan. 1944, 890F.51/57.

61. Memorandum by Leonard Parker, 15 Mar. 1944, 740.0011 Stettinius Mission/3-1944.

62. Foreign Office to Jordan, 16 Feb. 1944, E364/325/25 F.O.371:50379.

63. Kirk to secretary of state, 13 Jan. 1944, *FRUS 1944,* 5:672.

64. Baxter minute, 12 Feb. 1944, E1127/325/25 F.O. 371:40268.

65. Memorandum of conversation among Treasury representatives, White, Friedman, Bernstein, and Glendinning and State Department representatives Parker and McGuire, 12 Feb. 1944, 890F.51/60.

66. Minute by Maurice Peterson, 7 June 1944, E 2811/1407G F.O. 371: 40265. In August 1943, Jordan was appointed minister to Saudi Arabia to replace Stonehewer-Bird.

67. Moose to Hull, 27 Mar. 1944, 890F.5018/6, and Moose to Hull, 30 Mar. 1944, 890F.6363/113.

68. Hull to Moose, 3 Apr. 1944, ibid. According to Kirk, the proposed British subsidy for 1944 was 35 million riyals; anticipated American aid was 6 million riyals. Although Kirk noted that maintaining equality in Anglo-American aid might be difficult in view of the proximity of British supply bases, he recommended that Washington rectify the imbalance or "accept the consequences of permitting the inevitable growth of British influence. . . ." (Kirk to Hull, 28 Mar. 1944, 890F.515/94.)

69. Memorandum by Alling, 1 Apr. 1944, 890F.51/4-144.

70. NEA memorandum to Hull, 3 Apr. 1944, 890F.51/131. Hull to Roosevelt, 3 Apr. 1944, *FRUS* 1944, 5: 679–80. Upon NEA's recommendation, Hull also requested the president's approval to elevate the status of the U.S. diplomatic representative from minister resident to minister plenipotentiary (890 F.24/4-1044).

71. Other proposed Middle Eastern topics included Bahrain, the Arab federation, Palestine, Iranian oil, and the Arabian pipeline. For background papers on Saudi Arabia, see 740.0011 Stettinius Mission/ 3-1944.

72. The mission included: Stettinius, Murray, Isaiah Bowman, vice-chairman, Advisory Council on Post-War Foreign Policy; John L. Pratt, consultant on Commercial Affairs; H. Freeman Matthews, deputy director of the Office of European Affairs; Robert J. Lynch, special assistant to the undersecretary and executive secretary to the mission; and Louis J. Hector, assistant to the under secretary. The group arrived in London on 7 April and departed 29 April.

73. "Anglo-American Discussion—Saudi Arabia," Brief for the Murray conversations, E2678/325/25 F.O. 371:40269. The memo was based on a Baxter minute of 16 Mar. and revised by Peterson. E1775/ 128/25 F.O. 371:40265.

74. Butler Minute, 10 Apr. 1944, E2683/325/25 F.O. 371:39985. The "attached minute," written by Peterson on 5 April, argued that the British had a "predominant position" in the Middle East which was similar to the American position in Latin America. Peterson noted that Great Britain had no desire to interfere with American interests in Middle Eastern oil but would not accept the view that these oil interests entitled the United States to participate in security arrangements in the area—specifically on the matter of stationing troops.

75. Peterson to Eden, 14 Apr. 1944, E 2654/16/65 F.O. 371:39985. For the American record of discussions on Saudi Arabia, see meetings of 12 April (740.0011/Stettinius Mission/130) and 26 April (740.0011 Stettinius Mission/153).

76. For the text of the agreed minute of the conversations, see 740.0011 Stettinius Mission/120C. See also Stettinius to Hull, 22 May 1944, *FRUS 1944*, 3: 28–30.

77. During the conversations, Peterson had informed Murray that Ibn Saud was as usual concerned about his financial situation and had requested the British to provide a Sunni Muslim financial adviser. The king apparently preferred a Muslim because the Saudi Department of Finance was in Mecca. Peterson also noted that the king had requested Muslim military advisers, presumably because a mission led by Christian officers might provoke a reaction from traditionalists and weaken his influence. Peterson proposed a joint Anglo-American mission to be composed of Sunni Muslim Indian officers and Americans, but led by a British officer. In view of the fact that an American training mission under the leadership of Colonel Garrett B. Shomber was due to arrive in Saudi Arabia in mid-April, Murray could not endorse the British plan and requested more information. Although Moose was disturbed by the implications of withdrawing the Shomber mission in favor of a British-led operation, the Department of State did not seem particularly concerned. (Moose to secretary of state, 3 May 1944, *FRUS 1944*, 5: 697–98.) The Americans were far more interested in making sure that any financial reforms or missions were organized under the United States' auspices. Hull informed Winant in London that the Department of State, with War Department approval, accepted Britain's proposal provided that any economic or financial mission requested by the king would be headed by an American (Hull to Winant, 1 May 1944, ibid., p. 697).

78. Winant to Hull, 27 Apr. 1944, ibid., pp. 692–93. Stettinius's message was transmitted through the American ambassador in London.

79. Moose to secretary of state, 13 Apr. 1944, 890F.24/153.

80. Moose to secretary of state, 30 Apr. 1944, *FRUS 1944*, 5: 696–97.

81. Eddy to Merriam, 17 June 1944, 890F.50/6-1744. Born of missionary parents in Syria, Eddy was fluent in Arabic and had wide experience throughout the Middle East. He had headed the English department at the American University in Cairo (where he reportedly introduced the game of basketball to the Egyptians), and had also served as president of Hobart College. During the early years of the war he served as naval attaché in Cairo and later distinguished himself in the OSS throughout North Africa. In 1943, he was assigned to the Department of State and soon appointed as a special assistant to

Moose in the legation at Jidda. As part of his duties, Eddy was to visit other areas of the peninsula. (R. Harris Smith, OSS, pp. 41–42, and Name Index 123, Eddy, William 1940–1944, RG 59.) In August 1944, Eddy was appointed minister plenipotentiary to Saudi Arabia and assumed his duties in September 1944. Eddy, who developed a closer relationship with Ibn Saud than any other American official, became the most vocal advocate of closer American-Saudi ties. He became both a critic of British policy in Saudi Arabia and a virulent anti-Zionist. During 1946 and 1947, he helped reorganize the Research and Analysis Branch of oss (which had been transferred to the State Department) and later became a consultant to ARAMCO. According to Smith, he also served as an official of the CIA-funded American Friends of the Middle East (OSS, p. 365).

82. Memorandum of conversation between Hull and Halifax, 26 June 1944, *FRUS* 1944, 5: 710. Halifax requested that the department provide the British Embassy with the "full facts" and promised to "move in accordance therewith."

83. Jordan to Baxter, 11 May 1944 E3036/325/25 F.O. 371:40269.

84. Jordan to Baxter, 12 May 1944 E3029/325/25 F.O. 371:39985.

85. See Minutes of 23 May 1944, E3105/128/25 F.O. 371:40265. See also British Embassy in Washington to Foreign Office, 27 May 1944, E3398/128/25 F.O. 371:40265. The British Embassy argued that, as far as the Americans were concerned, unless Jordan were removed it would be impossible to conduct Anglo-American relations "with full confidence." The Foreign Office replied that changing representatives in Jidda would not only be "unjustifiable," but inconvenient in view of the shortage of Arab experts. (Foreign Office to British Embassy, Washington, 28 May 1944, ibid.)

86. Hankey minute, 2 June 1944, E3105/128/25 F.O. 371:40265.

87. Crofts to Peterson, 7 June 1944, E 3693/128/25 F.O. 371:40266. See also Minutes of 23 May 1944, E3105/128/25 F.O. 371:40265.

88. See Foreign Office to British Embassy in Washington, 28 May 1944, ibid.

89. Eddy to Merriam, 17 June 1944, 890F.50/6-1744.

90. For details of the fifty-fifty subsidy plan, see *FRUS* 1944, 5: 713–14.

91. Early in March, Ibn Saud, eager to secure a financial adviser but sensitive to the political consequences of a Christian officer working with Saudi finances, requested that the British consider supplying a British subject who was a Sunni Muslim. The Americans, however, convinced that London had forced the idea on the king, and determined to maintain the upper hand in economic matters, resisted. The State Department agreed to let London lead a military mission, provided that Washington take charge of an economic mission. (Minutes by Peterson, 10 Aug. 1944, E4201/325/25 F.O. 371:40271.)

92. Memorandum of conversation among State and Treasury Department representatives, 17 July 1944, 890F.515/24. See also Murray to the Policy Committee, 26 June 1944, 890F.50/6-2644.

93. Hull to Winant, 1 July 1944, FRUS 1944, 5: 711–13. Hull's message was transmitted through the American ambassador in London.

94. Memorandum of conversation between Murray and Peterson, 12 Apr. 1944, 740.0011 Stettinius Mission/130.

95. Winant to Hull, 21 July 1944, FRUS 1944, 5: 718–19. British Treasury officials pressed the Foreign Office not to yield to the Americans on the question of leadership of an economic mission. Writing to Peterson, a Treasury official observed: "If an American head of the Military Mission might conceivably cause trouble on the frontiers, so could the American subordinates contemplated in your proposal to Wallace Murray. A risk of this kind seems to be incidental to American intervention in the Middle East, and presumably was taken into account when you invited American cooperation. On the other hand our experience of the last two months has amply shown how much damage can be done on the economic side by ignorant and politically biased American advice." (Pinsent to Peterson, 15 July 1944, E 4201/325/25 F.O. 371:40271.)

96. Moose to Hull, 6 Aug. 1944, FRUS 1944, 5: 724–25. The department had been receiving reports as early as June that the king might turn to the oil companies for additional assistance (Tuck to secretary of state, 18 June 1944, ibid., pp. 706–7).

97. In late July, the War Department, with the State Department's assistance, had approached the Saudis with a request to begin aerial surveys of a route from Cairo to Dhahran as part of the longer Cairo to Karachi run. The military also requested permission to carry out surveys for an airport on the Persian Gulf coast within 150 miles of Dhahran. (Moose to Yassin, 29 July 1944, FRUS 1944, 5: 661–62.)

98. Memorandum of conversation by Murray, 19 Aug. 1944, 890F.24/8-1944.

99. Although department officials were not happy with Jordan's activities, they seemed somewhat concerned about Moose's relations with Jordan. According to the British Embassy in Washington, the decision to withdraw Moose was a result "not less by dissatisfaction over his capacity than by a feeling that he did not cooperate well with his British colleague." (Campbell to Foreign Office, 6 July 1944, E3976/128/25 F.O. 371:40266.) In August, Stettinius bluntly informed the legation at Jidda: "Moose is assigned to the Department. This transfer not made at his request nor for his convenience." (Stettinius to Legation at Jidda, 12 Aug. 1944, 123, Eddy, William, RG 59.)

100. Hankey minute, 7 July 1944; Cadogan minute 13 July 1944, E3976/128/125 F.O. 371:40266. Eden fully backed the decision to support Jordan.

101. Foreign Office to Jidda, 25 Aug. 1944, E5011/325/25 F.O. 371:40272.

102. Ibid.

103. Lawson to Hankey, 22 Sept. 1944, E5857/325/25 F.O. 371:40273. See also Anderson to Law, 18 Oct. 1944, E6499/325/25 F.O. 371:40274.

104. Jordan to Foreign Office, 6 Sept. 1944, E5672/128/25 F.O. 371:40266.

105. Hankey minute, 22 Sept. 1944, ibid.

106. Wikeley minute, 26 Oct. 1944, E6499/325/25 F.O. 371:40274.

107. Ibid.

108. According to Eddy, Jordan was insisting on reducing the subsidy from £3,000,000 to £2,000,000 (Eddy to secretary of state, 10 Sept. 1944, *FRUS* 1944, 5: 738–39). Early in October, Eddy reported that the "most authentic confidential" source confirmed that the British had advised the king not to permit the U.S. Army to construct an airfield in the vicinity of Dhahran or to fly its planes directly across Saudi Arabia. Eddy concluded that this constituted "anti-American coercion of Saudi Government." (Tuck to secretary of state, 6 Oct. 1944, *FRUS* 1944, 5: 663. Eddy's message was transmitted through the American minister in Egypt.) See also Hull to Winant, 17 Oct. 1944, ibid., pp. 666–67.

109. Eddy to secretary of state, 7 Sept. 1944, ibid., p. 734.

110. Eddy to Hull, 30 Oct. 1944, 890F.24/10-3044.

111. Memorandum by William Yale and P. W. Ireland, 14 Oct. 1944, 890F.50/10-1444. See also "Proposed Plan for Safeguarding American Interests in Saudi Arabia," 18 Oct. 1944, Folder: Memos re: Petroleum 1943–44 (with index), Box 1, *PED Records*.

112. Murray to Stettinius, 9 Nov. 1944, 711.90F/11-444.

113. Stimson to secretary of state, 27 Oct. 1944, *FRUS* 1944, 5: 748–49.

114. Murray to Stettinius, 11 Nov. 1944, Folder: Saudi Arabia—Proposed Loan to 1945, Box 6, *PED Records*. The new plan called for a $57,000,000 subsidy to balance the Saudi budget until 1950. Twenty million would be spent by the War Department in an "outright purchase" of airfield and overflight rights. Thirty-seven million would be used to acquire oil reserves for the navy. NEA had also considered the possibility of having the president request an Export-Import Bank loan to assist Saudi Arabia in its long-range development.

115. Memorandum of conversation among Rayner, Stettinius, Bard, Kane, and Patterson, 13 Nov. 1944, 890F.6363/11-1344. On the War Department's interest in Saudi Arabia, see *FRUS* 1944, 5: 748–51.

116. Memorandum of conversation among Sappington, McGuire, Phelps, and others, 8 Nov. 1944, 890F.6363/11-844. See also memorandum by McGuire, 7 Dec. 1944, 890F.24/12-744 and McGuire's memo-

randa of 3 and 7 Nov. 1944, 890F.51/11-344 and 890F.51/11-744, respectively.

117. Loftus to Sappington, 18 Oct. 1944, Folder: Memos re: Petroleum 1943–44 (with index), Box 1, *PED Records*. See also Hickerson to Dunn, 2 Dec. 1944, 890F.51A/2-244.

118. Memorandum of conversation among Rayner, Alling, Kane, and others, 22 Nov. 1944, 890F.6363/11-2244. See also memorandum of conversation, 23 Nov. 1944, 890F.51/11-2344.

119. Forrestal to secretary of state, 11 Dec. 1944, *FRUS 1944*, 5: 755–56. See also memorandum of conversation among Kane, Parker, and Brownell, 20 Dec. 1944, Folder: Saudi Arabia—Proposed Loan to 1945, Box 6, *PED Records*.

120. Stettinius to Roosevelt, 22 Dec. 1944, *FRUS 1944*, 5: 757–58. By 20 December both Forrestal and Stimson had approved NEA's plan.

121. Stettinius to Murray, 23 Dec. 1944, Folder: NEA-Office of Eastern and African Affairs (Mr. Wallace Murray, Dec. 1944), Box 221, Stettinius Papers. On 24 December, the department instructed Eddy to inform the king that pending legislative approval, a "comprehensive plan" had been developed for extending "substantial financial and economic assistance to Saudi Arabia on a long-range basis. . . ." (Stettinius to Eddy, 24 Dec. 1944, *FRUS 1944*, 5: 759.)

122. Murray to Stettinius, 6 Dec. 1944, 890F.24/11-244. The memorandum forwarded summaries of Eddy's telegrams.

123. Murray to Stettinius, 23 Nov. 1944, 890F.6363/11-1044.

124. Murray to Stettinius, 9 Nov. 1944, 711.90F/11-444.

Chapter 5

1. Christopher Tugendhat and Adrian Hamilton, *Oil: The Biggest Business*, p. 118.

2. Frey and Ide, *A History of the Petroleum Administration for War*, p. 1. See also U.S., Congress, Senate, Special Subcommittee Investigating Petroleum Requirements, *Petroleum Requirements—Postwar* (hereafter cited as *Petroleum Requirements—Postwar*), *Hearings before a Special Committee Investigating Petroleum Resources*, 79th Cong., 2d sess., 1945, pp. 77–78.

3. Dr. Walter H. Voskuil and Hope M. Meyers, "Can United States Oil Reserves Meet the Postwar Demand?" *American Interests in the War and the Peace*, July 1945 [located in Reports on the Petroleum Industry, #245, Central Files, General Classified Files, pt. 2, Box 119, Records of the Office of War Mobilization and Reconversion, RG 250 (hereafter cited as *OWMR Records*)]. See also *Wartime Petroleum Policy Under the PAW*, p. 254. According to American Petroleum Institute figures, U.S. crude production in 1945 totaled almost 4,695,000

b.p.d. World output exceded 7,100,000 b.p.d. (*Petroleum Facts and Figures*, 1950, pp. 444–48).

4. Ibid., pp. 51–52. See also *American Petroleum Interests in Foreign Countries*, p. 1 and *Petroleum Requirements—Postwar*, p. 65.

5. *Wartime Petroleum Policy Under the PAW*, pp. 6–8.

6. Wallace Pratt, "Our Petroleum Resources," pp. 120–28. See also Joseph Pogue, "Must an Oil War Follow this War?" pp. 41–47.

7. *American Petroleum Interests in Foreign Countries*, p. 5. See also *Petroleum Requirements—Postwar*, pp. 7, 89, and "Worldwide Petroleum Supply Survey," 4th Quarter 1945 and 1946, Program Division of PAW, Nov. 1945, Central Files, General Classified Files, pt. 1, Box 055, *OWMR Records*.

8. *American Petroleum Interests in Foreign Countries*, p. 35.

9. *Wartime Petroleum Policy Under the PAW*, pp. 117–18. During the early years of the war, Venezuela's contribution was hampered by German submarine activity and the difficulties of the convoy system. By 1944, Venezuela moved back into the position of the world's second greatest producer with a record output of 257,000,000 barrels—almost double the 1929 total. By 1945, Venezuelan wells produced over 323,000,000 barrels (Lieuwen, *Petroleum in Venezuela*, p. 98).

10. *Petroleum Facts and Figures*, 1950, pp. 448–49.

11. Some in OWMR calculated Middle Eastern proven reserves at 34,000,000,000 barrels and unproven between 240,000,000,000 and 281,000,000,000 barrels (Deutch to Russell, 22 June 1945, "Production —Oil," Central Files, General Classified Files, pt. 2, Box 098, *OWMR Records*). See also chapter 4 n.5.

12. "Middle Eastern Oil," London *Economist*, 30 June 1945.

13. Clayton to Roosevelt, 19 Jan. 1945, *FRUS 1944*, 5: 36–37. The memo was drafted in the Petroleum Division in connection with the Yalta conference, but never sent. See also Loftus to Haley, 31 Jan. 1945, 800.6363/1-3145.

14. Ickes to Pauley, 24 July 1945. File 1-188 Preparedness, *Interior Records*.

15. *New York Times*, 28 Jan. 1945, p. 1.

16. Murray to Stettinius, 27 Oct. 1944, *FRUS 1944*, 5: 624–26.

17. Memorandum of conversation among Ickes, Davies, Rayner, and Dunn, 8 Jan., Folder: Saudi Arabia—Proposed Loan to 1945, Box 6, *PED Records*.

18. Stettinius to Roosevelt, 8 Jan. 1945, *FRUS 1945*, 8: 847. See also memorandum of conversation among Wright, Murray, Alling, and Parker, 1 Jan. 1945, 890F.50/1-145.

19. Murray to Stettinius, 19 Jan. 1945, 890F.51/1-1945.

20. Rayner to Murray, 20 Jan. 1945, 890F.6363/1-2045. See also Dawson to Lend-Lease Board of Review, 30 Jan. 1945, Entry 445, Subject File of the Director, Folder: (Cables) Middle East Arabia and Ethiopia, *FEA Records*.

21. For the establishment of the military training mission and a survey of its activities see *FRUS* 1944, 5: 678 and *FRUS* 1945, 8: 888–90.

22. For a background memorandum on the Dhahran airfield, see Henderson to Acheson, 29 Dec. 1945, 890F.248/12-2955. For a detailed presentation of the War Department's views on the value of the airfield, see SWNCC 19 thru 19/18, 091 Saudi Arabia, pt. I, 7 Feb. 1945, State-War-Navy Coordinating Records (hereafter cited as *SWNCC Records*), Records of the Interdepartmental and Intradepartmental Committees of the Department of State, RG 353. In late 1944, by agreement of the secretaries of the Departments of State, War, and Navy a joint coordinating committee was established. In December, at the time the matter of long-range aid to Saudi Arabia was formally presented to the president, SWNCC held its first meeting. Although the committee was formed to deal with Far Eastern matters, the Saudi aid problem was among the first questions with which SWNCC had to deal. SWNCC's members included John McCloy, assistant secretary of war, James Dunn, and Artemus L. Gates, under secretary of the navy for air.

23. SWNCC 19/1, 091 Saudi Arabia, *SWNCC Records*.

24. Ibid.

25. Elsey to acting secretary of state, 3 Feb. 1945, 890F.001 ABDUL AZIZ/2-345. See also secretary of state to Jidda, 3 Feb. 1945, ibid.

26. Murray to Hull, 20 Dec. 1944, 890F.51/12-2044, and Stettinius to Murray, 23 Dec. 1944, Folder: NEA-Office of Eastern and African Affairs (Murray-December 1944), Stettinius Papers.

27. Landis to Roosevelt, 17 Jan. 1945, *FRUS* 1945, 8: 680–82. In January, the department was considering possible presidential gifts for the king. Eddy suggested a fleet of ten limousines or a naval vessel, but the Department of State decided upon a C-47 aircraft. Although the War Department questioned the propriety of such a gift, Acting Secretary of State Grew assured the general staff that Roosevelt himself had authorized it. (Memorandum of telephone conversation between Grew and Maddux, 8 Feb. 1945, 890F.001/ABDUL AZIZ/2-845 and Eddy to secretary of state, 8 Feb. 1945, ibid.)

28. The most detailed account of events surrounding the FDR-Ibn Saud encounter is William A. Eddy, *FDR Meets Ibn Saud*. See also, Reilly, *Reilly of the White House*, pp. 216–23; Sherwood, *Roosevelt and Hopkins*, pp. 871–72; James Byrnes, *Speaking Frankly*, p. 22; Edward R. Stettinius, Jr., *Roosevelt and the Russians*, pp. 272–78; Leahy, *I Was There*, pp. 325–27; Charles Bohlen, *Witness to History*, pp. 202–4; and Jim Bishop, *FDR's Last Year*, pp. 443–47.

29. Eddy, *FDR Meets Ibn Saud*, pp. 25–26.

30. Bohlen, *Witness to History*, pp. 202–4.

31. Eddy, *FDR Meets Ibn Saud*, pp. 29–30.

32. Eddy to secretary of state, 5 Feb. 1945, 890F.001 ABDUL AZIZ/ 2-545.

33. In November 1938, Ibn Saud had first expressed his opposition to Zionism in a letter to Roosevelt (Ibn Saud to Roosevelt, 29 Nov. 1938, *FRUS* 1938, 2: 994–98). In April 1943, the king again formally registered his opposition (Ibn Saud to Roosevelt, 30 Apr. 1943, *FRUS* 1943, 4: 773–75). In August 1943, Harold Hoskins, having recently returned from Riyadh, reported that Ibn Saud's attitude on Palestine had not changed. (Memorandum by Hoskins, 31 Aug. 1943, *FRUS* 1943, 4: pp. 807–10.)

34. Stettinius to Roosevelt, 9 Jan. 1945 *FRUS* 1945, 8: 679, and Landis to Roosevelt, 17 Jan. 1945, ibid., 680–82. In a memorandum to the president in early January, NEA noted: "The possibility that the King can be persuaded to alter his position with regard to Palestine is . . . so remote as to be negligible." ("Memorandum For the President, Subject: King Ibn Saud," 9 Jan. 1945, 890F.001/1-945.)

35. For the text of the agreed memorandum of the conversation, see *FRUS* 1945, 8: 2–3. Still, by all accounts, the president was very much impressed by Ibn Saud's views. According to Hopkins, Roosevelt was "overly impressed." Hopkins could never reconcile Roosevelt's later statement at a press conference, that he had learned more from Ibn Saud about Palestine in "five minutes" than in a lifetime, with his own impressions of the meeting. Hopkins noted that the conversation never dealt with the "real issues" and turned into a monologue by the king (Sherwood, *Roosevelt and Hopkins*, p. 872). According to Berle's recollection of Roosevelt's account of the meeting, "they apparently talked over the Palestine business, the President saying that they arrived at nothing at the moment though he hoped that he had begun to lay a base for the eventual solution of the problem." (Berle and Jacobs, *Navigating the Rapids 1918–1971*, pp. 475–76.)

36. Eddy, *FDR Meets Ibn Saud*, p. 33.

37. Eddy to the secretary of state, 3 Mar. 1945, *FRUS* 1945, 8: 7–9.

38. Sherwood, *Hopkins and Roosevelt*, pp. 871–72.

39. Feis to J. S. Davis, 22 Feb. 1945, Folder: Chronological File, January 1945, Box 30, Feis Papers.

40. *New York Times*, 22 Feb. 1945, p. 26.

41. SWNCC 19/3, 2 Mar. 1945; SWNCC 19/4, 3 Mar. and SWNCC 19/5, 19 Mar., *SWNCC Records*.

42. SWNCC 19/2, 1 Mar. 1945. See also Department of State memorandum, 6 Mar. 1945, 890F.51/3-645, and record of the 12th meeting of SWNCC, 3 Mar. 1945, JCS 381 Saudi Arabia (2–7–45), *JCS Records*.

43. Ibid.

44. Memorandum of conversation among Acheson, Kane, Bard, Vinson, Drewry, and McCormack, 8 Mar. 1945, *FRUS* 1945, 8: 861–63. See also memorandum by Dean Acheson, 4 Apr. 1945, 890F.00/4-

445, and Kane to Forrestal, 16 Mar. 1945, Folder: Middle East Oil, Box 22, Forrestal Papers.

45. McGuire to Collado, 24 Mar. 1945, 890F.51/3-2445.

46. Collado to Clayton, 1 Jan. 1945, 890F.51/1-145; McGuire to Collado, 10 Feb. 1945, 890F.51/2-1045; and Collado to Clayton, 12 Feb. 1945, 890F.51/2-1245.

47. Collado to Clayton, 27 Mar. 1945, 890F.6363/3-2745.

48. Clayton to Dunn, 7 Apr. 1945, *FRUS* 1945, 8: 869–71.

49. Eddy to secretary of state, 15 Apr. 1945, 890F.48/4-1545. See also Eddy to secretary of state, 20 Apr. 1945, 890F.24/4-2045.

50. Grew to Eddy, 22 Mar. 1945, 890F.51/3-1645. See also memorandum by Moose, 21 Apr. 1945, 890F.24/4-1745.

51. Eddy to secretary of state, 20 Apr. 1945, *FRUS* 1945, 8: 878–79.

52. Crowley to secretary of state, 20 Apr. 1945, ibid., pp. 879–81.

53. Henderson to Collado, 27 Apr. 1945, 890F.51/4-2445. The other priorities were airfields, radio communications, and American prestige in Saudi Arabia.

54. Grew to Crowley, 14 Feb. 1945, 890F.515/3-2345. Grew to Eddy, 7 May 1945, *FRUS* 1945, 8: 891–92.

55. Memorandum of conversation among Acheson, Brownell, Bard, Barkley, George, and Walsh, 17 May 1945, ibid., pp. 895–96. The idea of an Export-Import Bank loan had been part of the State Department's original proposal to Roosevelt in December 1944. The Export-Import Bank had since approved, in principle, extension of a $5,000,000 loan (memorandum by McGuire, 6 Feb. 1945, 890F.51/2-645 and 890F.51/4-1045).

56. Harry S. Truman, *Memoirs*, 1:126–27, 181–83. See also Nash, *United States Oil Policy*, p. 181.

57. Ickes to Truman, 7 May 1945, Secretary of the Interior File, Folder: Oil #40, Box 221, Ickes Papers.

58. Grew to Truman, 23 May 1945, *FRUS* 1945, 8: 900–901.

59. Memorandum of conversation among Truman, Bard, and Acheson, 28 May 1945, ibid., pp. 902–3. On 29 May, Acheson and Bard met with Senator Joseph C. O'Mahoney on Truman's recommendation. The senator was not particularly receptive and wondered whether the United States "as a matter of sound international interest," should not focus its interests on oil reserves closer to home. (Memorandum of conversation among O'Mahoney, Acheson, and Bard, 29 May 1945, 890F.51/5-2945.)

60. Bard to Forrestal, 26 May 1945, 36-1-30, *James Forrestal, General Correspondence*.

61. McGowan to Bard, 4 June 1945, 36-1-30, *James Forrestal, General Correspondence*. In addition to NEA's plan to loan money to Saudi Arabia for oil in the ground or for base rights, both Admiral Carter of the ANPB and Emilio Collado of OFD had proposed plans for handling the Saudi situation. Carter's plan focused on a naval reserve in Saudi

Arabia and the extension of American aid to the king via the companies. Collado's idea focused on a simple loan to the Saudis through the Export-Import Bank. Convinced that only direct government assistance could secure the concession, NEA was cool to both plans. To State Department officials, Carter, the alleged originator of the PRC pipeline venture, represented nothing but trouble.

62. Grew to Eddy, 18 June 1945, *FRUS* 1945, 8: 908–10.

63. Ibid.

64. Eddy to secretary of state, 21 June 1945, ibid., pp. 911–14.

65. For background and planning of the Dhahran airfield between 1943 and 1945, see SWNCC 19/19-19/22, 091 Saudi Arabia, *SWNCC Records*. See also Eddy to secretary of state, 29 May 1945, *FRUS* 1945, 8: 903.

66. SWNCC 19/12, 4 June 1945, 091 Saudi Arabia, *SWNCC Records*.

67. SWNCC 19/13, 14 June 1945, ibid.

68. SWNCC 19/14, 3 July 1945.

69. Grew to Truman, 26 June 1945, *FRUS* 1945, 8: 915–17.

70. Leahy to secretary of state, 28 June 1945, 890F.7962/6-2845.

71. The joint Anglo-American subsidy program totaled approximately $10,000,000. Washington's share was $5,000,000. In addition, the United States planned to grant supplementary aid totaling 10,000,000 riyals and $3,000,000 in commodities. (Grew to Eddy, 16 July 1945, *FRUS* 1945, 8: 930–31.)

72. Eddy to the secretary of state, 8 July 1945, ibid., pp. 923–26, and Grew to Eddy, 13 July 1945, ibid., pp. 928–29. See also SWNCC 19/15, 14 July 1945, 091 Saudi Arabia, *SWNCC Records*. In February, SWNCC had recommended that Colonel Voris H. Connor proceed to Saudi Arabia to assist in planning a military mission to aid the king. The mission was to assist with road construction, pilot training, and advising Eddy in his negotiations for the Dhahran airfield. (Report by the Ad Hoc Committee of SWNCC, 22 Feb. 1945, *FRUS* 1945, 8: 852–58.)

73. Eddy to secretary of state, 15 July 1945, ibid., pp. 929–30. Eddy noted that he had no "immediate evidence" of British complicity.

74. Sanger to Henderson, 17 Aug. 1945, 890F.51/8-1745. In June, Grew and Crowley had recommended that there be no immediate change in lend-lease policy toward Saudi Arabia. [Grew and Crowley to Truman, 14 June 1945, Official File (OF) 356 (1945), Truman Papers.]

75. Henderson to Thorp, 22 Aug. 1945, 890F.51/8-2245. The State Department felt particularly pressed to make good on its promises to Saudi Arabia in view of recent assurances given to Amir Faisal, who was visiting the United States as chief of the Saudi delegation to the United Nations. During meetings with Faisal, department officials had assured the foreign minister that the United States was working on a financial program to assist Saudi Arabia until oil royalties matured. (*FRUS* 1945, 8: 1000–1009.)

76. Truman authorized continuation of those special lend-lease programs to which the United States was committed before the termination directive of 17 August. The extension applied to Saudi Arabia, Liberia, and Italy (Clayton to Crowley, 4 Sept. 1945, ibid., pp. 951–52). See also memorandum of conversation, 28 Aug. 1945, 890F.1561/8-2845, and Byrnes to Vinson, 22 Oct. 1945, 890F.24/10-2245.

77. Eddy to secretary of state, 8 Aug. 1945, FRUS 1945, 8:943–45. All of Ibn Saud's objections to the accord, Eddy noted, were almost exclusively concerned with the appearance and reality of his sovereignty and jurisdiction. The agreement provided only for the use of Dhahran as a military facility. See also SWNCC 19/17, 21 Aug. 1945, 091 Saudi Arabia, SWNCC Records.

78. Assistant secretary of war to SWNCC Secretariat, 23 Aug. 1945, SWNCC 19/18 D, ibid.

79. On 10 August SWNCC's ad hoc committee became the subcommittee for the Near and Middle East. See SWNCC 19/20–19/22, ibid.

80. SWNCC 19/20, 1 Oct. 1945, ibid.

81. Truman to Grew, 28 Sept. 1945, FRUS 1945, 8: 958. Truman approved the completion at War Department expense on two conditions: first, that the U.S. Army control the field until completion and for at least a three-year period after completion; second, that Congress either approve the use of War Department funds or appropriate additional funds.

82. Eddy to secretary of state, 13 Sept. 1945, ibid., pp. 954–55, and Eddy to secretary of state, 2 Oct. 1945, ibid., pp. 958–59.

83. Byrnes to Winant, 8 Aug. 1945, ibid., pp. 940–42.

84. Sullivan to Forrestal, 16 Oct. 1945, 36-1-30, James Forrestal, General Correspondence.

85. ARAMCO's objections to an EXIM Bank loan seemed to focus on the company's unwillingness to guarantee advance royalties in dollars so that Saudi Arabia could pay interest on the loan. (Memorandum of conversation among Duce, Arey, Spurlock, and McGuire, 31 May 1941, 890F.51/5-3145.) See also memorandum of conversation among Thorp, Henderson, Duce, Spurlock, and others, 28 Sept. 1945, 890F.51/9-2845.

86. Collado to Taylor, 19 Oct. 1945, FRUS 1945, 8: 960–63.

87. Memorandum of converation among Tandy, Christelow, Merriam, McGuire, and others, 30 Nov. 1945, ibid., pp. 973–75.

88. Acheson to Eddy, 20 Dec. 1945, 890F.51/12-2045.

89. Eddy to secretary of state, 28 Dec. 1945, FRUS 1945, 8: 995.

90. Byrnes to Eddy, 4 Jan. 1946, ibid., p. 999. In view of Ibn Saud's unwillingness to accept Export-Import Bank control of the proposed funds, Eddy suggested, upon Amir Faisal's recommendation, that the loan "be permitted to die quietly without obituary." Eddy cited improved economic conditions in Saudi Arabia and the prospect of in-

creasing oil royalties as the principal reasons. (Eddy to secretary of state, 21 Mar. 1946, *FRUS* 1946, 7: 740–41.) In August 1946, agreement was reached between Saudi Arabia and the Export-Import Bank for a $10,000,000 line of credit.

91. Draft memorandum to Truman, *FRUS* 1945, 8: 45–48. The memo was prepared by Merriam and sent to Henderson early in August 1945.

92. Draft memorandum from Navy Department to the secretary of state, 25 Aug. 1945, "Saudi Arabia—Oil Resources," 36-1-30, *James Forrestal, General Correspondence*.

93. See Military Intelligence Report, XL-23528, "Succession Question in Saudi Arabia," 30 Oct. 1945, *Records of the OSS*.

94. Forrestal to secretary of state, 1 Aug. 1945, 36-1-30, *James Forrestal, General Correspondence*. See also Forrestal to Byrnes, 30 July 1945, Folder: Iran-Potsdam, Chapter 39, Feis Papers.

95. Murray to Hull, 6 Dec. 1944, 890F.24/11-244. Murray forwarded summaries of Eddy's reports from Jidda.

96. Eddy to secretary of state, 28 Dec. 1945, 890F.51/12-2845.

97. Clayton to Dunn, 7 Apr. 1945, *FRUS* 1945, 8: 869–71.

98. Henderson to secretary of state, 9 Oct. 1945, 890.50/10-945. Merriam's memorandum, entitled "Draft Memorandum to President Truman," was forwarded as an annex to a memorandum from Acheson to the secretary of state recommending that Congress create a special fund for promoting American interests in the Middle East. See also Acheson to Henderson, undated, 890.50/10-945.

Chapter 6

1. In 1945, Saudi Arabia produced 21,311,000 barrels of crude oil; by 1946, production almost reached 60,000,000 barrels. (*Petroleum Facts and Figures*, 1950, p. 449.) Saudi Arabia received $4,820,000 in direct oil revenue from ARAMCO in 1945; by 1946, the Saudis received $13,500,000. (Shwadran, *The Middle East, Oil and the Great Powers*, p. 350.)

2. Feis, *Seen From E.A.*, p. 184.

3. *Petroleum Requirements—Postwar*, p. 65.

4. Ibid., p. 69. Wilson noted that there was no reason imports should not be used to supplement supply, but he warned of the consequences of flooding the domestic market with cheap foreign oil.

5. "Worldwide Petroleum Supply Survey, 4th Quarter 1945 and the year 1946," Program Division of PAW, November 1945, Central Files, Central Classified Files, pt. 1, Box 055, *OWMR Records*.

6. *American Petroleum Interests in Foreign Countries*, p. 5 and U.S., Congress, Senate, Foreign Relations Committee, *Petroleum*

Agreement with Great Britain and Northern Ireland, Hearings June 2–25, 1947 (hereafter cited as *Hearings on Petroleum Agreement with Great Britain*), 80th Cong., 1st sess., 1947, pp. 119–22.

7. *Wartime Petroleum Policy Under the PAW*, pp. 10–11.

8. Memorandum for secretary of state, 25 Aug. 1945, 36-1-30, *James Forrestal, General Correspondence*. See also Forrestal to secretary of state, 3 Sept. 1945, Folder: Miscellaneous Files 1945, Box 48, Forrestal Papers.

9. *Hearings on Petroleum Agreement with Great Britain*, pp. 119–22.

10. Memorandum of conversation among Sheets, Harden, Clayton, and Rayner, 22 Mar. 1945, 890G.6363/3-2245. In 1931, SOCONY merged with the Vacuum Company to form Socony-Vacuum.

11. Memorandum by Loftus, 18 Jan. 1946, Folder: Policy (Foreign Policy Problems), Box 17, *PED Records*.

12. Loftus to Boardman, 18 Mar. 1946, 890.6363/3-1846. See also Loftus to Wilcox, 10 Jan. 1946, Folder: Policy (Foreign Policy Problems), Box 17, *PED Records*.

13. Hart to secretary of state, 10 Jan. 1945, 890F.6363/1-1045. The State Department's petroleum experts opposed the pipeline as a PRC-sponsored project, but had no objections to the facility as a private venture. (Rayner to Davies, 7 Jan. 1944, 890F.6363/91.)

14. Hare to secretary of state, 15 May 1945, 800.6363/5-1545.

15. Winant to secretary of state, 14 Feb. 1945, 867N.6363/2-1445. See also Winant to secretary of state, 27 Nov. 1945, *FRUS 1945*, 8: 60–61. According to Sir Nigel Bruce Ronald, assistant secretary of state in the Foreign Office, British military experts wanted to see the pipeline to the Mediterranean completed as soon as possible. See also Winant to secretary of state, 19 Nov. 1945, *FRUS 1945*, 8: 58–60.

16. Winant to secretary of state, 5 Dec. 1945, ibid., pp. 61–63.

17. Levy and Loftus to Henderson, 4 Feb. 1946, 890F.6363/2-446. See also Winant to secretary of state, 5 Dec. 1945, *FRUS 1945*, 8: 61–63.

18. Loftus to Henderson and Merriam, 5 Feb. 1946, *FRUS 1946*, 7: 18–22.

19. Loftus to Wilcox, 10 Jan. 1946, Folder: Policy (Foreign Policy Problems), Box 17, *PED Records*.

20. Loftus to Henderson and Merriam, 5 Feb. 1946, *FRUS 1946*, 7: 18–22.

21. Henderson and Loftus to Clayton and Byrnes, 11 Mar. 1946, 867N.6363/3-1146.

22. Byrnes to Gallman, 16 Mar. 1946, *FRUS 1946*, 7: 23–24.

23. Acheson to Gallman, 25 Mar. 1946, ibid., pp. 26–27.

24. Pinkerton to secretary of state, 24 June 1946, 867N.6363/6-2446. See also *FRUS 1946*, 7: 29–30. On 10 August, the Trans-Arabian Pipe-

line Company (TAPCO) signed an agreement with Lebanon. TAPCO had been created in July 1945 by SOCAL and the Texas Company.

25. Memorandum of conversation among Harden, Sheets, Rayner, McGhee, and Clayton, 27 Aug. 1946, ibid., pp. 31–34. For the oil company memorandum of the same meeting, see *Multinational Corporations*, pt. 8, p. 112.

26. This does not necessarily suggest the presence of an organized, tightly controlled cartel or conspiracy to dominate the world's oil. For almost ten years after the end of World War II, the major companies involved in Middle Eastern oil—SOCAL, Texas, Gulf, SONJ, AIOC, Dutch-Shell, and Socony-Vacuum faced virtually no competition. During a period of rising demand for petroleum, the companies realized that price competition could only hurt their marketing position. According to J. E. Hartshorn, no cartel agreements were required in the immediate postwar period because the major companies in the Middle East were without effective competition. What emerged was a kind of "orderly competition" which sought to adjust sources of supply with world market realities. (J. E. Hartshorn, *Politics and World Oil Economics*, p. 158–60.) The joint ventures, in a sense, were a manifestation of this view. The overlapping membership of the arrangements and the exchange of information and coordination of production could thus result in the control of Persian Gulf crude. See also Blair, *The Control of Oil*, pp. 36–38.

27. *Multinational Corporations*, pt. 7, p. 82.

28. Childs to secretary of state, 3 Jan. 1947, 890F.6363/1-347.

29. *Multinational Corporations*, pt. 8, pp. 94–95.

30. See memorandum of conversation by Harold Sheets, 28 Aug. 1946, ibid., p. 112.

31. Record of Informal Anglo-American Oil Talks, November 1946, *FRUS* 1946, 7: 44–46.

32. Secretary of state to Gallman, 29 Nov. 1946, ibid., pp. 38–40.

33. Memorandum of conversation among Clayton, Loftus, Rayner, Henderson, Harden, Sheets, and Jennings, 9 Jan. 1947, *FRUS* 1947, 5: 629–31.

34. Memorandum of conversation between Loftus and Webb, 14 Jan. 1947, 890.6363/1-1447. There were a number of American companies during these early years which made inroads into Middle Eastern oil. In 1948, the American Independent Oil Company (AMINOIL), composed of a number of smaller American companies, obtained a sixty-year concession for the Shaikh of Kuwait's rights over his undivided half of the Kuwait-Saudi Neutral Zone (*FRUS* 1948, pt. 1, 5: 19–20). In January 1949, the Pacific Western Oil Company, owned primarily by J. P. Getty, acquired the Saudi half of the neutral zone (a half which ARAMCO surrendered in return for rights over Saudi "continental waters"). SONJ and Socony-Vacuum purchased 30 percent and

10 percent respectively in the ARAMCO concession for $102,000,000—
$76,500,000 for SONJ's share and $25,500,000 for Socony-Vacuum's.
The two companies also, by a later agreement, became part owners of
the Trans-Arabian pipeline.

35. Eakens to Wilcox, 14 Feb. 1947, "Proposed Staff Committee
Paper on Middle East Oil Deals," Folder: Middle East Oil Deals (Proposed Staff Committee Papers), Box 2, *PED Records*. According to
Eakens, the paper was begun by Loftus, turned over to him for completion, and discussed in the office of Paul Nitze, the deputy director
of International Trade Policy. Although PED questioned the usefulness
of completing the paper because the department had already discussed
various aspects of the report with the oil companies, Nitze strongly
urged that it be completed in order to clarify the department's thinking
on the subject.

36. Ibid.

37. Nitze to Clayton, 21 Feb. 1947, *FRUS* 1947, 5: 646–47.

38. Ibid. See also Eakens to McGhee, 4 Mar. 1947, ibid., pp. 647–
51.

39. Memorandum of conversation among Harden, Jennings, Dar-
lington, Nitze, Loftus, Robertson, and Eakens, 7 Mar. 1947, ibid., pp.
651–54. In a letter to Gwin Follis, president of SOCAL, regarding the
proposed merger, Ickes noted that he saw no centralization of control
in the ARAMCO deal, only a broadening base for company operations.
Ickes added, however, that if the deal proved to be a cartel, "I could
not sit quietly by and see the ghost of the Standard Oil Trust walk with
a solid tread across the deserts of Saudi Arabia." (Ickes to Follis, 8 Feb.
1947, General Correspondence, Folder: Standard Oil 1946–1950, Box
86, Ickes Papers.)

40. Eakens to Wilcox, 14 Feb. 1947, "Proposed Staff Committee
Paper on Middle East Oil Deals." See also Eakens to McGhee, 4 Mar.
1947, *FRUS* 1947, 5: 647–51.

41. Stettinius to Roosevelt, 13 Dec. 1944, PSF, Folder: State Department, October-December 1944, Box 91, Roosevelt Papers.

42. Harriman to secretary of state, 13 Dec. 1944, *FRUS* 1944, 5:
646–48.

43. See memorandum "American Economic Policy in the Middle
East," 2 May 1945, *FRUS* 1945, 8: 34–39. For Merriam's comments,
see attached annex II, 15 Jan. 1945, 800.50 Middle East/5-245.

44. Grew to Roosevelt, 12 Jan. 1945, *FRUS* 1945, 8: 680.

45. See Hoskins to Alling, 5 Mar. 1945, ibid., pp. 690–91. According
to Hoskins, in a meeting with Roosevelt, the president agreed with
Hoskins's conclusion that a Zionist state in Palestine could be maintained only by force. See also Roosevelt to Ibn Saud, 5 Apr. 1945,
ibid., p. 698.

46. Henderson to secretary of state, 24 Aug. 1945, ibid., pp. 727–30.

47. Eddy to Henderson, 26 Oct., ibid., pp. 790–91.

48. See JCS comments of 21 Feb. 1946 on SWNCC's "Foreign Policy of the United States," 1 Dec. 1945, Folder: SWNCC Miscellaneous, Box 3, Records of the Military Adviser to the Office of Near Eastern, South Asian and African Affairs, 1945–1950, RG 59.

49. Patterson to Clifford, 27 July 1946, Folder: Russia (Folder 3), Clifford Papers.

50. "Memorandum of Information Re: Soviet Capabilities and Possible Intentions—Resume of," 21 Jan. 1946, prepared by Thomas B. Inglis, USN, Folder: Russia, Box 24, Forrestal Papers.

51. Memorandum by SWNCC to Hilldring, 12 Oct. 1946, *FRUS* 1946, 7: 529–32.

52. JCS to Clifford, 26 July 1946, Folder: Russia (Folder 2), Clifford Papers.

53. Memorandum by Henderson with annex, 21 Oct. 1946, 711.00/11-746. See also JCS to Patterson and Forrestal, 23 Aug. 1946, *FRUS* 1946, 7: 857–58.

54. See Weil, *A Pretty Good Club*, pp. 136–41.

55. Henderson to Acheson, Dunn, and Hickerson, undated, *FRUS* 1946, 7: 1–6.

56. Study on Soviet Objectives in the Middle East, 7 May 1946, prepared by R. F. Ennis, Colonel, GSC, Chief, Intelligence Group, Plans and Operations 092 Top Secret (7 May 1946), Section 3, Case 36, Records of the Army Staff, RG 319.

57. Memorandum by SWNCC to Hilldring, 12 Oct. 1946, *FRUS* 1946, 7: 529–32.

58. Smith to secretary of state, 24 May 1946, 867N.01/5-2446.

59. Memorandum by the JCS to SWNCC, 21 June 1946, *FRUS* 1946, 7: 631–33.

60. Henderson to Acheson, 21 Oct. 1946, ibid., pp. 710–13.

61. Eddy to secretary of state, 28 May 1946, ibid., pp. 615–16.

62. Hart to secretary of state, 14 June 1945, Folder: 800-Confidential, Dhahran Post Files, 1946–1949, Records of the Foreign Service Posts of the Department of State (hereafter cited as *Dhahran Post Files*), RG 84. See also Merriam to Rayner, 5 Dec. 1945, Folder: Saudi Arabia—Proposed Loan to 1945, Box 6, *PED Records*.

63. Childs to secretary of state, 22 Jan. 1947, 867N.01/1-2247. In December, Acheson had requested American posts in Beirut, Cairo, Damascus, and Jidda to report on their estimation of the possibilities for "coordinated" economic and political action by the Arabs against the United States (867N.01/12-1146).

64. Memorandum by the JCS to SWNCC, 21 June 1946, *FRUS* 1946, 7: 631–33.

65. Ibid. In a memorandum to Acheson, Henderson noted that the JCS viewed the oil reserves of Iran, Iraq, and Saudi Arabia as "absolutely vital" to the security of the United States (Henderson to Acheson, 8 Oct. 1946, *FRUS* 1946, 7: 523–25).

Chapter 7

1. See *Multinational Corporations*, pt. 7, p. 60. According to Shwadran, Saudi Arabia received $13,500,000 in "direct oil revenue" from ARAMCO in 1946; in 1947—$20,380,000 (Shwadran, *The Middle East, Oil and the Great Powers*, p. 350). Saudi production, according to ARAMCO's own figures totaled 164,229 b.p.d. in 1946; 246,169 b.p.d. in 1947; 390,309 b.p.d. in 1948; 476,736 b.p.d. in 1949; and 546,703 b.p.d. in 1950 (Lebkicher, et al., *ARAMCO Handbook*, p. 171).

2. U.S. Department of State, Secret Policy and Information Statement, "Arab Principalities of the Persian Gulf and the Gulf of Oman," 9 Apr. 1947, Folder: 711 Confidential, 120.3-523.1 *Dhahran Post Files*.

3. See "The Pentagon Talks of 1947," Statement by the United States and United Kingdom Groups, undated, *FRUS* 1947, 5: 597–99.

4. Acheson to Henderson, 15 Feb. 1947, ibid., pp. 1048–49.

5. Kennan to secretary of state, 22 Feb. 1946, *FRUS* 1946, 6: 696–709. For Kennan's thoughts on the "long telegram," see Kennan, *Memoirs 1925–1950*, pp. 292–97.

6. JCS to Clifford, 26 July 1946, Russia (Folder 2), Clifford Papers. For a concise account of the Iranian crisis, see John Lewis Gaddis, *The United States and the Origins of the Cold War 1941–1947*, pp. 309–12. See also Mark Lytle, "American-Iranian Relations 1941–1947 and the Redefinition of National Security," chaps. 7, 8.

7. Nimitz to Forrestal, 23 July 1946, and Forrestal to Clifford, 25 July 1946, Folder: Russia (Folder 3), Clifford Papers.

8. See "Arab Principalities of the Persian Gulf and the Gulf of Oman," 9 Apr. 1947, Folder: 711 Confidential, 120.3-523.1, *Dhahran Post Files*.

9. See memorandum prepared by NEA, 21 Oct. 1946, *FRUS* 1946, 7: 240–44. See also Royall and Forrestal to secretary of state, 5 Sept. 1947, *FRUS* 1947, 5: 327–29.

10. For documentation on the origins of the United States' aid to Greece and Turkey, see *FRUS* 1947, 5: 1–59. See also Joseph M. Jones, *The Fifteen Weeks*, pp. 129–47 and Kennan, *Memoirs 1925–1950*, pp. 313–24.

11. Henderson to Acheson, undated, *FRUS* 1947, 5: 52–55.

12. Acheson to Patterson, 5 Mar. 1947, ibid., pp. 94–95.

13. See Report by the Subcommittee on Foreign Policy Information of SWNCC, undated, ibid., pp. 76–78.

14. For the relationship between the Truman Doctrine's rhetoric and assumptions, see Gaddis, *The United States and the Origins of the Cold War*, pp. 350–51; Kennan, *Memoirs 1925–1950*, pp. 319–24; Richard Freeland, *The Truman Doctrine and the Origins of McCarthyism*, pp. 88–101; Jones, *The Fifteen Weeks*, pp. 148–70; and Daniel Yergin, *Shattered Peace*, pp. 279–86.

15. Report of the Special Ad Hoc Committee, 21 Apr. 1947, SWNCC 360, Folder: Ad Hoc Committee (Eddy), Box 3, Records of the Military Adviser to the Office of Near Eastern, South Asian and African Affairs.

16. Joint Strategic Survey Committee (JSSC) to SWNCC, 29 Apr. 1947, "United States Assistance to Other Countries from the Standpoint of National Security," JCS 1769/1, Folder: Ad Hoc Committee (Eddy), Box 3, Records of the Military Adviser to the Office of Near Eastern, South Asian, and African Affairs. Western Europe, JCS planners assumed, would be of "prime importance" in case of "ideological warfare." The Middle East was of "secondary strategic importance." See also JCS to SWNCC, 9 Sept. 1947, *FRUS 1947*, 1: 766–70.

17. Acheson to Henderson, 15 Feb. 1947, *FRUS 1947*, 5: 1048–49.

18. JSSC to SWNCC, 29 Apr. 1947, JCS 1769/1, Records of the Adviser to the Office of Near Eastern, South Asian, and African Affairs. See also report by the Joint War Plans Committee (JWPC), "Staff Study of the Bahrein-Trucial Oman Area," 25 Nov. 1946, JWPC 485/1, (9–6–45) CCS 463.7, Section 3, *JCS Records*.

19. Excerpt from NBC radio broadcast, "Our Foreign Policy Series," 12 June 1947, Folder: Daily July-Aug-Sept. 1947, Kenney Papers. See also ANPB to JCS, 3 July 1947, "Petroleum Supply Situation for Fiscal 1947 and 1948," JCS 1775/1 (3–2–47) CCS 463.7, Section 1, *JCS Records*.

20. Supply Report of the ANPB, 15 Dec. 1947, JCS 1775 (5-2-47) CCS 463.7, Section 1, *JCS Records*.

21. "Petroleum Crisis in Venezuela," 23 May 1946, *Intelligence Review*, pp. 2–7, Records of the Office of Assistant Chief of Staff for Intelligence, Records of the Collection and Dissemination Division, Document Library Branch, ID File 1944–1955, Records of the Army Staff, RG 319 (hereafter cited as ID File 1944–1955, *Records of the Army Staff*).

22. As a result of wartime destruction of mines, equipment, and the loss of the Silesian fields, as well as the lack of manpower, Europe was facing a probable coal deficit of some 55 million tons by 1948 (U.S., Congress, House, Select Committee on Foreign Aid, *Coal Requirements and Availabilities Report No. 1151*, 80th Cong., 1st sess., 25 Nov. 1947). See also *FRUS 1947*, 3: 485–514, for the United States' view of British and European coal shortages.

23. For the relationship among coal, petroleum, and European recovery in the European Recovery Program (ERP), see U.S. Department of State, *European Recovery Program: Commodity Reports, including Manpower*, Economic Cooperation Series, Publication 3093, Office of Public Affairs, 5 Jan. 1948, SI. 65, No. 4, Records of the Government Printing Office, RG 149.

24. For a detailed analysis of the role of petroleum in the ERP, see "Chapter G—Petroleum," prepared by the Petroleum Committee of

the Committee on European Economic Cooperation, 5 Nov. 1947, Folder: CEEC Reports, Box 22, *PED Records*.

25. Bonesteel to Clifford, 21 Sept. 1947, Chapter 3, The Production Effort, CEEC General Report, PSF, Box 163, Truman Papers.

26. Chapman to Wiley, 21 May 1948, Oil and Gas Division, Administrative, General File 1-322, pt. 6, Central Classified File: 1937–1953, Office of the Secretary, *Interior Records*.

27. U.S., Congress, House, Committee on Interstate and Foreign Commerce, *Fuel Investigation—Petroleum and the European Recovery Program, Report* 1438, 80th Cong., 2d sess., 25 Feb. 1948, p. 12.

28. Eugene Holman, president of SONJ, informed Forrestal that Middle Eastern reserves totaled 26,500,000,000 barrels (Holman to Forrestal, 21 Mar. 1947, Folder: Correspondence G-K 1947, Forrestal Papers). According to Secretary of Commerce Harriman, the proven reserves totaled 32,000,000,000 barrels [U.S., Congress, Senate, *Hearings before the Special Committee to Study Problems of American Small Business* (hereafter cited as *Problems of American Small Business*), pt. 33, 80th Cong., 2d sess., 17 Mar. 1948, p. 3669]. The American domestic "proved" reserves in 1950 were calculated at 24,649,489,000 barrels, comprising 32 percent of the world's total proven reserves (*Petroleum Facts and Figures*, 1950, p. 443).

29. In June 1947, Oscar Chapman informed the Senate Foreign Relations Committee that the United States was consuming 5,500,000 b.p.d.—a 41 percent increase over the 1941 level (Chapman Statement, 2 June 1947, Oil and Gas Division, Administrative, General File 1-322, pt. 2, Central Classified Files: 1937–1953, Office of the Secretary, *Interior Records*).

30. See Editorial Note, *FRUS* 1947, 5:664–65. Syria approved the pipeline convention on 1 September 1947 subject to ratification by Parliament.

31. Memorandum of conversation among Henderson, Sanger, Duce, Lenahan, and Miller, 22 Nov. 1946, 890B.6363/11-2246.

32. Memorandum of conversation among Duce, Miller, and Rugg of ARAMCO, and Villard, Merriam, Mattison, Rayner, Hamilton, Eakens, and Hoffman of the State Department, 29 July 1947, 890F.6363/7-2947.

33. Duce to Rayner and Villard, 6 Aug. 1947, 890F.6363/8-647. See also McWilliams to Lovett, Oct. 1947, Documents Regarding Saudi Arabian Pipeline, 890F.6363/10-247 (hereafter cited as *Documents Regarding Saudi Pipeline*).

34. Mattison to Henderson, 28 Aug. 1947, "Position Based on Political & Economic Repercussions in the Near East," Subject File, memos of conversation, July 1–December 31, 1947, Clayton-Thorp Papers.

35. Hoffman to Loftus, "Economic data re: Trans-Arabian pipeline," 3 Sept. 1947, ibid.

36. In September 1947, Captain Thomas Kelley, a navy logistics expert, having toured the Persian Gulf area while on a general trip throughout the Middle East, came back impressed with the potential of the area's reserves. (David Alan Rosenberg, "The U.S. Navy and the Problem of Oil in a Future War," pp. 53–61.) See also ANPB to JCS, 3 July 1947, "Petroleum Supply Situation for Fiscal Years 1947 and 1948," JCS 1775/1, (3–2–47) CCS 463.7, Section 1, *JCS Records*.

37. Ball to Krug, 17 Sept. 1947, Oil and Gas Division, Administrative General, File 1-322, pt. 2, Central Classified Files, 1937–1953, Office of the Secretary, *Interior Records*.

38. Memorandum of telephone conversation between Forrestal and Rodgers, 2 Sept. 1947, Folder: Correspondence P-S 1947, Forrestal Papers. In late July 1945, Forrestal remarked to Byrnes, that according to "oil people in whom I had confidence," Saudi Arabia was "one of the three great puddles left in the world." (Walter Millis, *Forrestal Diaries*, pp. 81–82.)

39. Ball to Krug, 17 Sept. 1947, Oil and Gas Division, Administrative General, File 1-322, pt. 2, Central Classified Files, 1937–1953, Office of the Secretary, *Interior Records*.

40. Lovett to Harriman, 8 Sept. 1947, *FRUS 1947*, 5: 665–66.

41. Meetings were held on 17 and 22 September at the Commerce Department for the purpose of reviewing the granting of ARAMCO's export licenses. See Sanger to Satterthwaite, 22 Sept. 1947, 890.6363/9-2247. The meeting, attended by more than 40 representatives of the Departments of Commerce, Agriculture, Navy, Interior, Defense Transportation, State, and the White House, lasted three hours.

42. See Report for the week of 14 Sept. to 20 Sept. 1947, 2d Decontrol Act Review Committee, Folder: Weekly Reports, Sept. 14–20, 1947 File 1-322, Central Classified Files, 1937–1953, Office of the Secretary, *Interior Records*.

43. Memorandum of conversation by Hoffman, 23 Sept. 1947, Subject File, memos of conversation, July 1–December 31, 1947, Clayton-Thorp Papers. At the conclusion of the meeting, David K. E. Bruce, under secretary of Commerce, announced that Harriman had decided to approve the export licenses for the pipeline on the basis of its "overall military and strategic importance." The final decision, he added, would be made by the Cabinet. According to Sanger, the support of the Interior Department was largely a result of the "good work on the part of PED." Harriman also reportedly favored the export licenses on economic grounds but wanted to be "reassured" of the political importance of the project. Sanger suggested that NEA or NE provide an officer for this purpose (Sanger to Satterthwaite, 22 Sept. 1947, 890.6363/9-2247).

44. Memorandum of conversation by Hoffman, 23 Sept. 1947. Subject File, memos of conversation, July 1-December 31, 1947, Clayton-Thorp Papers.

45. Henderson to Lovett, 24 Sept. 1947, 690F.119/9-2447. Henderson recommended that Lovett emphasize the political factors involved in the export license matter.

46. Nitze to Marshall, 24 Sept. 1947, Subject File, memos of conversation, July 1–December 31, 1947, Clayton-Thorp Papers. According to Nitze, the State Department's decision to recommend granting export licenses was cleared with NE, NEA, PED, ITP, the Office of the Under Secretary (U) and the assistant secretary of state for Economic Affairs (A-T). The War, Navy, and Interior Departments all recommended licenses; the Office of Defense Transportation opposed them; Agriculture expressed "mild concern"; the Commerce Department's Office of International Trade withdrew its objection but did not recommend the licenses; and other offices in Commerce neither opposed nor supported ARAMCO's request.

47. Forrestal Diary entry, 9 Oct. 1947, *Forrestal Diaries*, Forrestal Papers, vol. 8, p. 1862.

48. For the highlights of Lovett's testimony in executive session before the Wherry committee, 9 Oct. 1947, see Eakens to Thorp, 16 Mar. 1948, 890.6363/3-1648.

49. Duce to Harriman, 19 Sept. 1947, Folder: 420.3 Saudi Arab Training Mission, *Dhahran Post Files*.

50. Henderson to Lovett, 24 Sept. 1947, 690F.119/9-2447. The idea that the oil companies might be used to counter negative aspects of U.S. policy on Palestine gained considerable support among State Department officials. The Saudis seemed to draw a distinction, ARAMCO representatives informed the department, between company actions and Washington's policies. In a memorandum to Lovett in August 1948, in defense of ARAMCO's export licenses, Raymond Hare, NEA's Deputy Director concluded: "In the recent setback suffered by all American interests in the Near East as a result of our stand on Palestine American business firms have seemed to suffer less than either US Government or American cultural interests in the area. It may well be therefore, that the oil companies are in a position to recover lost ground in the Near East sooner than US Government or other private interests." (Hare to Lovett, 25 Aug. 1948, 890B.6363/8-2548.)

51. For the influence of political factors on Truman's Palestine policy, see John Snetsinger, *Truman, the Jewish Vote, and the Creation of Israel*. Clark Clifford, special counsel to Truman, claims politics was not a major factor. ("Factors Influencing President Truman's Decision to Support Partition and Recognize the State of Israel," paper delivered at the American Historical Association convention, Washington, D.C., 28 December 1976.) See also Margaret Truman, *Harry S. Truman*, pp. 388–89; Robert J. Donovan, *Conflict and Crisis*, pp. 386–87; and Lawrence S. Kaplan, "Ethnic Politics, the Palestine Question, and the Cold War," pp. 242–66.

52. Truman to Niles, 13 May 1947, PSF, Subject File, Folder: For-

eign-Palestine, Box 184, Truman Papers. Rabbi Abba Hillel Silver was president of the Zionist Organization of America and a member of the Jewish Agency for Palestine.

53. Yale to Kohler, 6 Aug. 1945, 867N.01/8-645 and Eddy to secretary of state, 13 Sept. 1947, 501.BB Palestine/9-1347.

54. Smith to secretary of state, 25 Aug. 1947, 867N.01/8-2547.

55. Eddy to secretary of state, 13 Sept. 1947, 501.BB Palestine/9-1347.

56. Excerpts from minutes of the sixth meeting of U.S. Delegation to the 2nd session of the General Assembly, 15 Sept. 1947, *FRUS 1947*, 5: 1147–51. On 3 October, representatives of the Saudi and Iraqi delegations to the UN informed State Department representatives that their countries were considering accepting Soviet overtures to work out a "voting" deal in the UN. Although the Arab representatives, particularly Faisal of Saudi Arabia and Jamali of Iraq, indicated that they were "loathe" to link themselves with Moscow, Palestine was of such vital importance that they would be willing to take the risk. (Memorandum of conversation by Kopper, 3 Oct. 1947, ibid., pp. 1171–73.)

57. Millis, *Forrestal Diaries*, 29 Sept. 1947, p. 322.

58. See Editorial Note, *FRUS 1947*, 5: 1180–81. In response to a letter from Senator Pepper congratulating him on the decision to support partition, Truman wrote, "I received about thirty-five thousand pieces of mail and propaganda from the Jews in this country while this matter was pending. I put it all in a pile and struck a match to it—I never looked at a single one of the letters because I felt the United Nations Committee was acting in a judicial capacity and should not be interfered with." (Truman to Pepper, 20 Oct. 1947, Folder: P, Confidential File, Box 59, Truman Papers.)

59. Henderson to Marshall, 22 Sept. 1947, *FRUS 1947*, 5: 1153–58.

60. The second memorandum, presumably a draft, dated 22 September 1947, was sent to Dean Rusk, director of the Office of Special Political Affairs (SPA). It is identical to the paper sent to Marshall, except that it adds twelve lines dealing specifically with the American position in Middle Eastern oil. During an interview with Henderson in August 1976, Henderson informed the author that the lines were omitted simply to shorten the memorandum. Upon further reflection, however, Henderson noted that he might have omitted the lines to avoid placing undue emphasis on any single factor. For the text of the draft memorandum, see 501.BB Palestine/9-2247.

61. On 24 September 1947, the Joint Strategic Survey Committee, in conjunction with the Joint Staff Planners, submitted a report to the JCS entitled the "Problem of Palestine." On 10 October, the JCS forwarded the report to the secretary of defense [JCS 1648/5, 1648/6, CCS 092 Palestine (5–3–46) Section 3, *JCS Records*].

62. Bailey to secretary of state, 5 Nov. 1947, Folder: Confidential

840.1, *Dhahran Post Files*. See also Bailey to secretary of state, 4 Nov. 1947, 867N.01/11-447.

63. Ibn Saud to Truman, 26 Oct. 1947, *FRUS 1947*, 5: 1212–13. Transmitting the king's message to Washington, Waldo Bailey, chargé in Jidda added: "In fairness to Arabs and by support of US policy to present both sides of question it seems only just this message ought to be released to press."

64. Memminger to secretary of state, 10 Nov. 1947, Folder: Palestine 1-15 November 1947, Records Relating to Palestine: Palestine Reference Book of Dean Rusk and Robert McClintock, RG 59 (hereafter cited as *Rusk-McClintock Files*).

65. Pinkerton in Beirut to consulate at Dhahran, 11 Oct. 1947, Folder: Confidential 840.1, *Dhahran Post Files*.

66. Smith to secretary of state, 14 Nov. 1947, *FRUS 1947*, 5: 1263–64.

67. See memorandum of conversation among Shertok, Epstein, Henderson, and Mattison, 22 Oct. 1947, ibid., pp. 1196–98. Henderson noted that the department had heard rumors about communist agents disguised as Jewish immigrants, but did not "place too great credence in them." Interestingly enough, on 12 May 1948, during a meeting at the White House to discuss the Palestine situation and the consequences of U.S. recognition of the proposed Jewish state, Lovett remarked that recognizing a Jewish state prematurely would be like "buying a pig in a poke." How would the United States know, Lovett continued, what kind of a Jewish state would be established. The under secretary then read excerpts from reports regarding Soviet agents disguised as immigrants coming from Black Sea ports to Palestine. (Memorandum of conversation among Truman, Marshall, Lovett, and others, 12 May 1948, *FRUS*, pt. 2, 5: 972–76.)

68. Rusk and Henderson to Marshall, 18 Nov. 1947, *FRUS 1947*, 5: 1264–66.

69. Memminger to secretary of state, 30 Nov. 1947, ibid., p. 1292. See also p. 1292 n.1.

70. Childs to secretary of state, 3 Dec. 1947, 501.BB Palestine/12-247. See also Childs to secretary of state, 28 Nov. 1947, Folder: Confidential 840.1 *Dhahran Post Files*.

71. Childs to secretary of state, 8 Dec. 1947, Folder: Palestine 1-15 Dec. 1947, *Rusk-McClintock Files*. Ibn Saud had reportedly ordered mobilization of the Saudi army—in part to protect American oil interests in the Dhahran area.

72. Childs to secretary of state, 30 Dec. 1947, 867N.01/12-3047. See also CIA Report 431706, 22 Jan. 1948, I.D. File 1944–1955, Central Intelligence Agency Reports, *Records of the Army Staff*.

73. Childs to secretary of state, 4 Dec. 1947, *FRUS 1947*, 5: 1335–37.

74. Memorandum of conversation among Jamali, Chorbachi, Hen-

derson, and Colquitt, 11 Dec. 1947, ibid., pp. 1310–11, and Rusk and Henderson to Marshall, 18 Nov. 1947, ibid., pp. 1264–66.

75. Memminger to secretary of state, 12 Dec. 1947, 890D.6363/12-1247.

76. Merriam to Henderson, 11 Dec. 1947, Folder: Palestine, 1-31 Jan. 1948, *Rusk-McClintock Files*.

77. Editorial Notes, FRUS 1947, 5: 1283, 1313–14. See also Kennan to Lovett, 20 Jan. 1948, FRUS 1948, pt. 2,5: 545–46.

78. "Possible Developments in Palestine," Report by CIA, FRUS 1948, pt. 2, 5: 666–75.

79. Forrestal Diary entry, 24 Jan. 1948, *Forrestal Diaries*, Forrestal Papers, vols. 9–10, p. 2040.

80. McClintock to Rusk, 14 Jan. 1948, 501.BB Palestine/1-1448.

81. Childs to secretary of state, 13 Jan. 1948, FRUS 1948, pt. 2, 5: 209–10.

82. See memorandum of conversation among Byrnes, Acheson, Henderson, Crown Prince Saud, and others, 17 Jan. 1947, FRUS 1947, 5: 738–41. See also Lovett to the legation in Saudi Arabia, 12 Dec. 1947, ibid., pp. 1338–40.

83. Childs to secretary of state, 21 Feb. 1948, FRUS 1948, pt. 2, 5: 220–21. On 15 March 1949, according to the terms of the Dhahran airfield agreement of 5-6 August, and as amended on 2 January 1946, the United States would formally turn the facility over to the Saudis.

84. See FRUS 1948, pt. 1, 5: 224 n.2.

85. Report by the Policy Planning Staff, 19 Jan. 1948, FRUS 1948, pt. 2, 5: 546–54.

86. Rusk to Lovett, 26 Jan. 1948, Folder: Palestine 15–31 Jan. 1948, *Rusk-McClintock Files*.

87. Draft Report by the Staff of the NSC, "The Position of the United States with Respect to Palestine," 17 Feb. 1948, Folder: Palestine Correspondence Misc. (Folder 1), Clifford Papers.

88. Ibid. For the conclusions of the staff report, see FRUS 1948, pt. 2, 5: 631–32.

89. Ibid.

90. The JCS study was apparently undertaken in early February at the request of Louis Denfeld, chief of Naval Operations. [JCS 1684/8, 1684/9, 1684/10, CCS 092 Palestine (5–3–46), Section 3, *JCS Records*.]

91. See Henderson to Grew, 29 May 1945, 867N.01/5–2545, and Merriam to Henderson, 28 July 1945, 867N.01/7–2845.

92. Whether Truman directly or indirectly approved Austin's statement is a matter of considerable debate. Although there is little doubt that the president had endorsed the principle of trusteeship in the event partition was unworkable, it seems there was considerable confusion over the timing of Austin's address. See Editorial Note FRUS 1948, pt. 2, 5: 744–46, and Donovan, *Conflict and Crisis*, pp. 375–79. Both Marshall and Lovett claimed that Truman had endorsed the idea

of trusteeship and approved Austin's speech. (Humelsine to Marshall, 22 Mar. 1948, *FRUS* 1948, pt. 2, 5: 749–50.) According to Donovan, Truman approved Austin's speech but misjudged the impact that trusteeship would have on the Zionists. (*Conflict and Crisis*, p. 378.)

93. Merriam to Henderson, 14 Apr. 1948, 867N.01/4–1448.

94. Smith to secretary of state, 21 Feb. 1948, Folder: Palestine 15–29 Feb., *Rusk-McClintock Files*.

95. Kennan to Marshall and Lovett, 24 Feb. 1948, PPS 23, Records of the Policy Planning Staff, 1947–1953, RG 59.

96. *Problems of American Small Business*, pt. 33, 17 Mar. 1948, p. 3669, and *Fuel Requirements—European Recovery Program*, 6 Feb. 1948, p. 12.

97. Memorandum of conversation among Duce, Kidd, and Eddy of ARAMCO and Sanger, Jenkins, and Breakey of the State Department, 28 Jan. 1948, 890F.6363/1–2648.

98. Henderson to Marshall and Lovett, 29 Jan. 1948, 867N.01/1–2948. Duce had written to Henderson regarding his recent trip to the Middle East. Henderson informed the secretary of state that according to Duce, anti-Zionism was not a movement of a "fringe of fanatics" but a "deep seated resentment nurtured by all Arab peoples from government officials and important financiers down to the peasants in the fields."

99. Mattison to Rusk, 2 Jan. 1948, Folder: Palestine 1–31 Jan. 1948, *Rusk-McClintock Files*.

100. Statement of J. A. Krug before the Senate Foreign Relations Committee, 13 Jan. 1948, Folder: Senate Appropriations Committee, Files of N. H. Collison 1947–1949, Records of the Office of Secretary of the Interior, *Interior Records*.

101. Marshall to Koegler, 8 Mar. 1948, *FRUS* 1948, pt. 1, 5: 7.

102. Memorandum, NSRB Petroleum Staff, 27 Feb. 1948, JCS 1754/7 (3–6–47), CCS 678 Section 1, *JCS Records*.

103. Eakens to Thorp, 12 Mar. 1948, 890.6363/3–1248. PED with the support of NEA, NE, and ITP recommended that the department continue to support ARAMCO's requests for export licenses for steel.

104. Deale to Forrestal, 19 Mar. 1948, JCS 1754 series (3–6–47), CCS 678, Section 1, *JCS Records*.

105. *Problems of American Small Business*, pt. 33, 17 Mar. 1948, p. 3667. See also excerpt of a telephone conversation between Kenney and Krug, Subject File, Folder: Conference Record May 1948, Box 49, Krug Papers.

106. On 19 March, the JCS informed Forrestal that national security would be "better served" if only the part of the Saudi section of the line linking present and projecting oil fields were constructed. [JCS 1754/9 (3–6–47), CCS 678, Section 1, *JCS Records*.]

107. "Study on the Military and Strategic Value to our National Security of Middle East Oil Developments," 23 Mar. 1948, Folder 44,

January-April 1948, JCS Correspondence, Leahy Papers (Naval History Division, Washington Navy Yard).

108. In June, the Department of State recommended that ARAMCO's requests for steel pipe for the second quarter of 1948 be postponed rather than risk "outright rejection" of the project as a result of congressional and executive opposition. The postponement, Marshall informed the legation in Saudi Arabia, was requested with the understanding that it would not prejudice the company's applications in the future. (Marshall to American legation, Jidda, *FRUS* 1948, pt. 1, 5: 23–24. See also Draft memo, Henderson and Brown to Lovett and Thorp, 1 June 1948, 890B.6363/6-148.) According to the June memo, Forrestal, Thomas Blaisdell, acting assistant secretary of commerce, and Max Ball of the Interior Department agreed with the State Department's approach. In February 1949, upon the recommendation of the Departments of State, Interior, the Economic Cooperation Administration, and the national military establishment, the interdepartmental Export Review Board granted ARAMCO's export license for the second and third quarters of 1949. In May, the TAPLINE convention was ratified by the Syrian Parliament and in September 1950, construction was completed. By November, the 300,000 b.p.d. facility was carrying its first barrel of oil from the Persian Gulf to the terminus at Sidon on the Lebanese coast.

109. Intelligence Division to Department of the Army, "Petroleum Supply and Demand," May 1948, P&O 463 (May 1948) F/W 17, pt. 2, *Records of the Army Staff*.

110. See SANACC 398/4, 25 May 1948, Enclosure "Preparations for Demolition of Oil Facilities in the Middle East." The oil resources of Saudi Arabia, the JCS concluded in early May, are of "major importance" to the United States and her allies both in peace and in a war with the Soviet Union. [JCS 1881, P&O 091 Arabia TS 6/4 Section 1, (Cases 1-), *Records of the Army Staff*.]

111. "Review of the World Situation as it Relates to the Security of the United States," 8 Apr. 1948, Report of the Central Intelligence Agency, *Records of the Army Staff*.

112. Epstein to Truman, 14 May 1948, *FRUS* 1948, pt. 2, 5: 989, and secretary of state to Epstein, 14 May 1948, ibid., p. 992.

113. Truman, *Memoirs*, 2:149,162.

114. Niles memorandum, 26 May 1946, OF 204, Truman Papers.

115. Memorandum by Clifford, 8 Mar. 1948, *FRUS* 1948, pt. 2, 5: 687–96.

116. Statement of Owen Brewster, 2 Apr. 1948, Folder: Congressional Action, March–April File, 1-322, Central Classified Files, 1937–1953, Office of the Secretary, *Interior Records*.

117. Secretaries of state, interior, and acting secretary of commerce to Truman, 3 Mar. 1948, Oil and Gas Division, Administrative General, File 1-322, pt. 4, Office of the Secretary, *Interior Records*. See

also *Petroleum Facts and Figures*, 1950, p. 339. In 1948, the United States imported 10,694,710 barrels of Saudi crude; 93,850,822 barrels from Venezuela; and 8,648,675 barrels from Colombia. The total for the year was 128,557,486 barrels.

118. Memorandum of conversation among Duce, Henderson, and others, 28 May 1948, 890F.6363/5–2848. See also Childs to secretary of state, 29 May 1948, Folder: Palestine 15–30 May 1948, *Rusk-Mc-Clintock Files*.

119. Childs to secretary of state, 15 May 1948, *FRUS* 1948, pt. 2, 5: 995–96.

120. Childs to secretary of state, 9 June 1948, 890F.6363/6–948. According to ARAMCO officials, Childs informed the department, Faisal and Saud were prepared to adopt any sanctions proposed by the Arab League against American interests (Childs to secretary of state, 9 June 1948, 890F.6363/6–948.) Also, interview with Parker T. Hart, Sept. 1976. Hart was consul general at Dhahran.

121. Marshall to the legation in Saudi Arabia, 3 July 1948, *FRUS* 1948, pt. 1, 5: 241–42.

122. Childs to the secretary of state, 12 June 1948, Folder: Palestine 1–15 June 1948, *Rusk-McClintock Files*.

123. Childs to secretary of state, 21 Feb. 1948, *FRUS* 1948, pt. 1, 5: 222–23.

124. Childs to secretary of state, 19 Apr. 1948, ibid., pp. 234–35.

125. Childs to secretary of state, 27 Dec. 1948, 890F.20 Missions/12–2748. See also Kopper to Satterthwaite, 17 Nov. 1948, Folder: Palestine 15–30 Nov. 1948, *Rusk-McClintock Files*.

126. JCS 1881, 4 May 1948, P&O 091 Arabia TS (Section 1) (Cases 1-) 6/4, *Records of the Army Staff*.

127. Joint Logistics Plans Committee to JCS, 18 May 1948, "The Military Necessity for Middle East Oil and Planning Factors Used in Computing POL Requirements," JCS 1741/2, *JCS Records*.

128. Forrestal to Marshall, 8 Nov. 1948, *FRUS* 1948, pt. 1, 5: 252.

129. Joint Strategic Survey Committee to JCS, 11 May 1948, JCS 1689/1, P&O 091 Arabia, TS (Section 1) (Case 1), *Records of the Army Staff*.

130. Moline's memorandum, "Effect of the Loss of Arab League Oil," 25 May 1948, was received in the Office of United Nations Affairs on 25 May 1948, Folder: Palestine 15–31 May 1948, *Rusk-McClintock Files*. See also Brown to Humelsine 28 July 1948, Folder: 15–31 July 1948, *Rusk-McClintock Files*. Brown's memorandum, "Possible Loss of Middle East Oil," was forwarded to the NSRB for consideration (Lovett to Hill, 19 Aug. 1948, 890.6363/8–1948).

Chapter 8

1. Pierre l'Espagnol de la Tramerye. *The World-Struggle for Oil*, p. 10.
2. Truman, *Memoirs*, vol. I, p. 164.
3. McClintock to Rusk, 1 July 1948, *FRUS* 1948, pt. 2, 5: 1171–79.
4. For a brief discussion of the tax arrangement, see Sampson, *Seven Sisters*, pp. 110–12. For the State Department's interest in the arrangement, see *FRUS* 1950, 5: 106–21. See also *Multinational Corporations*, pt. 8, pp. 341–50.

BIBLIOGRAPHICAL ESSAY

Any examination of American policy toward Saudi Arabia and its oil must begin with the massive collection of State Department records (RG 59) located in the National Archives. The State Department records used in this study generally fall into two categories—the indexed decimal or central file and the special or lot files. The decimal file provides the most complete record of the department's attitudes and actions toward Saudi oil and contains the record copies of memoranda, policy papers, and telegrams. The large collection of material on Saudi Arabia in the general and petroleum files (890F.oo and 890F.6363 respectively), not only contain the cable traffic between Jidda and Dhahran and Washington, but also include the majority of information on the development of United States policy toward Saudi oil. The general file on Palestine (867N.o1) contains a great deal of material on Middle Eastern oil and particularly on Ibn Saud's reaction to the Palestine problem. For interesting insights into official attitudes toward the partition of Palestine, the 501.BB/Palestine file is particularly good. Finally, for Anglo-American discussions on petroleum and for documentation on general petroleum questions see the 800.6363 file. Information on Stettinius's 1944 mission to London is in file 740.0011/Stettinius Mission.

Perhaps some of the most fascinating documentation on Arabian oil and American attitudes and policies toward the entire Middle Eastern area can be found in the State Department special or lot files. These files were maintained by the various divisions and offices of the department and often retired independently of the central file. Particularly rewarding are the records of the Department's Petroleum Division. This material, maintained jointly by the Petroleum Division and the Office of International Trade Policy, contains new information on the development of Middle Eastern oil policy; lend-lease and the various departmental oil committees are particularly emphasized. For information on American policy toward Saudi Arabia and American aid programs between 1944 and 1949, the State-War-Navy-Coordinating Committee records are essential.

American policy toward the Middle East in the postwar years can also be followed through the records of the Policy Planning Staff. This series contains important information on Palestine and American security interests in the Middle East and eastern Mediterranean. The records of SWNCC's ad hoc subcommittee on the Near and Middle East throw some light on political and military planning between 1947 and 1948. Finally, the Rusk-McClintock file is especially rich in material on Palestine and its relation to American security interests.

The second largest source of information on Saudi Arabia and its oil during the 1940s are the files of the various military and intelligence agencies. For high-level strategic thinking and planning on the Middle East, the Records of the Joint Chiefs of Staff (RG 218) are particularly instructive. There is also a good deal of material in the files of the lower-level committees such as the Army-Navy Petroleum Board and the Munitions Board (RG 330). The OSS files are also useful when supplemented by the army intelligence files—the Regional File 1933–1944 (RG 165) and the ID File 1944–1955 (RG 319). The CIA also cleared a number of intelligence reports which provided interesting information on Saudi Arabia and Arab reaction to events in Palestine. The navy's view of Middle Eastern oil as well as naval intelligence reports can be found in the Naval History Division's Operational Archives, located at the Washington Navy Yard. Particularly useful for the navy's view of Arabian oil is the general correspondence of James Forrestal in the General Records of the Department of the Navy (RG 80).

Because Middle Eastern petroleum attracted the interest of numerous government agencies during the war and postwar years, various Record Groups in the National Archives contain a great deal of important information. The Records of the Foreign Economic Administration (RG 169) contain material on lend-lease and subsidies to Saudi Arabia. The two richest sources, outside of State Department and military files, are the Records of the Office of Secretary of the Interior (RG 48) and the massive Records of the Petroleum Administration for War (RG 253). Neither have been adequately explored and contain a wealth of information on the domestic petroleum industry and economy and their relationship to foreign petroleum. The Chapman Files and the Collisson Files of RG 48 contain a considerable amount of material on Middle Eastern oil. The Records of the Foreign Service Posts of the Department of State (RG 84) often include interesting material not found in the Decimal File on the situation in Saudi Arabia as viewed from Jidda and Dhahran. Finally, the Records of the Reconstruction Finance Corporation (RG 234) contain the Minutes of the Petroleum Reserves Corporation, 1943–1944.

Although the primary focus of this study is the formation of American attitudes and policies toward Arabian oil, I have also incorporated material from the Public Records Office in London. I have concentrated largely on the years 1943 to 1945, the period of greatest Anglo-American tension in Saudi Arabia, in order to provide some sense of British thinking on Saudi oil and the increasing United States interest in the area. My research was selective, concentrating primarily on cable traffic from Jidda and Washington to London, Foreign Office memoranda of discussion and policy papers, and minutes of the War Cabinet.

In addition to the rich archival sources now available on Arabian oil, there is a great deal of congressional material on domestic and foreign oil policy. The best single source on Saudi Arabia for the 1940s is the record of the hearings of the Senate Special Committee Investigating the National Defense Program, *Petroleum Arrangements with Saudi Arabia*, pt. 41. For a wealth of information on domestic and foreign oil, see the hearings of the Special Senate Committee Investigating Petroleum Resources for the years 1945 to 1947. Information on the relationship between Middle Eastern oil and European recovery can be found in the Committee on Interstate and Foreign Commerce, *Fuel Investigation—Petroleum and the European Recovery Program*.

Research in oil company records has not been possible. SOCAL and ARAMCO's Washington representatives were helpful in suggesting secondary source material, but access to the companies' files is restricted. What information is available on company activities during the 1940s is drawn from government records and congressional hearings. Particularly useful, though clearly anticompany, is the Federal Trade Commission's staff report *The International Petroleum Cartel*. Similarly, the hearings and supporting material of Senator Frank Church's Subcommittee on Multinational Corporations (*Multinational Corporations and United States Foreign Policy*, pts. 7,8), provide valuable information and documentation on the activities of ARAMCO, SOCAL, SONJ, and Socony-Vacuum from the 1940s to the 1970s.

The private papers of the various personalities in the Roosevelt and Truman administrations provide an important source of information on American oil policy in the Middle East. The papers of Harry Truman at the Truman Library do not contain much material on Middle Eastern oil, yet hold important material on Palestine. Similarly, the Clifford, Acheson, Clayton, and Elsey papers and those of the assistant secretary and under secretary for economic affairs (Clayton-Thorp), include interesting insights into the formation of American oil policy in the Middle East and on the emerging cold war atmosphere of the postwar years.

Roosevelt's papers at Hyde Park, particularly the Official File and President's Secretary File, contain valuable documentation on a number of petroleum matters, including the PRC, pipeline, and Anglo-American petroleum agreement. There is little material on oil or Middle Eastern affairs in the Jones or Hopkins collections. The Morgenthau diaries and the Rosenman papers do include material on Palestine and on Saudi Arabia.

The Cordell Hull papers in the Library of Congress shed little light on Arabian oil or Middle Eastern policy. Similarly, the Ickes papers reveal a number of personal observations on oil company and PRC matters, yet contain little information on petroleum policy. Ickes's diary, however, includes important information on the Petroleum Reserves Corporation. The papers of Herbert Feis and Robert Patterson include little on Middle Eastern petroleum.

Although James Forrestal had a deep interest in the Middle East and its oil, his papers at Princeton add little to the understanding of the formation of American policy in the Middle East. They do provide material on the development of Forrestal's attitude toward the Soviet Union. His diaries at Princeton include a number of interesting references to Palestine and Saudi oil. Finally, the Stettinius papers at the University of Virginia offer a massive collection of State Department correspondence and policy memoranda for the period 1943 to 1945. There is considerable material on Anglo-American petroleum negotiations and on the Stettinius mission to London.

Personal memoirs do not add much to the primary sources yet they serve as useful background material. Particularly helpful are Herbert Feis, *Seen From EA*, for the development of policy toward the PRC, pipeline, and petroleum agreement; Joseph Jones, *The Fifteen Weeks* for the development of the Truman Doctrine; and William Eddy, *FDR Meets Ibn Saud* for Roosevelt's much acclaimed meeting with Ibn Saud. Harry Truman's *Memoirs* contain little on oil but much on Palestine. Cordell Hull's *Memoirs* include helpful background material on both petroleum and Palestine. Dean Acheson, *Present at the Creation*, provides useful information on Truman's Palestine policy.

The secondary literature available on the Middle East and Saudi oil is exhaustive though generally dated. There are a number of sources, however, that provide indispensable background material on the development of the oil concessions and the role of the great powers. Benjamin Shwadran, *The Middle East, Oil and the Great Powers*, 3rd ed., is the most comprehensive examination of the concessions, and contains a good overview of American oil policy toward Saudi Arabia. Stephen Longrigg, *Oil in the Middle East*, 3rd ed., contains much useful information but is limited by a lack of analysis. Longrigg, a former IPC employee is predictably sympathetic to both the IPC and the British government.

Within the last five years a great many works have appeared on the economics of international oil and the behavior of the major companies. Particularly good is John M. Blair's *The Control of Oil*. Blair, a government economist who coauthored and directed the FTC cartel report, sees cartel, consolidation, and control as the major legacies of the companies' involvement in Middle Eastern oil. For a more detached view of company behavior and market structure, see M. A. Adelman, *The World Petroleum Market*. Anthony Sampson, *Seven Sisters*; Leonard Moseley, *Power Play*; and Christopher T. Rand, *Making Oil Safe for Democracy*, provide very readable accounts of the major companies in the Middle East. Moseley, however, should be read with caution for interpretation and detail. Robert Engler's *The Politics of Oil* offers a good deal of material on the relationship between oilmen and government. For a good overview of American policy toward foreign oil see Gerald Nash, *United States Oil Policy 1890–1964*.

The development of American foreign policy in the Middle East in the war and immediate postwar years has only recently received the attention of scholars and journalists. John A. DeNovo's *American Interests and Policies in the Middle East 1900–1939* is the best work on the subject before 1939. Philip J. Baram, *The Department of State in the Middle East 1919–1945*, deals with the department's attitudes and policies, particularly during World War II. Both William R. Polk, *The United States and the Arab World*, and Robert W. Stookey, *America and the Arab States*, provide general overviews of American policies in the Middle East.

There has been no detailed study of American policy toward Middle Eastern oil during World War II. Mark Lytle's "American-Iranian Relations 1941–1947 and the Redefinition of National Security" (Ph.D. dissertation, Yale University, 1973), includes chapters on American policy toward Iranian oil. Joseph William Walt's "Saudi Arabia and the Americans, 1926–1951" (Ph.D. dissertation, Northwestern University, 1960), has a good deal of information on oil as does Malcolm C. Peck's, "Saudi Arabia in United States Foreign Policy to 1958" (Ph.D. dissertation, Fletcher School of Law and Diplomacy, 1970). Both were written without the benefit of the mass of archival material on Saudi Arabia and its oil which became available in the 1970s. Shoshana Klebanoff's *Middle East Oil and U.S. Foreign Policy with Special Reference to the U.S. Energy Crisis* contains a general overview of American policy toward Middle East oil in the war and immediate postwar years, and Burton I. Kaufman's *The Oil Cartel Case* deals briefly with oil diplomacy during the 1950s.

Saudi Arabian oil has not figured heavily in the literature dealing with American policy in the war and cold war years. Gaddis Smith's *American Diplomacy During the Second World War* briefly describes the new American interest in Saudi Arabia. Daniel Yergin's *Shattered Peace* deals with American policy toward Iran, but largely ignores the Middle East. Philip Baram's *The Department of State in the Middle East* has two chapters which survey the new American interest in Saudi Arabia. Only the revisionists deal in any greater detail with the importance of Middle Eastern oil, presumably in an attempt to demonstrate the predominance of "economic interests." Lloyd Gardner's *Economic Aspects of New Deal Diplomacy* and Gabriel Kolko's *Politics of War* both deal briefly with Saudi Arabian oil. Richard Freeland's *The Truman Doctrine and the Origins of McCarthyism* suggests the importance of Middle Eastern oil in United States strategic planning.

BIBLIOGRAPHY

Manuscript Sources

PERSONAL PAPERS

Charlottesville, Virginia
  University of Virginia Library
  Edward Stettinius Papers
Hyde Park, New York
  Franklin D. Roosevelt Library
  Harry L. Hopkins Papers
  Jesse Jones Papers
  Henry M. Morgenthau, Jr. Papers and Diary
  Franklin D. Roosevelt Papers
Independence, Missouri
  Harry S. Truman Library
  Dean Acheson Papers
  Assistant Secretary for Economic Affairs and the Under Secretary for
    Economic Affairs (Clayton-Thorp)
  Oscar L. Chapman Papers
  William L. Clayton Papers
  Clark M. Clifford Papers
  Ralph K. Davies Papers
  George M. Elsey Papers
  Joseph M. Jones Papers
  W. John Kenney Papers
  President's Committee on Foreign Aid Papers
  Samuel I. Rosenman Papers
  John W. Snyder Papers
Princeton, New Jersey
  James Forrestal Papers and Diary
Washington, D.C.
  Library of Congress
  Tom Connally Papers
  Herbert Feis Papers
  Cordell Hull Papers
  Harold Ickes Papers
  Julius Krug Papers
  James Landis Papers
  William Leahy Papers and Diary
  Robert Patterson Papers

GOVERNMENT ARCHIVES

Great Britain
  Public Records Office, London
  Foreign Office
    General Correspondence, Political (Eastern) 1941–1944
      F.O. 371/27265
            371/34975
            371/39985
            371/40265–69
            371/40271–74
            371/50379
Washington, D.C.
  National Archives
  Department of State Decimal File, Record Group (RG) 59
    800.6363 General Petroleum File 1940–1944; 1945–1949
    841.6363 Great Britain Petroleum File 1945–1949
    891.6363 Iran Petroleum File 1940–1944; 1945–1949
    890G.6363 Iraq Petroleum File 1945–1949
    890E.6363 Lebanon Petroleum File 1940–1944; 1945–1949
    867N.01 Palestine General File 1940–1944; 1945–1949
    867N.6363 Palestine Petroleum File 1940–1944; 1945–1949
    501.BB/Palestine United Nations File 1945–1949
    890F.00 Saudi Arabia General File 1940–1944; 1945–1949
    890F.6363 Saudi Arabia Petroleum File 1940–1944; 1945–1949
    861.6363 Soviet Union Petroleum File 1945–1949
    740.0011/Stettinius Mission Stettinius Mission File
    890D.6363 Syria Petroleum File
    867.00 Turkey General File 1945–1949
    890B.6363 Western Arabia Petroleum File 1945–1949
    State Department Decimal File 123 (Name Index)
  Department of State Lot Files
    Harley A. Notter Files, 1939–1945
    Military Adviser to the Office of Near Eastern, South Asian and
      African Affairs, 1945–1950
    Office of the Assistant and Under Secretary of State Dean Acheson,
      1941–1950
    Office of European Affairs (Matthews-Hickerson) 1935–1947
    Office of Near Eastern Affairs—Palestine, 1946–1949
    Office of The Petroleum Division, 1940–1949
    Records of the Policy Planning Staff, 1947–1953
    Reports of the Research and Analysis Brance (OSS) and the Bureau of
      Intelligence and Research (Department of State), 1941–1961
    Rusk-McClintock Files, 1947–1949

Records of the State-War-Navy Coordinating Committee (SWNCC) and the State-Army-Navy-Air Force Coordinating Committee (SANACC), 1944–1949.

Modern Military Records Branch

National Security Council Memoranda (numbered documents)

Records of the Joint Chiefs of Staff, 1942–1945, 1946–1947, 1948–1950, RG 218

Records of the Munitions Board and the Army-Navy Petroleum Board, Records of the Office of Secretary of Defense, RG 330 (located at the Federal Records Center, Suitland, Maryland)

Records of the Office of Assistant Chief of Staff for Intelligence, Documents Library Branch, I.D. File 1944–1955, Records of the Army Staff, RG 319 (located at Suitland, Maryland)

Records of the Office of the Director of Intelligence (G-2), Regional File 1933–1944, Records of the War Department General and Special Staffs, RG 165

Records of Headquarters, Army Service Staff, RG 160

Records of the Office of Strategic Services, RG 226

Records of the Army Staff, RG 319

Record Groups (Additional)

General Records of the Department of the Navy, 1798–1947, RG 80.

Records of the Office of Secretary of the Navy, James Forrestal, General Correspondence

Records of the Foreign Economic Administration, RG 169

Records of the Foreign Service Posts of the Department of State, RG 84

Records of the Government Printing Office, RG 149

Records of the Interdepartmental and Intradepartmental Committees of the Department of State, RG 353

Records of the Office of the Secretary of the Interior, RG 48

Records of the Office of War Mobilization and Reconversion, RG 250

Records of the Petroleum Administration for War, RG 253

Records of the Reconstruction Finance Corporation, RG 234

Records of the U.S. Senate, RG 46

OPERATIONAL ARCHIVES, NAVAL HISTORY DIVISION

Navy Yard, Washington, D.C.

Command File Post 1946

Papers of Fleet Admiral William D. Leahy, JCS Correspondence, 1946–1948

Published Government Documents

U.S. Congress. House. Committee on Interstate and Foreign Commerce.
*Petroleum Investigation—Petroleum Products for National
Defense.* H. Rept. 2744, 77th Cong., 2d sess., 1942.
U.S. Congress. House. Committee on Interstate and Foreign Commerce.
*Petroleum Investigation (Gasoline and Rubber), Hearings before a
subcommittee of the House Committee on Interstate and Foreign
Commerce.* 77th Cong., 2d sess., 1942.
U.S. Congress. House. Committee on Naval Affairs. *Investigation of the
Progress of the War Effort (Petroleum Investigation, Volume 3),
Hearings before a subcommittee of the Committee on Naval Affairs.*
78th Cong., 1st sess., 1943.
U.S. Congress. House. Committee on Appropriations. *Hearings on Navy
Department Appropriations Bill for 1945.* 78th Cong., 2d sess.,
1944.
U.S. Congress. House. Select Committee on Foreign Aid. *Coal
Requirements and Availabilities.* H. Rept. 1151, 80th Cong., 1st
sess., 1947.
U.S. Congress. House. Committee on Interstate and Foreign Commerce.
*Fuel Investigation—Petroleum and the European Recovery
Program.* H. Rept. 1438, 80th Cong., 2d sess., 1948.
U.S. Congress. House. Special Subcommittee on Petroleum of the
Committee on Armed Services. *Petroleum for National Defense.
Hearings before the Special Subcommittee of the Committee on
Armed Services.* 80th Cong., 2d sess., 1948.
U.S. Congress. House. Committee on Interstate and Foreign Commerce.
*Current Petroleum Outlook. Progress Report of the Committee on
Interstate and Foreign Commerce.* H. Rept. 2460, 80th Cong., 2d
sess., 1948.
U.S. Congress. Senate. Special Committee Investigating Petroleum
Resources. *American Petroleum Interests in Foreign Countries,
Hearings before a Special Committee Investigating Petroleum
Resources.* 79th Cong., 1st sess., 1945.
U.S. Congress. Senate. Special Committee Investigating Petroleum
Resources. *Wartime Petroleum Policy Under the Petroleum
Administration for War, Hearings Before a Special Committee
Investigating Petroleum Resources.* 79th Cong., 1st sess., 1945.
U.S. Congress. Senate. Special Committee Investigating Petroleum
Resources. *Petroleum Requirements—Postwar, Hearings before a
Special Committee Investigating Petroleum Resources.* 79th Cong.,
1st sess., 1945.
U.S. Congress. Senate. Special Committee Investigating Petroleum
Resources. *Diplomatic Protection of American Petroleum Interests
in Mesopotamia, the Netherlands East Indies and Mexico. A Staff*

Report Prepared for the Special Committee Investigating Petroleum Resources. S. Doc. 43, 79th Cong., 1st sess., 1945.

U.S. Congress. Senate. Special Committee Investigating Petroleum Resources. *Investigation of Petroleum Resources in Relation to the National Welfare*. Intermediate S. Rept. 179, 79th Cong., 2d sess., 1945.

U.S. Congress. Senate. Special Committee Investigating Petroleum Resources. *Investigation of Petroleum Resources in Relation to the National Welfare*. Final S. Rept. 9, 80th Cong., 1st sess., 1947.

U.S. Congress. Senate. Foreign Relations Committee. *Petroleum Agreement with Great Britain and Northern Ireland. Hearings, June 2–25, 1947.* 80th Cong., 1st sess., 1947.

U.S. Congress. Senate. Small Business Committee. *Problems of American Small Business, Parts 21, 33. Hearings before the Special Committee to Study Problems of American Small Business.* 80th Cong., 2d sess., 1948.

U.S. Congress. Senate. Special Committee Investigating the National Defense Program. *Petroleum Arrangements with Saudi Arabia, Part 41, Hearings before a Special Committee Investigating the National Defense Program.* 80th Cong., 1st sess., 1948.

U.S. Congress. Senate. Committee on Foreign Relations. *Multinational Corporations and United States Foreign Policy, Parts 7, 8. Hearings before the Subcommittee on Multinational Corporations.* 93rd Cong., 2d sess., 1974.

U.S. Congress. Senate. Committee on Foreign Relations. *A Documentary History of the Petroleum Reserves Corporation 1943–1944, Prepared for the use of the Subcommittee on Multinational Corporations.* Committee Print, Washington, D.C.: Government Printing Office, 1974.

U.S. Department of the Army. Office of the Chief of Military History. *The United States Army in World War II. The Middle East Theater. The Persian Corridor and Aid to Russia,* by T. H. Vail Motter. Washington, D.C.: Government Printing Office, 1952.

U.S. Department of State. *Assistance to European Economic Recovery, Statement by Secretary George C. Marshall, Secretary of State, before Senate Committee on Foreign Relations, January 8, 1948 and the President's Message to Congress, December 19, 1947.* Economic Cooperation Series, Publication 3022, Public Affairs Office, Publications Division, 1948.

U.S. Department of State. *European Recovery Program: Commodity Reports, Including Manpower.* Economic Cooperation Series, Publication 3093, Public Affairs Office, Publications Division, 1948.

U.S. Department of State. *Foreign Relations of the United States.* Washington, D.C., 1861— (cited below as *FRUS*).

FRUS 1937, Vol. II, *British Commonwealth, Europe, Near East, Africa.* Washington, 1954.

FRUS 1938, Vol. II, *British Commonwealth, Europe, Near East, Africa*. Washington, 1955.

FRUS 1939, Vol. IV, *The Far East, The Near East and Africa*. Washington, 1955.

FRUS 1940, vol. III, *British Commonwealth, the Soviet Union, Near East, Africa*. Washington, 1958.

FRUS 1941, Vol. III, *British Commonwealth, The Near East and Africa*. Washington, 1959.

FRUS 1942, Vol. IV, *The Near East and Africa*. Washington, 1963.

FRUS 1943, Vol. IV, *The Near East and Africa*. Washington, 1964.

FRUS 1943, *Conferences at Cairo and Tehran*. Washington, 1961.

FRUS 1944, Vol. III, *The British Commonwealth, Europe*. Washington, 1965.

FRUS 1944, Vol. V, *The Near East, South Asia, Africa, The Far East*. Washington, 1965.

FRUS 1945, Vol. VIII, *The Near East and Africa*. Washington, 1969.

FRUS 1945, *The Conferences at Malta and Yalta*. Washington, 1955.

FRUS 1946, Vol. VII, *The Near East and Africa*. Washington, 1969.

FRUS 1947, Vol. I, *General; The United Nations*. Washington, 1973.

FRUS 1947, Vol. III, *The British Commonwealth; Europe*. Washington, 1972.

FRUS 1947, Vol. V, *The Near East and Africa*. Washington, 1971.

FRUS 1948, Vol. V, (Part 1), *The Near East, South Asia and Africa*. Washington, 1975.

FRUS 1948, Vol. V, (Part 2), *The Near East, South Asia and Africa*. Washington, 1976.

FRUS 1949, Vol. VI, *The Near East, South Asia and Africa*. Washington, 1977.

FRUS 1950, Vol. V, *The Near East, South Asia, and Africa*. Washington, 1978.

U.S. Federal Trade Commission. *The International Petroleum Cartel. Staff Report Submitted to the Subcommittee on Monopoly of the Select Committee on Small Business.* Committee Print, Washington, D.C.: Government Printing Office, 1952.

Interviews

Harold Glidden, Washington, D.C., October 1975.
Raymond Hare, Washington, D.C., August 1976.
Parker T. Hart, Washington, D.C., September 1976.

Loy Henderson, Washington, D.C., October 1975, August 1976.
Herbert Liebesny, Washington, D.C., October 1975.
Richard Sanger, Washington, D.C., November 1975 (by telephone).
Joseph Satterthwaite, Washington, D.C., November 1975 (by
   telephone).

Books, Articles, and Dissertations

Acheson, Dean. *Present at the Creation: My Years in the State
   Department*. New York: W. W. Norton, 1969.
Adelman, M. A. *The World Petroleum Market*. Baltimore: The Johns
   Hopkins University Press, 1972.
Adler, Selig. "American Policy vis à vis Palestine in the Second World
   War," in James O'Neill and Robert W. Krauskopf, eds. *World
   War II: An Account of its Documents*. Washington, D.C.:
   Howard University Press, 1976, pp. 43–58.
Albion, Robert G., and Connery, Robert H. *Forrestal and the Navy*.
   New York: Columbia University Press, 1962.
American Petroleum Institute. *Facts and Figures*. (9th Edition) New
   York, 1951.
Anderson, Irvine. *The Standard-Vacuum Oil Company and United
   States East Asia Policy, 1933–1941*. Princeton: Princeton
   University Press, 1975.
Badeau, John S. *The American Approach to the Arab World*. New
   York: Harper & Row, 1968.
Baker, Robert L. *Oil, Blood and Sand*. New York: D. Appleton-
   Century Company, Inc., 1942.
Baram, Phillip J. *The Department of State in the Middle East 1919–
   1945*. Philadelphia: University of Pennsylvania Press, 1978.
Barger, Thomas C. "Middle Eastern Oil Since the Second World
   War." *America and the Middle East. Annals of the American
   Academy of Political and Social Science* 401 (May 1972): 31–34.
Berle, Beatrice Bishop, and Jacobs, Travis Beal, eds. *Navigating the
   Rapids 1918–1971*. New York: Harcourt Brace Jovanovich,
   Inc., 1973.
Bishop, Jim. *FDR's Last Year, April 1944–April 1945*. New York:
   Morrow, 1974.
Blair, John M. *The Control of Oil*. New York: Pantheon Books, 1976.
Bohlen, Charles E. *Witness to History 1929–1969*. New York: W. W.
   Norton & Company, Inc., 1973.
Bolles, Blair. "Oil: An Economic Key to Peace." *Foreign Policy
   Reports* 20 (1 July 1944): 86–95.
Brooks, Benjamin T. *Peace, Plenty and Petroleum*. Lancaster,
   Pennsylvania: Jacques Cattell Press, 1944.
Bryson, Thomas A. *American Diplomatic Relations with the Middle*

East, 1784–1975: A Survey. Metuchen, New Jersey: Scarecrow Press, 1977.

Buhite, Russell D. *Patrick J. Hurley and American Foreign Policy*. Ithaca: Cornell University Press, 1973.

Burns, James MacGregor. *Roosevelt. The Soldier of Freedom 1940–1945*. New York: Harcourt Brace Jovanovich Inc., 1970.

Byrnes, James F. *Speaking Frankly*. New York: Harper & Brothers, 1947.

Campbell, John C. *Defense of the Middle East: Problems of American Policy*. New York: Praeger, 1961.

Caroe, Olaf. *Wells of Power: The Oilfields of South-Western Asia*. London: Macmillan & Co., 1951.

Childs, J. Rives. *Foreign Service Farewell: My Years in the Near East*. Charlottesville: University of Virginia Press, 1969.

Chisholm, Archibald, H. T. *The First Kuwait Oil Concession Agreement: A Record of the Negotiations 1911–1934*. London: Frank Cass, 1975.

Churchill, Winston S. *The World Crisis*. New York: Charles Scribner's Sons, 1931.

Clifford, Clark M. "Factors Influencing President Truman's Decision to Support Partition and Recognize the State of Israel." Paper delivered at the annual meeting of the American Historical Association, 28 December 1976, Washington, D.C.

Daniel, Robert L. *American Philanthropy in the Near East, 1820–1960*. Athens: Ohio University Press, 1970.

DeGaury, Gerald. *Faisal: King of Saudi Arabia*. New York: Frederick A. Praeger, 1967.

De La Tramerye, Pierre l'Espagnol. *The World-Struggle for Oil*. New York: Alfred A. Knopf, 1924.

DeNovo, John A. *American Interests and Policies in the Middle East 1900–1939*. Minneapolis: University of Minnesota Press, 1963.

———. "Petroleum and the United States Navy Before World War I." *Mississippi Historical Review* 41 (March 1955): 641–56.

———. "The Movement for an Aggressive American Oil Policy Abroad, 1918–1920." *American Historical Review* 61 (July 1956): 854–76.

Dickson, H. R. P. *Kuwait and Her Neighbors*. London: George Allen & Unwin Ltd., 1956.

Donovan Robert J. *Conflict and Crisis*. New York: W. W. Norton & Company, Inc., 1977.

Eddy, William A. *FDR Meets Ibn Saud*. New York: American Friends of the Middle East, Inc., 1954.

Elwell-Sutton, L. P. *Persian Oil: A Study in Power Politics*. Westport, Conn.: Greenwood Press, 1975.

Engler, Robert. *The Politics of Oil: A Study of Private Power and*

Democratic Directions. New York: The Macmillan Company, 1961.

Evans, Laurence. *United States Policy and the Partition of Turkey 1914–1922*. Baltimore: Johns Hopkins Press, 1965.

Fanning, Leonard M. *American Oil Operations Abroad*. New York: McGraw-Hill Book Co., Inc., 1947.

————. *Foreign Oil and the Free World*. New York: McGraw-Hill Book Co., Inc., 1954.

Feis, Herbert. *Petroleum and American Foreign Policy*. Stanford: Stanford University Press, 1944.

————. *Seen From E.A.: Three International Episodes*. New York: Alfred A. Knopf, 1947.

————. *The Birth of Israel: The Tousled Diplomatic Bed*. New York: Norton, 1969.

Field, James A., Jr. *America and the Mediterranean World, 1776–1882*. Princeton: Princeton University Press, 1969.

Finnie, David H. *Desert Enterprise: The Middle East Oil Industry in Its Local Environment*. Cambridge, Mass.: Harvard University Press, 1958.

————. *Pioneers East: The Early American Experience in the Middle East*. Cambridge, Mass.: Harvard University Press, 1967.

Frechtling, Louis E. "Oil and the War." *Foreign Policy Reports* 17 (1941): 70–80.

Freeland, Richard M. *The Truman Doctrine and the Origins of McCarthyism 1946–1948*. New York: Alfred A. Knopf, 1972.

Frey, John W., and Ide, H. Chandler. *A History of the Petroleum Administration for War*. Washington, D.C.: United States Government Printing Office, 1946.

Friedwald, Eugene Marie. *Oil and the War*. London: William Heineman, 1941.

Gaddis, John Lewis. *The United States and the Origins of the Cold War, 1941–1947*. New York: Columbia University Press, 1972.

Gardner, Lloyd C. *Economic Aspects of New Deal Diplomacy*. Boston: Beacon Press, 1971.

Grabill, Joseph L. *Protestant Diplomacy and the Near East: Missionary Influence on American Policy, 1810–1927*. Minneapolis: University of Minnesota Press, 1971.

Grobba, Fritz. *Männer und Mächte im Orient: 25 Jahre diplomatischer Tätigkeit im Orient*. Göttingen: Musterschmidt-Verlag, 1967.

Gulbenkian, Nubar. *Portrait in Oil: The Autobiography of Nubar Gulbenkian*. New York: Simon & Schuster, 1965.

Hamilton, Charles W. *Americans and Oil in the Middle East*. Houston: Gulf Publishing Company, 1962.

Hare, Raymond A. "The Great Divide: World War II." *America and the Middle East. Annals of the American Academy of Political and Social Science* 401 (May 1972): 23–30.

Hartshorn, J. E. *Politics and World Oil Economics: An Account of the International Oil Industry in its Political Environment.* New York: Frederick A. Praeger, 1962.

Henderson, Loy W. "American Political and Strategic Interests in the Middle East and Southeastern Europe." *Department of State Bulletin* 17 (23 November 1947): 996–1000.

Hewins, Ralph. *Mr. Five Per Cent: The Biography of Calouste Gulbenkian.* New York: Rinehart, 1958.

Hirszowicz, Lukasz. *The Third Reich and the Arab East.* London: Routledge & Kegan Paul, 1966.

Hogan, Michael J. *Informal Entente: The Private Structure of Cooperation in Anglo-American Economic Diplomacy 1918–1928.* Columbia: University of Missouri Press, 1977.

Holt, P. M. *Egypt and the Fertile Crescent 1516–1922.* Ithaca: Cornell University Press, 1966.

Hopwood, Derek, ed. *The Arabian Peninsula: Society and Politics.* Totowa, N.J.: Rowman and Littlefield, 1972.

Hoskins, Halford L. *Middle East Oil and United States Foreign Policy.* Washington, D.C.: Legislative Reference Service, Library of Congress, 1950.

Howard, Harry N. *The King-Crane Commission: An American Inquiry in the Middle East.* Beirut: Khayats, 1963.

———. *Turkey, the Straits and U.S. Policy.* Baltimore: The Johns Hopkins University Press, 1974.

Howard, Michael. *The Mediterranean Strategy in the Second World War.* London: Weidenfeld and Nicolson, 1968.

Howarth, David A. *The Desert King: Ibn Saud and His Arabia.* New York: McGraw-Hill, 1964.

Hull, Cordell. *The Memoirs of Cordell Hull.* 2 vols. New York: Macmillan, 1948.

Hurewitz, J. C. *The Struggle for Palestine.* New York: W. W. Norton & Company, 1950.

Ickes, Harold L. *The Secret Diary of Harold L. Ickes.* 3 vols. Vol. 3, *The Lowering Clouds 1939–1941.* New York: Simon and Schuster, 1954.

———. *Fightin' Oil.* New York: Alfred A. Knopf, 1943.

Iqbal, Dr. Sheikh Mohammad. *Emergence of Saudi Arabia (A Political Study of King Abd al-Aziz ibn Saud 1901–1953).* Srinagar, Kashmir: Saudiyah Publishers, 1977.

Israel, Fred, ed. *The War Diaries of Breckinridge Long.* Lincoln: University of Nebraska Press, 1966.

Jacoby, Neil H. *Multinational Oil: A Study in Industrial Dynamics.* New York: Macmillan Publishing Co., Inc., 1974.

Jones, Joseph M. *The Fifteen Weeks.* New York: Viking Press, 1955.

Kaplan, Lawrence S. "Ethnic Politics, the Palestine Question, and the Cold War," in Morrell Heald and Lawrence Kaplan, eds. *Culture and Diplomacy: The American Experience*. Westport, Conn.: Greenwood Press, 1977.

Kaufman, Burton I. *The Oil Cartel Case: A Documentary Study of Antitrust Activity in the Cold War Era*. Westport, Conn.: Greenwood Press, 1978.

Kennan, George F. *Memoirs, 1925–1950*. Boston: Little, Brown & Co., 1967.

Kent, Marian. *Oil and Empire: British Policy and Mesopotamian Oil 1900–1920*. London: The London School of Economics and Political Science, 1976.

Kimche, Jon. *The Second Arab Awakening*. New York: Holt, Rinehart and Winston, 1970.

Kirk, George E. *The Middle East in the War*. London: Oxford University Press, 1952.

———. *The Middle East, 1945–1950*. London: Oxford University Press, 1954.

Klebanoff, Shoshana. *Middle East Oil and U.S. Foreign Policy with Special Reference to the U.S. Energy Crisis*. New York: Praeger Publishers, 1974.

Kolko, Gabriel. *The Politics of War*. New York: Vintage Books, 1968.

Kolko, Joyce and Kolko, Gabriel. *The Limits of Power: The World and United States Foreign Policy 1945–1954*. New York: Harper & Row, 1972.

Krasner, Stephen D. *Defending the National Interest, Raw Material Investments and U.S. Foreign Policy*. Princeton: Princeton, University Press, 1978.

Krueger, Robert B. *The United States and International Oil: A Report for the Federal Energy Administration on U.S. Firms and Government Policy*. New York: Frederick A. Praeger, 1975.

LaFeber, Walter. *America, Russia and the Cold War*. New York: John Wiley and Sons, Inc., 1976.

Larson, Henrietta M., ed. *The History of Standard Oil Company (New Jersey)* 3 vols. Vol. 1. *Pioneering in Big Business, 1882–1911*, by R. W. Hidy. Vol. 2., *The Resurgent Years, 1911–1927*, by G. S. Gibb and E. H. Knowlton. Vol. 3., *New Horizons, 1927–1950*, by H. M. Larson and E. H. Knowlton. New York: Harper & Row, 1955–1971.

Leahy, William D. *I Was There*. New York: McGraw-Hill Book Company, 1950.

Lebkicher, Roy; Rentz, George; and Steineke, Max. *ARAMCO Handbook*. Haarlem, The Netherlands: J. Enschede, 1960.

Lenczowski, George. *Oil and State in the Middle East*. Ithaca: Cornell University Press, 1960.

————. *Russia and the West in Iran 1918–1948.* New York: Greenwood Press, 1968.

Leuchtenburg, William E. *Franklin D. Roosevelt and the New Deal.* New York: Harper & Row, 1963.

Lieuwen, Edwin. *Petroleum in Venezuela, A History.* New York: Russell & Russell, 1954.

Loftus, John A. "Middle East Oil: The Pattern of Control." *The Middle East Journal* (January 1948): 17–33.

Long, David. *Saudi Arabia.* Beverly Hills/London: Sage Publications, 1976.

Longrigg, Stephen H. *Oil in the Middle East: Its Discovery and Development.* London: Oxford University Press, 1968.

Lytle, Mark H. "American-Iranian Relations 1941–1947 and the Redefinition of National Security." Ph.D. dissertation, Yale University, 1973.

Malone, Joseph J. "America and the Arabian Peninsula: The First Two Hundred Years." *The Middle East Journal* (Summer 1976): 406–24.

Manuel, Frank E. *The Realities of American-Palestine Relations.* Washington, D.C.: Public Affairs Press, 1949.

Mazuzan, George T. "United States Policy Toward Palestine at the United Nations, 1947–1948: An Essay." *Prologue: The Journal of The National Archives* (Fall 1975): 163–76.

McCarthy, W. Barry. "Ibn Saud's Voyage." *Life* (19 March 1945): 59–64.

Mikesell, Raymond, and Chenery, Hollis B. *Arabian Oil: America's Stake in the Middle East.* Chapel Hill: University of North Carolina Press, 1949.

Miller, Aaron David. "The Influence of Middle East Oil on American Foreign Policy: 1941–1948." *Middle East Review* (Spring 1977): 19–23.

Millis, Walter, ed. *The Forrestal Diaries.* New York: Viking, 1951.

Monroe, Elizabeth. *Philby of Arabia.* London: Faber and Faber, 1973.

Moseley, Leonard. *Power Play: Oil in the Middle East.* Baltimore: Penguin Books, Inc., 1973.

Motter, T. H. Vail. *The Persian Corridor and Aid to Russia.* Washington, D.C.: The Government Printing Office, 1952.

Murray, Wallace S. "The Division of Near Eastern Affairs." *The American Foreign Service Journal* 10 (1933): 16–19.

Nash, Gerald D. *United States Oil Policy 1890–1964.* Pittsburgh: University of Pittsburgh Press, 1968.

Odell, Peter R. *Oil and World Power.* New York: Taplinger, 1970.

Peck, Malcolm C. "Saudi Arabia in United States Foreign Policy to 1958: A Study in the Sources and Determinants of American

Policy." Ph.D. dissertation, Fletcher School of Law and
Diplomacy, 1970.

Pogue, Joseph E. "Must An Oil War Follow This War?" *The Atlantic Monthly* 173 (March 1944): 41–47.

Polk, William R. *The United States and the Arab World*. Cambridge, Mass.: Harvard University Press, 1969.

Philby, H. St. J. B. *Arabian Jubilee*. London: Robert Hale Limited, 1952.

————. *Arabian Oil Ventures*. Washington, D.C.: Middle East Institute, 1964.

————. *Saudi Arabia*. New York: Frederick A. Praeger, 1955.

Pratt, Wallace. "Our Petroleum Resources." *American Scientist* 32 (April 1944): 12–28.

Rand, Christopher T. *Making Democracy Safe for Oil: Oilmen and the Islamic East*. Boston: Little, Brown & Company, 1975.

Reilly, Michael F. *Reilly of the White House*. New York: Simon and Schuster, 1947.

Rentz, George. "Wahhabism and Saudi Arabia." in Derek Hopwood, ed., *The Arabian Peninsula: Society and Politics*. Totowa, N.J.: Rowman and Littlefield, 1972.

Rihani, Ameen. *Ibn Sa'oud of Arabia*. Boston: Houghton-Mifflin Company, 1928.

Rogow, Arnold A. *James Forrestal: A Study of Personality, Politics and Policy*. New York: The Macmillan Company, 1963.

Rosenberg, David A. "The U.S. Navy and the Problem of Oil in a Future War: The Outline of a Strategic Dilemma, 1945–1950." *Naval War College Review* (Summer 1976): 53–64.

Sachar, Howard M. *A History of Israel: From the Rise of Zionism to Our Time*. New York: Alfred A. Knopf, 1976.

————. *Europe Leaves the Middle East, 1936–1954*. New York: Alfred A. Knopf, 1972.

Sampson, Anthony. *The Seven Sisters, The Great Oil Companies & The World They Shaped*. New York: Viking Press, 1975.

Sanger, Richard H. *The Arabian Peninsula*. Ithaca: Cornell University Press, 1954.

Sherwood, Robert E. *Roosevelt and Hopkins: An Intimate History*. New York: Harper & Brothers, 1948.

Shwadran, Benjamin. *The Middle East, Oil and the Great Powers*. New York: John Wiley & Sons, Inc., 1973.

Smith, Gaddis. *American Diplomacy During the Second World War 1941–1945*. New York: John Wiley and Sons, Inc., 1965.

Smith, R. Harris. *OSS: The Secret History of America's First Central Intelligence Agency*. Berkeley: University of California Press, 1972.

Smyser, William R. "The Formation of the Iraq Petroleum

Company, 1888–1928." M.A. Thesis, Georgetown University, 1960.

Snetsinger, John G. *Truman, The Jewish Vote, and the Creation of Israel*. Stanford: Hoover Institution Press, 1974.

Stettinius, Edward R., Jr. *Roosevelt and the Russians*. Garden City, N.Y.: Doubleday, 1949.

Stevens, Richard P. *American Zionism and United States Foreign Policy, 1942–1947*. New York: Pageant Press, 1962.

Stocking, George W. *Middle East Oil. A Study in Political and Economic Controversy*. Nashville: Vanderbilt University Press, 1970.

Stookey, Robert W. *America and the Arab States: An Uneasy Encounter*. New York: John Wiley & Sons, Inc., 1975.

Stork, Joe. *Middle East Oil and the Energy Crisis*. New York: Monthly Review Press, 1975.

Stuart, Graham H. *The Department of State: A History of its Organization, Procedures, and Personnel*. New York: Macmillan Company, 1949.

Sweet, Louise E. "The Arabian Peninsula." in Louise E. Sweet, ed. *The Central Middle East*. New Haven: Human Relations Area Files Press, 1971, pp. 202–206.

Sykes, Christopher. *Crossroads to Israel 1917–1948*. Bloomington: Indiana University Press, 1965.

Tibawi, A. L. *American Interests in Syria, 1800–1901: A Study of Educational, Literary, and Religious Work*. London: Oxford University Press, 1966.

Time. "Oil—In Search of a Policy." (27 December 1943): 77–78.

Trask, Roger R. *The United States Response to Turkish Nationalism and Reform 1914–1939*. Minneapolis: University of Minnesota Press, 1971.

Troeller, Gary. *The Birth of Saudi Arabia: Britain and the Rise of the House of Sa'ud*. London: Frank Cass, 1976.

Truman, Harry S. *Memoirs: Year of Decisions*. Garden City, N.Y.: Doubleday, 1955.

―――. *Memoirs: Years of Trial and Hope, 1946–1952*. Garden City, N.Y.: Doubleday, 1956.

Truman, Margaret. *Harry S. Truman*. New York: William Morrow & Company, Inc., 1973.

Tugendhat, Christopher, and Hamilton, Adrian. *Oil: The Biggest Business*. London: Eyre and Spottiswoode, 1968.

Twitchell, Karl S. *Saudi Arabia*. Princeton: Princeton University Press, 1958.

Ulam, Adam B. *The Rivals: America and Russia Since World War II*. New York: The Viking Press, 1971.

―――. *Expansion & Coexistence: The History of Soviet Foreign Policy 1917–1967*. New York: Frederick A. Praeger, 1968.

Walpole, Norman C.; Bastos, Alexander J.; Eisele, Frederick R.; Herrick, Allison Butler; John, Howard J.; and Wieland, Tura K. *Area Handbook for Saudi Arabia.* Washington, D.C.: United States Government Printing Office, 1971.

Walt, Joseph W. "Saudi Arabia and the Americans 1928–1951." Ph.D. dissertation, Northwestern University, 1960.

Ward, Thomas E. *Negotiations for Oil Concessions in Bahrain, El Hasa (Saudi Arabia), The Neutral Zone, Qatar, and Kuwait.* New York: Ardlee Service, Inc., 1965.

Watt, D.C. "The Foreign Policy of Ibn Saud, 1936–1939." *Journal of the Royal Central Asian Society*, 50 pt. 2 (1963): 152–160.

Weil, Martin. *A Pretty Good Club: The Founding Fathers of the U.S. Foreign Service.* New York: W. W. Norton & Company, Inc., 1978.

Wilkins, Mira. *The Emergence of Multinational Enterprise: American Business Abroad from the Colonial Era to 1914.* Cambridge, Mass.: Harvard University Press, 1970.

———. *The Maturing of Multinational Enterprise: American Business Abroad from 1914 to 1970.* Cambridge, Mass.: Harvard University Press, 1974.

Williamson, Harold F.; Andreano, Ralph L.; Daum, Arnold R.; and Klose, Gilbert C. *The American Petroleum Industry.* 2 vols. Vol. 1, *The Age of Illumination*, 1859–1899, by Harold F. Williamson and Arnold R. Daum. Vol. 2, *The Age of Energy*, 1899–1959, by Harold F. Williamson, Ralph L. Andreano, Arnold R. Daum, and Gilbert C. Klose. Evanston: Northwestern University Press, 1963.

Wilmington, Martin W. *The Middle East Supply Centre.* Albany: State University of New York Press, 1971.

Winder, R. Bayly. *Saudi Arabia in the Nineteenth Century.* New York: St. Martin's Press, 1965.

Van der Meulen, D. *The Wells of Ibn Saud.* London: John Murray, 1957.

Yergin, Daniel. *Shattered Peace: The Origins of the Cold War and the National Security State.* Boston: Houghton-Mifflin Company, 1977.

INDEX

Acheson, Dean, 59, 65, 72, 149, 160, 168, 169, 173, 175; and Saudi subsidy, 127; meets with congressional leaders, 132, 135–36; meets with Truman, 136–37
Abdullah (Amir and King of Transjordan): and Trans-Arabian Pipeline, 155–56
Alling, Paul H., 36, 40, 43, 47, 48, 50, 58, 60, 87, 109; background of, 23
American Independent Oil Company, 273–74 (n. 34)
Anglo-American Petroleum Agreement, xv, 99–107, 160, 207; origins of, 83–84, 250 (n. 82); technical discussions, 102–4; Memorandum of Understanding, 103–4; cabinet negotiations, 104; final accord, 104–6; opposed by Congress, 106, 258 (n. 56); and consultation with oil industry, 256 (n. 40); and British, 256 (n. 42), 257 (nn. 49, 50); fate of, 258 (n. 57)
Anglo-Iranian Oil Company (AIOC), 69, 93, 111, 153, 155, 158, 161, 205. See also Anglo-Persian Oil Company
Anglo-Persian Oil Company (APOC), 7, 9, 12, 16, 30
Arab League, 185, 188, 195, 200, 201
Arabian American Oil Company (ARAMCO), xiin, xiv, 19, 92, 94, 119, 133, 135, 138, 145, 147, 153, 154, 155, 156, 158, 159, 160, 162, 163, 173, 179, 205, 206, 209, 211, 213; name changes from CASOC, 92, 252 (n. 2); and PRC pipeline, 96, 97, 98; and Export-Import Bank loan, 143; and transit rights in Transjordan, 157; participation in joint ventures, 158–63; lobbies for TAPLINE, 180–81, 182; and TAPLINE export licenses, 196–98; and State Department, U.S., 211. See also California Arabian Standard Oil Company; State Department, U.S.
Armstrong, Hamilton Fish, 49

Army-Navy Petroleum Board (ANPB), 60, 73, 74, 79, 93, 177; and PRC pipeline, 98–99; and TAPLINE, 181; origins of, 239 (n. 105); and Middle East oil, 247 (n. 48)
"As Is" Agreement, 12, 158
Atlantic Charter, 75, 78, 99, 105, 153, 204

Bahrain: and oil, xviii, 4, 13, 14–15, 48, 54
Bahrain Petroleum Company (BAPCO), xiin, 15
Balfour Declaration, 210
Ball, Max: and TAPLINE, 181, 182
Bard, Ralph, 119, 134, 135, 136, 137
Barkley, Alben W., 135
Baxter, C. W., 108, 112, 117
Beaverbrook, Lord, 104
Ben-Gurion, David, 199
Berenger, Henri, 204
Berle, Adolf, 35, 47, 59; and Moffett proposal, 41–42; and Saudi oil, 60, 64, 65, 78, 241–42 (n. 8)
Bonesteel, C. H., 177
Brewster, Owen, 70, 200
Britain. See Great Britain
British Foreign Office. See Foreign Office
Brown, Sir William, 103
Brownell, George, 135
Bullitt, William, 74, 76, 90, 247 (n. 51)
Butler, Neville, 41, 45, 111
Byrnes, James, 76, 156, 157, 160; and PRC pipeline, 96

Cadogan, Alexander, 115–16
California Arabian Standard Oil Company (CASOC), xii, xiv, 5, 20, 73, 82, 84; and financial crisis in Saudi Arabia, 34–35, 36–37; lobbies for U.S. aid (1941), 35–50; view of British, 37–38, 50; fear of British influence, 67–68, 236 (n. 73), 243 (n. 22); and proposals of February 1943, 68–71; lobbies for

meeting, 130; and State
Department concern about, 164–
66; plan to partition, 169, 184; and
United Nations, 176; and U.S.
strategic interests, 179, 184–91,
186–87, 190, 191, 192, 193, 209,
275 (n. 63); Soviet exploitation of,
185, 187, 188, 193, 194, 195, 209,
281 (n. 56), 282 (n. 67); and loss of
Middle East oil, 186–87, 192, 193,
194, 202–3; and Arab world, 188–
89; and U.S.-Saudi relations, 199–
202. *See also* Ibn Saud; State
Department
Parker, Leonard, 107, 108
Patchin, Philip, 24, 36, 226 (n. 81)
Patterson, Robert, 166, 175
Pauley, Edwin, 124
Peterson, Sir Maurice, 111, 115
Petroleum. *See* Oil
Petroleum Administration for War
(PAW), xiii, 71, 72, 73, 88, 122, 123,
207, 211, 240 (n. 1)
Petroleum Division (PED), State
Department, 16, 87, 100, 161, 203;
and Anglo-American Oil
Agreement, 100; and Middle East
oil, 124; and oil policy, 153; and
TAPLINE, 156, 181
Petroleum Industry War Council,
(PIWC): and PRC pipeline, 97–98
Petroleum Reserves Corporation
(PRC), xv, 74, 76, 79, 80, 81, 82, 84,
88, 89, 95, 206, 207, 211, 249 (n.
66); origins of, 73, 76–77, 245 (n.
41), 246 (n. 45), 248 (n. 58); Ickes
interest in, 74; military's interest
in, 74; and negotiations with oil
companies, 78–82, 249 (nn. 67, 70,
71), 250 (nn. 74, 75, 79); and
pipeline, 97, 98, 254 (n. 22); 254–
55 (n. 25), 255 (n. 27)
Philby, H. St. John, 4, 16, 19, 20, 24,
35, 189, 221 (n. 49)
Phillips, Sir Frederick, 45
Pierson, Warren, 44
Pinsent, Gerald Hume, 113
Policy Planning Staff, State
Department, 192–93
Pratt, Wallace, 123

Rayburn, Sam, 132
Rayner, Charles, 99, 100, 124, 127,
152, 160
Reconstruction Finance Corporation
(RFC), 42, 45, 75, 77, 232 (n. 35)
Red Line Agreement, 12, 14, 15, 30,
83, 100, 103, 104, 105, 158, 159,
160, 220–21 (n. 36)
Reilly, Michael, x
Rihani, Ameen, 24, 225 (n. 78)
Robertson, D. H., 85
Rodgers, W. S. S., 45, 67, 68, 69, 79,
81, 180, 181, 231 (n. 29)
Roosevelt, Franklin Delano, x, xii,
28, 29, 38, 39, 40, 42, 43, 44, 50,
52, 55, 70, 71, 76, 77, 79, 90, 94,
124, 130, 164, 170, 204, 233 (n. 49),
226 (n. 80), 227 (n. 89); meets with
Ibn Saud, x–xii, 128–31; interest in
oil, 38; and Moffett, 38–39, 229–30
(n. 19); interest in Saudi Arabia,
39, 43; and failure of Moffett
proposal, 44; discussions with
Britain, 89, 101, 101–2, 253 (n. 10);
and PRC, 95, 97, 98, 248 (n. 62);
and aid to Saudi Arabia, 110, 120–
21, 126–27, 207; and Palestine
problem, 164–65, 274 (n. 45)
Royal Dutch-Shell, 7, 8, 9, 12, 158,
161
Royall, Kenneth C., 177
Rusk, Dean, 186, 188, 189, 193, 196

al-Sabah, Ahmad al-Jabir, 15–16
Salha, Najib, 109, 112
Sanger, Richard, 140, 182
San Remo agreement, 10–11
Sappington, James, 72, 87, 89
Saudi Arabia: special relationship
with U.S., xiv, xvii–xviii, 125–26,
211–12; geography of, 13–14;
history of, 16–18; and diplomatic
relations with U.S., 28, 52, 225 (n.
74), 246–47 (n. 47), 259 (n. 70);
and pilgrimage, 34, 223 (n. 58), 229
(n. 8); strategic importance of, 34,
51–52, 176, 212; economic crisis
in, 35; oil company aid to, 36–37,
229 (n. 13); U.S. aid to, 38–48,
126, 239 (n. 104), 242 (n. 14), 243